YOUR READING

A Booklist for Junior High Students

YOUR READING

A Booklist for Junior High Students

New Edition

Prepared by

Jerry L. Walker, Editorial Chairman,
and the Committee on the Junior High School Booklist
of the National Council of Teachers of English

National Council of Teachers of English
1111 Kenyon Road, Urbana, Illinois 61801

Fifth Edition
NCTE Stock Number 59370

Library of Congress Cataloging in Publication Data
National Council of Teachers of English. Committee on
  the Junior High Book List.
  Your reading.

  Includes indexes.
  1. Children's literature—Bibliography. I. Walker,
Jerry L. II. Title.
Z1037.N346 1975 [PN1009.A1]   028.52   75-21358
ISBN 0-8141-5937-0

ACKNOWLEDGEMENTS

I wish to acknowledge first the professional dedication of all the members of the NCTE Committee on the Junior High School Booklist. Given the amount of work they had to do in a very short period of time, I'm sure they must have sacrificed many, many hours of personal leisure time in order to complete the task. Not only have the quantity and the speed of work been impressive, but so, too, has been the quality. The selection of books and the writing of annotations has been excellent, making my job as chairman relatively easy.

A fortuitous event occurred toward the end of the Committee's work which had a significant effect on both the scope and quality of this booklist—namely, the arrival at NCTE of an unsolicited manuscript containing hundreds of excellent annotations prepared by Claire Rosser, a librarian from Wellesley Hills, Massachusetts. Since her listing included books which had not been reviewed as yet, we asked for, and received, permission to include her annotations of those books. We are especially indebted, therefore, to Claire Rosser, for over two hundred and fifty of the finest annotations included here.

Additionally, credit must be accorded a prior junior high school booklist committee who, under the direction of Grace Maertins, prepared a number of the annotations for books published before 1970.

Acknowledgement is due also to the NCTE editorial staff for all the aid and encouragement which was given so willingly throughout the work on this project. Much of the quality of this publication is directly attributable to their efforts.

Many individuals and groups deserve special mention for the assistance they gave to various committee members in reading and annotating books. Among those providing substantive assistance were the following: Dorothy D. Grant, Treva Hunter Jacobs, Helen Griffith Minteer, Lillian Kachel, Marily Simon, Lynn Myers, Anita Musser, Mrs. Arlis Christock, Conrad Case, Francis Goschy, Doris Schumacher, George Strand, Ruth

Goslin, Douglas Stotter, and Nancy Dillingham. Many students also provided assistance in reading and annotating, especially Jane Christensen's seventh and eighth grade students, Janice Bengtson's accelerated ninth-grade students, Zora Rashkis's accelerated students, and Alan Madsen's English education students.

To those and all others who contributed to this project, I and the students who will use this book owe sincere thanks.

Jerry L. Walker, Chairman

CONTENTS

INTRODUCTION TO THE STUDENT

This book was written for you. Teachers and librarians can use it, of course, but they are not the audience we had in mind as we selected and wrote about books for this volume. We believe that you prefer to select what you read all by yourself—at least part of the time. Reading is a private act, and so too is selecting a book. There's nothing wrong with taking people's advice about books; in fact, some of your best reading tips will come from friends, parents, teachers, and librarians. Still, there will be times when the advice you receive proves to be wrong. Sometimes you will not like a book that others liked, and sometimes you will like books that others didn't. Since no one else is exactly like you, it's impossible for anyone else to know exactly how you will react to a particular book.

People choose to read for different purposes at different times; sometimes we read to be entertained; sometimes we read to be informed about some topic; sometimes we read because we like a particular writer; sometimes we read because we want to escape from the conditions in which we find ourselves; sometimes we read because our jobs demand it; and sometimes we read just to pass the time. There are probably more reasons than that even, but they are all good reasons. Maybe that's why, in spite of television, movies, and all of the other things around for us to spend our time on, reading continues to be important in our lives.

Because readers and their purposes are so different, in order for a book like this to be useful to young readers all across the country, it must contain descriptions of books representing a very wide range of subjects and types. It must also be put together in such a way that it doesn't take too long to find out if it contains a description of a book of a particular type on a particular subject. If you look at the Contents, you can easily see how wide the range of books is and how they are organized.

In the Fiction section, you will find that the books are grouped according to what the basic story deals with. Usually, that means that the main characters in the book are somehow involved in what the topic suggests. In books included within the topic, "On being adventurous," for instance, you can assume that the main characters at some point or other in the story find themselves in a daring and perhaps threatening situation that tests their strength and courage. Because in some books the characters are involved in more than one main activity or situation, the same book appears in two different categories.

Books that present factual information on different subjects are included in the Nonfiction section, and books that deal with the same subject are, of course, grouped together. In this section, too, some books are included in two categories when they deal with two different subjects. The subjects dealt with in the "Biography" section are the lives of people, some famous and some not-so-famous. Because there are so many biographies included, we have divided them into subgroups to make the biography of a particular person easier to locate.

Books included in the Poetry section are simply listed alphabetically according to the poet's or the editor's name. Every book in this section is a collection of poetry, and the range of things dealt with in the poems is so varied that subcategories wouldn't make much sense.

Books included in the Reference Tool section are those that you can use to locate specific information quickly. If you want to find out who holds a certain sports record or who invented a certain thing, you can probably find a book in this section to give you that information.

The section on Short Stories lists authors, titles, and bibliographic information. Descriptions of these books are found in other sections. Consult the title index for the page.

Whatever your purpose for reading, we hope that YOUR READING will help you achieve it. We have tried in our annotations, or descriptions of what the books contain, to give you all the information you will need to make your selection. We have not told you whether a particular book is exciting or dull: that is your decision to make. We have not indicated whether a particular book is difficult to read: that, too, is your decision. All that we have tried to do is to give you as much information about a particular book as we could in about fifty words.

One final thing needs to be said about this book. Many of the standards, books that have been read and enjoyed by millions of young people over the years, are not annotated here. The reason for that is that we wanted primarily to give you information about newer books that are available to you. Your parents, teachers, or librarians can tell you about the standards or direct you to other sources for descriptions of them. An incomplete List of Standards is included. You will probably want to get acquainted with at least some of the books your parents and their parents considered the best of the books available to them. At the same time, you and other young people like you will decide which of the newer books annotated in YOUR READING deserve to be cherished and reprinted for future generations to read, enjoy, and grow by.

FICTION

The books described in this section are novels, which means that they are lengthy pieces of fiction. Not everything in a novel has to be fiction, of course. Some stories are actually based on people who really lived, on events that really happened, or on places that really exist. What makes them fiction is the writer's imagination. The author imagines and writes what the characters must have thought, done, or said in real situations; or exaggerates what really happened; or sometimes just invents characters and events and puts them in real places. A writer is usually successful when the imagined seems real to the reader.

Writers make up stories about their own and others' experiences for many reasons. Of course they write to make money, but they also write because there is a point they want to make to their readers, because they like to make up good, interesting stories, and because they are fascinated by the characters they have created. You will find that certain writers keep writing the same kinds of stories again and again and that others seldom repeat themselves. Sometimes it is fun to read two books by the same author to see if you can find similarities in them. When you find the same characters, places, or situations occurring in two or more books, you can bet that those are the things that have fascinated the author. Maybe you will become fascinated by the same things.

Hopefully you will find many things that intrigue you in the books which are annotated in this section. To help you find them, we have grouped the books in categories. Some of the categories, such as "Growing up male" and "Growing up female," will help you find books according to the main character or characters. Other categories, such as "On being adventurous," will help you locate certain types of fiction. And still other categories, such as "On being free," will help you find stories according to the theme or point of a story. Some books easily fit into two categories, and when they do, you will find them annotated in two places.

Generally, you will find stories which are set in modern times and places located in the section entitled HERE AND NOW. Stories which take place in the past can be found in the section entitled, of course, THE PAST. Science fiction stories can be found in THE FUTURE section, and stories that could take place anywhere, at any time, are included in OF ALL TIME, OF NO TIME.

Choose wisely, and have fun!

HERE AND NOW
On being adventurous

Aiken, Joan, et al. **Authors' Choice 2.** T Y Crowell 1974.

Each of seventeen well-known authors chooses his or her favorite short story for this collection and gives reasons for the selection. There are stories about a monster from another world; Lobo, king of the grey wolves; and Big John and the Water Woman. Also included are a story about a yellow dog who tangles with dynamite; one about an old lady who makes a boy invisible; and another about a bee–man who uses his bees to save a child.

Almedingen, E. M. **Young Mark.** FS&G 1968.

Many adventures, often dangerous ones, befall young Mark, who sets out in April of 1742 to walk from the Ukraine to St. Petersburg, determined to become a singer.

Arthur, Ruth M. **After Candlemas.** Atheneum 1974.

An unexpected vacation gives Harriet a chance to visit her friend Nancy in her home on the English seacoast. When Nancy gets sick, Harriet is left to explore on her own. Her adventures lead her to stone caves on the seashore, where she encounters a boy who is in trouble with the law. She also finds there a sacred staff which apparently is used by local witches in their ceremonies. Gramma Cobbley warns Harriet and Nancy to stay away from the caves on Candlemas (February 2) since that's the time witches observe their sabbath. Harriet disregards this warning and her adventures begin.

Arthur, Ruth M. **A Candle in Her Room.** Atheneum 1972.

When her father inherits a large sum of money, Melissa Mansell, along with the rest of her family, moves out of London to a 300-year-old house on the coast of Wales. Trouble begins when Melissa's youngest sister discovers an ancient, beautifully carved doll in the attic of the old house. The three sisters, Melissa, Judith, and Briony, have never been close, and the doll mysteriously causes tension among them to become even greater. The novel is made up of four stories—two told by Melissa, one told by Judith's daughter, and one told by Judith's granddaughter—and covers the loves and misfortunes that take place over a period of forty years.

Bawden, Nina. **The Runaway Summer.** Lippincott 1969.

Mary knows, though no one has actually told her, that her parents are unhappy together and that neither really wants her. This hurts so much, she feels like being angry and nasty most of the time even to her grandfather and aunt who love her and take care of her. She lies often and even steals candy bars just to do something to try to get even with fate. This summer she finds friends, an adventure, and an escape from her own plight: she hides an illegal immigrant from the police. And she gets far enough away from her own problems to face the truth.

Bawden, Nina. **The White Horse Gang.** Lippincott 1966.

Rose, Sam, and Abe decide to raise some needed cash by kidnapping a spoiled seven-year-old whose parents are wealthy and over-protective. The plot takes a bewildering turn when just as the kids give up the plan as too dangerous, their "victim" decides he wants to be kidnapped. He has never had an adventure before and the thrill of sleeping out in the woods, riding a horse, and eating chocolates seems the greatest excitement in the world. There is an escaped wolf in the vicinity to add more thrills, and a grand finale of heroism and friendship confirmed.

Bell, Margaret E. **Watch for a Tall White Sail.** G&D 1972.

Florence's father has dragged his family away from a posh, comfortable life so that he can begin an adventurous business in the Alaskan wilderness. This means isolation, brutally hard work, and even the death of one brother because of lack of adequate medical care. The family often quarrel, but they have a great loyalty for one another and they love each other deeply.

Bennett, Jay. **The Long Black Coat.** Delacorte 1973.

This is a tense suspense story of a boy caught in the evil organized by his older brother, a tough amoral loner reported killed in Vietnam. Strange men start pressuring Phil for the package Vinnie left behind when he went overseas. They are ruthless, torturing for information, killing for protection. Phil is totally confused, wanting to be loyal to his brother, but gradually facing the knowledge of his corruption. Edgar Allen Poe Award.

Blades, Ann. **A Boy of Tache.** Tundra Bks 1973.

When spring finally comes, Charlie gets up every morning and goes down to Stuart Lake to see if the ice has melted. When the ice melts at last, Charlie and his grandparents, Za and Virginia, set out on the long trip up river to the cabin on Trembleur Lake to begin the yearly beaver hunt. But after they arrive, Za, who is seventy-four years old, becomes very sick with pneumonia, and Charlie has to make the lonely, dangerous trip back to radio for a plane to take his grandfather to the hospital.

Bodsworth, Fred. **The Sparrow's Fall.** Signet 1967.

Jacob Atook, member of an Indian tribe in the Canadian far north, is also a Christian who hates to kill. He and his wife are married by a Christian priest, but because she had been promised to another hunter, Jacob and Niska are exiled and must choose between trying to survive on their own—tracking down caribou in the freezing snow—or surrendering to starvation.

Bonham, Frank. **The Vagabundos.** Dutton 1969.

Eric Hansen leaves his luxurious southern California home with his motorcycle and $100 to find his father, who has taken off for the Baja peninsula in Mexico. Eric is forced to trade his motorcycle for a sailboat where the road ends, and he becomes a *vagabundo* too, taking his food from the sea and sleeping under the stars.

Brown, Joe David. **Addie Pray.** G K Hall 1972.

This book from which the film *Paper Moon* was created is the story of a young orphan girl travelling around the South during the Depression in the company of an imaginative con-man. But don't think young Addie is being taken advantage of. No, rather, she shares the brain-work necessary to dream up and execute elaborate swindles. The culmination of their money-making schemes is passing Addie off as the missing heiress of a wealthy old woman in New Orleans. Addie is loyal, loving, independent, and intelligent. And Moses, the con-man who refuses to accept the role of "father," does make a loyal, protective friend and companion.

Brown, Roy. **Escape the River.** Seabury 1970.

Twelve-year-old Paul Nolan "finds himself" through an attempt at juvenile crime with Brad Crotchet as his accomplice. Paul's concern for his fourteen-year-old retarded brother Ken helps him learn that the father who adopted him really loves him.

Brown, Roy. **No Through Road.** Seabury 1974.

Barry leaves home on his Honda after his girlfriend disappoints him and after being involved in a crime he didn't commit. This is a story about motorcycle gangs—their love of their motorcycles and their hate of the other gang.

Burroughs, Edgar Rice. **Back to the Stone Age.** Ace Bks 1973.

Entering the subterranean world of Pellucidar with other men, Wilhelm Van Horst is left behind for dead when they depart. His friendship for La Ja, who has the homing instinct of the natives, finally leads him to safety. Various adventures lie between his realization of being left and his final safety in Sari, Pellucidar's main kingdom.

Burroughs, Edgar Rice. **The Cave Girl.** Ace Bks 1973.

Washed ashore in a strange land, a young Bostonian learns to live in the primitive world of the jungle. His love for a beautiful native girl compels him to many adventures. Their final adventure reveals a mystery in the girl's past.

Burroughs, Edgar Rice. **The Eternal Savage.** Ace Bks 1972.

A visit to Africa, a twist in time, and Victoria Custer enters a Stone Age adventure. With her is the mighty warrior Nu. Their lives are threatened by the prehistoric life surrounding them. Emotions and senses are attacked in their strange encounters. Can time again be twisted to release its captives?

Burroughs, Edgar Rice. **The Lad and the Lion.** Ace Bks 1974.

From a royal court to a derelict steamer to an African nation, a young man finds his greatest friend is a giant lion. A series of adventures brings Michael from youth to maturity and eventual love. A parallel story details the intrigue occurring in the country from which the young prince fled. Together, they provide a clear picture of the contrast between civilization and the law of the wild.

Burroughs, Edgar Rice. **The Land of Hidden Men.** Ace Bks 1973.

Lost in a Cambodian jungle, Gordon King discovers an ancient civilization. His involvement becomes nearly his death and his salvation as he falls in love with the Princess Fou-tan. Magnificent jungle cities, vicious battles and dangerous treachery interfere in his search for happiness and peace.

Burroughs, Edgar Rice. **Land of Terror.** Ace Bks 1973.

David's ship is overtaken by the savage tribe of Oog, and all crewmen are taken captive. The warriors of Oog are all muscled, bearded women. David fights for his life and that of his beautiful Dian against the Oogs, the mad Jukans and later the man-eating ants, in their adventures in the world of Pellucidar at the earth's core.

Burroughs, Edgar Rice. **The Mad King.** Ace Bks 1972.

On a visit to his mother's homeland, Lutha, Barney Custer of Beatrice, Nebraska, becomes involved in the intrigue surrounding that kingdom. An escaped mad king, an ambitious prince, and a lovely princess add to the excitement of the story. A coronation and royal wedding end the story, but only after much excitement.

Burroughs, Edgar Rice. **The Mucker.** Ace Bks 1974.

Billy Byrne, from the slums of Chicago, finds himself sought by head hunters in a Far East jungle. His ruthlessness provides salvation for many whom he would never before have helped. The experiences he has cause him to become more aware of himself, and his vicious nature is turned to worthwhile pursuits.

Burroughs, Edgar Rice. **Pellucidar.** Ace Bks 1972.

David, Emperor of Pellucidar, uses the great burrowing machine to again penetrate the earth's crust and return to the land of unending sun. He seeks the beautiful Dian and his former companion Perry, and to re-establish the federation begun on his first visit. Again the Mahars are his opponents as he tries to establish a civilization using earth's twentieth-century skills.

Burroughs, Edgar Rice. **Savage Pellucidar.** Ace Bks 1973.

In the vast subterranean world of Pellucidar, David Innes, its emperor, and the warriors of his empire are involved in an attempt to calm angry tribes. The inventor, Perry, creates problems by causing people to become lost in his inventions. A young hero and his mate are separated and seek to find each other. These and many other adventures fill the novel.

Burroughs, Edgar Rice. **Tanar of Pellucidar.** Ace Bks 1973.

After battling the Korsar sea-rovers and subduing them, Tanar is taken prisoner by them. He is held captive as they flee in their ships. His escape and capture of a lovely maiden make up this novel. Unmapped jungles and strange, fierce beasts lie between him and his homeland in the world of Pellucidar.

Burroughs, Edgar Rice. **Tarzan at the Earth's Core.** Ace Bks 1973.

Tarzan enters the inner-earth world of Pellucidar to help free David, its emperor, from his captors. With others of the crew which accompanies him, he faces the savage terrors of the primitive land. Tarzan's jungle skills are tried to the utmost in endeavoring to free the ruler.

Burroughs, Edgar Rice. **The Wizard of Venus & Pirate Blood.** Ace Bks 1973.

Two separate stories make up this book. The first provides further adventures of Carson Napier on Venus, as he combats evil forces using magic to enslave people. The second story is earth-bound and deals with modern-day piracy. It includes many adventures and some emotional scenes.

Burton, Hester. **The Flood at Reedsmere.** World Pub 1968.

Left alone for the evening, Mark and Mary are horrified to see the ocean coming into their home. They find a boat and escape, but the great storm continues, sweeping over the coast of England and taking many lives. Suspense and fear mount as friends are marooned on roofs, in the church, and in their homes.

Butler, William. **The Butterfly Revolution.** Ballantine 1961.

"From the diary of Winston Weyn, camper, former Cabin Leader and Chief of Propaganda in the revolution at High Pines" comes this frightening story of social interaction at a boys' camp. Some of the older boys revolt against a planned activity to catch butterflies. Thirteen-year-old Winston's diary details the revolt.

Canning, Victor. **The Runaways.** Morrow 1972.

When Smiler got into trouble and was sent to reform school, there was no one around to help him prove his innocence. As soon as he can, he escapes and hopes to somehow keep on the run until his father comes home from sea to fight the authorities for him. For months he survives, tinting his hair and skin, making up stories to protect his identity, finding work, and gaining people's respect and friendship.

Caras, Roger. **Sarang.** Little 1968.

An American teenager, a blind village boy she befriends in Pakistan, the seeing-eye dog she gets for him, the tiger who kills the dog, and the tiger who comes to take the place of the dog—these are only some of the ingredients which make this book a memorable experience.

Carlsen, Ruth Christoffer. **Ride a Wild Horse.** HM 1970.

Barney and Julie, a yellow-eyed wild horse from another world, have a summer full of adventure in this entertaining blend of fantasy and reality.

Cohen, Peter Zachary. **Foal Creek.** Atheneum 1972.

While the sheriff and his men stake out an old barn containing sacks of marijuana, two neighborhood boys try to remove it. A sudden, heavy storm, a flood, and a night in the wilderness confront the lawbreakers. Friends of American Writers Award.

Cohen, Peter Zachary. **The Muskie Hook.** Atheneum 1969.

Eager to spend his summer in timber country, Aaron resents having to work as a guide for muskie fishermen. But it turns out to be a challenge as he pits his skill against the personalities of the men, the weather, and the muskie itself.

Corcoran, Barbara. **Don't Slam the Door When You Go.** Atheneum 1974.

Judith and two of her friends have been planning their escape for months. They have a car, money, and a destination in Montana. Plunketville, Montana, is not what they expect, but the girls, just out of high school, are determined to make it on their own.

Corcoran, Barbara. **Sasha, My Friend.** Atheneum 1969.

Hallie's mother dies accidentally, and she and her father leave their home and friends in California to begin anew in the wilderness. At first Hallie is lonely and bored, filled with grief and homesickness. Slowly she becomes accustomed to the strangeness of the north, with the help of a wolf puppy whom she finds abandoned in the forest. The wolf gives her the companionship she so desperately needs and also ties her emotionally to the wildlife of her new environment.

Davis, Verne T. **The Devil Cat Screamed.** Morrow 1966.

Ray McClung has many adventures living on a ranch and learning to be a cowboy, but always in the background is the deadly cougar which Ray has made his enemy. Ray knows that sooner or later he and the cougar must confront each other.

DeJong, Meindert. **The House of Sixty Fathers.** Dell 1973.

Tien Pao's family sail their sampan steadfastly upriver to escape the Japanese attacks on the Chinese coast, but during a storm the sampan breaks loose with Tien Pao alone on board. Separated from his family, he drifts back into occupied territory. As he searches for his family, he encounters many hardships as well as sixty American airmen friends. Child Study Association of America/Wel-Met Children's Book Award; International Board on Books for Young People Honor List.

DeTrevino, Elizabeth Borton. **Casilda of the Rising Moon.** FS&G 1967.

Medieval Spain with Moors and Christians at war provides the background for this historical adventure romance involving a Moorish princess who falls in love with a prince of Jewish ancestry.

Duncan, Lois. **They Never Came Home.** Avon 1969.

A terrifying novel of a strange camping trip during which two boys vanish for very different reasons. It becomes a nightmare before the weekend is over. Larry has to fill Dan's shaken memory with facts too frightening to be believed. The boys are the objects of a desperate search, then fugitives from the law. They are living in fear of the future and of each other.

Duncombe, Frances Riker. **The Quetzal Feather.** Lothrop 1967.

Luis, a Spanish boy, accompanies Pedro Alvarado in the Spanish conquest of Guatemala in 1523, but changes his views toward Indians as he gradually comes to realize the greed of his hero.

Eckert, Allan W. **Incident at Hawk's Hill.** Little 1971.

This incredible book is based on a true incident, the account of a six-year-old boy's survival in the wilderness for several months. He always has been a strange child. The youngest in a large family, he is little for his age and rarely speaks. He spends most of his time with the animals he finds in his hours of wandering.

Edwards, Sally. **Isaac and Snow.** Coward 1973.

Small Isaac Jenkins lives on the coast of South Carolina and works in the summers on a patrol boat for Captain J. C. of the State Wildlife Association. He finds and becomes friends with an albino dolphin, Snow, and begins to train her. When she is discovered by others who want to use her as a tourist attraction, her life is endangered. It is necessary to take Snow to a seaquarium for safety, but Isaac does not like the idea. An adventure begins which includes complications such as a shooting attempt.

Ellis, Mel. **Caribou Crossing.** HR&W 1971.

Johnny and Danny are good friends who share a love for the wilderness. At eighteen, they have taken on the job of opening up a beautiful site for a resort, but it entails tunnelling a road through a mountain in a difficult and dangerous undertaking. After all their efforts, they do succeed in establishing a fishing camp and they act as guides for a party of fishermen. Soon the garbage piles up and one of the tourists is gun happy, shooting animals indiscriminately. The boys watch helplessly as their paradise turns into a violent, ugly place.

Finlay, Winifred. **Danger at Black Dyke.** S G Phillips 1968.

Three young boys, who have formed a secret society in Northumberland, offer Bud Riley, an American, a place to hide when he seems to be followed by some sinister characters. Edgar Allen Poe Award.

Fitzgerald, John D. **Brave Buffalo Fighter.** Independence Pr 1973.

This story is based on the diary of Susan Parker, who traveled by wagon train from St. Joseph, Missouri, to Ft. Laramie. Indian fights, illness, and frustration plague the family's trip. Her brother Jerry's bravery earns him the Indian name of Brave Buffalo Fighter. That name carries a responsibility that no one on the wagon train wanted to face, and sets the stage for a moving climax.

Fitzgerald, John D. **Private Eye.** Nelson 1974.

Wally Stone, a ten-year-old boy who has a skill for finding things, forms a private detective business. He solves several cases during the course of the story.

Fox, Paula. **How Many Miles to Babylon?** D White 1967.

James, a ghetto boy, his father gone, his mother ill in the hospital, falls into a fantasy that his mother has gone to Africa, leaving him a ring to guide him there where he will be a prince. As he wanders out of school and around the streets, he is kidnapped by some bigger boys, who use him in their dog-stealing racket. James is trapped, in trouble either way he turns.

Garfield, Leon. **The Strange Affair of Adelaide Harris.** Pantheon 1971.

Adelaide Harris has a way of affecting many lives— and she is only a baby. The tale begins when Adelaide's brother decides to leave her in a field where she might be suckled by a she-wolf, just like the Roman infants in ancient history. But Adelaide is found by Tizzy and Ralph, two young lovers, who take her away. The story becomes tangled and funny as people at the Academy and in town get involved.

George, Jean Craighead. **Julie of the Wolves.** Har-Row 1972.

Miyax (Julie) is lost on the North Slope of Alaska when she tries to run away to her pen pal in San Francisco. She is adopted by a pack of wolves which feed and protect her as she travels. The story is rich in information about the habits of wolves, survival techniques, and Eskimo rituals. John Newbery Medal; National Book Award.

George, Jean Craighead. **My Side of the Mountain.** Dutton 1959.

Sam Gribley decides to leave his family and city life and head for the woods. And so, one chilly spring night, he finds himself in the Catskill Mountains trying to get a fire started with no success. But Sam comes a long way in the knowledge of survival, and in fact succeeds in spending a year alone, making a cozy shelter in a spacious hemlock tree, fishing, trapping, and foraging for his food and clothes, taming and training a falcon for help and company.

Golding, William. **Lord of the Flies.** Putnam 1954.

An airplane carrying a group from a British boys' school crashes on a deserted island, killing all the adult crew members. At once the boys begin to build a democratic society, assigning duties and electing a leader. Gradually, however, as they realize their great freedom, two factions develop: one, led by Ralph, who tries desperately to maintain a civilized group; the other, led by Jack, who leads a tribe of "savages," becoming more and more primitive every day. Ralph's group tries to keep a big signal fire burning on top of a mountain, but as more and more boys join Jack's "tribe," Ralph becomes a hunted animal.

Hallstead, William F. **Ghost Plane of Blackwater.** HarBraceJ 1974.

Youth and inexperience combine to cause Greg Stewart many troubles as an agricultural pilot. Neither, however, causes as much trouble as his search to help his friend Roy prove his innocence in a long-ago plane crash. As their search for the downed plane narrows, both men realize that more than nature opposes their success. Tense adventure in the air and on the ground makes this an exciting mystery to solve.

Harris, Christie. **You Have To Draw the Line Somewhere.** Atheneum 1964.

Linsey Ross-Allen, who wanted to be an artist, recalls her art school adventures in Vancouver and Los

Angeles, a honeymoon in Jamaica at the time of its worst earthquake in fifty years, and life in New York, where she learned to "draw the line" between home duties and a career.

Harris, Marilyn. **The Runaway's Diary.** Four Winds 1971.

Cat (Catherine Anne) runs away from Harrisburg, Pennsylvania, to nowhere and ends up in Canada. Along the way she picks up Mike, a German shepherd pup, and Robber and Ruthie. Robber and Ruthie ride around from town to town in a VW bus. They're the same age as Cat's parents, but have dropped out of society. Much as Cat dislikes her parents, she discovers she is glad not all people are like Robber and Ruthie. Cat finds peace on a mountain all her own, and finally is ready to start home. This diary is a record of her journey.

Havrevold, Finn (translator Cathy Babcock Curry). **Undertow.** Atheneum 1970.

Jorn, a Norwegian boy, can't understand why his parents are upset that he isn't spending the summer with them, nor why they don't like his friend Ulf. Ulf is a little strange, but Jorn feels this is just because he is older. Jorn is excited, if not apprehensive, about the sailboat trip they plan to take, off the Norwegian coast. Later Jorn realizes he is in the midst of a test of wills that can only result in disaster.

Hodges, Elizabeth Jamison. **A Song for Gilgamesh.** Atheneum 1971.

Adaba is a potter and poet in ancient Sumer. When he discovers the art of writing through his business visits to the temple, he wants to learn. When he does, however, he is accused of stealing temple magic, and his adventures begin. He escapes violence and goes on a mission for the queen with Gilgamesh. The story is made even more exciting by the fact that history recognizes the Sumerians as the first known to develop a system of writing and a primitive democracy. They are also responsible for the first great folk epic, *The Epic of Gilgamesh.*

Huffaker, Clair. **The Cowboy and the Cossack.** S&S 1973.

The year is 1880 and the place is Siberia, where fifteen cowboys from Montana and fifteen Russian cossacks must learn to coexist during a 4,000-mile cattle drive. They soon learn that they haven't time for the instant hatred each feels for the other. There are worse problems, such as wolf packs, tigers, flash floods, wars, and an entire Tartar army.

Hunt, Irene. **No Promises in the Wind.** G&D 1971.

Josh Grondowski, fifteen years old, finds he must face like a man the greatest depression in the history of the United States. His home life in shambles, and with lack of food and money making it worse all the time, Josh launches into his own adventure with Joey, his little brother. Sickness, loneliness, and despair plague their journey, and a close shave with death teaches them tolerance and appreciation for what they left behind.

Jeffries, Roderic. **Trapped.** Har-Row 1972.

Gerry, trying to prove his courage and friendliness, goes hunting with Bert, one of his classmates. After stealing a boat, the two boys are trapped on the mudflats in a snowstorm.

Kiddell, John. **Euloowirree Walkabout.** Chilton 1968.

To win a bet, three eighteen-year-olds travel nine hundred miles from Sydney to Adelaide with a dollar each and a minimum of equipment.

Konigsburg, E. L. **From the Mixed-up Files of Mrs. Basil E. Frankweiler.** Atheneum 1967.

This is a madcap runaway story about two resourceful kids who hide out in the Metropolitan Museum of Art for a week without being discovered, sleeping on the antique beds and washing in the lavatories. Claudia, the older sister (only eleven) who is the designer of the runaway plan, never fully explains why she does it, but she seems to be yearning for a challenging, dramatic adventure. Well, she has one! Not only is it a unique survival story, but the children use their formidable intelligence and imagination to help solve a mystery as well. John Newbery Medal.

L'Amour, Louis. **The Californios.** Bantam 1974.

If Sean Mulkerin is to save his family's ranch, he knows he will have to find his way to some gold his father discovered long ago. Since his father is dead, Sean has to rely on Old Juan, the mysterious Indian whom all the other Californios fear and respect, to lead him to the gold. His search for the treasure leads him to remote parts of the California hills, where Sean has to confront not only the men who pursued him but also the "old ones" that Juan seems to know.

Leach, Christopher. **Free, Alone, and Going.** Crown 1972.

One afternoon after school, Dave dumps all his school books in the river, picks up his knapsack, and—with his buddy Gregg—leaves his home in London. Hitch-hiking to a seaport town where they plan to catch a ship to America, Dave and Gregg get caught in a heavy rain, steal food from a party given by very rich people, and see two men fight over a woman. Gregg chickens out and returns home. Dave wants to go on, but he mistakenly tries to hitch a ride in a police car.

Lee, S. C. **Best Basketball Booster.** Strode 1974.

Moving with his family into eastern Kentucky, young Paul Daley learns quickly that his life will be very different. Basketball and new neighbors occupy much of his time in this story which intertwines the sports influence and the strange feelings of the mountain people.

Lefebure, Molly. **The Loona Baloona.** Nelson 1974.

Cat astronauts plan an expedition to the moon, and two opposing teams pursue the same goal. The writer has very cleverly poked fun at the space program and at pompous people. If you like cats and love to laugh, you'll like this "moon" trip.

L'Engle, Madeleine. **The Arm of the Starfish.** FS&G 1965.

Adam is an intelligent young scientist about to enter college. He gets a summer job in Portugal as a lab assistant to a renowned biologist who is working on the regeneration of missing limbs by studying the starfish. Adam becomes mixed-up in an intrigue in which he doesn't know who is telling the truth. Slowly he sorts it out, using his good mind and his instinct about people. There is danger everywhere from men greedy for power and wealth.

L'Engle, Madeleine. **The Young Unicorns.** FS&G 1968.

As in the previous book, a scientist is threatened by power-hungry villains who want to use technology to gain control over mankind. The Austin family (of

Meet the Austins) and two other young people are drawn into a struggle with the hostile, raw culture of the street gangs of New York City.

McKay, Don. **On Two Wheels: An Anthology about Men and Motorcycles.** Dell 1971.

Low-pitched rumble veering into a screech, chrome tracing the curves of a powerful engine, the threat of speed on the road—motorcycles exert a mystique equally over those who ride them and those who fear them. The prize-winning stories, poems, and essays collected here offer a glimpse of the many-faceted world of cycling, from the drama of a town overrun by a cycling club to the tension and courage of a novice rider's first race and the humor of Arlo Guthrie's *Motorcycle Song*.

Ney, John. **Ox Goes North: More Trouble for the Kid at the Top.** Bantam 1973.

Fifteen-year-old Ox comes from a very eccentric rich family. He is fat, big, and a year behind in school. For the summer, he goes to Camp Downing in New England. This boy, who has everything and still isn't happy, confounds everyone. But Ox finds adventure by helping Tommy Campbell, whose grandparents have schemed to take his trust fund money.

Nichole, Christopher. **Operation Manhunt.** HR&W 1970.

A British intelligence agent tracks down a Polish general who has disappeared behind the Iron Curtain.

Nixon, Joan Lowery. **The Mysterious Red Tape Gang.** Putnam 1974.

Mike, Linda Jean, and the rest of their gang decide to take care of some community problems without going through the usual "red tape." When the gang boards up a dangerous abandoned house, they find themselves threatened by some tough-looking men who are involved in stealing auto parts.

Norman, Lilith. **Climb a Lonely Hill.** Walck 1972.

Uncle Bert's jeep is wrecked in the Australian desert. He is killed, and Sue and Jack are left alone with few supplies. The two know that they must get to a water supply even though the desert is brutal both day and night. Sue compounds their difficulties by accidentally dropping the water barrel on her foot, spilling their

precious supply of water and crippling herself, making
the trek across the bush for water both essential and
agonizing. Jack has always relied on his sister for
making decisions and organizing their projects; now
he must prove strong enough to lead them through
their ordeal, or they will die.

Norton, Andre. **Lavender-Green Magic.** T Y Crowell
1974.

Holly, Judy, and Crock must leave Boston when their
father is reported missing in Vietnam and live with
their grandparents at a rural place called Dimsdale.
Since the children are black, they experience difficult
adjustments to the new school and town. They feel
compelled to explore the garden, where their adventure begins. They are taken back to colonial days
where a feud is going on between two witches of good
and evil. The ancient curse on Dimsdale brings the
threat of disaster to everyone.

Norton, Andre. **Operation Time Search.** HarBraceJ
1967.

Have you ever wondered whether Atlantis could have
existed? The scientists in this book invent a time
machine for bringing back films of the past, but accidently Ray Osborne, newspaper photographer, walks
into the path of the time beam. He is knocked right
into the middle of a war between the Atlanteans and
the Murians.

O'Connor, Patrick. **Seawind from Hawaii.** Washburn
1965.

Pete Warner, sixteen, and his kid brother are employed as crew members on the *Seawind*. Pete finds
that in spite of his past experience with ships, he has
much to learn about seamanship—or at least that's
what Tony, the young captain, tells him.

O'Dell, Scott. **The Black Pearl.** HM 1972.

Ramon is the son of a prosperous fisherman who is
training him in the business. Ramon isn't satisfied
with desk work and wants to dive for pearls. He
bribes an old Indian to teach him, and then dares to
dive and enter a cave which the Indian avoids because
he believes it to be the cave of the Manta Diablo.
Ramon finds the largest black pearl in the cave, but
even though his family give the pearl to the Madonna,
their fortunes turn and they are ruined. Ramon, who

at first laughed at the idea of a devil, now believes that somehow he must appease the angered monster.

O'Dell, Scott. **Island of the Blue Dolphins.** Dell 1973.

This novel is based on the true story of a young girl who was abandoned on the Island of the Blue Dolphins and managed to survive until she was rescued almost twenty years later. The girl, named Karana in the novel, sees her father and most of the warriors in her tribe killed by foreigners who come to hunt sea otters. The novel tells about her adventures—with wild dogs, devil fish, sea otters—and the way she manages to survive with only her wit and courage to rely on. John Newbery Medal.

O'Hara, Mary. **Green Grass of Wyoming.** Dell 1974.

In this story, Ken McLaughlin, the main character in two previous novels by Mary O'Hara, has to deal with an outlaw stallion. Ken recaptures the stallion after a series of adventures in which his fiancée nearly freezes to death. The adventure theme is complicated by romance and by Ken's efforts to become a mature, self-reliant young man.

Olsen, Jack. **Night of the Grizzlies.** Putnam 1969.

Two girls are killed in Glacier National Park when grizzlies attack their campground. This account re-creates the atmosphere in the park that summer of 1967, and makes it clear why the grizzly turned against man.

Peck, Robert Newton. **Millie's Boy.** Knopf 1973.

Tit Smith has grown up in two rooms over the restaurant with a mother who makes a living entertaining men in the big double bed. He comes home from a dance one night to the blast of a shotgun which wounds him but kills his mother. Gus, the sheriff, digs out the bullet and gives him some hints inadvertently about his origins. As soon as Tit can walk, he heads toward the town his mother had come from. On the way, his wound opens and the trail of blood incites a pack of wild dogs to hunt him down.

Pedersen, Elsa. **House Upon a Rock.** Atheneum 1968.

The people of a small Alaskan fishing village know that a tidal wave will come later and they scurry to the nearby hills to watch in horror as the wall of water comes into the harbor and smashes against the land, destroying their homes and businesses. The disaster changes their characters as well as their lives. Derrick's once weak father suddenly takes charge of the new plans; and his sturdy mom seems to crumble under the knowledge that all things familiar to her are now destroyed.

Peyton, K. M. **Thunder in the Sky.** World Pub 1967.

When World War I begins, Sam and Gil are brothers working as mates on barges crossing the English channel. The cargo changes to munitions and other war supplies for the British troops fighting in Europe, and so the brothers find themselves directly involved in the war. Sam begins to suspect that one of the men he knows must be a spy, carrying information to traitors in France. To his dismay, he discovers that Gil is informing for money even as their older brother is fighting in the trenches. Sam is forced into the horrible position of deciding whether or not to expose his own brother as a traitor.

Phipson, Joan. **The Boundary Riders.** HarBraceJ 1963.

After the Thompsons settle in on their property on the edge of the "Outback," the children ride off on a week's camping trip to inspect the boundary fences. Their cousin Vincent, fifteen, takes command during the adventure because he is the oldest and most experienced. Jane, at thirteen, is cheerful and adventurous, and Bobby, eleven, is shy and quiet, but remarkably level-headed and steady. After three days of following fences, their job is finished and they decide to explore some falls which they discovered earlier. The weather turns stormy, they lose their way, and their efforts to return to a familiar landmark are hopeless. Somehow they must survive, with only a packet of matches and their wits to help them.

Phipson, Joan. **The Way Home.** Atheneum 1973.

As Richard, Prudence, and Prudence's little brother Peter are driving through the Australian countryside, the car in which they are riding is swept off the road by a flash flood. This incident begins a series of incredible adventures that take them far back in time, to the Ice Age, and far ahead into the future. Through all this, they are guided and protected by some mysterious force, which Prudence and Peter accept but which Richard refuses to believe in.

Portis, Charles. **True Grit.** S&S 1968.

A fourteen-year-old girl from Yell County, Arkansas, leaves home and goes off in the wintertime to avenge her father's death. A lively, uproarious high adventure in which the girl never loses her nerve—not even when she finds herself sinking fast into a cave where bats are brushing her legs. Basis for the popular movie.

Rawls, Wilson. **Where the Red Fern Grows.** Doubleday 1961.

An adventure story of astonishing beauty and amazing power about Billy and his two dogs—Old Dan and Little Ann. They range the dark hills and river bottoms of Cherokee County. Billy trains them to be the finest hunting team in the valley. Glory and victory are coming to them, but sadness waits, too.

Rodgers, Mary. **Freaky Friday.** Har-Row 1972.

Annabel does not think she has enough freedom. So her mother fixes that by turning Annabel into her! Annabel is delighted to wake and find this out; but she doesn't know what's ahead for her, and she has a real surprise! Book World Children's Spring Book Festival Award; Christopher Award Children's Book Category.

Roueché, Berton. **Feral.** Har-Row 1974.

A stray cat becomes the focus of a tale of horror and fear in this chilling novel. Dumped by tourists and living in the wild, cats breed in a remote section of Long Island until they are formidable in number. They eliminate their natural food supply of birds and small mammals and must turn to larger game for survival. Jack and Amy Bishop become a central part of the novel, which builds to a terrifying climax, then tapers to a surprising anticlimax.

Sachs, Marilyn. **A Pocket Full of Seeds.** Doubleday 1973.

Living in southern France, Nicole and her family feel safe from the Nazis. Although they are making very little money, they find enough for food, and they manage to stay together. Their tiny apartment is filled with Jewish refugees from the occupied areas, and they have heard the horror stories, but they feel cer-

tain that it is only a matter of time until the Nazis
are defeated and life returns to normal. Then one day
Nicole returns home from school to a deserted home.
The landlady says the Nazis are rounding up all the
Jews and have taken her parents and little sister.
Unless Nicole finds a place to hide, they will capture
her too. Jane Addams Children's Book Award.

Shaefer, Jack. **Mavericks.** Dell 1974.
Old Jake Hanlon sits on the edge of a mesa, overlooking the rundown ranch where he worked as a young
man and where—unwanted by townspeople who think
of him as a troublesome old maverick—he has come to
spend his last days. Sometimes he sees the super-
highway that cuts across the plains in front of him.
But mostly he sees the men and horses—all long-since
dead—that exist only in his memory. Even though
his memories are almost all he has left, he has more
than most people, for the stories that run through his
head are good ones, filled with adventure and courageous men and animals.

Sherry, Sylvia. **A Snake in the Old Hut.** Nelson 1972.
Mugo, a twelve-year-old "man," must lead his criminal
uncle through the dense Kenyan forest. The white
police and Uncle Joshua's bitter enemy are searching
for the pair, but Mugo must continue to keep his
family safe.

Smith, Beatrice S. **Don't Mention Moon to Me.** Nelson
1974.
Holly Woodworth, who is traveling in Europe, gets
involved with Emily Fortsaker, who is smuggling
moondust. Holly ends up being followed by Ross
Belanca, an FBI agent, and Frank Hoffman, a scientist, who are racing each other to get the moondust.

Snyder, Zilpha K. **The Velvet Room.** Atheneum 1965.
Ever since Robin's family were forced to leave their
home during the Depression, Robin has had an ache
of wanting something beautiful, wanting to belong
somewhere. When the car breaks down, Robin's family
get jobs working in fruit orchards; and Robin is given
an old key which opens a deserted mansion. She
doesn't hesitate to investigate, and inside she finds a
special room. She calls it "the velvet room" and it
becomes her comfort and escape from the uncertainties in her life.

Stevenson, William. **The Bushbabies.** HM 1965.

Jackie, an English girl raised in Kenya, feels that she must return her pet bushbaby to his own home when her family leaves Africa. This she does with the help of an African tribesman who is her friend. Their week-long trek through the wilderness exposes the inadequacy of the education Jackie possesses in contrast to the African's intimate knowledge of nature. Jackie is a perfect heroine: brave, strong, intelligent, sensitive, but a bit gawky and stubborn too, which makes her quite human.

Symons, Geraldine. **Miss Rivers and Miss Bridges.** Macmillan 1971.

Atalanta and Pansy, two thirteen-year-old girls, are on holiday in England in the early 1900s. Free from a strict private girls' school, they seek adventure masquerading as suffragettes. The girls are determined to help women gain the vote even if they must "rot in jail" to get it done.

Symons, Geraldine. **The Workhouse Child.** Macmillan 1969.

Atalanta and Pansy are on summer holiday from school in London in the early 1900s. Aunt invites the girls to the seashore for a week. What seems a pleasant, innocent trip turns into a madcap adventure of mistaken identity and suspense. As usual, Pansy must "think on her feet" to get out of what could be a really bad situation.

Townsend, John Rowe. **Pirate's Island.** Lippincott 1968.

A slum in an English city is the setting for this unusual book. Gordon Debbs, the overfed, pampered son of a butcher, mostly spends his time eating, reading comics, and avoiding the neighborhood bullies. A strange nine-year-old girl telling fantastic stories about a buried treasure gets Gordon on his feet and doing things—even such extraordinary deeds as outsmarting thugs and recovering an old man's life savings.

van Iterson, Siny R. **Pulga.** Morrow 1971.

For most of his fifteen years, Pulga roamed the slum streets of Bogotá, Colombia. Roused from his apathy by the experiences he has while working as a truck driver's helper, Pulga feels the first glimmers of self-respect. This adventure tale turns into one of self-discovery. Mildred L. Batchelder Award.

Verne, Jules. **Tigers and Traitors.** Assoc Bk 1959.

The vision of Jules Verne has created a steam elephant pulling luxurious houses on wheels through the deep Indian jungles. This, with a tiger hunt, a white goddess, and rampaging elephants, creates an exciting novel written years before such technical wonders were developed.

Walsh, Jill Paton. **The Dolphin Crossing.** Macmillan 1967.

Two British boys who are too young for military service hear the call for small boats to cross the Channel to France to help bring the defeated British army home from Dunkirk. They know it is something they can do, and so they take John's family boat. When they reach the French beaches they encounter the exhausted troops. There is constant shelling, and death and injury are all around them, but the boys find strength in themselves to keep working, shuttling the boat full of soldiers back and forth as long as their gasoline supply lasts.

Wechter, Nell Wise. **Taffy of Torpedo Junction.** Blair 1973.

This tale of New England during World War II blends history, adventure and lifestyle into a story centering around a small girl, her grandmother and a dog.

Weiss, M. Jerry, editor. **Tales Out of School.** Dell 1973.

A collection of fourteen short stories written by American humorists. Among them are "Hi, Teach" by Bel Kaufman; "The Great Cherokee Bill" by Jesse Stuart; "Eloquence and the Master's Guilding Dome" by Mark Twain; "Boy Bites Man" by Max Shulman. The stories center around pranks and troubles in the classroom. All have something to do with forms of education from grade school to college.

Welch, Ronald. **Tank Commander.** Nelson 1974.

This story of World War I tells what life in the trenches is like for a young British officer, John Carey. The introduction of the tank marks a turning point in the war.

White, Robb. **Deathwatch.** Dell 1972.

Wealthy Madec hires a desert-wise youth to help him shoot bighorn sheep for sport. An accidental killing pits Madec and the youth, Ben, against each other. Survival in the scorching desert depends on possession of a .358 magnum. Edgar Allen Poe Award.

Woods, George A. **Catch a Killer.** Har-Row 1972.

Andrew Morgan, searching for a place to hide after a scene with his mother, climbs through the window of an empty house and finds himself the captive of a deranged murderer. Dorothy Canfield Fisher Children's Book Award.

York, Carol Beach. **Takers and Returners.** Nelson 1973.

A group of kids, bored by the length of the summer, devise a new game. Called Takers and Returners, the game contains dangerous elements that they fail to see until too late.

On being a family

Alcock, Gudrun. **Turn the Next Corner.** Lothrop 1969.

Richie's father is a successful lawyer, and the family have always lived in beautiful homes in the suburbs. Now he has been accused of embezzlement, and Ritchie watches in horror and disbelief when his father is found guilty and sentenced to one year in prison. While the father is in prison, Richie's mother finds a job in the city and they move into a tiny apartment on the border of a tense, miserable, black neighborhood. Richie's greatest fear is that someone will discover that his father is a criminal and in prison.

Allen, Elizabeth. **You Can't Say What You Think and Other Stories.** Dutton 1974.

The high school students in these stories struggle with many problems. They include parents remarrying, moving into a new neighborhood, imitating the popular friend, having no real friends, and having parents disapprove of friends. The students find they can't say what they think—and often don't even know what they themselves think in the first place. They all solve their problems and learn more about what life is really like and who they are.

Armer, Alberta. **Troublemaker.** Collins-World 1966.

Joe's father is serving time in prison, and his mother is an overworked, immature woman who loves Joe but cannot deal with him. Once she beats him so hard, a neighbor reports her to the police; she is sent to a mental hospital, and he ends up in a foster home. Joe doesn't warm to his foster parents, but he feels easy with the younger kids in the family. He misses his mother and invents a science fiction plot to account for his parents' absence from his life.

Arthur, Ruth M. **The Little Dark Thorn.** Atheneum 1971.

When Merrie's father and mother are separated, Merrie's father brings her to England to stay with some of his relatives. Merrie resents being separated from her mother and acts in a way that causes people to refer to her as "the little dark thorn." Although Merrie does learn to love her stepmother, Bergit, many years go by before she can forgive her father. They become close only after she has grown up and has gained a sense of her value as a person.

Arthur, Ruth M. **Requiem for a Princess.** Atheneum 1972.

Just when British schoolgirl Willow Forrester is having trouble with her parents over her choice of music as a career, she discovers that she is adopted. She becomes ill, so her "parents" take her out of school for a term and allow her to go to Penliss, a beautiful, ancient estate on the coast, to recover. At Penliss, Willow gains two really close friends. She also has a series of fantastic dreams that help her realize who she is and make being adopted seem less terrible.

Arundel, Honor. **The Blanket Word.** Nelson 1973.

When Jan is called home from her student life in Edinburgh to the bedside of her dying mother, she obeys the summons with a mixture of guilt, anger, and impatience which is in fact her usual reaction to her family. Her mother has always seemed a distant drudge to Jan, but her sickness makes Jan feel guilty that she can't love her mother more. Jan's brother and sisters are there to share the nursing and await the death.

Baker, Laura Nelson. **The Dahlbe Family Horse.** Hale 1964.

Because all their neighbors are buying cars, Sarah is afraid that her father will get rid of their horse Birdie. Sarah's love and affection and the crisis that Birdie helps the family to withstand prove the worth of the horse.

Benary-Isbert, Margot. **The Long Way Home.** Har-BraceJ 1959.

An East German teenager is invited to America by the American soldier who had saved his life during the war. Immediately there is a problem: the soldier's new wife is unable to love and take care of the war orphan her husband has adopted. The German boy is old enough to live on his own, struggling with a new culture and a new language. But he yearns to be a part of the family, and he tries to help his foster father with his family responsibilities.

Benary-Isbert, Margot. **Rowan Farm.** HarBraceJ 1954.

Margot is the oldest daughter in a family which faces many problems. Since she loves animals, she is content to leave school to work on a farm, tending show dogs and taking care of other animals. When Margot is given the opportunity to go to America, she finds it difficult to leave her family and the farm.

Blue, Rose. **Grandma Didn't Wave Back.** Watts 1972.

Debbie's grandmother always was waiting for her at home after school with good things to eat and warm, special love. Recently Grandmother has been saying and doing strange things, like setting a place at the table for a cousin who died long ago, and wandering out on the street at night in her nightgown. Other times, Grandmother seems the same as before, so Debbie thinks of the strange times as "when Grandma is sick." Her parents explain that Grandma is becoming senile, and they worry about whether it might be best to put her in an old-folks' home. Debbie feels this would be turning Grandma out, and only Grandma can help her understand what is best. Easy to read.

Blue, Rose. **A Month of Sundays.** Watts 1972.

Divorce and a move from the suburbs to the city sever Jeffrey from the life he has always known. Everything is different now. His mother works and isn't home to greet him when he gets home from his new bewilderingly different school. His father spends Sundays with him, but they always do something special, not just the comfortable, ordinary things they did when they lived together. Gradually the variety of things to do in the city starts to be as attractive as

the usual activities in his old town. Jeffrey starts to
find ways to feel close to his parents again, even
though they don't feel close to each other.

Blume, Judy. **It's Not the End of the World.** Bradbury
Pr 1972.

Karen's parents call each other names; her mother
throws dishes; her father stops coming home nights.
But Karen would prefer having her parents fight, cry,
anything rather than get a divorce. How would she
ever get over the pain of the family breaking up? The
author tells how Karen, her sister, and brother learn
to survive.

Bonzon, Paul-Jacques. **The Orphans of Simitra.** Hale
1962.

Earthquakes, as we know, occur with frequency in
certain parts of the world and Greece is one of these
areas. The two Greek children in this story are the
only survivors from their entire village after an earthquake strikes. They first become a part of a refugee
camp and later are taken into a friendly Dutch home
as foster children. The grief of losing their family and
being away from the country they love ties them
especially close together.

Bradbury, Bianca. **Two on an Island.** HM 1965.

Jeff, his sister Trudy, and their dog are stranded on a
small harbor island, within sight of a large city. However, since no one is actually missing them (because
everyone believes they are safely somewhere else),
they are really in a bad way, with only the remnants
of a picnic lunch. Jeff, after sharing hunger, thirst, and
sunburn with Trudy for a few days, resolves some of
the jealousy he has always felt for her. Now he sees
her as a person, and not just as an intruding little
sister. Easy to read.

Byars, Betsy. **The House of Wings.** Dell 1973.

The house of wings is grandfather's old house, where
he lives with birds: geese, an owl, a parrot. When
Sammy's parents drive off one morning leaving him
alone in this place, he blames his grandfather and tries
to run away. A blind, wounded crane halts the chase
and in fact draws together the grandfather and the
boy, as they share common concern for the bird and
a common joy when they see he will survive. National
Book Award.

Calhoun, Mary. **It's Getting Beautiful Now.** Har-Row 1971.

This is the story of Bert, an appealing, rebellious sort of fellow who seems to have everyone buzzing around him trying to understand and help him—everyone, that is, except his truck driver father who just wishes he would be tougher and more obedient. When Bert gets arrested for possession of drugs, he is placed for a time with a "normal" family who are sympathetic and helpful. Bert surprises himself when he realizes he misses his father and the slapdash, often explosive life they shared.

Childress, Alice. **A Hero Ain't Nothing but a Sandwich.** Avon 1974.

Benjie tells the story, as he sees it, of why and how he takes to "fooling" a little with "the stuff." He shares with the reader the way he sees his mother, whom he loves dearly, her relationship with her boyfriend, his grandmother, his friends, and his teacher at school. At the same time, the reader is allowed to hear the story from the other people's viewpoints. Jane Addams Book Award.

Cleaver, Vera, and Bill Cleaver. **The Mimosa Tree.** Lippincott 1970.

Zollie, the stepmother, organizes the family move from a rundown farm to Chicago, where a job is waiting. She doesn't stay with them long, though, and soon Marvella, her little brothers and blind father are alone, ignorant of the ways of survival in a city slum. A young tough initiates the kids to petty thievery; and even Marvella, who knows stealing is wrong, can't see another alternative to provide the basic needs of the family.

Cleaver, Vera, and Bill Cleaver. **Where the Lilies Bloom.** Lippincott 1969.

Mary Call, at fourteen, is appointed head of the family by her dying father, with instructions. First she must get his body up the mountain to bury him in the grave he has already dug for himself. Second, she must never allow her older sister, whom he believes to be retarded, to marry. And third, absolutely accept no charity from anyone. With his death, their adventure in independence begins. The children maintain an elaborate lie that their father is still alive and well. They bamboozle their neighbor, Kiser, into

signing the farm over to them, and they begin making
money by gathering wild plants from the mountains
to sell for drugs. Mary Call turns into a hard, nagging
shrew, but she doesn't know how else to keep the
family fighting for survival. National Book Award.

Clymer, Eleanor. **My Brother Stevie.** HR&W 1967.

With a minimum of fuss, we learn of Annie's plight:
responsibility for her younger brother, who is in constant trouble. The kids live with their grandmother,
but she is stiff and unsympathetic, and her efforts at
discipline drive Stevie into more rebellion. Annie
knows that Stevie needs something or somebody desperately, but being a child herself, she can't solve the
problem. Stevie begins to be happier and better be-
haved, and Annie realizes the difference is a new
teacher, a young woman who seems to understand
Stevie's needs. Unfortunately just as Annie begins to
relax, this teacher has to leave. In desperation, Annie
is driven to find some solutions of her own.

Constant, Alberta Wilson. **The Motoring Millers.** T Y
Crowell 1969.

The two daughters of an absent-minded professor suddenly acquire a young, beautiful stepmother. They
get along well enough to decide to drive across the
country at a time when motor cars are new and unpredictable. The result of the trip is a rollicking adventure in which the new mother proves that she is
as strong and independent as she is beautiful. Sequel
to *Those Miller Girls.*

Constant, Alberta Wilson. **Those Miller Girls!** T Y
Crowell 1965.

Lou Emma and Maddy are trying to take good care
of their father to avoid having to put up with a house-
keeper. They have moved to Kansas, where their
father teaches at a small college. They have fun, the
three of them, but Lou Emma feels the burden of always being pitied by the neighbors and having so
much responsibility. Their father adores them, but
he needs time for research. Lou Emma sees the answer in the warm, charming Kate, an independent
business woman, who seems to love them and be
interested in their father.

Crane, Caroline. **Don't Look at Me That Way.** Random
1970.

Rosa's mother is a loving woman who is raising her

seven children without a husband or much money.
Now she is pregnant with the eighth child and her
strength has disappeared. Rosa leaves home to work
because her family needs the money she can earn
babysitting for a wealthy family across town. She
desperately wants to permanently escape the hopeless
poverty of her Puerto Rican neighborhood, but she
quickly sees that she doesn't belong with the "gringos."
A telephone call pulls her back to her family—her
mother has not survived the birth of the eighth baby.
Rosa must now make a home for all those little
brothers and sisters, including the newborn baby.

Crane, Caroline. **A Girl Like Tracy.** McKay 1966.

Kathy faces the problem of having a sister like
Tracy—beautiful, strong-willed, indulged, and retarded. Kathy fights to give Tracy the feeling of doing
something useful, even though at times it is almost
too much for her to bear.

Erwin, Betty K. **Behind the Magic Line.** Little 1969.

Dozie's family are warm, loving people, but they do
have a lot of problems. They live in a cramped
apartment in a city, and Dozie's father decides to
buy an old car and drive across the country to a
new city and a new life for them all. Dozie wants
desperately to believe in a fairytale solution to all
their hardships, but when she sees her family work
together to take some real steps toward a better life,
she believes they can make it.

Erwin, Betty K. **Go to the Room of the Eyes.** Berkley
Pub 1969.

A large family moves from the sameness of the suburbs to a big Victorian house in the inner city. The
children have a big adjustment to make, meeting
children who are quite different from those they left
behind in their old neighborhood. The parents are
great; the house is fascinating and even provides the
children with a treasure hunt and a mysterious man
who insists on stealing the baby's teddy bear. Dorothy
Canfield Fisher Children's Book Award.

Eyerly, Jeannette, **The Phaedra Complex.** Lippincott
1971.

It is an awkward situation when a girl's mother
marries an attractive man who has never had a
daughter before, and when the girl has never lived

with a father before. The girl is just starting to date and discover romantic love; and she gets this feeling all confused with the feeling she has for Michael, her new stepfather. The mother senses the tension between her husband and daughter, and interprets it as a love affair. It takes a psychiatrist to sort out the ambivalent feelings, a process especially fascinating to those of us who are interested in psychological intricacies.

Falk, Ann Mari. **Who Is Erika?** HarBraceJ 1963.

Erika's mother remarries and the new "family" moves away from Stockholm, leaving behind Erika's friends. The adjustment is very painful. Erika thinks her new stepfather, a chubby man who laughs a lot, is ridiculous. She hates life in the village, where everyone seems to know her business. With the help of a new boyfriend and time, she comes to accept her new life.

Fenton, Edward. **Duffy's Rocks.** Dutton 1974.

Timothy Brennan, a thirteen-year-old boy, lives in Duffy's Rocks, Pennsylvania, with his grandmother, his aunt, and a cousin. His father, Bart, has deserted them, and Timothy has only a few momentos of him. He decides to find his father, and the journey takes him away from Duffy's Rocks. He returns to a situation that causes him to realize a new beginning.

Fiedler, Jean. **A Break in the Circle.** McKay 1971.

Six months ago, the father died suddenly. His death means a change for each member of the family, especially because he was a very strong, dominant person. His daughter, Julie, is a college student, anxious for security with people and a meaningful career. She is not only coping with the tremendous grief she feels; she is also trying to understand the changes in their lives. Her brother, Pete, is a pre-med student who loves music, and who is now free to give up medicine because his father is no longer around to prevent him from doing what he wants. The mother is turning back to her acting career, which she had abandoned during her marriage.

Fox, Paula. **Blowfish Live in the Sea.** Bradbury Pr 1970.

Twelve-year-old Carrie tells about life with her long-haired, rebellious stepbrother Ben. When Ben's father writes to him for the first time in thirteen years, Ben and Carrie take the bus to Boston to see him. The visit changes Ben's life. National Book Award.

Fox, Paula. **The Stone-Faced Boy.** Schol Bk Serv 1972.

Gus, in the middle of five children, learned years ago that he can escape teasing by not registering any feeling at all. However, at ten, he is beginning to wonder if he could smile or cry even if he wanted to. The children call him "stone-face" and that is the way things stand until the sudden visit of an old great aunt and a midnight adventure rescuing an old dog.

Friis-Baastad, Babbis. **Don't Take Teddy.** Scribner 1967.

Teddy is a fifteen-year-old who is mentally retarded. He lives at home with his parents and his younger brother Mikkel, who tells the story. The day comes that they have all dreaded—Teddy throws a stone and accidently hurts a boy. Mikkel is sure this means Teddy will have to be "put away." He runs away with him, but their flight is disastrous, and running away doesn't solve the dilemma. Mildred L. Batchelder Award.

Frolov, Vadim. **What It's All About.** Doubleday 1968.

A Russian boy is caught up in the mess his parents have made of their marriage. No one tells him what's going on, and he decides to try to find answers for himself. He gets tangled in all kinds of misunderstandings until finally he learns the truth. The book is translated from the Russian and is an interesting close-up view of a teenager's life-style in modern Russia.

Gardam, Jane. **The Summer after the Funeral.** Macmillan 1973.

The death of sixteen-year-old Athene's father brings about an unusual summer for her and her two brothers. While her mother is off looking for a new place for them to live, Athene drifts from one strange situation to another, meeting eccentric people and getting into bizarre experiences.

Gates, Doris. **Blue Willow.** Viking Pr 1940.

Just about the only thing beautiful in Janey's life is the china plate which was her mother's. The plate has a picture of a home, three people, and a willow tree, which represents what Janey wants for herself, her father, and her stepmother. They are victims of the Depression and are forced to wander from farm job to farm job to have enough money to live. In a new neighborhood, Janey makes a friend, loves her teacher, and finds a river with willows just like those on her plate. If only she could stay! Easy to read.

George, Jean Craighead. **Gull Number 737.** T Y Crowell 1964.

Many kids would envy Luke because of the opportunity he has to be involved in important research on animal behavior. His father is a scientist, and the family spend their summers on an island off Nantucket, banding sea gulls, testing the birds' instincts, and observing their behavior. The father is well-meaning, but he tries to force his own theories and career on his son; and the son is struggling for recognition for his own work, independent from his father.

Greene, Constance C. **The Un-Making of Rabbit.** Viking Pr 1972.

Paul has been living with his grandma because his divorced mother lives in New York City and really doesn't want to accept the responsibility of her son. Paul persists in fantasizing about his mother taking him to live with her. Finally, after a visit with his mother and her new husband, Paul realizes that he doesn't really enjoy being with her as much as with his grandma, who loves him and likes to take care of him.

Hamilton, Dorothy. **The Blue Caboose.** Herald Pr 1973.

After Jody's father leaves home to look for steady work, Jody and his mother have to find a cheaper place to live. A train caboose on the edge of town, painted and fixed up with flowers and curtains, makes a perfect place to live. This easy-to-read story tells how Jody and his mother change the old caboose into a home.

Harnden, Ruth. **The High Pasture.** HM 1964.

Tim is living in the Colorado mountains with his aunt for the summer while his mother is ill in the hospital in New York. He befriends a semi-wild dog who later saves his life, and this adventure helps him to put aside the fact that he is being excluded from his parents' lives, even though he knows they are trying to shield him from the misery. When his father appears alone, Tim knows that he will never see his mother again. He feels not only the grief, but a resentment at being kept away while his mother was dying. Easy to read. Child Study Association of America/Wel-Met Children's Book Award.

Holland, Isabelle. **Heads You Win, Tails I Lose.** Lippincott 1973.

This teenage girl feels like a rejected lump of fat. Her skinny mother is always trying to get her on a diet. Nothing helps until she starts sneaking her mother's diet pills, hidden upstairs (her mother's secret "willpower"). Her figure soon begins to shape up, but her nerves are jittery, and her behavior more and more erratic. In the midst of this, her parents have a particularly bitter fight which results in her father moving out and her mother becoming depressed enough to get drunk every day.

Howard, Elizabeth. **A Girl of the North Country.** Morrow 1957.

Calista and her family settle in upper Michigan in a new town where the father hopes to start a new life as a farmer. Even though Calista is only sixteen, she is asked to teach in the new little school. There is no money for school books, and Calista has had no experience, but her folks need the money and the children need a teacher, so she tries her best. When a tree cripples her father, Calista's earnings help them through a miserable winter.

Jarunkova, Klara. **Don't Cry for Me.** Schol Bk Serv 1968.

Olga is fifteen; she is a talented artist and a serious student. She falls for a boy she meets on the street, and her parents are shocked and disapproving. This means fights and sneaking around without their knowing she is meeting him. Olga begins to realize that her parents are not just tense about her affairs, they are also quarrelling with each other, and are in fact on the verge of a separation. She can't understand what has happened to their love for each other. An English translation of a Czechoslovakian story.

Johnston, Norma. **Glory in the Flower.** Atheneum 1974.

This book is a sequel to *The Keeping Days*. Being

fourteen is fun when it means a major role in a play; but it's no fun helping mother have a baby. Tish Sterling copes with the problems of jealousy at school and responsibility at home in the ways she thinks best. In spite of many troubles, she does manage to find a day now and then that's worth "keeping."

Johnston, Norma. **The Keeping Days.** Atheneum 1974.

Being a teenager is hard for Tish Sterling. She has a great deal of responsibility in a family of eight and nothing she does pleases her mother. Worries pile up— there are quarrels with high school friends; her father loses his job; her brother skips classes and has rejected the church. Still Tish finds there are some special days which need to be kept in her memory forever and treasured as her sister treasures her add-a-pearl necklace. This book has a dominant religious theme and presents a strong statement about Christianity.

Kerr, Judith. **When Hitler Stole Pink Rabbit.** Dell 1973.

Anna's parents, being Jews and outspoken against Hitler, decide wisely to leave Germany immediately before Hitler is elected to power. The family first spends an idyllic summer in Switzerland, but things get tougher when they move to Paris. There they must learn a new language, and the father has a difficult time making a decent income with his writing. But it isn't a horror story; it's a warm story of growth under strain, of a family getting closer together because of their struggles coping in a new culture. Easy to read.

Kerr, M. E. **Dinky Hocker Shoots Smack!** Har-Row 1972.

(Dinky doesn't, really, but she writes this all over town to embarrass her do-gooder mother, who spends more time with dope addicts than with her own daughter.) Dinky's mother will drive you wild, just as she drives Dinky to compulsive eating and hostile withdrawal. She picks at, analyzes, and generally interferes with the lives of Dinky and her friends as well as the addicts who hang around. In fact, Dinky's friends are the best possessions she has, but even they have a hard time protecting her from her mother.

Klein, Norma. **Mom, the Wolf Man and Me.** Pantheon 1972.

Brett does not have a father. The twelve-year-old girl enjoys a close relationship with her mother. When her mother finally meets a man whom she would consider marrying, Brett questions her mother about her relations with "the Wolf Man" and the possible results of marrying him.

Klein, Norma. **Taking Sides.** Pantheon 1974.

Nell and her five-year-old brother Hugo live with their father in the city during the winter and with their mother in the country on weekends. Nell, who is twelve, tells the story of their family life after her parents are divorced for the second time.

Koob, Theodora. **The Deep Search.** Lippincott 1969.

The Fontaine family, especially the teenage daughter Dee, don't accept their mentally handicapped son until a neighborhood child shows that the boy needs love and acceptance.

Lawrence, Mildred. **Once at the Weary Why.** HarBraceJ 1969.

Although Crammy's mother and father have been divorced for some time, Crammy feels quite comfortable in her world, which includes a best friend, her mother's undivided attention, and her interest in creating projects and making things. During Crammy's junior year, her mother marries the principal of the high school. Crammy begins to feel desolate and somewhat angry that "Mr. D." now claims some of her mother's attention. In her need to belong, she turns to an "in" crowd at school whose values and ideas are really different from hers. The novel tells what happens in this relationship between Crammy and Gogi's gang, and how Crammy handles that relationship.

Lawrence, Mildred. **Walk a Rocky Road.** HarBraceJ 1971.

Silvy Kershaw lives with her family in the Appalachian Mountains. She wants to go to college but knows her parents do not have the money to send her. It is when she tries to help a friend, Kel McLeod, get a scholarship to study mineralogy that she works out her own problems, too. The land, her own hobby, and a rough-talking Pa all have their places in the final solution to Silvy's problems about college and herself.

Lee, Harper. **To Kill a Mockingbird.** Popular Lib 1972.

Atticus Finch, a lawyer in a small Southern town, defends a black man wrongly accused of rape. The

town reacts violently against this, putting Atticus and
his two children, Scout and Jim, in danger. Seen
through Scout's eyes, the story shows us the bigotry
present in the town and forces us to evaluate our
own attitudes. Pulitzer Prize.

L'Engle, Madeleine. **Meet the Austins.** Vanguard 1960.

There are four Austin children living together happily
in a large house with their father, who is a doctor,
and their mother, who is a singer. Everyone is loving,
sensitive, although at times quarrelsome. Their easy,
fun times are disrupted by the arrival of an orphan
who needs a temporary home. This girl, Maggie, is a
selfish, insecure little thing whom the Austins can't
stand, even though they know they should feel sorry
for her. Sequels to this book include *The Moon by
Night* and *The Young Unicorns*.

Little, Jean. **Home from Far.** Little 1965.

There has been a car wreck, and Jennie's twin
brother is dead. The family is loving and close, but
Jennie feels that no one else misses Michael as she
does. When her parents decide to take two foster
children into the family, Jennie thinks they are trying
to replace Michael and she resents the intrusion of
the strange kids.

Maddock, Reginald. **Danny Rowley.** Little 1970.

This book is full of British slang and customs, but
the reaction of Danny to his mother's remarriage is
easy to understand, especially since the adults don't
do much explaining or show much patience. First in
a rage, Danny runs on the streets, smashing all the
lights. Then he settles down to a smoldering hatred
that occasionally erupts, and things stay that way
until his mother and stepfather try to see things from
his point of view. Easy to read.

Madison, Arnold. **Think Wild!** HR&W 1968.

Frustrated by his father's refusal to let him drive the
family car alone, Ted concentrates on fixing up Blue
Monster, a wreck he and a friend bought at a junkyard. Everyday problems of cars and dating take a
back seat, however, when student rioters rampage
Ted's suburb and a right-wing group lashes out at all
teenagers. Ted matures through his first confrontation
with bigotry and violence and he and his father come
to a new understanding.

Mathis, Sharon Bell. **Listen for the Fig Tree.** Viking Pr 1974.

A sensitive and powerful narrative of a blind girl's world which includes a mother tormented by the murder of the girl's father, good adult friends who give her a sense of family, and a young male companion, Ernie, who helps her realize the true meaning of Kwan, the traditional black African celebration that takes place a few days after Christmas. The book moves quickly, and though its subject matter is black life, it talks of the anxieties, dreams, and hopes of all teenagers.

Mazer, Harry. **Guy Lenny.** Dell 1972.

Guy has all the problems most twelve-year-olds have and then some. His girl likes an older boy, a tough who has a way of causing many problems. Guy has lived the past seven years with his father, but now Emily is taking his father away and destroying their way of life. His mother has come back and wants him to live with her at his father's request. Guy feels he is being bought, bounced around, and that everyone is a cheat and a liar.

Mazer, Norma. **A Figure of Speech.** Delacorte 1973.

Jenny's grandfather lives with them, and he has always been the most special person in her life. When she was a baby, he moved in and took care of her to help her busy mother. Even though she is growing up, she still needs him and feels close to him. He's past eighty now, and Jenny's older brother is married and bringing home his new wife. Everyone but Jenny wants to crowd Grandfather out and into a home for the aged. When Grandfather decides to return to his old farm and support himself once again, Jenny agrees to go too, unable to bear a separation. When they get there, they see that the place has gone to ruin and their efforts can't change it.

Mazer, Norma. **I, Trissy.** Dell 1972.

Trissy is a monster. She ruins her brother's birthday, smears chocolate all over the kitchen of her father's apartment, and loses her best friend through bizarre actions—such as wearing one red sock, one white. Trissy's problem is that she is eleven and her parents are getting a divorce. Her mother plans to remarry, leading Trissy to ask, "But what will I be? I mean, who will I be?"

Murphy, Shirley R. **Poor Jenny, Bright as a Penny.** Viking Pr 1974.

Only her dream of becoming a writer and having a stable home for her young brother keeps Jenny from despair. Her father has died, her mother drinks too much, her older sister is on hard drugs, and the family moves often to avoid welfare inspection. Help comes to Jenny from the police in an unusual and heart-warming way.

Murray, Michele. **The Crystal Nights.** Seabury 1973.

Getting along with a large family in a small Connecticut farmhouse is further complicated for Elly when German relatives escape Hitler's persecution of the Jews and come to live with them. Money is scarce as Elly and her older brother try to plan for college and careers.

Neufeld, John. **Edgar Allan.** S G Phillips 1968.

A book that examines, through the story of "E.A.," the relationships between a ten-year-old Michael and his father, between a mother and father, between sisters and brothers. It further probes the feelings of all of the members of a family as they adjust to the possible adoption of a newcomer, Edgar Allan, who is black, three years old, and eager. This is Michael's story of how the problems and concerns surrounding the acceptance of Edgar Allan are worked out. Michael further shares with the reader his concerns about how a boy works out the problems of reconciling adults' behavior with what they *say* is right.

Ogilvie, Elizabeth. **The Pigeon Pair.** McGraw 1967.

A tarpaper shack on the back road is home for twins Ingrid and Greg, but they have a life dream of buying a real home for their parents and brothers and sisters. This is their fight to overcome poverty and prejudice.

Peck, Richard. **Don't Look and It Won't Hurt.** HR&W 1972.

Carol Patterson learns to cope with the problems of being the middle child in a very poor family. Living in a small town brings additional problems when her older sister becomes involved with a drug pusher and becomes pregnant. There are not many good things in Carol's life, but she finds enough to handle the bad.

Peck, Robert Newton. **A Day No Pigs Would Die.** Dell 1972.

A moving story about Robert Newton Peck, a Vermont boy who, in the course of the story, becomes a man. The usual problems of his age are helped by an understanding family and friends. The book is a New England rendition of the Waltons. Each chapter encompasses one episode in Robert's life. The characters are so well portrayed that you begin to feel you know them as people. Characters' language may offend some readers.

Phipson, Joan. **The Family Conspiracy.** HarBraceJ 1964.

In the Australian outback, a family of individualists face the problem of lack of funds for their mother's needed operation. Each child finds his or her own way of earning money and each gets some experience of life in the process. Not every project is successful even though the enthusiasm is there. In fact, the children's strange behavior is beginning to worry their parents, who don't know what they are trying to do. Easy to read.

Phipson, Joan. **Threat to the Barkers.** HarBraceJ 1965.

A family is threatened by sheep thieves who might carry off their best animals. Edward accidentally stumbles on their hideout and sees for himself who is involved and learns their plans. But the thieves discover him there and threaten to burn his family's farm if he informs. For days Edward is crippled with indecision. He tries to protect the sheep without looking suspicious either to his family or to the thieves. Easy to read.

Platt, Kin. **Chloris and the Creeps.** Chilton 1973.

Her parents' divorce and her father's subsequent suicide have left Chloris bitter. She particularly resents her mother's suitors, each of whom she calls a creep. Chloris, with the help of a psychiatrist and Fidel, one of the creeps, comes to know more about herself and the false image of her father she has created.

Rabin, Gil. **Changes.** Har-Row 1973.

Changes are coming so fast in Chris's life, he hardly knows what he is feeling. After his father's sudden death he, his mother, and grandfather move from South Dakota to New York City. Chris adjusts to

the city, falls in love, and begins a full-time job, even
though he is only fourteen. Then Grandfather has a
stroke which blinds and slowly disorients the old man.
Chris can't forgive his mother for putting him into a
nursing home, but on the other hand, he knows
that school is starting soon and his mother must work,
so there will be no one at home to nurse Grandfather.

Sorenson, Virginia. **Miracles on Maple Hill.** HarBraceJ
1972.

Marly's father has returned from a prisoner-of-war
camp in Korea, but he is depressed and withdrawn.
The family moves to a farm in rural New England,
hoping that nature and solitude will help him to
regain an interest in life. The miracles are the usual
ones provided by nature as the seasons change and
the father slowly heals. John Newbery Medal.

Stolz, Mary. **By the Highway Home.** Har-Row 1971.

Nothing in Catty's family has been the same since
Beau, the oldest son, was killed in Vietnam. The
laughter and love seem to have dissolved into a silent
tension. Now Catty's father has lost his job and they
move to rural Vermont to help in a guest house. From
the beginning they love the place and the aching
grief is eased by the natural beauty around them. The
only one who is still miserable is Gloria, Catty's glamorous but nasty older sister.

Streatfeild, Noel. **The Family at Caldicott Place.**
Random 1968.

There is a car accident and the father is seriously
injured. The children and their mother are miserable
when they find out that it will be many months before
he can leave the hospital. They decide to change their
old life by moving to a big house in the country with
three wealthy children paying board to provide the
family income. It is a difficult move, but an adventurous one. The father is able to come from the hospital
to recuperate in the quiet guesthouse on the large
estate. The boarding children bring problems with
them, but they also bring fun and companionship to
the family in trouble.

Summers, James L. **The Long Ride Home.** Westminster
1966.

Todd, a junior, and his sister Ann, a sophomore, with
their alcoholic father and his wife, Cora, move to a
small town, where Todd and Ann try to keep from

getting involved in school life because they are sensitive about their home life. But then they do become involved and find Alcoholics Anonymous a big help.

Sykes, Pamela. **Our Father!** Nelson 1970.

A family constantly on the move, a hotel in France, and a young girl's dream—all add up to a summer that is far from ordinary. This story is written with warmth and humor.

Townsend, John Rowe. **Trouble in the Jungle.** Lippincott 1969.

A steady fellow is the hero of this story set in a British slum. He and his equally resourceful sister, along with their younger cousins, have been deserted by their irresponsible guardians, an uncle and his current woman. In order to stay together instead of being split up into foster homes, the children try desperately to hide the fact that they have no adult looking after them. Unfortunately, their hideout is also the hideout of a gang of thieves and smugglers, one of whom is their uncle.

Uchida, Yoshiko. **Hisako's Mysteries.** Scribner 1969.

Hisako is a girl growing up in modern Japan. She has led a quiet life with her traditional grandparents, who have always sheltered her from troubles and provided a good life for her. Hisako is stunned to discover that her father is alive, struggling as a poor artist. Her grandparents have never approved of him, and so she is faced with the decision of either leaving her grandparents or giving up her father once again. Easy to read.

Uchida, Yoshiko, **In-Between Miya.** Scribner 1967.

Twelve-year-old Miya has a chance to leave her poor but lively family in a Japanese village to stay with her rich aunt and uncle in Tokyo. At first she is fascinated with the luxury, but she soon learns that it does not automatically mean happiness. She is impulsive and vivacious, and her way of life is fascinating to us, whose lives are quite different and yet in ways quite similar.

Ward, Martha Eads. **Ollie Ollie Oxen-Free.** Abingdon 1969.

Ollie Wellingham is loyal to his father—a man who is often dishonest and lazy. When they are caught stealing dirt, Ollie's father joins a crew working on a

levee to save the farmland from the flooding Mississippi River. Mr. Wellingham risks his life when the
levee breaks.

Warren, Mary Phraner. **Walk in My Moccasins.** Westminster 1966.

Five Indian children have lost their mother and father
in an accident. Miraculously they are all adopted together by two loving novice parents. But there are
many difficulties when a new family is formed so
suddenly: the mother isn't used to the mess and noise
five children can make; the children, particularly
the oldest girl, are concerned about holding onto their
Indian identity. Easy to read.

Weaver, Stella. **A Poppy in the Corn.** Pantheon 1961.

The Poppy is a French orphan who joins a happy,
normal English family when she is thirteen. She
is experienced and competent in comparison to the
English children because she has had to fight to
survive throughout her life, but she has never known
love. She steals and does not understand why. This
is her story of gradual understanding of herself, and
her new family's love and acceptance of her.

Weverka, Robert. **Apple's Way.** Bantam 1975.

George Apple moves his family back to Appleton, Iowa,
his boyhood home. The whole family loves the peace
and quiet of the country. They are glad to get
away from the smog and into the fresh air. But a
developer comes up with a multimillion dollar scheme
that will turn Appleton into a big city. Now the
whole family must struggle to save the small town they
love, and to make others understand what they would
be losing. Based on the television series *Apple's Way*.

Weverka, Robert. **The Waltons.** Bantam 1974.

John-Boy of the Walton family is on spring vacation.
He doesn't figure anything will be different on this
vacation. Then he gets odd jobs, helps to catch a
criminal, and, best of all, meets Jenny, a runaway
girl. The novel is based on the television series "The
Waltons."

Willard, Barbara. **Storm from the West.** HarBraceJ
1964.

This story tells what happens when a British mother
of two marries an American father of four and the
eight of them try spending their holiday together on

the Scottish coast. The fights and fears are believable; the dangers are real (falls, storms, swimming accidents). The parents get so exasperated with the kids and their constant bickering, they decide to leave them alone for a few days to find a workable arrangement for living together.

Wojciechowska, Maia. **Hey, What's Wrong with This One?** Har-Row 1969.

This is really in a format for younger kids, but it is so hilarious and so filled with raw child behavior, you might like to glance through it or recommend it to someone. Three brothers, gone slightly wild without the influence of a mother, chase even the paid housekeepers away with their madcap projects. The seven-year-old decides what they need is a new mother, and he starts the search with an unabashed directness. Easy to read. Georgia Children's Book Award.

On being free

Arnold, Elliott. **A Kind of Secret Weapon.** Scribner 1969.

Peter is eleven in 1943; he can hardly remember what it was like in his country, Denmark, before the Nazis came. One day he interrupts his parents printing an illegal newspaper in their basement, and he begs to help them in their underground activities. He delivers papers to a "connection" and has the horrifying experience of being chased by the Gestapo. Peter and his mother and father become very close in the weeks that follow, sharing their struggle, working together at great risk to themselves. Then one night, the Gestapo arrests his father and he and his mother must go into hiding to avoid being captured.

Benchley, Nathaniel. **Bright Candles: A Novel of the Danish Resistance.** Har-Row 1974.

This is more detailed than *A Kind of Secret Weapon,* but it too is the story of a young Dane's involvement in his country's resistance to the Nazi occupation. The narrative concentrates on methods, attitudes, and people during the five years Jens is committed to the struggle. It is honest, recognizing Jens' first actions as little more than schoolboy pranks. As Jens matures, his moral philosophy is formed. He knows why he fights, and he is willing to make any sacrifice, even to give his own life, in order to bring about the defeat of an evil force.

Bloch, Marie Halun. **Aunt America.** Atheneum 1972.
Lesya is a Russian child whose parents have spent time in prison because of their protest against the government. She is ashamed of this and also of their present refusal to take part in the community. Instead she admires her prosperous uncle, who has succeeded because he takes care not to offend anyone in power. When Lesya's American aunt visits the family and shows sympathy and even respect for Lesya's parents, Lesya begins to reconsider the situation. She starts looking at the way they live through her aunt's eyes, and can no longer ignore the political repression in evidence everywhere. Easy to read.

Coles, Robert. **Saving Face.** Dell 1972.
When black students are bussed to Andy's school, parents, teachers, and students react. The tensions increase until a teacher overreacts to a black student who has not done his homework. A protest demonstration brings the police. Andy's father is one of the policemen.

Courlander, Harold. **The Son of the Leopard.** Crown 1974.
In an African village, the people think the dead are reincarnated in the living. Each new baby born is told who he was in an earlier life. The witch doctor says one new baby was Solde Nebri, a former leader who killed many people. So when the boy is ten years old, he is thrown out of the village. He tries to perform good deeds but in his anger fulfills a strange prophecy that he will fail three times. He finally finds his true identity and receives a new name.

Crosby, Alexander L. **One Day for Peace.** Dell 1971.
Jane Simon writes to the President to ask, "Why are we at war in Vietnam?" Encouraged by her father, Jane and her junior high school friends organize a parade protesting the war in Vietnam. Many leading citizens join the young people in their protest.

Deyneka, Anita. **Tanya and the Border Guard.** D C Cook 1973.
This religious story is about a Christian family in Russia. Three Russian soldiers interrupt a secret

prayer meeting in the woods which Tanya and her family are attending. Tanya trusts one soldier and prays that he will help her get her father a Bible.

Ellis, Mel. **Sidewalk Indian.** HR&W 1974.

Charley Nightwind has lived in Milwaukee for most of his life. He is a "sidewalk Indian." But when Charley is falsely accused of murdering a policeman during an Indian protest, he is forced to flee the city and seek refuge on his people's reservation. Helped by Betty Sands, an Indian girl, Charley hides out from the law on Spirit Flowage, lake of floating islands. Charley learns what it means to be an Indian and become involved in a dangerous plan to blow up the hated power dam which has robbed the Indians of some of their best farmland on the reservation.

Hayes, William D. **Project: Scoop.** Atheneum 1966.

A clash of ideals and a contest of will between a school principal and a student editor leads to a series of incidents involving the principal, Mr. Hanhauser, vs. crusading editor Pete. A hilarious "trial" involves Hanhauser as judge, Pete as defense attorney for perennially tardy Burchmore Weems, and a large part of the student body. Easy to read.

Hentoff, Nat. **In the Country of Ourselves.** Dell 1971.

A group of high school students experiment with political ideas in a school situation. Sophisticated conversations reveal their revolutionary plans against an authoritarian principal. When a guest speaker for a black students' club is not allowed to give his talk, the student revolutionaries plan their campaign for the next school year.

Hesse, Hermann (translator Ralph Manheim). **Stories of Five Decades.** FS&G 1973.

This book is a collection of twenty-three short stories written by the German author, Hermann Hesse, over a fifty-year period and now translated into English. "The Steppenwolf" is probably the most familiar title in the collection.

Johnson, Annabel and Edgar Johnson. **The Last Knife.** S&S 1971.

Rick cannot understand why his older brother, Howard, chooses to go to jail rather than be drafted. Howard's friends try to explain the reason to Rick by telling true stories of dissenters in American history: a young Indian boy's defiance of his forefathers' code, a black Mountain Man's refusal to be a servant, and a lawyer's defense against mob rule in Montana Territory.

Leach, Christopher. **Free, Alone, and Going.** Crown 1972.

One afternoon after school, Dave dumps his school books into the river, picks up his knapsack, and—with his buddy Gregg—leaves his home in London. Hitchhiking to a seaport town where they plan to catch a ship to America, Dave and Gregg get caught in a heavy rain, steal food from a party given by very rich people, and see two men fight over a woman. Gregg chickens out and returns home. Dave wants to go on, but he mistakenly tries to hitch a ride in a police car.

Maddock, Reginald. **Thin Ice.** Little 1971.

The hardest part of Bill's move away from London is finding friends he really likes. A negative, cynical fellow erroneously named Angel insistently pursues his friendship, and succeeds through petty blackmail in getting Bill to be in his gang. Bill finally manages to break with Angel, but in doing so puts his new friends and himself in danger.

Solzhenitsyn, Aleksandr (translator Keith Armes). **Candle in the Wind.** Bantam 1974.

This short play by Solzhenitsyn has autobiographical touches. Alex, a brilliant mathematician and teacher, returns to freedom after years of fighting at the front, prison, and exile. Alex persuades his cousin Alda to undergo "neurostabilization," a biofeedback experiment. As a result, Alda loses her capacity for emotional experience.

Sommerfelt, Aimeé. **Miriam.** Schol Bk Serv 1972.

A story of Norway during the Nazi occupation. Because they are Jews, Miriam and her family leave their home and live nearby until the threat of arrest sends them over the border to neutral Sweden. During the tense months of hiding in Oslo, Miriam makes friends with Hanne and Rolf. She idealizes Rolf's sophisticated, beautiful mother until she overhears her tell her husband that "Miriam is sweet now; but think when she becomes a fat old Jew-lady." Miriam is horrified to discover anti-semitism even in people she knows and trusts.

Tunis, John R. **His Enemy, His Friend.** Morrow 1967.
The brutality of war is brought home through the experiences of a German sergeant who befriends the people of an occupied village but is later forced to kill six hostages. He is only able to face his conscience when the French and German teams meet in a World Cup soccer game.

Twain, Mark. **Pudd'nhead Wilson.** Airmont 1966.
Roxana, a white-looking slave, switches her son, Valet de Chambre, for Thomas a Becket Driscoll, a white baby, so that her son will have a better chance in life. After twenty-three years, circumstances restore each to his rightful place, but Tom is uneasy in the white community, having been a slave all his life, and Valet de Chambre, thief and murderer, gets "sold down the river." Pudd'nhead Wilson is the first detective to make use of the science of fingerprinting to solve his friend's murder.

Wuorio, Eva-Lis. **To Fight in Silence.** HR&W 1973.
Thor Eriksen is eager to fight the Germans occupying Denmark in 1940. He is too young for the army. After several mistakes, he becomes part of a daring and successful plan to ship the Danish Jews out of Denmark before the Germans send them to concentration camps.

Zei, Alki. **Petro's War.** Dutton 1972.
Petro's rather ordinary life as a schoolboy in Athens is disrupted by the war and Nazi occupation. He and his family soon find themselves, along with their friends and neighbors, involved in a desperate struggle to survive hunger and brutality. During the long years of the war, Petro matures and takes on duties in the Resistance.

On being friends

Allen, Elizabeth. **The Loser.** Dutton 1969.
Deitz, a high school girl, likes Denny very much. But he is different from other suburban high school boys. His cowboy boots, torn shirt and long hair mark him as a "loser" to the others. He had just "up and walked out of Harvard" which is only a part of his nonconformity. Deitz learns about other people's attitudes toward the nonconformist and about her own.

Through many episodes she learns more about what Denny is truly like.

Allen, Elizabeth. **You Can't Say What You Think and Other Stories.** Dutton 1974.

The high school students in these stories struggle with many problems. They include parents remarrying, moving into a new neighborhood, imitating the popular friend, having no real friends, and having parents disapprove of friends. The students find they can't say what they think—and often don't even know what they themselves think in the first place. They all solve their problems and learn more about what life is really like and who they are.

Anckarsvärd, Karin. **Doctor's Boy.** HarBraceJ 1965.

A doctor's son who has always lived in comfort becomes awakened to the fact of desperate poverty when he sees how some of his father's patients must live. There is a scholarship student from the slum whom Jon admires, but it seems impossible to overlook the huge gap in their backgrounds in order to become friends.

Arthur, Ruth M. **Requiem for a Princess.** Atheneum 1972.

Just when British schoolgirl Willow Forrester is having trouble with her parents over her choice of music as a career, she discovers that she is adopted. She becomes ill, so her "parents" take her out of school for a term and allow her to go to Penliss, a beautiful, ancient estate on the coast, to recover. At Penliss, Willow gains two really close friends. She also has a series of fantastic dreams that help her realize who she is and make being adopted seem less terrible.

Arundel, Honor. **The Girl in the Opposite Bed.** Nelson 1971.

Jane checks into a hospital for the first time and misses her sheltered home. No one is interested in her at all, except Jeannie, who is definitely "lower class." As she fights to overcome her snobbery, Jane begins to see more good in people, and less prejudice in herself.

Blume, Judy. **Then Again, Maybe I Won't.** Bradbury Pr 1971.

This story tells frankly and warmly the adjustments that must be made by thirteen-year-old Tony in a single summer. He moves from the working class neighborhood in Jersey City where he grew up to a wealthy New York suburb, and begins to change from a boy into a young man.

Bonham, Frank. **Cool Cat.** Dell 1971.

Dogtown is a hard place to live—not enough jobs, not enough money, but a whole lot of drugs. Buddy is making it as a lifeguard, Little Pie as a police cadet. The others just drift along until they can get enough money to start a hauling business. But there's trouble with the Machete gang. The gang shoot out the tires of the truck and firebomb it. Little Pie retaliates by destroying the gang leader's car.

Brink, Carol. **Two Are Better than One.** Macmillan 1968.

This is a gentle story of the friendship of two girls who are growing up at the beginning of this century. The girls have two dolls, much like our modern "Barbie" dolls, and they invent fantastic adventures for them. They write these adventures down, chapter by chapter, to make an exciting novel. Easy to read.

Brown, Joe David. **Addie Pray.** G K Hall 1972.

This book from which the film *Paper Moon* was created is the story of a young orphan girl travelling around the South during the Depression in the company of an imaginative con-man. But don't think young Addie is being taken advantage of. No, rather, she shares the brain-work necessary to dream up and execute elaborate swindles. The culmination of their money-making schemes is passing Addie off as the missing heiress of a wealthy old woman in New Orleans. Addie is loyal, loving, independent, and intelligent. And Moses, the con-man who refuses to accept the role of "father," does make a loyal, protective friend and companion.

Burnett, Frances Hodgson. **The Secret Garden.** Dell 1971.

Mary doesn't even know what it is to have a friend. She has grown up in India and her only playmates have been servants who dressed her and obeyed her every little wish. Small wonder it's a shock to her to be in England, where no one seems to pay much attention to her and everyone thinks she is a selfish sour-faced brat. What seems to be a miracle happens to this child and her new friend, a strange boy hidden away in the vast mansion which is their home. Easy to read.

Caras, Roger. **Sarang.** Little 1968.

An American teenager, a blind village boy she befriends in Pakistan, the seeing-eye dog she gets for him, the tiger who kills the dog, and the tiger who comes to take the place of the dog—these are only some of the ingredients which make this book a memorable experience.

Carlson, Natalie Savage. **Ann Aurelia and Dorothy.** Dell 1970.

These two are the kind of friends who can always think up something interesting to do, like making outrageous monster masks for Halloween, creating new recipes by drastic experimentation, choosing a week's groceries and then leaving the full cart at the store. The friendship means much more than such fun, however, because Ann Aurelia's mother has left her with a foster mother and Ann Aurelia has a deep hurt inside. Easy to read.

Carlson, Natalie Savage. **Luvvy and the Girls.** Har-Row 1971.

This well-written book is about an eighth-grade girl who goes to boarding school for the first time. Luvvy worries about her popularity. Will she make friends? Will she do well in school?

Carpelan, Bo. **Bow Island.** Delacorte 1971.

Johan loves the sea and the isolation of his family's summer cottage. It is their first year here, and soon they meet the few neighbors in the area. Marvin is a huge boy who lives on a nearby island. It is evident that he is different, and in fact he is mentally retarded, but the boys are good companions for gardening, fishing, and boating. Two other children are summer people, but unlike Johan they are unable to relate to Marvin. Instead of being friends, they tease him as they would a dumb animal. They are senselessly cruel and Johan is repelled by their cruelty, yet attracted by their energy and excitement.

Cleaver, Vera, and Bill Cleaver. **Ellen Grae.** Dell 1969.

In the small town where Ellen lives, her incredible stories are considered one of the major entertainments. But even Ellen's vivid imagination could never have created the terrible story Ira told her about the circumstances of his parents' death. Ira is a slow, quiet man who never speaks to anyone but Ellen, and after hearing his story, she's sorry he spoke to her. She feels she must protect him, and yet the horror of the secret is literally making her sick. She is irritable with her friends, has nightmares, can't concentrate on her schoolwork, doesn't feel like eating, and is, in fact, miserable. Easy to read.

Cleaver, Vera, and Bill Cleaver. **The Mock Revolt.** Lippincott 1971.

Back in 1939 Ussy Mock was having many of the problems that are around thirty years later. First, minor rebellions consume his energy. For instance, as a protest against the haircut his father demands, he cuts it Mohawk style to aggravate the old man. This kind of activity falls away when he gets involved with a kid his age named Luke. Luke's father is an angry loser; his mother lies around, pale, looking as if she is dying. Ussy wishes he could avoid their problems, but he keeps getting pulled back by their helplessness. The more he helps, the more he feels responsible toward them. Sometimes he could scream with frustration at their mistakes, but he is unable to give them up.

Clewes, Dorothy. **A Boy Like Walt.** Coward 1967.

What are boys who wear motorcycle jackets and shaggy hair really like? Norma thinks she knows what Walt is like, and she is determined to help him.

Clewes, Dorothy. **Storm over Innish.** Nelson 1973.

This Irish tale centers around a mysterious young man with amnesia and broken bones. It tells of his struggle to remember and heal with the help of a girl. A background of family conflict, and gun-smuggling enlivens the story.

Clymer, Eleanor. **Me and the Eggman.** Dutton 1972.

The eggman is an old farmer determined to remain independent even though his health is poor and money is scarce. His plight is discovered by Donald, a city boy with problems of his own, who stows away in the eggman's truck to escape his own family. Living a few days with the old man causes Donald to put aside his own difficulties for a time and see life as the egg-

man sees it. Donald is in the country for the first
time, and though he has always dreamed of a freshly
painted farm and clean animals, he never realized
the immense hard labor that is necessary to maintain
a farm. Easy to read.

Cole, Sheila R. **Meaning Well.** Watts 1974.

For as long as Lisa can remember, Peggy Hatch has
been the outcast at school. Now, in sixth grade, Lisa
and Susan befriend her. But when Susan changes her
mind and decides to torment and tease Peggy, Lisa
is caught between them. Should she follow what she
has been taught to be right, or should she follow
Susan, the group leader, the most popular girl in
class?

Corcoran, Barbara. **Don't Slam the Door When You Go.**
Atheneum 1974.

Judith and two of her friends have been planning
their escape for months. They have a car, money,
and a destination in Montana. Plunketville, Montana,
is not what they expect, but the girls, just out of
high school, are determined to make it on their own.

Corcoran, Barbara. **A Trick of Light.** Atheneum 1972.

Cassandra and Paige are twins who have always
understood each other and done everything together.
Now Paige seems to ignore her for new friends and
new interests, and Cassandra often feels hurt and
angry. He rebels at her possessiveness. When the
story begins, they are temporarily united in their
search for their missing dog. They follow the trail
of his blood into the woods and must spend the night
camping out. As they struggle together against the
cold and against their fears for the dog, they know
once more how special they are to each other.

Donovan, John. **Remove Protective Coating a Little at a
Time.** Har-Row 1973.

When you grow up with parents who treat you more
like a kid brother, there are bound to be some things
missing in life. Harry is like this, and when his
parents begin to have problems, he meets and befriends the strange, seventy-year-old Amelia. From
her he learns many of the realities of life. The novel
is realistic in identifying a fourteen-year-old boy's
problems and solutions.

Ellis, Ella Thorp. **Celebrate the Morning.** Atheneum 1974.

April and her mother are on the welfare roll of the small California town in which they live. Still, life wouldn't be half bad for April if only her mother would stay in the real world and not become so confused. April fears she'll be placed in a foster home and lose her friends if people find out about her mother.

Fitzhugh, Louise. **Harriet the Spy.** Har-Row 1964.

Harriet's home is usually empty and boring and so she roams the streets and other people's homes to find some excitement. She spies on people, entering their homes secretly or positioning herself so that she can eavesdrop on conversations and observe people when they think they are alone. All the information Harriet uncovers is carefully recorded in her special notebooks. Unfortunately her friends get hold of the notebooks and discover what Harriet is up to, and worse, what she really thinks of them. Harriet has become one of the most popular characters ever created for young readers, and if you start her story, you will soon see why.

Graham, Gail. **Cross-Fire: A Vietnam Novel.** Pantheon 1972.

When Harry regains consciousness in a jungle in Vietnam, he finds he is separated from his platoon. He also finds that he has four new companions: a girl, two small children, and a young boy who wants to kill him. They are enemies in war, but they have to cooperate to survive.

Greene, Bette. **The Summer of My German Soldier.** Dial 1973.

Patty Bergen is an only child. Her parents spend most of their time at their store. In the small Southern town where they live, they are a Jewish family in a sea of Gentiles, and Patty's parents are nervous about calling attention to themselves. You can imagine their horror when their daughter is arrested for helping a German prisoner of war hide in their back yard. It is an outrage to them that while Jews are struggling to survive the Nazi policy of extermination, one little Jewish girl tries to assist a Nazi soldier. The truth is that this soldier is one of the few people in her life to care about her and pay attention to her. Society of Children's Book Writers Golden Kite Award.

Greene, Constance C. **A Girl Called Al.** Viking Pr 1969.
Al is on the fat side, neglected by her parents in a benevolent sort of way. She moves into a city apartment and makes friends with another girl living there. The two of them become close companions and their friendship makes a very warm, often humorous story.

Hall, Lynn. **The Siege of Silent Henry.** Follett 1972.
An unexpected friendship develops between Robert Short and the old man, Silent Henry. At first, Robert plans to win Henry's friendship and deceive the old man into letting him share the profitable crop of ginseng herbs that grows behind Henry's house. But Robert learns more from the old man about strength and honesty, not knowing that Henry is himself troubled by secret failures in his own past.

Hamilton, Virginia. **The Planet of Junior Brown.** Macmillan 1971.
Buddy and Junior are friends in a big city. Buddy has no family and lives within a cooperative system of runaway boys. He sponsors a "planet" of younger boys, working to provide clothing, food, and a hideaway for them. When Junior, a 300-pound musical prodigy, leaves home, Buddy takes him to his planet. Lewis Carroll Shelf Award; National Book Award.

Harris, Marilyn. **The Peppersalt Land.** Four Winds 1970.
Tollie is black and Slocum is white. The two girls always spend their summers together. When they are twelve, Tollie shouts, "I'm a nigger, and you're not!" Their friendship seems doomed until they become interested in the stories a young black student architect tells them about the dangerous swamp called Peppersalt Land.

Havrevold, Finn (translator Cathy Babcock Curry). **Undertow.** Atheneum 1970.
Jorn, a Norwegian boy, can't understand why his parents are upset that he isn't spending the summer with them, nor why they don't like his friend Ulf. Ulf is a little strange, but Jorn feels this is just because he is older. Jorn is excited, if not apprehensive, about

the sailboat trip they plan to take, off the Norwegian coast. Later Jorn realizes he is in the midst of a test of wills that can only result in disaster.

Hinton, S. E. **The Outsiders.** Dell 1967.

After their parents die, the three Curtis brothers stay together in their home. They are poor and, therefore, "greasers." The youngest brother tells the story of constant fighting between Socs and Greasers, resulting directly in the death of one boy and indirectly in the destruction of several others.

Hinton, S. E. **That Was Then, This Is Now.** Dell 1971.

Gang wars, drugs, and everyday teenage existence in a slum neighborhood are a part of this story. Mark and Bryon grow up together like brothers—close friends. They are very different, but they are good buddies. After Bryon falls in love with Cathy, their lives change.

Hooker, Ruth. **Gertrude Kloppenberg II.** Abingdon 1974.

Gertrude Kloppenberg ends her fifth grade school year by starting her second notebook diary. Throughout the summer, the entries tell of sad and happy days, including the friendship she develops with the teasing neighbor boy she teaches to read by writing stories about him.

Jeffries, Roderic. **Trapped.** Har-Row 1972.

Gerry, trying to prove his courage and friendliness, goes hunting with Bert, one of his classmates. After stealing a boat, the two boys are trapped on the mudflats in a snowstorm.

Jones, Cordelia. **Nobody's Garden.** Scribner 1966.

Hilary talks too much and most of her classmates get sick of her. However when a new girl named Bridget comes to class, it takes someone as persistent as Hilary to break through her reserve. No one knows exactly why Bridget is so timid and withdrawn; they only know that she has lost her parents in the war. Hilary discovers that Bridget likes growing plants, and inspired by *The Secret Garden,* she searches all over London for an abandoned garden which she and Bridget can work on together. The garden does help; but not until Bridget can talk about what happened to her parents in the war is she able to be a real friend.

Jones, Weyman B. **Edge of Two Worlds.** Dial 1968.

A young boy is the only survivor of an ambush on
a wagon train. In his attempt to find his way back
to civilization he becomes involved with an old Indian
who is on a journey to Mexico. Through this friendship, understanding grows. Western Heritage Juvenile
Book Award.

Konigsburg, E. L. **Jennifer, Hecate, Macbeth, William
McKinley, and Me, Elizabeth.** Atheneum 1967.

Elizabeth is new and hasn't found any friend worth
knowing until she finds Jennifer, dressed in an old
pilgrim costume, in a tree on the way to school.
Jennifer is fascinating; she is mainly interested in
witchcraft, and she starts Elizabeth on a program
of initiation rites. Jennifer is a domineering person,
but the two finally decide they can trust each other
and admit their friendship. Easy to read.

Lawrence, Mildred. **Once at the Weary Why.** HarBraceJ
1969.

Although Crammy's mother and father have been
divorced for some time, Crammy feels quite comfortable in her world, which includes a best friend, her
mother's undivided attention, and her interest in
creating projects and making things. During Crammy's
junior year, her mother marries the principal of the
high school. Crammy begins to feel desolate and somewhat angry that "Mr. D." now claims some of her
mother's attention. In her need to belong, she turns
to an "in" crowd at school whose values and ideas
are really different from hers. The novel tells what
happens in this relationship between Crammy and
Gogi's gang, and how Crammy handles that relationship.

Lee, Mildred. **Fog.** Seabury 1972.

This adventure story tells how Luke, his club friends,
his girl Milo, Milo's mother and Luke's father, Henry
Sawyer, all face life and grow up. Incidents from the
clubhouse fire to Henry's death force Luke to look
at himself and see what he is doing with his life.

Lingard, Joan. **The Twelfth Day of July: A Novel of
Modern Ireland.** Nelson 1972.

Sadie and Tommy are Protestants. Kevin and his
sister, Brede, are Catholics. In Northern Ireland, they

are supposed to be enemies, and they do play tricks on each other. However, when a riot develops on the twelfth day of July, a Protestant day of celebration, and Brede is injured, they all realize how much they care for each other. *Across the Barricades* and *Into Exile* by the same author continue the story.

Little, Jean. **Look Through My Window.** Har-Row 1970.

Emily is the only child in a quiet family. Her life suddenly changes when four little cousins need to live with them, and they move to a big house in a new town. It is chaos for the most part until Emily meets Kate, her first real friend. Their warm relationship stimulates their shared interests and provides support when each needs help. Easy to read.

Little, Jean. **One to Grow On.** Archway 1974.

Janie is a quite, rather plain girl who feels no one could be interested in her for herself. She often elaborates stories to make her life seem more attractive. Her family doesn't really understand her, although they do try. In her loneliness she is extremely vulnerable to the selfishness of other girls who just want to use her for one reason or another. Slowly Janie does begin to learn to believe in herself enough to be a good friend.

Neville, Emily C. **Berries Goodman.** Har-Row 1965.

When Berries and his family move to the suburbs from New York City, they are unprepared for the narrow-minded anti-semitism so ingrained in the culture of their new neighborhood. The people next door are original Archie Bunkers and their daughter who plays with Berries is contaminated by their bigotry. Ironically the only other friend Berries finds is a Jewish boy whose mother is an up-tight neurotic, forbidding her son to play with non-Jews. Believe it or not, there are plenty of laughs here too, and the Goodman family find a perfect revenge as they move out with a flair. Jane Addams Book Award.

Neville, Emily C. **The Seventeenth-Street Gang.** Har-Row 1966.

Minnow and her friends share a passionate "in" feeling and decide to reject a new boy who has a fierce-looking dog and doesn't seem to care about being friends. Actually the boy, Hillis, really doesn't know how to make friends. He can swim though, and the day arrives when Minnow falls into the East River and needs rescuing.

Ney, John. **Ox Goes North: More Trouble for the Kid at the Top.** Bantam 1973.

Fifteen-year-old Ox comes from a very eccentric rich family. He is fat, big, and a year behind in school. For the summer, he goes to Camp Downing in New England. This boy, who has everything and still isn't happy, confounds everyone. But Ox finds adventure by helping Tommy Campbell, whose grandparents have schemed to take his trust fund money.

Ottley, Reginald. **The War on William Street.** Nelson 1973.

A story of Australian youth during the Depression is the basis of this book. It centers around three boys from wide-ranging backgrounds, involved in gang warfare in Sydney, Australia, of the thirties. The author describes the lifestyle of the well-off and the poor, and the way boys from three backgrounds can get along.

Parker, Richard. **A Time to Choose.** Har-Row 1973.

A glimpse of a world other than theirs is shared by Stephen and Mary, and they must answer their questions themselves. This novel is set in England and deals with typical teenage problems which are solved in a most unusual way.

Parkinson, Ethelyn M. **Rupert Piper and Megan, the Valuable Girl.** Abingdon 1972.

Megan Donahue is valuable to the baseball team even though she is a girl. She can read minds. The summer she moves to Wakefield, movie scouts are looking over the town to see if it is the typical American town. Rupert and his friends decide to help Wakefield get chosen by doing many "typical" things like raising a goose.

Peck, Robert Newton. **Soup.** Knopf 1974.

These are gentle but boisterous stories of a friendship between two young boys, living some years ago in a small town. The chapters are full of minor incidents, many funny, but nothing so different from many ordinary, happy childhoods. Easy to read.

Perl, Lila. **Me and Fat Glenda.** Seabury 1972.

Sara Mayberry's parents look like what some people have called "bohemians" and "hippies." They move into the conservative town of Havenhurst in a garbage truck, and Sara's father sets up his junk sculpture in the yard, while her mother stirs her tie-dyeing vats. The only person to become Sara's friend is lonely Fat Glenda.

Perl, Lila. **That Crazy April.** Seabury 1974.

A month of crazy events, including a fashion show and an episode involving Women's Lib, leads an eleven-year-old girl, Cress Richardson, to think more about herself as a person and to resolve some problems.

Perrin, Blanche C. **Hundred Horse Farm.** St Martin 1973.

This is the story of Suzy Taylor, whose parents own Cherrydale Farm, and her two cousins, Ann and Roddy, who come to live there after their parents are killed in an automobile accident. Suzy teaches her cousins how to ride the horses, and the three of them have many adventures. A farm that raises and races thoroughbred horses is an exciting place to grow up.

Pevsner, Stella. **Call Me Heller, That's My Name.** Seabury 1973.

Hildegarde loves her nickname, Heller, and does her best to live up to it. She resists admitting she is a girl until the boys she pals around with gradually ease her out of the gang. Her proof of courage is to set off fireworks in the cemetery one midnight. Heller finally breaks her self-imposed exile from the feminine world.

Putcamp, Luise, Jr. **The Christmas Carol Miracle.** Abingdon 1970.

It is cold winter and the children in the orphanage will have no place to go when their building is condemned. Luckily, it is also Christmas. Christmas is a time for miracles.

Rogers, Pamela. **The Rare One.** Nelson 1974.

Upset about his father's remarriage, thirteen-year-old Toby finds friendship with Josh, who lives alone in the woods. When an essay contest is announced, Toby writes one on Josh and, as a result, changes both of their lives.

Ruark, Robert. **The Old Man and the Boy.** Fawcett World 1971.

The Old Man knows pretty nearly everything. He's

willing to talk about what he knows, and he never talks down to a kid who wants to find things out. The essence of this story, however, is the most precious legacy the old can convey to the young—a sense of the satisfaction, dignity, and joy inherent in everyday living.

Sachs, Marilyn. **Peter and Veronica.** Doubleday 1969.

Peter's family doesn't approve of his friendship with a non-Jewish girl. When he insists that she should be invited to his Bar Mitzvah, his mother just about goes nuts. Peter feels that it is a matter of principle and fights on, never even considering that shy, gawky Veronica might not even want to come. After all the struggle and final victory, Veronica doesn't show up and Peter is so angry he is ready to explode. It takes some real honesty for both of them to work this out in order to continue their friendship.

Schellie, Don. **Me, Cholay and Co. Apache Warriors.** Four Winds 1973.

When the lieutenant puts seventeen-year-old Joshua Thane in charge of a young Apache prisoner, no one realizes that the boys will become good friends. Together they rescue the Apache's little sister from a Papago tribe, which had massacred 125 Apache women and children.

Schmidt, Kurt. **Annapolis Misfit.** Crown 1974.

"I used to think a man was a guy who could drink hard stuff, swear good, and be a big deal with the women," Charlie Hammel, fourth classman at Annapolis says. Charlie changes his attitude about what it means to be a man, as well as his attitude about what life at Annapolis is really like.

Shotwell, Louisa R. **Magdalena.** Viking Pr 1971.

Magdalena is a lovely, well-behaved girl who is quietly rebelling against the rigid Puerto Rican traditions which her grandmother insists upon. When the principal at school asks her to be friendly to a new girl, Spook, Magdalena thinks at first she will do her "duty" by befriending the bedraggled, unruly girl. Oddly enough, her grandmother, so afraid of all American influences, takes one look at Spook and loves her. The two girls soon are good friends, each one influencing the other for the better. Easy to read.

Snyder, Zilpha K. **The Changeling.** Atheneum 1970.

Marty's family is solid middle class; Ivy's family is a grouping of failures, constantly on the move. But both girls share a similar loneliness and build exciting worlds of their own by pretending, acting, and creating. As they get older (their story begins when they are seven and ends when they are fifteen), their play-acting becomes more complex and sophisticated and finally gives each girl an identity to be proud of: one as an actress, the other as a dancer.

Snyder, Zilpha K. **The Egypt Game.** Atheneum 1967.

April and Melanie have a rare friendship which revolves around an intricate pretend game which they invent. The secret language, costumes, and oracles lead them into involvement with a neighborhood murder. Although the two girls share a vivid imagination and numerous adventures, they are very different. April is insecure and hides under false eyelashes and loud boasting. Luckily Melanie is capable of overlooking these faults and giving April a chance to learn to belong. Easy to read.

Snyder, Zilpha K. **The Witches of Worm.** Atheneum 1972.

Jessica is alone most of the time in the apartment she shares with her attractive, young working mother. She has recently lost her best friend, Brandon, through a violent argument, and has even been thrown over by the only school friend she has. One day she finds a strange kitten, and even though it is exceptionally ugly and not at all affectionate, she raises it, names it Worm, and Worm gradually becomes her only companion. Jessica begins doing hateful, spiteful acts against her mother and the neighbors, and she is convinced that Worm has some evil power which causes her to act against her will. It is Brandon who returns in time to help her figure out the truth. Easy to read. National Book Award.

Spence, Eleanor. **The Nothing Place.** Har-Row 1973.

In this Australian suburb, the children have no organizations or recreational facilities until they form their own. One of the boys is recovering from a serious illness and his hearing has been impaired. He can only understand when he lip-reads, and he hates to admit his handicap to his new friends.

The kids decide to raise some money for a "community" project, and when the deaf boy finds out the project is a hearing aid for him, he is furious.

Stolz, Mary. **Lands End.** Har-Row 1973.

This book is about a twelve-year-old boy, Joshua, who lives on one of the Florida Keys. He is very talkative, and gets upset easily at parents and friends. Then he meets the Arthurs, who accept him immediately as though he were a member of their family. They live simply and are very poor. After a hurricane, Joshua realizes that the Arthurs have changed his life in a strange way. The book is very well written.

Stolz, Mary. **Leap Before You Look.** Dell 1973.

Divorce is always a painful experience, and more so if one is not prepared for it. Jimmie Gavin isn't. Her mother is moody and intellectual, taken to spending most of her time alone. Her father is affectionate and easygoing, the direct opposite. Jimmie is so busy being fourteen, and with the problems of her friends, she doesn't see the growing antagonism between her parents. It is a shock when the Gavins announce they are going to get a divorce and Jimmie learns she will be living with her snobbish grandmother. A new friendship and a new awareness of life bring Jimmie and her father back together.

Stolz, Mary. **The Noonday Friends.** Har-Row 1965.

Franny and her friend Simone both have such inadequate lives that they expect each other and their friendship to be a perfect oasis from their problems. Of course they are disappointed, and this leads to fights and sulks which add to the general misery of their family situations. Franny's home-life worsens as her father loses yet another job and her mother becomes tense and critical. Simone's home is a crowded apartment full of children and relatives from Puerto Rico, and she has little time to spare from her household responsibilities. Easy to read.

Taylor, Theodore. **The Cay.** Avon 1970.

An old man and a boy are the only survivors of a shipwreck, and they find refuge on a small island in the Caribbean. The boy has been blinded by a blow on his head during the wreck, which makes him helpless and completely dependent on the old man. The man is a gentle, wise black man who knows he must prepare the boy to be self-sufficient in case anything should happen to himself. He has infinite patience, despite the boy's understandable frustrations. The two build a beautiful relationship together, giving an added dimension to an already fascinating survival adventure. Jane Addams Book Award.

Thiele, Colin. **Fire in the Stone.** Har-Row 1974.

Fourteen-year-old Ernie Ryan, working a mine in Australia, discovers opal. Someone robs his claim, but Ernie and his Aboriginal friend Willie Winowie set out to find the thief.

Towne, Mary. **The Glass Room.** FS&G 1971.

Two boys unhappy with their own families meet and become friends. One is from a chaotic family of musicians who are always practicing music rather than organizing their daily existence. The other boy is an only child whose parents are separated, mainly because the father demands quiet and order to the point of isolation and intolerance of others. The boy who craves an end to the uproar of his home finds his oasis in the other household; and his friend finds his longing for some vitality fulfilled in the home of the musicians.

Vining, Elizabeth G. **The Taken Girl.** Viking Pr 1972.

When Veer reaches fifteen, she is eligible to leave the orphanage to become a servant with a family. The first family she is with prove to be an even uglier situation than the barren growing-up years in the orphanage. But life changes for the better when a Quaker family take Veer to help with their boarding house in Philadelphia and love her as their own daughter. Veer slowly responds to the warmth of that love and becomes totally engrossed in the family's participation in helping runaway slaves. John Greenleaf Whittier, the fiery young abolitionist poet, is one of the boarders and Veer adores him, helping him faithfully with his newspaper and copying his poems.

Wallace, Barbara Brooks. **Victoria.** Follett 1972.

Dilys Rattenbury and Victoria Corcoran are sent unwillingly to a New York boarding school. They curb their homesickness by forming a club with their roommates Scarlett and Eugenia. Victoria runs the secret

club whose purpose is to ward off "evil forces" at the
school. The Black Book is Victoria's guide for club
rules and secret signals. When she tries to oust Scarlett from the club, Dilys examines her own motives and
comes to terms with herself and her definition of
friendship.

Walsh, Jill Paton. **Fireweed.** FS&G 1970.

London during the bombing in 1940 is not exactly
the most logical place and time for running away from
home, but Bill and Julie are rebelling teenagers and
don't really care what happens. They meet in an
underground station one night during a bombing
raid and join forces, determined to try to survive on
their own and enjoy some freedom. They spend the
next few months literally on the London streets, watching the destruction expand until it nearly engulfs them.
They are above all loyal to each other, but when
a tiny waif becomes their responsibility, they realize
they can only enjoy their own freedom when they
aren't causing hurt to someone else.

Watson, Sally. **Other Sandals.** HR&W 1966.

Devra has grown up on a kibbutz in Israel and harbors
a real hatred for all Arabs. When her parents send
her to Haifa one summer, she is lonely at first until
she meets a girl in the park one day. She discovers
later that her new friend is an Arab, and they both
become fascinated by the contrasts of their cultures.
Devra, being such a provincial, and an impulsive one
at that, jumps right into maneuvers within the Arab
family to get a better life for her friend. She learns
how shallow her knowledge was which fed her
prejudice, and involvement and friendship make a
new person of her.

Wells, Rosemary. **The Fog Comes on Little Pig Feet.**
Dial 1972.

A witty, rebellious thirteen-year-old named Rachel
is sent to a snob boarding school by her parents who
want to give her the "best." She hates almost everything about the school, especially the lack of privacy
and freedom of movement. Inadvertently she becomes
involved with an older, hip girl who runs away to
New York City, telling Rachel where to find her. This
unwanted knowledge catches Rachel between the
"Honor Code" of the school and her personal feeling
of loyalty to the girl. She is pressured even farther

when she learns that the runaway has a reputation for
emotional instability and may really need help.

Wersba, Barbara. **The Dream Watcher.** Atheneum
1968.

Albert Schully has no friends. His mother believes
that she sacrificed herself in suburbia for him. His
father is a sympathetic man who drinks to dull his
own disappointment in himself and his life. Albert
thinks he is the only kid around who is critical of
suburban materialism, who loves "culture" and who
has no competitive spirit. Luckily he meets a great
old lady who teaches him somehing about enjoying
life and other people.

Westheimer, David. **My Sweet Charlie.** NAL 1966.

Marlene, an uneducated southern white girl, and
Charlie, a black northern intellectual, are both running.
When they meet they hate each other, but their
plight forces them to trust and even love each other.
They begin to see each other as individuals and find
they must re-examine their own attitudes.

Windsor, Patricia. **Something's Waiting for You, Baker
D.** Har-Row 1974.

In this mystery for mature readers, Baker D. knows
something is after him. He names the something
Slynacks, not knowing who or what they are. Mary
the Hulk, who makes following people a compulsive
hobby, follows Baker and his kidnappers from New
York to Sawtruck, Maine, where the two of them
make some startling discoveries.

Windsor, Patricia. **The Summer Before.** Har-Row 1973.

The death of a very special friend removes Alexandra
from reality. When she comes home after being
hospitalized, her parents are so concerned that they
almost suffocate the few sparks of life she has
left. This novel traces her gradual regaining of
stability and a sense of reality and of herself. Desperately, Alexandra fights isolation as she seeks life.

Winthrop, Elizabeth. **Walking Away.** Har-Row 1973.

Emily has always spent her summers on her grandparents' farm, helping with the work and enjoying
their company. This summer her best friend from the
city is coming for a visit, and Emily expects that the
vacation will be especially good. But when Nina

arrives, she doesn't fit into the pattern. She likes adventure and risk more than chores and quiet talks with grandparents. Emily feels guilty because she goes off with Nina to explore rather than help as she usually does on her visits. Her warm, easy relationship with her grandfather turns chilly and uncomfortable. Then during the winter, it is too late to make amends.

Young, Bob, and Jan Young. **Across the Tracks.** Messner 1958.

Betty Ochoa is a popular senior at Bellamar High. As the conflicts between the Chicano students and the white students increase, Betty finds herself torn between her white friends and her Mexican heritage.

Zindel, Paul. **The Pigman.** Har-Row 1968.

Two high school sophomores have a story to tell about a very disturbing incident in their lives. Both John and Lorraine come from unhappy homes and, together, become involved with a lonely old man they nickname the Pigman. Their story concerns what happens between them and the Pigman and what they do which causes Lorraine to feel that they murdered him. The story is sad, in that it makes one realize that trust is very fragile.

On being in love

Allen, Elizabeth. **The Loser.** Dutton 1969.

Deitz, a high school girl, likes Denny very much. But he is different from other suburban high school boys. His cowboy boots, torn shirt and long hair mark him as a "loser" to the others. He had just "up and walked out of Harvard" which is only part of his nonconformity. Deitz learns about other people's attitudes toward the nonconformist and about her own. Through many episodes she learns more about what Denny is truly like.

Arthur, Ruth M. **After Candlemas.** Atheneum 1974.

An unexpected vacation gives Harriet a chance to visit her friend Nancy in her home on the English seacoast. When Nancy gets sick, Harriet is left to explore on her own. Her adventures lead her to stone caves on the seashore, where she encounters a boy who is in trouble with the law. She also finds there a sacred staff which apparently is used by local witches in their ceremonies. Gramma Cobbley warns Harriet and

Nancy to stay away from the caves on Candlemas (February 2) since that's the time witches observe their sabbath. Harriet disregards this warning and her adventures begin.

Arthur, Ruth M. **The Autumn People.** Atheneum 1974.

Karasay—the old-timers call it the Island of the Witches. It was here that Romily William's great-grandmother met Rodger Graham, a mysterious young man who practiced witchcraft in a cave not far from his parents' home. Rodger cast an evil influence on Romily's family that is not broken until Romily visits the island on a summer vacation. While at Karasay, Romily comes to know the Autumn People, ghosts of the family and friends of Romily's great-grandmother. Rodger's influence is ended when Romily meets her future husband—a descendant of the man her great-grandmother had loved.

Arthur, Ruth M. **Dragon Summer.** Atheneum 1967.

Kate Barclay returns to Stone Place, the seaside cottage where she spent many happy times as a young girl. Her memories take her back to her friendship with Romily, her love for Stephen, her interest in the stone dragon that stood in a nearby field, and her affection for Merrity, the servant girl who saved Kate's life. Kate returns to the present when Romily's children come to visit and she sees that they, too, will know the delight and mystery of another dragon summer.

Arundel, Honor. **The Terrible Temptation.** Dell 1974.

Janet, the youngest daughter of divorced parents, resolves to lead a cold, scholarly life at the University of Edinburgh. She lives with her Aunt Agnes, also a loner, and goes out with cool, superficial friends. Then she meets Thomas, and the struggle to keep safe from emotional entrapments begins in earnest.

Benary-Isbert, Margot. **Dangerous Spring.** HarBraceJ 1961.

Karin's love story runs parallel to the Allied invasion of Germany during the last Nazi spring. She and her family are caught up in the turbulence of the bombing and the fighting, and they take refuge in the village where her fiance is the pastor. Thrown together as they are, Karin is forced to see the complexity of serious love relationships. She realizes she is too young to be the kind of wife she would like to be, and wonders whether she should leave her lover in order to learn more about herself.

Burroughs, Edgar Rice. **The Cave Girl.** Ace Bks 1973.
Washed ashore in a strange land, a young Bostonian learns to live in the primitive world of the jungle. His love for a beautiful native girl compels him to many adventures. Their final adventure reveals a mystery in the girl's past.

Burroughs, Edgar Rice. **The Mad King.** Ace Bks 1972.
On a visit to his mother's homeland, Lutha, Barney Custer of Beatrice, Nebraska, becomes involved in the intrigue surrounding that kingdom. An escaped mad king, an ambitious prince, and a lovely princess add to the excitement of the story. A coronation and royal wedding end the story, but only after much excitement.

Capps, Benjamin. **A Woman of the People: A Novel.** Hawthorn 1966.
Helen, who was captured by the Comanches as a young child, tries to fight tribal customs until she falls in love with a warrior.

Cone, Molly. **The Real Dream.** Schol Bk Serv 1970.
This love affair is a vivid example of the dangers of projecting ideals of romance and fantasy onto real people and real situations. Every person must face this at some time: to be forced to see someone objectively and not as you wish them to be. When an attractive new fellow moves to her town, the girl falls for him without really knowing much about him. She seems blind to his faults which everyone else soon sees. Her parents are exceptionally cool; instead of going berserk when their daughter gets serious about a fellow they can't stand, they communicate their disapproval without actually forbidding the romance or forcing a showdown.

Crane, Carolyn. **Wedding Song.** McKay 1967.
Those of you with a romantic view of teenage marriage should have a look at this story. April's family have always been serious scholars and she feels left out and inferior. When the family moves, she meets and falls in love with a handsome college student. She feels so warm and secure in his love she agrees to a secret marriage. At first it is just like dating, but

then the secret is out. April has to leave high school and the two begin living together in a small cottage, with little money, no friends, and no hope for the future.

DeTrevino, Elizabeth Borton. **Casilda of the Rising Moon.** FS&G 1967.

Medieval Spain with Moors and Christians at war provides the background for this historical adventure romance involving a Moorish princess who falls in love with a prince of Jewish ancestry.

Eyerly, Jeannette. **Drop-Out.** Berkley Pub 1969.

Donnie Muller and Mitch Donaldson are two high school students in love. They decide to escape the pressures at home and school by running away to get married. Almost immediately their troubles begin and, with no money, they set about finding jobs. It's not long before they find that there are no jobs available to dropouts. Their experience makes them realize they must make a mature decision.

Freedman, Benedict, and Nancy Freedman. **Mrs. Mike.** Berkley Pub 1968.

Kathy meets a young Mountie, Mike, during her visit to the Canadian Northwest in 1907. She loves him so much she agrees to marry him and live with him on his post, three months by dog sled into the wilderness. In the years that follow, Kathy is tested almost to the breaking point by the reality of violence, illness, and death in her chosen home. Her love for Mike changes from shining romance to deep trusting love as she bears children and faces the daily hardship and beauty of the wilderness.

Head, Ann. **Mr. and Mrs. Bo Jo Jones.** NAL 1973.

July and Bo Jo are just getting to know each other after a few months of dating when they find themselves in a nightmare situation: July becomes pregnant. The choices of abortion or giving the baby away are untenable to them both, and so they decide to accept the responsibility for the baby and get married. July is sixteen, Bo Jo is seventeen; both had planned to go to college, but instead they find themselves trapped into housekeeping, a dreary job with no future, and imminent parenthood. Oddly enough, their difficulties bring them close together, and the strangers become true lovers.

Henry, O. **The Gift of the Magi.** Hawthorn 1972.

Della and Jim want to give each other gifts of love at Christmastime. But they each have to make a sacrifice to get the money. Their sacrifices give a strange twist to the final gifts.

Holland, Isabelle. **Cecily.** Lippincott 1967.

Cecily is a whining, fat schoolgirl who is almost impossible to tolerate. Elizabeth Marks is a lovely, intelligent teacher, in love for the first time, who becomes almost obsessed by her dislike of Cecily because she compares so unfavorably to the other English schoolgirls who are cheerful, stoical, and generally uncomplaining. Elizabeth's fiancé is an easy-going American who is teaching at a boys' boarding school nearby. He comes to Cecily's defense because he does not have the same rigid traditional standards for children, and can be more sympathetic. Elizabeth senses his criticism of her and her standards of behavior, and finds her own confidence ebbing away, and a childish jealousy and temper taking its place.

Houghton, Norris. **Romeo and Juliet/West Side Story.** Dell 1973.

The second of these two stories is a modern reimagining of Romeo and Juliet. When read together, each story helps make the other one clearer and more meaningful. In both, two young lovers are caught in a larger conflict, a struggle between their families, their closest friends. Both pairs of lovers make plans to cut their ties with family and friends and depend only on each other. But they can't. Their lives are influenced by people around them, and their love can only end tragically. In addition to the love theme, mature readers will find that these two works raise interesting questions about why people fight and hate as well as why people love.

Hull, Eleanor. **The Second Heart.** Atheneum 1973.

This is the story of Marina, a young girl who is caught between the new and the old of present day Mexico. Her grandmother, a heroine of the revolution, expects Marina to attend the university. Geraldo expects her to marry him and become a village wife. Out of the turmoil this creates in her life, Marina comes to a decision compatible with her spirit.

Jordan, June. **His Own Where.** Dell 1973.

Two black adolescents who have both been battered by life seek a refuge in their love for each other. Buddy's father has been hurt in an accident and lies unconscious, near death in a hospital room. Angela's parents work, leaving her at home responsible for the younger children. They constantly abuse her, accusing her of being a "whore" in their absence. Her father beats her severely after one incident of mistaken distrust, and this brings down the wrath of social agencies who place Angela in an institution for her own protection. Angela's confinement drives both kids together in desperation, and they find comfort in making love and even in hoping for a baby. National Book Award.

Kerr, M. E. **If I Love You, Am I Trapped Forever?** Dell 1974.

Alan Bennett is very handsome and very cool. But things don't turn out the way they should his senior year. It starts with the publication of a weird newspaper that seems to have a strange effect on all the girls and ends with the loss of his girlfriend. The book takes an honest look at divorce, a boy's attraction to an older woman, and growing up, frustrations and all.

Kerr, M. E. **The Son of Someone Famous.** Har-Row 1974.

Brenda Belle is coming of age in a small town in Vermont, raised by her widowed mother who is constantly urging her to be more "ladylike." When Adam Blessing comes to live with his grandfather, the kindly village drunk, no one knows that he is actually the son of one of the most powerful men in America. (No names mentioned, but it sure sounds like Henry Kissinger.) Adam is constantly measuring himself by his father's enormous public image, and the result is shattering to what ego he has. Brenda Belle and Adam come together in their belief that they are both nothings, a belief based on their failings in the eyes of their parents.

Klein, Norma. **Sunshine.** Avon 1974.

Kate is a young pregnant girl who has just left her husband when she meets Sam. She is honest with him and he still loves her, and she feels everything is perfect. The nagging problem with her leg is just a nuisance until doctors diagnose cancer. From then on Sam and she must face a terrible reality. This warm and sad story is based on the true story of Jacquelyn Helton, who died in 1971.

Lessing, Doris. **The Temptation of Jack Orkney & Other Stories.** Bantam 1974.

This collection of short stories for mature readers covers a broad range of subjects. Most concern love or love affairs.

Lyons, Dorothy. **Pedigree Unknown.** HarBraceJ 1973.

Jill Howell is pretty, vivacious, popular, an expert horsewoman, and engaged to the most eligible bachelor of the Hotspur Hunt Club. Hadley S. Winslow III is a fanatic about "proper breeding" both for animals and people. When a change of honeymoon plans requires Jill to present her birth certificate for a passport and her own background is questioned, Jill calls off the wedding. She devotes herself to rehabilitating a broken down horse she calls Granite. Together, Jill and Granite prove that a pedigree is not necessary for their success and happiness.

Madison, Winifred. **Growing Up in a Hurry.** Archway 1975.

No one has ever seemed too interested in Karen, including her own family. Her sisters are slim, vivacious girls who obviously please their mother. Karen, overweight and quiet, never has done more than irritate her mother and bemuse her busy father. A secret love affair suddenly changes her life, and she eagerly makes love with no thought of the consequences. Then, just as their passion is cooling and Steve is thinking ahead to exams and the university, Karen finds out that she is pregnant. She realizes that she must make the decisions alone, and that she must enlist her family's support.

McKay, Robert. **Dave's Song.** Bantam 1969.

Kate Adams doesn't understand Dave Burdick's eccentric individuality any better than anyone else in town. Dave talks back to the teachers, quits the football team, and seems oblivious to the social conventions of dress, dance, and dating observed by the town's other teenagers. But as Kate comes to terms with her own resentment of the confines of small town Ohio life, she learns to appreciate the depth behind Dave's inner convictions as he stands up to the local bullies, the school board, and the corrupt town leaders.

McKay, Robert. **The Troublemaker.** Dell 1972.

Garfield High is stirred up by the arrival of a new boy, Jesse Wade. Soon he is in trouble and the rumours start flying about his past. It seems he was expelled from school in California because he was a student organizer, a "troublemaker." Also he was briefly a rock singer and made a lot of money from one successful record. Gina is a townie who is attracted to Jesse mainly because he brought her an injured bird which he found on the sidewalk, and she sees the tender side of him. He responds to her quiet warmth and beauty, but is afraid to get involved because his life is so complicated.

Mehdevi, Anne. **Parveen.** Knopf 1969.

A sixteen-year-old American girl goes to pay a six-month visit to her father on his estate in Iran. During her visit she gains understanding of her father's country and falls in love with a young Iranian.

Newman, Daisy. **Mount Joy.** Atheneum 1968.

Maris loves medieval history. She loves Jim, too, but is rejected because she won't "prove she is a woman." Maris rejects college and rushes off to Europe on a modern pilgrimage. Although scoffing at the faith of medieval pilgrims, she nevertheless follows their routes through France and Spain. She experiences loneliness, fear, and even danger, but she finds friends who restore her belief in herself and her values.

Peyton, K. M. **The Beethoven Medal.** T Y Crowell 1972.

Ruth has always been consumed by her interest in wild horses until at sixteen she falls in love with Pat, unable to resist his restless wildness. Pat is an aggressive, hostile person, yet capable of great love and tenderness. These contradictions enable him to create exceptionally fine music as a concert pianist, and they also make him a fascinating person to love. His aggression and rebellion, however, have gotten him into constant trouble with the police, and even now he faces a prison term for assaulting a policeman. (This is the sequel to *Pennington's Last Term*.)

Peyton, K. M. **The Edge of the Cloud.** Collins-World 1969.

Will and Christina do not find their dreams easily. Their marriage is impossible because they are too young to be married without parental consent. Will wants to work at an air field until he has enough money to buy a plane of his own. Then he plans to fly stunts in air shows to earn enough money to design planes. Christina joins the social revolution to become a working girl at a hotel near the air field where Will works, and waits for the chance to be married.

Peyton, K. M. **Flambards.** Collins-World 1968.

Christina's uncle insists that she come to live at Flambards with his two sons, hoping that there will eventually be a marriage between her and the oldest son, Mark. She has been an orphan for years, living with gentle aunts, and nothing has prepared her for the masculine dominance at the country estate. It is 1908, but only the second son, Will, seems aware of the changes that the automobile, airplane, and a world war will soon bring. Christina does love the old way of life full of horses and hunting, but by 1912 she is so infuriated with her uncle and Mark, and so in love with Will, she decides to leave with him to make a life together.

Peyton, K. M. **Flambards in Summer.** Collins-World 1970.

This is Will and Christina's story continued. Christina must return to Flambards alone after Will goes off to France in the war. She aches to see the old place deserted and in ruin. She is determined to bring the home to life, make the fields produce food, and give her baby a secure nest. Many characters weave in and out of the three books, returning when least expected. Christina's life changes completely, in a way which would have been impossible before the war.

Rayner, William. **Stag Boy.** HarBraceJ 1972.

Jim returns to his childhood home in England in the hope that the fresh air may cure his asthma. One day he finds a dark chamber that has in it a helmet and a pair of antlers. He is soon a person under magical powers of a stag. The stag helps him to control his own life and his love for a childhood playmate, Mary. The famous black stag becomes a legend in town, and when he is finally hunted, the legend and ritual are revealed.

Segal, Erich. **Love Story.** NAL 1970.

Jenny and Oliver, two college students of completely different backgrounds, fall in love and get married, over protests from Oliver's wealthy parents. They are struggling but very happy when they find out that Jenny has a terminal illness. In an effort to make her last days as happy as possible, Oliver swallows his pride and asks his father for money, only to realize his father will never understand what Jenny means to him. Oliver's grief after her death brings them closer together.

Southall, Ivan. **Matt and Jo.** Macmillan 1973.

Love strikes these two as they are riding to school on the trolley. It is a new experience for each and their excitement, fears, shyness, and disappointments are tumbled out of each in turn.

Stolz, Mary. **A Love, or a Season.** Har-Row 1964.

Nan Gunning and Harry Lynch have been friends since early childhood, but one summer, friendship turns to love. They don't know how to cope with the people who think their love is something to be scoffed at. This is a story of love between teenagers and the hardships that accompany it.

Stolz, Mary. **Second Nature.** Har-Row 1958.

Anne Rumson is a teenager in the 1950's writing about her own life. Her easy confidence in herself is shattered when the first guy she really loves wants her "for a friend" and chooses to get serious with Anne's best friend instead. Somehow she has to maneuver through this experience, hiding her hurt from everyone.

Storr, Catherine. **Thursday.** Har-Row 1972.

Bee is home sick with mononucleosis when she hears that her boy friend, Thursday, has disappeared. She can't imagine that he would run away without telling her, so she is afraid something terrible has happened to him. As soon as she can, she begins her search, but when she finds him, he isn't the same person. He is unfeeling, like a computer, and he doesn't want to see her again. Bee helps the authorities find him, and they put him into a mental institution. When Bee sees how much worse he is there, she starts believing in superstitions and "possession," and by a drastic method she tries to get Thursday "back."

Weverka, Robert. **The Waltons.** Bantam 1974.

John-Boy of the Walton family is on spring vacation. He doesn't figure anything will be different on this vacation. Then he gets odd jobs, helps to catch a criminal, and, best of all, meets Jenny, a runaway girl. The novel is based on the television series "The Waltons."

Windsor, Patricia. **The Summer Before.** Har-Row 1973.

The death of a very special friend removes Alexandra from reality. When she comes home after being hospitalized, her parents are so concerned that they almost suffocate the few sparks of life she has left. This novel traces her gradual regaining of stability and a sense of reality and of herself. Desperately Alexandra fights isolation as she seeks life.

Wood, Phyllis Anderson. **Song of the Shaggy Canary.** Westminster 1974.

Sandy, at seventeen, is trying to finish school and raise her baby alone when she meets John. She is uncertain about trusting any man since her young husband left her after a short disastrous marriage. John is just as hesitant as Sandy to trust anyone else. At first they are friends, and then John returns to an old girlfriend, putting Sandy back down in a bitter loneliness. This is the story of how they find each other again, this time more ready to trust and love.

Zindel, Paul. **I Never Loved Your Mind.** Har-Row 1970.

A dropout, Dewey Daniels works in inhalation therapy at a local hospital. Yvette Goethals, also a dropout, works at the same place. This novel puts these oddly-matched teenagers together in a funny, sad, frustrating story of love and loss. Their problems are similar, but their methods of attack are very different. This love story is told from the boy's point of view and does not necessarily end happily—or does it? The lives of teenagers are more realistic for this handling.

Zindel, Paul. **My Darling, My Hamburger.** Har-Row 1969.

Life and love in the teenage world can be very devastating, particularly when you are not the best looking or most popular. This novel deals with two couples who are friends but opposites. Serious problems plague the good-looking, popular pair and shatter their lives completely. The other couple moves forward, touched by their friends, toward realization of true maturity. The story is not completely pleasant, but it is realistic.

On being a member of a racial, ethnic, or religious minority

Adoff, Arnold, editor. **Brothers and Sisters.** Macmillan 1970.

This collection of twenty short stories by black American writers tells about black youth in many different situations. Some of the stories are retrospective and involved—aimed at an older audience. However, "The Sky Is Gray" by Ernest J. Gaines, "African Morning" by Langston Hughes, "Neighbors" by Diane Oliver, and "A Love Song for Seven Little Boys Called Sam" by C. H. Fuller, Jr. tell about common problems such as a trip to the dentist and neighborhood fights.

Armstrong, William H. **Sounder.** Har-Row 1972.

This is the way life was for poor black families before the Civil Rights movement—a horror. When the father is caught stealing meat to feed his starving family, the sheriff comes and drags him out of his home, beating and insulting him. The family watches in helpless agony; and when the dog tries to help his master, the sheriff shoots him. Somehow the dog survives, just as the family and the prisoner survive, kept alive by hope and love. When the son goes to the prison with some food for his father, he is humiliated by the guard, and as a defense, he fantasizes brutal, violent revenge. In actuality, of course, they are all defenseless against the system which supports injustice. John Newbery Medal.

Baker, Betty. **And One Was a Wooden Indian.** Macmillan 1970.

This is a journal of the wanderings of a small band of Apache Indians consisting of the shaman (wise one), his superstitious nephew, and Hatilshay who has poor eyesight but greater inner vision. The story tells about their struggle for survival in what is doomed to be an impossible way of life with the coming of the white man. Western Heritage Juvenile Book Award.

Baker, Betty. **A Stranger and Afraid.** Macmillan 1972.

Although the Indians of the Cicuye pueblo treat the Wichita Indian boy, Sopete, and his brother Zabe well after taking the boys captive in a raid on their village, Sopete yearns to escape and return to his family's lodge on the plains. He is worried that Zabe, younger than he, has become too attached to the ordered life of the pueblo Indians. Then word comes that "strangers riding monsters," Spanish conquistadores, have attacked a nearby Zuni pueblo. Sopete gets his chance to return home, not by escaping but as a guide for the Spanish.

Baum, Betty. **Patricia Crosses Town.** Knopf 1965.

Many children are bussed to new schools and are adjusting to racial integration, something quite difficult with the amount of fear and prejudice all around. Patricia seems to have a reasonable share of these fears when her family decides to send her to a better, all-white school across the city. The school *is* better, the teacher more helpful and more understanding, channeling Pat's energy into creative projects. However, trying to make friends and understand the white kids is complicated and confusing.

Benchley, Nathaniel. **Only Earth and Sky Last Forever.** Har-Row 1972.

Dark Elk has lived on Indian reservations and has seen the starvation, alcoholism, and psychological defeat of his people there. He decides to join Crazy Horse's warriors in an effort to prove his courage in the traditional Indian way. He feels that the Indian has no choice but to fight, even if defeat is certain. The author chose to bring the Indian culture closer to us today by "making the people speak what sounds most natural to the modern ear." The resulting dialogue is interesting, if slightly unnerving. Western Writers of America Spur Award.

Bennett, Jay. **The Deadly Gift.** Hawthorn 1969.

Finding $10,000 can cause many problems. Where did it come from? What should be done with it? John-Tom, a Mohawk Indian living in New York City, must make the decision, a decision that could change his life. He must also deal with Carey, a man without scruples, who tells John-Tom, "People have been murdered for a lot less. A whole lot less." On the other hand, $10,000 could do a lot for John-Tom's people and maybe mean college for himself.

Blume, Judy. **Are You There, God? It's Me, Margaret.** Dell 1974.

Margaret is almost twelve and has just moved from fantastic New York City to a small town in New Jersey. She's also a bit confused about religion. Should she join the "Y" or the Jewish community center? Her parents aren't much help; one is Jewish, the other Catholic. Margaret wrestles with the problem of growing up without the sense of belonging that her friends have.

Blume, Judy. **Iggie's House.** Bradbury Pr 1970.

Winnie's best friend has just moved away, and into her house moves a black family with three kids, the first black family in the neighborhood. Winnie is consumed with excitement and sets out to be a good neighbor. The new kids seem to resent her efforts almost as much as they are upset by the local bigots who are trying to pressure them to get out. Winnie has some rethinking to do.

Bonham, Frank. **Chief.** Dell 1973.

Henry Crowfoot, hereditary chief of a small band of downtrodden Indians, attends high school in Harbor City. Chief has several schemes to improve the lives of his people on the reservation. One scheme involves his Science Fair project—making glue. The other scheme involves an old treaty.

Bonham, Frank. **The Nitty Gritty.** Dell 1968.

Should he go to school today or earn a little money by shining shoes, Charlie Matthews wonders. When his favorite uncle comes to town, clever Charlie manages to earn almost two hundred dollars in two weeks in order to go into business with him. Charlie longs to escape the slum where his family lives.

Bonham, Frank. **Viva Chicano.** Dell 1970.

Keeny Duran is a victim of the slums, his family's instability, and most of all the system. He has been in trouble since age seven and has even been in juvenile prison. This story tells of his struggle to get right with himself and the system, but on his own terms.

Borland, Hal. **When the Legends Die.** Bantam 1972.

Because Tom Black Bull's father killed a man who stole from him, his wife and young son flee with him into isolation on Horse Mountain, where they live in the old ways. Tom's father dies in an avalanche and later his mother dies of illness. For a time young Tom lives by himself in the old ways with a young bear as his brother, but Blue Elk, a fellow Ute, persuades him to attend reservation school, where his pet is taken from him. He finally joins Red Dillon, a crooked promoter, as a bronc buster. With Dillon he learns to throw some meets as Red wants him to, but after Red's death he is on his own, riding hard and taking out his anger against the world and white society on the horses. After a serious injury, he returns to Colorado to the old life.

Brooks, Charlotte, editor. **The Outnumbered.** Dell 1967.

An anthology of stories, poems, and essays about the plight of minority groups. The selections are by well-known American writers. Among the minority groups represented are the Bohemians, Irish, Italians, Jews, Puerto Ricans, Indians, and blacks.

Carlson, Natalie Savage. **Marchers for the Dream.** Har-Row 1969.

A black family in New England can't find low income housing to replace their apartment which is being torn down for highway construction. It is during the days of the Civil Rights marches, and the grandmother and Bethany decide to join the group at Resurrection City that summer of 1968. Protest, polemics, returning home, and a small-scale protest of their own finally bring them in touch with someone willing to honor the Fair Housing Law and rent them a house.

Cavanna, Betty. **Jenny Kimura.** Morrow 1964.

Jenny has always lived in Tokyo with her American father and Japanese mother. Her Japanese grandparents have never accepted her father and Jenny because they are different. When her American grandmother invites Jenny to spend the summer in America, she accepts with great eagerness and excitement. Once there, she soon sees that her grandmother is ashamed of her, but in the face of attack from some "old friends," her grandmother unites behind her with loyalty and the beginning of love.

Clark, Ann Nolan. **Santiago.** Viking Pr 1955.

Santiago is a South American Indian whose life is divided three ways. Although he is an Indian by birth, he knows little of Indian life because he has spent his first twelve years in the home of a Spanish lady. A wealthy American family know him and love him as well, offering him a place in their home, an American education, and a future job of importance on their immense plantations. Santiago spends several years trying to decide where he belongs and what to do with his future. His adventures begin when his Indian family insist that he return home to his people. At first they seem completely alien to him, but as he shares the hardships of their exploited lives, he too becomes hostile to the Spaniards and the Americans who have conquered his people and treated them as servants for centuries.

Clark, Ann Nolan. **Secret of the Andes.** Viking Pr 1970.

Cusi is an Inca Indian who lives with an old herdsman and a herd of llamas isolated high in the Andes mountains. He wonders who his parents are and misses the warmth of a loving family. Chuto, his guardian, gradually introduces him to the outside world, to the Inca culture, and to his own identity, and finally to the great secret of their people hidden since the invasion of the Spaniards four hundred years before. John Newbery Medal.

Coles, Robert. **Saving Face.** Dell 1972.

When black students are bussed to Andy's school, parents, teachers, and students react. The tensions increase until a teacher overreacts to a black student who has not done his homework. A protest demonstration brings the police. Andy's father is one of the policemen.

Colman, Hila. **The Girl from Puerto Rico.** Morrow 1961.

Felicidad and her brother are restless on their family farm in Puerto Rico. They urge their widowed mother to come with them to New York, but once there they find that being Puerto Rican makes it almost impossible to discover the glamorous "American way of life." They can get jobs only in Puerto Rican neighborhoods because the others they apply for are suddenly "filled" when the employer discovers their identity. Felicidad becomes friendly with a boy whose parents soon forbid him to date her when they find out she is Puerto Rican. Their neighborhood is seething with threats of violence and the strong cultural traditions are weakening. Felicidad realizes that they were better off in Puerto Rico, perhaps with less money, but with the familiar beauty of their land and customs. Child Study Association of America/Wel-Met Children's Book Award.

Cone, Molly. **Number Four.** HM 1972.

The Indians from a nearby reservation have been attending this school system for years, but only three have ever finished high school. Number four is Benjamin Turner, a boy slowly awakening to his own identity as an Indian after eighteen years of trying to be "white." He sees the Indian students dropping out because of the constant barrage of subtle and not-so-subtle humiliation they face every day they are in the white culture. Most of the whites are not even aware of their own prejudice, and when Benjamin proposes a new Indian Culture Club to encourage pride in their heritage among the Indians, the whites see it as a threat, and the distrust and hatred fly out into the open.

Cone, Molly. **The Other Side of the Fence.** HM 1967.

When Joey arrives for his yearly visit with his aunt, he finds the neighborhood nervous and evasive. It seems that a new family has moved on the block and they are black. Joey sees ugliness in some of the neighbors' attitudes, and during a wretched afternoon of fence building, he goes berserk and tears down the fence, defying everyone. This is especially difficult because he wants everyone to like him, but his sense of fairness wins out.

Coolidge, Olivia. **Come by Here.** HM 1970.

Back in 1900, life in a Baltimore slum wasn't much for black people; and for Minty Lou it was about as bad as it could be. Her mother had been on the way up, holding a job in a hospital, but she was killed accidentally leaving Minty Lou an orphan and an unwanted responsibility on relatives who have few resources to share, spiritual or material.

Craig, John. **Zach.** Coward 1972.

Zach has grown up on an Ojibway Indian Reservation in Canada, but when his only relatives die in a fire, the chief tells him that he has a different heritage: that in fact he is an Agawa Indian, the last of a group which had joined the Ojibway some years ago. Zach decides to take his old truck and try to find his own people. He heads south, into the Midwest, and the Southwest, asking in Indian communities, at libraries and universities. There are no answers and Zach feels more and more alienated, haunted by the fact that he is the last of his kind, a dying race. He meets other people who come from vastly different backgrounds, and soon he sees that yearning for a special niche in the world is not his search alone.

Ellis, Mel. **Sidewalk Indian.** HR&W 1974.

Charley Nightwind has lived in Milwaukee for most of his life. He is a "sidewalk Indian." But when Charley is falsely accused of murdering a policeman during an Indian protest, he is forced to flee the city and seek refuge on his people's reservation. Helped by Betty Sands, an Indian girl, Charley hides out from the law on Spirit Flowage, lake of floating islands. Charley learns what it means to be an Indian and becomes involved in a dangerous plan to blow up the hated power dam which has robbed the Indians of some of their best farmland on the reservation.

Feldmann, Susan, editor. **The Storytelling Stone: Myths and Tales of the American Indians.** Dell 1965.

A collection of myths and folktales of the American Indian. The stories tell of how the earth was formed and how mankind came to be, about the theft of fire, the flood, and how the Indians' unique cultures came to be. Also included are tales of mythological heroes and supernatural journeys. The short, readable tales, which resemble Aesop's fables, show the value structures of the tribes.

Fife, Dale. **Ride the Crooked Wind.** Coward 1973.

Po Threefeathers loves his Indian heritage. He wants to stay with his grandmother on the reservation and learn the way his people, the Paiutes, used to do things. When Po's grandmother becomes ill and has to go to the hospital, Po's uncle insists that he go to an Indian boarding school. Po hates his uncle and the school at first. He cannot understand why he has to learn the white man's ways like his uncle. Gradually Po learns that he must learn and accept the white man's ways and preserve his Indian heritage too.

Gaines, Ernest J. **A Long Day in November.** Dial 1971.

Sonny lives on a plantation in the rural South in the 1940s. His parents, who work on the plantation, have fought and his mother wants to leave and go to Gran'mon's. When Sonny's father finally talks his way back into the house, he goes with Sonny to Madame Toussaint, a lady who knows voodoo. She tells him how to get Sonny's mother back. Easy to read.

Glasser, Barbara, and Ellen Blustein. **Bongo Bradley.** Hawthorn 1973.

Bongo Bradley, a kid from Harlem, spends the summer with relatives in North Carolina. He learns a lot about himself, his family, and his heritage as a black person. Bongo also learns that his country cousin, Vernon, knows a few things that life in the big city can't teach. The plot contains some mystery, but the novel is mainly interesting for its account of Bongo's thoughts and feelings.

Godden, Rumer. **The Diddakoi.** Viking Pr 1972.

One busy-body reports Kizzy, a gypsy girl living with her old grandmother in a nearby meadow, to the school authorities. After that Kizzy has to go to school even though she doesn't want to, and the children make matters worse by constant teasing and beatings. Then Kizzy's Gran dies and the authorities once more enter her life, insisting that they find a "proper" home for her. By a great stroke of luck, a very special woman agrees to take her home, and soon Kizzy begins to love her even though she still hates school and misses the ways of her people. Most of the village habits she finds confining and silly after the freedom of living outdoors with few possessions.

Graham, Lorenz. **South Town.** NAL 1966.

In an almost documentary style, this is an account of the struggle of a black family in the South before the Civil Rights Movement. A simple request for equal wages results in tragedy for the Williams family. It is an accurate, well-written, and interesting story which can help us to understand the effects of racial bigotry on good people. Charles W. Follett Award; Child Study Association of America/Wel-Met Children's Book Award.

Guy, Rosa. **The Friends.** Bantam 1973.

The story of two black girls in New York City ghettos:
one struggling to find her identity, the other trying
to cope with it. Phyllisia depends on Edith for protection in school, and Edith in turn defends and befriends her. Phyl's father calls Edith a ragamuffin and
forbids their friendship. After her mother dies, Phyl
realizes the importance of friendship and the irrelevance of her father's prejudice.

Hamilton, Dorothy. **Jim Musco.** Herald Pr 1972.

Jim Musco doesn't completely understand why he
and his father and mother are shunned by the other
Delaware Indians. But Jim knows he likes working for
Mr. Reese on his farm. When Mr. Reese gives Jim
and his mother the little cabin that had been the
Reese's first home when they settled in Indiana, Jim
is determined to stay. But there is talk that his tribe
plans to carry him off when they move west, because
they will need young men to be hunters and warriors
in their new home.

Hamilton, Virginia. **M. C. Higgins, the Great.** Macmillan 1974.

While his parents work, M.C., who is thirteen years
old and black, helps take care of the younger children.
He steals off to play when he can and likes to
sit atop a forty-foot pole so that he can survey his
domain, the strip-mine-scarred mountain his family
owns. M.C. dreams that the folklorist who visits them
will offer his mother a fortune to leave the mountain
and become a recording star. Then his family would
be away from the danger of the slow-moving spoil heap
which was left from strip mining. A girl who comes
from "outside" helps M.C. realize that he can take
the initiative to help mold his fate, right where he is.
John Newbery Medal; National Book Award.

Hamilton, Virginia. **The Planet of Junior Brown.** Macmillan 1971.

Buddy and Junior are friends in a big city. Buddy has
no family and lives within a cooperative system of
runaway boys. He sponsors a "planet" of younger
boys, working to provide clothing, food, and a hideaway for them. When Junior, a 300-pound musical
prodigy, leaves home, Buddy takes him to his planet.
Lewis Carroll Shelf Award; National Book Award.

Harris, Christie. **Raven's Cry.** Atheneum 1966.

This is the story of the Haidas, the Lords of the Northwest Coast of America, a proud and cultured people whose art has come to be admired throughout the world. It is the story of how they lived before the coming of the white man and how their culture declined and almost disappeared after the white man settled British Columbia and the Queen Charlotte Islands. The story is told through the eyes of three generations of Haida Eagle Chiefs.

Harris, Marilyn. **Hatter Fox.** Bantam 1973.

A young doctor with the Bureau of Indian Affairs tells the story of a seventeen-year-old Navajo girl. At their first meeting, Hatter stabs him. After the doctor is called to the State Reformatory for Girls to tell about the stabbing, he stays for several months to help Hatter regain her sanity.

Harris, Marilyn. **The Peppersalt Land.** Four Winds 1970.

Tollie is black and Slocum is white. The two girls always spend their summers together. When they are twelve, Tollie shouts, "I'm a nigger, and you're not!" Their friendship seems doomed until they become interested in the stories a young black student architect tells them about the dangerous swamp called Peppersalt Land.

Harrison, Deloris. **Journey All Alone.** Dial 1971.

Mildred Jewell lives in Harlem with her parents and her brother Michael. One night Mildred hears her parents arguing fiercely because her father has decided to leave them to make money as a jazz musician. Mildred tries to help her mother keep the family together. When summer comes, she escapes from the hardships of reality into her own world of fantasies. Suddenly summer fades, and in a burst of violence, Mildred learns that the journey each of us must take is a journey all alone.

Hentoff, Nat. **Jazz Country.** Har-Row 1965.

Many stories probe the feelings, fears and frustrations of young blacks as they try to negotiate living in a white world. By way of contrast, this novel deals with Tom Curtis, a young white boy who tries to live in the black world because his major interest is jazz music. The book shows what happens and what is resolved.

In addition, readers interested in jazz will have plenty of opportunity to reminisce through this book. Book World Children's Spring Book Festival Award.

Hickman, Janet. **The Valley of the Shadow.** Macmillan 1974.

This novel is based on historical records of Moravian missionaries, who taught Christian doctrine to Indian tribes in early America. Through the eyes of a thirteen-year-old boy, we see their pilgrimage to find safe and neutral land for a group of Delaware Indian converts. The story explores the boy's difficulty in communicating with his father and in understanding why white men (Long Knives) trained in Christian ways like the Moravians, treat Indians so cruelly. Differences in tribal customs are pictured.

Hunter, Kristin. **Guests in the Promised Land.** Scribner 1973.

The eleven stories in this book tell how it feels to be young and black in the ghetto. The kids Kristin Hunter writes about cope spiritedly with the put-downs of life in the housing projects, on welfare, in menial jobs for white people. Fast-moving and realistic, the stories show boys and girls learning to survive in a hostile world. Book World Children's Spring Book Festival Award.

Hunter, Kristin. **The Soul Brothers and Sister Lou.** Scribner 1968.

This is how it is to be young, talented, and black, with no place to go. Louretta and her friends do find an old storefront with a piano where they take rock and their own heritage of soul music and make a sound of their own. While they are practicing they get a lot of harassment from the police. Emotions finally explode into violence resulting in the death of one of the friends. Even their eventual success and money can't ease the pain and feeling of hopelessness. Lewis Carroll Shelf Award.

Jackson, Jesse. **Tessie.** Dell 1968.

Tessie, a young black girl living in Harlem, gets a scholarship to an exclusive private school. The story centers around Tessie's belief that she can "make it" both there and back home in the neighborhood. Her mother believes that she won't be happy at the school and can't make new friends that "matter," in a different world. The story pictures Tessie's struggles, disappointments, successes, and triumphs.

Kissin, Eva H., editor. **Stories in Black and White.** Lippincott 1970.

Of these fourteen short stories about race relations, for mature readers, eight are by white authors and six by black authors. Each story gives insight into the way each group thinks and reacts. The varied characters include an "almost white boy" in Chicago, a sheriff in the South, a Jewish shopkeeper, and a black superstar who returns to the United States with his white wife and their son. The writers include John Updike, Ralph Ellison, Richard Wright, and William Faulkner.

Knudson, R. R. **Jesus Song.** Dell 1974.

This is a funny-crazy story of a girl in search of Jesus who follows the trail of a group of Jesus freaks to the wilderness of Canada. The commune spends most of its time starving and singing, with pauses for "witnessing" which often end in street fights with unwilling converts. Alma, our heroine, decides the answer to their financial problems lies in song, and she even steals a local piano in desperation. Then comes the miracle she has sought for so long: as the angry miners attack to retrieve their piano, a new song bursts from the lips of the singers.

Kuber, Jack. **Child of the Holocaust.** Doubleday 1968.

In order to escape Nazi persecution in Poland, a young Jewish boy poses as a Christian. After the war his troubles are not yet over, for he still has to make the journey back to his family and his religion.

Laklen, Carli. **Migrant Girl.** McGraw 1970.

When Juan begins to speak up to the crew boss and demand some basic rights, the other migrant workers shake their heads at his naiveté. But Dacey, a sixteen-year-old who has also known only the helplessness of the migrant's life, believes that Juan is right—they must protest to change their conditions. One camp along their route has free, decent cabins, day-care for the children, and schools for both children and adults. This wakes the whole group up; even Dacey's conservative father begins to seriously consider protesting for a better life for them all. The story has no cushions. It is the cold facts about the way many

Americans must live. And yet, these same workers are
essential to any of us who buy food because they are
the ones who make the harvest possible.

Levitin, Sonia. **Journey to America.** Atheneum 1970.

Lisa is the middle sister of a well-to-do Jewish family
in Berlin during Hitler's rise to power. The family
realize they must leave Germany. The father goes
first to America to get the money and papers to bring
the girls and their mother. While they wait, they go
to Switzerland where they are safe but penniless, since
the Nazis didn't allow them to take anything of value
from Germany. The insecurities of moving, the horror
of hatred for Jews in Nazi Germany, the separation of
the family are all portrayed vividly by an author,
whose family lived through similar experiences. Jewish
Book Council of the National Jewish Welfare Board,
Charles & Bertie G. Schwartz Juvenile Award.

Levoy, Myron. **The Witch of Fourth Street and Other
Stories.** Har-Row 1972.

Magic or mystery enter into each of these stories about
families who, living now in the Lower East Side of
New York City, originated from Russia, Italy, Greece,
Ireland, and Lithuania.

Lipsyte, Robert. **The Contender.** Bantam 1969.

Alfred Brooks, a teenage boy in the ghetto, knows
the rules. Stay away from Whitey; your life could
depend on it. But Alfred wants to make it straight.
Then one night he sees a sign on a window: "Donatelli's Gym." He climbs the stairs and walks into his
new life. He trains to be a fighter, trying harder when
he feels like quitting, until the big fight. He finally
knows what Donatelli meant that first night when he
said, "Everybody wants to be a champion. That's
not enough. You have to start by wanting to be a
contender." Alfred knows he isn't just prepared for
the fight, but for life. Winner of the 1967 Children's
Book Award; ALA Notable Children's Book of 1967.
Child Study Association of America/Wel-Met Children's Book Award.

Little, Jean. **Kate.** Har-Row 1971.

Kate becomes curious about her Jewishness. She has
always known that her father is a Jew who married
a Protestant, her mother, but she never really had
thought about what that means for them and for

herself. She meets people who have known her father before his marriage and exile from his family. Her parents suddenly become people to her, not just parents. She wants to discover what their background means to her life.

Lockett, Sharon. **No Moccasins Today.** Nelson 1970.

Jay Williams wins an athletic scholarship to Pacific College to play basketball. To Jay, college meant escape—from the Chuala Indian Reservation, from the tourists who come to gape at his people, from having to think about friends who had to drop out of school to support their families and about unemployment among the older men. In a way, Jay wants to escape from being Indian. He thinks that once he has left the reservation, he will never return. But as he struggles during the summer to earn the extra money he will need to go to college, he comes to see his Indian heritage in a different light and changes his decision about his future.

Mather, Melissa. **One Summer in Between.** Avon 1971.

Harriet Brown, a black college student from South Carolina, takes a job for the summer with a white Vermont family in order to study Caucasians for a sociology course. The story is told in diary form; and one can see the change in Harriet from an unsure, cautious girl to a witty, relaxed young lady.

Meltzer, Milton. **Underground Man.** Bradbury Pr 1972.

The story of a young, white farm boy who leaves his upstate New York home during the period when America was divided into free states and slave states. Josh Bowen hopes to find a life of his own. After a chance meeting with a runaway slave on a raft on the Ohio river, Josh spends the years between 1835 and 1861 helping slaves escape from the state of Kentucky. The story depicts slave trading and experiences of escaping slaves, as well as Josh's life in prison, after he is convicted of helping slaves escape.

Mohr, Nicholasa. **Nilda.** Bantam 1973.

This story takes place in New York City's barrio or Spanish ghetto during World War II. Nilda, twelve years old when the story begins, watches and some- times understands the problems that exist around her— her brother's arrest for pushing dope, the gangs, the prejudice, her mother's sorrow. The language of the street may offend some readers, but the novel gives a good insight into life in the barrio and into one young girl's reaction to that life. Jane Addams Book Award.

Momaday, Natachee Scott, editor. **American Indian Authors.** HM 1971.

This is a collection of stories by American Indians. The stories tell in different ways what it means to be an Indian and how the Indian sees the world he lives in. There are also several poems and legends included in the book.

Murray, Michele. **The Crystal Nights.** Seabury 1973.

Getting along with a large family in a small Connecticut farmhouse is further complicated for Elly when German relatives escape Hitler's persecution of the Jews and come to live with them. Money is scarce as Elly and her old brother try to plan for college and careers.

Randall, Florence Engel. **The Almost Year.** Atheneum 1972.

An unnamed black girl of fifteen, full of fear and hatred of white people, is forced to accept the charity of a wealthy white family for a school year when her mother dies. Fear and guilt within the house trigger strange, unexplained, ghostlike happenings. Only when fear and hatred disappear can things return to normal.

Rodman, Bella. **Lions in the Way.** Avon 1967.

Robby is one of eight black children attending an all-white school for the first time. Robby's tension and turmoil are finally surmounted by determination to continue in spite of demonstrations of hate and violence.

Smith, Patrick. **Forever Island.** Dell 1973.

Charlie Jumper is eighty-six years old when his whole way of life is threatened again by the greed of the white man. Charlie, an Indian, has a rare and beautiful feeling for nature and life which cannot be destroyed by man or progress.

Sneve, Virginia Driving Hawk. **When Thunders Spoke.** Holiday 1974.

Norman Two Bull doesn't accept the old beliefs of his people, the Sioux. But when Norman finds an ancient Sioux relic, a coup stick, on Thunder Butte, strange things begin to happen. Norman's father hangs the

coup stick on the wall, and each day the old stick
seems to change and look newer. The coup stick
brings Norman's family luck.

Sommerfelt, Aimeé. **My Name is Pablo.** Criterion Bks
1965.

Pablo is a Mexican peasant who is clenched in a
fist of poverty. He has troubles with the police and
with tough juvenile criminals from the slums. A
Norwegian family help Pablo and his family ease their
worst problems and start them on a course toward a
better life. We still have the sense of the enormity
of the poverty of the masses of people who are not so
fortunate as Pablo in finding help. Easy to read.

Suhl, Yuri. **Uncle Misha's Partisans.** Four Winds 1973.

After the death of his parents, Motele, a twelve-year-
old Jewish boy, joins Uncle Misha's partisans—a band
of Jews resisting the Nazis. Motele receives a dangerous assignment, risks his life, and avenges his parents'
deaths. Jewish Book Council of the National Jewish
Welfare Board, Charles & Bertie G. Schwartz Juvenile
Award.

Turner, Frederick W., III. **The Portable North American
Indian Reader.** Viking Pr 1974.

A collection of literature of and about the American
Indian: myths, tales, poetry, oratory and autobiography
from the Iroquois, Cherokee, Sioux, Navaho and many
other tribes.

Turner, Mary, editor. **We, Too, Belong: An Anthology
about Minorities in America.** Dell 1973.

This anthology of short works reveals a lot about
minorities in America. It contains poetry, short stories,
and descriptive passages which present the problems
faced by these minority groups. Martin Luther King,
Jr., James Baldwin, and Countee Cullen are some of
the writers included.

Ward, Frederick. **Riverslip.** Tundra Bks 1974.

This book gives the reader the opportunity to look
into some of the experiences of black people who
lived near the edges of many of our famous American
cities. Through poems, letters, jobs, diary entries,
through the words of people themselves, the reader
can understand how they feel. These are real people
with real stories to tell.

Westheimer, David. **My Sweet Charlie.** NAL 1966.

Marlene, an uneducated Southern white girl, and Charlie, a black Northern intellectual, are both running. When they meet they hate each other, but their plight forces them to trust and even love each other. They begin to see each other as individuals and find they must re-examine their own attitudes.

Wier, Ester. **Easy Does It.** Vanguard 1965.

Two new families move into a neighborhood. One is black; one is white. Chip and his white parents are accepted easily, but A. L. and his family are ostracized. Chip himself is glad to have a friend next door who shares his passion for baseball, and he is bewildered by the reactions of his parents and the up-tight white neighbors. Easy to read.

Wiesel, Elie. **Dawn.** Avon 1970.

John Dawson, a British officer in Palestine, has been kidnapped by a terrorist group as a reprisal for the British execution of one of their group. Elisha, a young survivor of a Nazi prisoner-of-war camp and a member of the terrorist group, has been chosen to execute him. He is tormented, torn between the need to help his cause and his natural abhorrence of murder. He is only eighteen years old and must kill a man at dawn.

Witt, Shirley Hill, and Stan Steiner editors. **The Way: An Anthology of American Indian Literature.** Knopf 1974.

This is a collection of speeches, prophecies, poems, songs, prayers, legends, essays, proclamations and underground parodies and satires written by American Indians. The selections reflect the Indians' pride in their heritage and their anger at what the white man has done to them from the time of Tecumseh to the Red Power movement of today.

Wuorio, Eva-Lis. **To Fight in Silence.** HR&W 1973.

Thor Eriksen is eager to fight the Germans occupying Denmark in 1940. He is too young for the army. After several mistakes, he becomes part of a daring and successful plan to ship the Danish Jews out of Denmark before the Germans send them to concentration camps.

Young, Bob, and Jan Young. **Across the Tracks.** Messner 1958.

Betty Ochoa is a popular senior at Bellamar High. As the conflicts between the Chicano students and the white students increase, Betty finds herself torn between her white friends and her Mexican heritage.

On being in sports

Christopher, Matt. **Long Shot.** S&S 1974.

An easy-to-read novel about a mentally retarded boy and how, through long practice and his brother's encouragement, he becomes a full-fledged member of the basketball team.

Cox, William. **The Running Back.** Bantam 1974.

After Frank Conover is dropped from a college football team and has to leave school, he joins a semi-pro team in California. His teammates accept him, and his troubles seem to be overcome. Detailed plays are given for each football game.

Glanville, Brian. **Goal Keepers Are Different.** Crown 1972.

Ron Blake, a talented young goalkeeper, finally gets his chance to become an apprentice to the Borough Soccer team. When the first team's goalie breaks his arm, Ron takes over. During the season, Ron learns to cope with both failure and success.

Heath, W. L. **Most Valuable Player.** HarBraceJ 1973.

Pete Stallings, the team quarterback his senior year, wants the Most Valuable Player Cup. For someone who is good at just about everything, he suddenly has trouble with his girlfriend Patsy, becomes jealous of his team friend Billy Foxx, and breaks training rules. Through the experience he learns more about the spirit of football and about his own feelings.

Jackson, Jesse. **Charley Starts from Scratch.** Har-Row 1968.

A young man named Charles leaves home to get a job as a soda jerk. While on the job, he starts training in track. He buys a pair of track shoes that begins his lucky career. He knows that all the good things will not come at once, so he accepts the good with the bad, and strives to become a track star.

Keith, Harold. **Go, Red, Go!** Nelson 1972.

This is a story about an eighth-grade boy on a basketball team. He is short but has guts, and can make a basketball do anything. He is tough and emotional; if the coach won't let him start out in the game, he cries. But Red surprises his teammates, and a girl named Peggy.

Konigsburg, E. L. **About the B'nai Bagels.** Atheneum 1973.

Mark is embarrassed when his mother becomes the manager of his Little League team. But she has a passion for baseball and she does a superb job with the team. Soon the boys are playing better and fighting to win each game. The team wins the championship, but Mark discovers that there has been some subtle cheating. He doesn't know whether to report it, because it would mean betrayal to his friends and disappointment to his mother. Easy to read.

Lee, S. C. **Best Basketball Booster.** Strode 1974.

Moving with his family into eastern Kentucky, young Paul Daley learns quickly that his life will be very different. Basketball and new neighbors occupy much of his time in this story which intertwines the sports influence and the strange feelings of the mountain people.

Lockett, Sharon. **No Moccasins Today.** Nelson 1970.

Jay Williams wins an athletic scholarship to Pacific College to play basketball. To Jay, college means escape—from the Chuala Indian Reservation, from the tourists who come to gape at his people, from having to think about friends who had to drop out of school to support their families and about unemployment among the older men. In a way, Jay wants to escape from being Indian. He thinks that once he has left the reservation, he will never return. But as he struggles during the summer to earn the extra money he will need to go to college, he comes to see his Indian heritage in a different light and changes his decision about his future.

Rutherford, Douglas. **The Gunshot Grand Prix.** Bradbury Pr 1972.

A young racing driver is trying for his second Grand Prix win when he realizes that more than the race is at stake. Politics are involved as well.

Spach, John T. **Time Out from Texas.** Blair 1969.

Seven-foot-tall Josh Wash and his shorter but smarter brother Gabe, from Tucumcari, New Mexico, "take over" New York City in a really funny basketball story.

On coping with physical handicaps

Baker, Betty. **And One Was a Wooden Indian.** Macmillan 1970.

This is a journal of the wanderings of a small band of Apache Indians consisting of the shaman (wise one), his superstitious nephew, and Hatilshay who has poor eyesight but great inner vision. The story tells about their struggle for survival in what is doomed to be an impossible way of life with the coming of the white man. Western Heritage Juvenile Book Award.

Branfield, John. **Why Me?** Har-Row 1973.

Sarah just cannot come to terms with the fact that she is a diabetic and has to begin each day with a shot of insulin in her leg. Her mother tries to discipline her into taking care of herself; her father tends to pity her and give in to her demands. Her older sister, Jane, resents every bit of extra attention Sarah receives. Sarah finds a measure of relief in riding her pony along the beach every afternoon, in happy escape from the pressure. One day she finds a dog in an empty mine shaft, and by fighting to save its life, she forgets her own illness. Sarah gets older, relaxes with boys, and eventually takes her condition as a diabetic in stride.

Christopher, Matt. **Long Shot.** S&S 1974.

An easy-to-read novel about a mentally retarded boy and how, through long practice and his brother's encouragement, he becomes a full-fledged member of the basketball team.

Lee, Mildred. **The Skating Rink.** Dell 1970.

Constant friction with his father, rejection by his classmates, and a speech defect make Tuck Faraday's life miserable until he becomes friends with Pete Degley and his wife. Pete is building a roller skating rink billed as "Elysium on Wheels," and Tuck becomes the star on opening night after keeping it a secret that he has been learning how to skate.

Little, Jean. **From Anna.** Har-Row 1972.

Her family calls her "Awkward Anna" because she is always stumbling around. She can't read, she can't sew properly. Her hair is untidy, and she never looks neat and pretty. The family lives in Germany at the beginning of the Nazi era, and the father insists that they emigrate to Canada to get away from the horror. Anna can't imagine leaving what is familiar to her, even though she has been so unhappy as a failure in school and the laughing-stock of her family. But Canada isn't so bad after all. A kindly doctor discovers that Anna is almost blind, which has been the reason for her failures. A new school, meeting other children with sight problems, and a warm, loving teacher all give Anna a chance to like herself. Easy to read.

Little, Jean. **Mine for Keeps.** Little 1962.

Sal has cerebral palsy and has been at a special school, learning how to be independent and as adept as possible, physically. But now the doctors and her family decide that she is ready to go home and attend a regular school. The thought of squeaking braces, awkwardness with normal kids, and the inevitable pity and stares is almost as paralyzing to Sal as her physical disease. She tries, but her sensitivity and embarrassment cause her to fail often. Finally she realizes that it is her attitude that is putting a barrier between her and kids who would like to be her friends. Easy to read.

Mathis, Sharon Bell. **Listen for the Fig Tree.** Viking Pr 1974.

A sensitive and powerful narrative of a blind girl's world which includes a mother tormented by the murder of the girl's father, good adult friends who give her a sense of family, and a young male companion, Ernie, who helps her realize the true meaning of Kwan, the traditional black African celebration that takes place a few days after Christmas. The book moves quickly, and though its subject matter is black life, it talks to the anxieties, dreams, and hopes of all teenagers.

Platt, Kin. **Hey, Dummy.** Dell 1971.

Twelve-year-old Neil meets Alan Harper, a brain-damaged boy who talks and acts like a small child. Neil longs to understand the problem and becomes involved when "the dummy" is cruelly teased and falsely accused. Neil is beaten up when he tries to protect the brain-damaged boy.

Rayner, William. **Stag Boy.** HarBraceJ 1972.

Jim returns to his childhood home in England in the hope that the fresh air may cure his asthma. One day he finds a dark chamber that has in it a helmet and a pair of antlers. He is soon a person under magical powers of a stag. The stag helps him to control his own life and his love for a childhood playmate, Mary. The famous black stag becomes the legend in town, and when he is finally hunted, the legend and ritual are revealed.

Robinson, Veronica. **David in Silence.** Lippincott 1965.

David is deaf; and if you are interested in the problems of deaf people, how they learn to understand and communicate, their frustrations, their emotional problems, then this book is for you. The story isn't earth-shattering, but David and the kids in the neighborhood who must get accustomed to his deafness are all realistic and interesting.

Witheridge, Elizabeth. **Dead End Bluff.** Atheneum 1966.

The hero of this story is a remarkably able blind boy who seems to be able to do almost anything better than most people, despite his handicap. The mystery and adventure of this story are unlikely, but nevertheless make good escape reading. Quite realistic, however, are the emotions of the blind boy trying to cope with life and with his parents' difficulties in giving him independence which he craves but which may lead to his physical harm. Easy to read.

Woods, Hubert C. **Child of the Arctic.** Follett 1962.

An Eskimo boy is deaf and believed insane. He disturbs the tribe by his erupting tantrums caused by the frustration of his handicap, and they are ready to send him far away to an institution. His brother loves him and believes in his intelligence. He promises to take full responsibility for him. The two boys have designed a way to communicate, and they are quite capable of having good times together, playing and hunting. The arrival of a young American doctor and his adventurous wife means the presence of people who can understand and help the boys. It also creates some amusing incidents as the people from two vastly different cultures try to understand each other.

On growing up female

Arthur, Ruth M. **Dragon Summer.** Atheneum 1967.

Kate Barclay returns to Stone Place, the seaside cottage where she spent many happy times as a young girl. Her memories take her back to her friendship with Romily, her love for Stephen, her interest in the stone dragon that stood in a nearby field, and her affection for Merrity, the servant girl who save Kate's life. Kate returns to the present when Romily's children come to visit and she sees that they, too, will know the delight and mystery of another dragon summer.

Arthur, Ruth M. **The Little Dark Thorn.** Atheneum 1971.

When Merrie's father and mother are separated, Merrie's father brings her to England to stay with some of his relatives. Merrie resents being separated from her mother and acts in a way that causes people to refer to her as "the little dark thorn." Although Merrie does learn to love her stepmother, Bergit, many years go by before she can forgive her father. They become close only after she has grown up and has gained a sense of her value as a person.

Arundel, Honor. **The Girl in the Opposite Bed.** Nelson 1971.

Jane checks into a hospital for the first time and misses her sheltered home. No one is interested in her at all, except Jeannie, who is definitely "lower class." As she fights to overcome her snobbery, Jane begins to see more good in people, and less prejudice in herself.

Arundel, Honor. **The Terrible Temptation.** Dell 1974.

Janet, the youngest daughter of divorced parents, resolves to lead a cold, scholarly life at the University of Edinburgh. She lives with her Aunt Agnes, also a loner, and goes out with cool, superficial friends. Then she meets Thomas, and the struggle to keep safe from emotional entrapments begins in earnest.

Bach, Alice. **They'll Never Make a Movie Starring Me.**
Har-Row 1973.

Boarding school presents many problems to Alice
Rodgers, a sophomore at an all-girl school. She faces
many difficult stiuations while becoming adjusted—
making friends, gettting used to new rules and old
traditions. Her problems increase as she becomes
attracted to a senior named Wendy. Mischief becomes
the ruler in their lives!

Bachman, Evelyn Trent. **Tressa.** Viking Pr 1966.

Tressa isn't as beautiful and brave as the heroines in
the books she reads. She is an ordinary girl who has
her share of fears and shyness. This story of her
adjustment to a west Texas farm after living in a
city apartment takes place in the 1920s, but she is
an easy character to feel close to now. The new neighbors are tough farm kids, used to riding horses, tending
farm animals and many other activities which seem
impossible feats to Tressa. When she finds out that
even these new friends have fears too, this knowledge
gives her confidence to try to overcome some fears of
her own.

Benary-Isbert, Margot. **Castle on the Border.** HarBraceJ
1956.

It is as difficult for the reader to feel close to Leni
as it is for her family and friends. She survived the
war, the escape from Berlin, and the death of her parents by maintaining a cool defense of quiet, determined
ambition. The only outlet she has for her feelings
is through acting, and this ambition to become a great
actress is the strongest force driving her. Over several
years she learns to open herself to people. She begins
to discover all kinds of love again, and she finds a
home.

Blume, Judy. **Are You There, God? It's Me, Margaret.**
Dell 1974.

Margaret is almost twelve and has just moved from
fantastic New York City to a small town in New
Jersey. She's also a bit confused about religion.
Should she join the "Y" or the Jewish community
center? Her parents aren't much help; one is Jewish,
the other Catholic. Margaret wrestles with the problem of growing up without the sense of belonging that
her friends have.

Blume, Judy. **Deenie.** Dell 1974.

Deenie is the beautiful sister. Her mother and aunt have been waiting for her to enter her teens to launch her modeling career. Deenie isn't positive that this is what she wants, but she is incapable of resisting her domineering mother. People begin noticing that she walks "funny," and a gym teacher recommends that Deenie have a thorough physical exam. The doctor discovers that she has curvature of the spine which, if not corrected, will develop into a disfiguration. The mother at first refuses to face the fact that this beautiful daughter of hers must give up any hope of modeling, and in fact must wear an awkward back brace for the next four years. Deenie finds some strength in herself that she wasn't aware of before, and is curious to continue to find out more about herself as a person and not just a beautiful image.

Blume, Judy. **It's Not the End of the World.** Bradbury Pr 1972.

Karen's parents call each other names; her mother throws dishes; her father stops coming home nights. But Karen would prefer having her parents fight, cry, anything rather than get a divorce. How would she ever get over the pain of the family breaking up? The author tells how Karen, her sister, and brother learn to survive.

Blume, Judy. **Otherwise Known as Sheila the Great.** Dutton 1972.

Sheila is constantly working to hide her fears and inadequacies from other people, and even from herself. For instance, she claims that she is highly allergic to dogs in order to avoid getting near them and revealing to one and all that she is terrified. Her family moves to the suburbs for the summer and she makes some new friends. One of her best friends actually has the nerve to tell Sheila the truth about herself, and then to admit that she too is often afraid and feels like a "nothing." At first Sheila is crushed, but then she realizes that her friend was not being critical, just helping her to relax and be a human being.

Bolton, Carole. **Never Jam Today.** Atheneum 1972.

Maddy Franklin, seventeen years old, is among the suffragists—not suffragettes—arrested for picketing the White House in 1917. America is at war, and many

Americans cannot understand how these women can be so unpatriotic as to question the government at such a time. Among those refusing to take seriously women's right to vote are Maddy's father and Jamie, her boyfriend.

Bradbury, Bianca. **Goodness and Mercy Jenkins.** Washburn 1963.

A fever sweeps through Puritan New Haven, taking away everyone in Mercy's family except her young brother. The town fathers immediately take over the responsibility of Mercy, arranging her marriage, and making arrangements for their property. Mercy is stunned with grief and numbly goes along with plans to marry an older widower with five children, knowing that at least she and her brother can find security in the new arrangements. Then, a young sailor from Cornwall meets her on the street, starts flirting with her, and arouses some passions she didn't know existed.

Brink, Carol. **The Bad Times of Irma Baumlein.** Macmillan 1974.

Irma has moved to the oppressive house of her great-uncle: no pets and no friends allowed. Her father is always busy with his new job, and her mother hasn't joined them yet. In order to impress a classmate, Irma confides that she owns the biggest doll in the world. Now she has to either produce this doll or be discovered a liar. Things get worse and worse, but Irma shows a lot of imagination and spirit in solving her problems.

Bro, Margueritte H. **Sarah.** Doubleday 1949.

Sarah's father, the strength in her family, dies when she is only eleven, and this story begins then as she learns to rely more and more upon herself. She is influenced by a wealthy doctor and his wife who encourage her career in music, introducing her to New York and famous musicians, arranging lessons. Sarah's dedication to music is unbroken until she falls in love. Even then she and Alan promise each other that she will continue as a musician after their marriage. World War I halts their dreams of happiness together because Alan is one of the first Americans in the European trenches. Sarah tries to live through her music, playing for soldiers in Europe. After the fighting stops, her family needs her, and all of her discipline and work are in conflict with her responsibilities to others.

Burch, Robert. **Queenie Peavy.** Viking Pr 1966.

Queenie is a poor child in rural Georgia who is trying to understand why her father is in prison. As most children, she idealizes her father, but must see him eventually as the weak, selfish man that he really is. In the meantime she is a defiant, disobedient child who is incapable of expressing what she feels, and whose emotions are in an unrecognizable tangle. Child Study Association of America/Wel-Met Children's Book Award; Jane Addams Book Award; Georgia Children's Book Award.

Burton, Hester. **In Spite of All Terror.** Dell 1971.

Liz has had a bleak time since her father's death, spending three years with a rigid, nagging, unloving aunt. When the Second World War begins, Liz sees it at first as a great escape from her aunt's household, because the government pays for the evacuation of all London school children to the country. As the war comes closer and becomes more terrible, Liz would like to leave school to get a job in the war effort, but a teacher persuades her to stay in school and keep studying because she will be more valuable in the work force with a trained mind. Even so, there comes a time when she can participate directly.

Burton, Hester. **Time of Trial.** Dell 1970.

Margaret, like most young girls, would rather think about a happy future, but her father, a kindly bookseller, is committed to a protest against the glaring poverty and ignorance around them in London, 1801. His publications lead to trial and imprisonment, and Margaret must sort out her life alone.

Byars, Betsy. **The Summer of the Swans.** Avon 1974.

Sara is a fourteen-year-old trying to survive the emotional mysteries of adolescence. She is worrying about her looks and sensitive to the emotional undercurrents at home. Her younger brother is mentally retarded, and this story centers around a search for him after his disappearance one afternoon. Sara is responsible for him and in a near panic trying to find him. A boy whom Sara knows from school volunteers to help search, and she is surprised that he seems sincerely interested in her and her brother. John Newbery Medal.

Cameron, Eleanor. **A Room Made of Windows.** Dell 1972.

Julia is an introspective girl who loves words and loves to write. She sees the world, her mother, and her brother only in terms of herself. When her mother wants to marry and move the family away to a new home, Julia can't face it. She selfishly wants things to go on the same because she is satisfied with her own room and her friends and doesn't want to change. Boston Globe-Horn Book Award.

Campbell, Hope. **No More Trains to Tottenville.** Dell 1972.

Lots of people drop out, but not mothers. And when Jane's mother drops out to India, Jane dislikes the change—especially in her father—and her new responsibilities. Jane is confused. Seeking answers, she travels by train to Tottenville, finds Scorpio, gets drunk, stays out all night, and comes home to a furious father who has already phoned the police and threatens to send her away. Also awakening in Jane is a feeling of inequality. It's the females, not the men, who carry things constantly—groceries, handbags, clothes baskets. No wonder her mother dropped out to India.

Carlson, Natalie Savage. **Luvvy and the Girls.** Har-Row 1971.

This well-written book is about an eighth-grade girl who goes to boarding school for the first time. Luvvy worries about her popularity. Will she make friends? Will she do well in school?

Carlson, Natalie Savage. **School Bell in the Valley.** HarBraceJ 1963.

Belle Mundy is an orphaned child who comes to live with her warm-hearted aunt and uncle in western Maryland at the turn of the century. She is illiterate and her joy at being able to attend school is soon squelched by the jeers of her schoolmates, because she is ten but must start with the little children. Belle quits school, unable to face the teasing. She fills her life with work, but her desire to learn to read wars with her pride until she looks closely at destructive pride in others.

Clarke, Mary S. **The Iron Peacock.** Viking Pr 1966.

Joanna Sprague is from a good family, used to beautiful clothes and servants, but she and her father are
political refugees from Cromwell. They must leave
for New England with no money, clothes, or supplies.
The father dies at sea, and to pay the passage Joanna
has no alternative but to become an indentured servant. She starts with no skills and no money, but
soon she is capable of working efficiently, and wins
her way into a family of iron workers who have hired
her.

Clarke, Mary S. **Petticoat Rebel.** Viking Pr 1964.

In Gloucester, Massachusetts, on the eve of the Revolutionary War, the troubles with Britain make a
difference in everyone's lives. Dacie's father has been
a merchant seaman, but now the harbors are closed.
Dacie, who has never been allowed in the local public
school because she is a girl, now is asked to teach
there because the schoolmaster has joined the militia.
She agrees and other girls are accepted as pupils.

Cleaver, Vera, and Bill Cleaver. **I'd Rather Be a Turnip.**
Lippincott 1971.

Annie is sophisticated, perceptive, articulate and thus
remote from the narrow-minded gigglers who are her
"friends." Her life is further complicated by the arrival of Calvin, her illegitimate nephew, a kindly little
genius. The small town gossips and stares. Annie
hates the bigots, but there is a lonely part of her which
wants their approval. The whole situation is so involved and so unresolved that Annie takes to a type-
writer to try to organize the story of her life.

Cleaver, Vera, and Bill Cleaver. **The Whys and Where-
fores of Littabelle Lee.** Atheneum 1974.

When Aunt Sorrow goes away to live with the man
she loves, Littabelle Lee suddenly finds herself responsible for caring for her poor, aged grandparents
as well as Aunt Sorrow's patients, who relied on her
knowledge of herb doctoring.

Colman, Hila. **Dangerous Summer.** Bantam 1966.

Gaby Captivo, in her first job as a newspaper woman,
finds it hard to be a woman rather than a fun-loving
girl. Decisions must be made as to what she is going
to do in the future.

Colman, Hila. **Daughter of Discontent.** Morrow 1971.

Katherine has grown up with strong women: her divorced mother, her aunts, her grandmother. Her father is a successful judge in New York City, and this summer he is campaigning for the U.S. Congress and has invited her to join him and help. He is a stranger to Katherine, and she finds herself torn in her reaction to the man. He is charming, powerful, and attractive; one part of her craves his love and protection, but another voice inside is wary of masculine dominance and rebels against his authority.

Colman, Hila. **Diary of a Frantic Kid Sister.** Crown 1973.

This novel, in diary form, offers a slice of life as experienced by Sarah, the younger daughter of an apartment-dwelling family in New York City. Sarah suffers the conflicts and frustrations of an eleven-year-old who feels overshadowed by her glamorous older sister and unimportant to her parents and teachers. One thing she has learned, she tells her diary, is that "everybody lies." Sarah recounts her ups and downs through twelve months, but as her diary year ends, she discovers she has become much more a person in her own right.

Cone, Molly. **Annie, Annie.** HM 1969.

Annie's parents are intellectuals who have raised their children with a minimum of interference, trusting them to make wise decisions for themselves. Annie is tired of being responsible for herself and interprets her parents' attitude as indifference. She has a yen for some rules and regulations, and when she finds a summer job in an orderly (actually rigid) household, she welcomes it—at first.

Cooper, Gordon. **An Hour in the Morning.** Dutton 1974.

Twelve-year-old Kate leaves school to be trained as a maid to a well-to-do English farm family. She is allowed to visit her own family every Sunday. When the farm is sold and her employers move away, Kate returns home until she is able to find another job.

Corcoran, Barbara. **This Is a Recording.** Atheneum 1971.

Marianne's parents are going to Europe on a long trip and they have decided that she should go to live with her grandmother in Montana while they are away. After Boston, the small town in Montana is like another country. Marianne's closest friends are Indian neighbors, who introduce her to the beauty of the wilderness. Marianne's grandmother is a strong, elegant person who used to be an actress. She is a very private person, and at first Marianne is awe-struck, feeling that she is unwanted. It takes some time, but the two become very close and are glad to be together.

Crawford, Deborah. **Somebody Will Miss Me.** Crown 1971.

Abby van Eyk has many things to learn during the Depression of the 1930s. It's hard enough to learn to do without and manage for three people to live on fifteen dollars a month, but that's the least of Abby's worries. Why do Uncle Aaron and Grandma hate her? Why can't she have a friend? And most of all, what do these changes within herself mean?

Dizenzo, Patricia. **Phoebe.** Bantam 1970.

Phoebe lives for two months alone with her secret, as if the truth could be blotted out by silence. She is sixteen when she realizes there will be no turning back to childhood games. She is pregnant and ter-ribly frightened. There is only a raw, aching reality and the agonizing search for a way out.

Eyerly, Jeannette. **Bonnie Jo Go Home.** Bantam 1973.

This is the account of one girl's degrading, frightening abortion, a story which realistically reflects the ex-periences of many girls in the past before laws and attitudes toward abortion were changed to allow girls and women more choice about their bodies. Bonnie Jo is young, sixteen, and away from home in a strange city, trying to rid herself of a totally unwanted preg-nancy. After breaking up with a special guy, she was so emotionally low, she slid into a masochistic rela-tionship with the father of the baby. The abortion details are described step-by-step. It is a complicated, painful operation because Bonnie Jo is more than three months pregnant and the relatively simple abor-tion is impossible in an advanced pregnancy.

Eyerly, Jeannette. **Escape from Nowhere.** Berkley Pub 1970.

Carla's father gets a promotion which moves them into an expensive suburb but keeps him traveling away from home. Her mother drinks more than she should, and Carla misses her older sister, who is away at college. Carla is overweight and shy, and getting into the new high school social life seems an impossibility. She is disoriented and miserable. There is an attractive guy at school who catches her in a moment of panic and sees her as a potential soul-mate. The two of them smoke marijuana constantly, and Carla's life takes on a hazy, unreal dimension. Dexter wants to keep on experimenting with other drugs; he figures he has nothing to lose. Carla begins to see him objectively and then takes a good look at herself. Christopher Award Children's Book Category.

Eyerly, Jeannette. **A Girl Like Me.** Lippincott 1966.

Robin's beautiful friend, Cass, is crazy in love with a handsome, wealthy fellow who gets her pregnant and tries to avoid responsibility. Cass's family feels disgraced and at the first opportunity they bundle her away to a home for unwed mothers. Robin is sympathetic to Cass, particularly after her recent infatuation with a fellow whom she found disturbing and yet sexually attractive. Robin has always known that she herself was adopted, but now that she is close to Cass's experience, she realizes that her own "natural" mother may have been a young girl in the same dilemma. She starts to search for her.

Faulkner, Nancy. **Undecided Heart.** Doubleday 1969.

Drusilla's father is sympathetic to the British during the Revolutionary War, and Drusilla is devoted to him and to his beliefs. When her brother joins General Washington's army, she is dismayed and confused. Her boyfriend, Peter, is a Quaker, but sympathetic to the Americans, and in fact wrestles with his own beliefs until he too goes off to join the fighting. Drusilla knows that somewhere inside herself is a personal conviction, aside from her love and respect for other people, and she tries to discover that inner truth.

Feagles, Anita Mac Rae. **Me, Cassie.** Dell 1968.

Cassie is a beautiful eighteen-year-old girl. Exciting, zany things are always happening in her world. She tells her own happy story about growing up, making commercials, and living in a suburban town.

Fitzhugh, Louise. **The Long Secret.** Har-Row 1965.

Harriet (the spy) and Beth Ellen are at their summer houses in a resort town. Beth Ellen is very upset because her selfish, jet-setter mother is coming for a visit and might take her away. In the midst of this anxiety, she gets her period for the first time which adds to her general confusion about herself. Harriet is not much help because she is consumed in a project to find out who is leaving devastating notes around town. She drags a reluctant Beth Ellen with her, trying to solve the mystery, infuriated that the writer of the notes seems to know a great deal about them all.

Friermood, Elizabeth H. **Doc Dudley's Daughter.** Doubleday 1965.

Em, the doctor's daughter in a small American town at the end of the nineteenth century, finds herself with time on her hands after her high school graduation. She starts work in the town library and organizes a bicycle club with her girl friends. Her brother returns home from the Spanish-American War stricken with yellow fever. He gets worse, and the family finally realizes that he is going to die. It seems impossible to accept, but somehow they get through the winter, with Em working hard to cope with her grief.

Friermood, Elizabeth H. **Focus the Bright Land.** Doubleday 1967.

Vicky is a girl of nineteenth-century America who pushes her independence and talents to the limits in a very twentieth-century sort of way. She wants to be a photographer like the men in her family, and so she tries every wile in the book to get her way. A summer jaunt through the rural Midwest—living, working, and travelling with her brothers as they all take photographs—is full of adventure and achievements. She ceases thinking about her career long enough to get interested in a struggling young photographer in one of the towns they visit; but her idea about marriage includes working together taking pictures.

Gardam, Jane. **A Long Way from Verona.** Macmillan 1974.

You'll meet a fascinatingly unique heroine here: a determined, maverick English schoolgirl. Her talents center more on observation, analysis, and writing than in making friends and influencing people. There are some very funny scenes arising from ludicrous social relationships.

Gold, Sharlya. **Amelia Quackenbush.** Seabury 1973.

Amelia Quackenbush's father builds her a tree house, where she can hide when life gets rough. She wants to outgrow the tree house, but now she is in a new school with no friends. Her older sister, Courtney, has announced that she will soon become an unwed mother. Amelia's parents and other sister are also too busy to help.

Greene, Constance. **Leo the Lioness.** Dell 1974.

Tibb is just fourteen, in that transition time when she shuns the clothes/boys preoccupation, but isn't a child anymore. We all have some good laughs over the disaster of Tibb's pretty sister's first formal dance. Another major incident is Tibb's perhaps naive horror at the discovery that a girl whom she has always idolized has to get married suddenly because she is pregnant.

Guy, Rosa. **The Friends.** Bantam 1973.

The story of two black girls in New York City ghettos: one struggling to find her identity, the other trying to cope with it. Phyllisia depends on Edith for protection in school, and Edith in turn defends and befriends her. Phyl's father calls Edith a ragamuffin and forbids their friendship. After her mother dies, Phyl realizes the importance of friendship and the irrelevance of her father's prejudice.

Hamilton, Dorothy. **Kerry.** Herald Pr 1973.

Kerry Paige, an eighth grader, has a close, loving family, and so when she wants to do things without them once in a while, she has to struggle with a sense of disloyalty. Ironically, her father, who takes Kerry and her twin brothers camping every weekend, is trying to break away from the family business, but is afraid to tell Grandpa.

Harris, Marilyn. **The Runaway's Diary.** Four Winds 1971.

Cat (Catherine Anne) runs away from Harrisburg, Pennsylvania, to nowhere and ends up in Canada. Along the way she picks up Mike, a German shepherd pup, and Robber and Ruthie. Robber and Ruthie ride around from town to town in a VW bus. They're the same age as Cat's parents, but have dropped out of society. Much as Cat dislikes her parents, she discovers she is glad not all people are like Robber and Ruthie. Cat finds peace on a mountain all her own, and finally is ready to start home. This diary is a record of her journey.

Hinchman, Jane. **A Talent for Trouble.** Doubleday 1966.

Ann, nicknamed "Clam" (short for Calamity Jane) by her brother, tells her story in this amusing novel of a fifteen-year-old girl who, because she always seems to attract trouble, feels a "strong kinship" with Mary of Scotland and Anna Karenina.

Holland, Isabelle. **Amanda's Choice.** Lippincott 1970.

Her behavior has been so outrageous for so many years, her father finally gives Amanda an ultimatum: either shape up or face a school for "emotionally disturbed" children in September. Amanda's family is wealthy, and her life is made of a townhouse in New York, a summer estate on Long Island, nannies, housekeepers, private planes and boats. What Amanda doesn't have is a mother. Even so, no one's sympathy for Amanda can survive her constant tantrums and general nastiness. A young Cuban musician is living on the family estate this summer. He can't stand Amanda either, but he isn't shocked by her, and he helps her get her feet on the ground.

Holman, Felice. **A Year to Grow.** Norton 1968.

Julia is a shy person who feels a barrier between herself and the rest of the world, a barrier especially imposing at the horribly antiquated boarding school where she lives. One understanding teacher tells her not to give up, that someday something will happen which will encourage her to get involved with life. But when she develops a passion for her English teacher, she soon realizes how unsubstantial such feelings can be. She finds an old graveyard where she can escape, and there she finds someone else who also likes to clean up weeds and put flowers on graves. Now Julia feels that she has been "in touch" and is committed to finding other meaningful relationships someday.

Howard, Elizabeth. **Winter on Her Own.** Morrow 1968.

Amantha loves to draw but her penny-pinching father and the circumstances of living on an isolated farm in the 1820s leave small hope of her finding time or

means to become an artist. At sixteen she is restless
and eager to escape her predictable future, including
marriage to steady Thad, with whom she grew up.
A handsome young peddler comes by and, discovering
Amantha's talent, persuades her father to let her go
to a nearby town to work in a family business making
hand-painted tinware. Amantha soon discovers that
all change is not necessarily for the better.

Hunt, Irene. **Up a Road Slowly.** G&D 1968.

Julie begins her reminiscence of her life as it continued after her mother's death. She moves in with
her aunt in the well-polished family house in a small
town and attends the country school taught by this
same aunt. The story is full of precisely-drawn scenes,
characterizations, and emotional nuances. Julie lives
with her aunt until high school graduation and along
the way sees the shadow of an old love affair between
the aunt and a former student, learns to understand
her alcoholic uncle, adjusts to her father's remarriage,
and survives a disastrous bout of first love. John
Newbery Medal; International Board on Books for
Young People Honor List.

Hunter, Mollie. **A Sound of Chariots.** Har-Row 1972.

Birdie McShane came into the kitchen. The other
children were huddled into a group and they looked
frightened. Then her mother told them all, "Your
father's dead." For a long time Birdie is devastated
by grief and haunted by time passing toward the
moment of her own eventual death. Birdie loves
words and her mind is creative. Finally, through her
desire to be a writer, she is able to come to terms with
her fear of grief and her fear of time passing. She
learns to use her feelings as a constructive force instead of allowing them to block her creative gift.
Child Study Association of America/Wel-Met Children's Book Award.

Jackson, Jesse. **Tessie.** Dell 1968.

Tessie, a young black girl living in Harlem, gets a
scholarship to an exclusive private school. The story
centers around Tessie's belief that she can "make it"
both there and back home in the neighborhood. Her
mother believes that she won't be happy at the school
and can't make new friends that "matter," in a different world. The story pictures Tessie's struggles,
disappointments, successes, and triumphs.

Johnston, Norma. **Glory in the Flower.** Atheneum 1974.

This book is a sequel to *The Keeping Days.* Being fourteen is fun when it means a major role in a play; but it's no fun helping mother have a baby. Tish Sterling copes with the problems of jealousy at school and responsibility at home in the ways she thinks best. In spite of many troubles, she does manage to find a day now and then that's worth "keeping."

Johnston, Norma. **The Keeping Days.** Atheneum 1974.

Being a teenager is hard for Tish Sterling. She has a great deal of responsibility in a family of eight and nothing she does pleases her mother. Worries pile up—there are quarrels with high school friends; her father loses his job; her brother skips classes and has rejected the church. Still Tish finds there are some special days which need to be kept in her memory forever and treasured as her sister treasures her add-a-pearl necklace. This book has a dominant religious theme and presents a strong statement about Christianity.

Kay, Mara. **Masha.** Lothrop 1968.

For nine years Masha attends the Smolni Institute for Noble Girls in St. Petersburg, in czarist Russia. She develops from a shy country girl into a young woman chosen to be lady-in-waiting to Grand Duchess Charlotte.

Kingman, Lee. **The Peter Pan Bag.** Dell 1971.

Wendy wants out this summer—to be away from her family and on her own. She joins a group living in Boston and soon is initiated into a way of living totally different from what she has known before. She lives in a small apartment with several girls and a guy. She smokes marijuana; she sells merchandise for money to buy groceries; she meets speed freaks, mystics, people trying to run away from life, and people trying to grasp meaning in life. Her friend's brother, Peter, seems to have a special interest in her, and it doesn't seem romantic. She meets a boy on Boston Common and spends a blissful forty-eight hours with him, but can't remember what happened later.

Klein, Norma. **It's Not What You Expect.** Avon 1974.

Life, that is, is not what you expect. Especially if you are a girl like Carla, who expects quite a bit. This summer no one seems to be acting the way she'd like them to. Her parents are separated, but won't explain why; her twin brother has a girlfriend; her older brother's girl is pregnant and decides to have an abortion. The only thing that has been a success is the family summer restaurant, but that has meant a lot of work for them all. This is an honest novel, though perhaps lacking some depth in the abortion sequence, which is presented primarily as a financial problem.

Knudson, R. R. **Zanballer.** Dell 1974.

Zan is a girl in the eighth grade who has been waiting for years to get on the basketball team. This season the gym is being remodelled, and no one seems to care that the girls have to forfeit their ball games for the winter. Zan and a few friends grab a corner of the boys' playing field and start practicing soccer until the boys' coach catches a glimpse of their athletic ability and urges them to try touch football. The girls throw themselves into the game, and this time they turn up winners.

Lawrence, Mildred. **Walk a Rocky Road.** HarBraceJ 1971.

Silvy Kershaw lives with her family in the Appalachian Mountains. She wants to go to college but knows her parents do not have the money to send her. It is when she tries to help a friend, Kel McLeod, get a scholarship to study mineralogy that she works out her own problems, too. The land, her own hobby, and a rough-talking Pa all have their places in the final solution to Silvy's problems about college and herself.

Lee, Mildred. **The Rock and the Willow.** Lothrop 1963.

Enie and her large family are struggling farmers in the South during the Depression. Enie loves to write and cherishes her few moments of solitude when she can think and dream. Mostly she is busy helping her mother with the little kids and working in the fields. Her father is a stern disciplinarian who finally shouts Enie's oldest brother off the land. Enie is a good student and her teachers encourage her to go to college, but she has no idea where to get the money. A young man ambles along, looking for work from her father. He is an attractive, original fellow and when he falls for Enie, she is tempted to give up her dreams and settle with him. Child Study Association of America/Wel-Met Children's Book Award.

L'Engle, Madeleine. **Camilla.** T Y Crowell 1965.

When Camilla becomes aware of her parents' weaknesses and the ways they have failed each other, she looks outside her home for the love and companionship she craves. Her friend's older brother suddenly becomes the most important person in the world, a refuge from the agony at home. Their love is a positive force, each one expanding the other's experience of life. Frank introduces her to some very open people in the Greenwich Village community, people whom Camilla has always been sheltered from. She realizes that she is now willing to shed her own childhood and grapple with adult problems.

L'Engle, Madeleine. **The Moon by Night.** FS&G 1963.

Though it is not the author's best book, those who liked *Meet the Austins* will probably appreciate this sequel. The family is travelling across the country, camping along the way, but the focus is on Vicki, who for the first time is attracting boys' attention. She is baffled as well as flattered by it all. One crazy rich kid, whom the rest of the family hates, insists on following Vicki from campsite to campsite, spouting cynicism, atheism, and affection for Vicki along the way. Another admirer is an attractive, comfortable guy whom the rest of the family likes. Vicki just doesn't know how to deal with the hassle.

Lenski, Lois. **Texas Tomboy.** Lippincott 1950.

It is difficult to resist this kid's refusal to be coerced into a sex role. Charley Boy (actually Charlotte Clarissa) has the toughness needed for the hard work and physical demands of outdoor Texan ranch life. Charley's father approves of her rough ways even though her mother and the other females around are shocked. Instead of eventually conforming to the standards of ladylike behavior as did Laura Ingalls and Caddie Woodlawn, Charley just seems to persist in her style. Her selfishness, however, is somewhat eroded by a gradual awareness that other people's lives have value too.

Lowrey, Janette S. **Margaret.** Pyramid Pubns 1964.

Margaret McLeod, uprooted from the only home she has ever known, in a small town, goes to live with her great aunt and uncle. Confused and unsure of herself, she longs to belong to the fashionable clique of young girls in the school. When one of her new "friends," Laura, accuses her of stealing her jewelry, Margaret is hurt and terrified. Through her experience Margaret begins to develop poise and self-confidence.

Lyle, Katie Letcher. **I Will Go Barefoot All Summer for You.** Dell 1974.

This is the story of the summer when Jessie learns about people—about her mother, who died when she was born, about the father she feels deserted her, and about her aunt, uncles and grandmother, all of whom take care of her. But Jessie feels she doesn't belong. Then Tony Beight comes for a visit, kisses her and leaves. Jessie runs away to Baltimore to find him, but never gets there. Instead she meets Bob Brunelli, a CPA turned cab driver, and spends a wonderful afternoon at the Smithsonian, talking, acting, searching. Bob takes Jessie home, and she learns that the best things must end and it's better that they do end.

Lyons, Dorothy. **Pedigree Unknown.** HarBraceJ 1973.

Jill Howell is pretty, vivacious, popular, an expert horsewoman, and engaged to the most eligible bachelor of the Hotspur Hunt Club. Hadley S. Winslow III is a fanatic about "proper breeding" both for animals and people. When a change of honeymoon plans requires Jill to present her birth certificate for a passport and her own background is questioned, Jill calls off the wedding. She devotes herself to rehabilitating a broken down horse she calls Granite. Together, Jill and Granite prove that a pedigree is not necessary for their success and happiness.

Mazer, Norma. **I, Trissy.** Dell 1972.

Trissy is a monster. She ruins her brother's birthday, smears chocolate all over the kitchen of her father's apartment, and loses her best friend through bizarre actions—such as wearing one red sock, one white. Trissy's problem is that she is eleven and her parents are getting a divorce. Her mother plans to remarry, leading Trissy to ask, "But what will I be? I mean, who will I be?"

McGraw, Eloise Jarvis. **Greensleeves.** HarBraceJ 1968.

Shannon Lightley feels she doesn't belong anywhere—not in Europe with her parents or in her "native" America. Uncle Frosty, a prominent Portland lawyer and friend of her father's, rescues her from her despair by asking for help in finding out about the beneficiaries of a very unusual will that is being contested. After changing her appearance, Shannon lives among these people for an entire summer. On her own for the first time in her life, Shannon discovers who she is and what she wants to do about her future.

Mohr, Nicholasa. **Nilda.** Bantam 1973.

This story takes place in New York City's barrio or Spanish ghetto during World War II. Nilda, twelve years old when the story begins, watches and sometimes understands the problems that exist around her— her brother's arrest for pushing dope, the gangs, the prejudice, her mother's sorrow. The language of the street may offend some readers, but the novel gives a good insight into life in the barrio and into one young girl's reaction to that life. Jane Addams Book Award.

O'Dell, Scott. **Island of the Blue Dolphins.** Dell 1973.

This novel is based on the true story of a young girl who was abandoned on the Island of the Blue Dolphins and managed to survive until she was rescued almost twenty years later. The girl, named Karana in the novel, sees her father and most of the warriors in her tribe killed by foreigners who come to hunt sea otters. The novel tells about her adventures—with wild dogs, devil fish, sea otters—and the way she manages to survive with only her wit and courage to rely on. John Newbery Medal; International Board on Books for Young People Honor List.

O'Neill, Janet. **The Other People.** Little 1970.

Kate's mother has just remarried and Kate is sent to spend some time with her aunt, who runs a boarding house on the English coast. The boarders are a group of characters probably unfamiliar to American readers, but they are well-drawn and successfully interesting. Kate spends these three weeks getting to know these people who began as strangers. She gets some confidence in herself by coping well in this new situation. At thirteen, she is just at the edge of entry into adult lives and problems, beginning now to think of adults as people in their own right.

Perl, Lila. **That Crazy April.** Seabury 1974.

A month of crazy events, including a fashion show and an episode involving Women's Lib, leads an eleven-year-old girl, Cress Richardson, to think more about herself as a person and to resolve some problems.

Pevsner, Stella. **Call Me Heller, That's My Name.** Seabury 1973.

Hildegarde loves her nickname, Heller, and does her best to live up to it. She resists admitting she is a girl until the boys she pals around with gradually ease her out of the gang. Her proof of courage is to set off fireworks in the cemetery one midnight. Heller finally breaks her self-imposed exile from the feminine world.

Platt, Kin. **Chloris and the Creeps.** Chilton 1973.

Her parents' divorce and her father's subsequent suicide have left Chloris bitter. She particularly resents her mother's suitors, each of whom she calls a creep. Chloris, with the help of a psychiatrist and Fidel, one of the creeps, comes to know more about herself and the false image of her father she has created.

Prince, Marjorie M. **The Cheese Stands Alone.** HM 1973.

The Pack, three boys and two girls, have always spent summers together on Elmer's Island for as long as anyone can remember. Daisy knows this summer is going to be different when the boys change Stinky's name to Boobs after she appears on the beach in a bikini. The only thing that makes the summer bearable for Daisy is the portrait Mr. Potter paints of her.

Randall, Florence Engel. **The Almost Year.** Atheneum 1972.

An unnamed black girl of fifteen, full of fear and hatred of white people, is forced to accept the charity of a wealthy white family for a school year when her mother dies. Fear and guilt within the house trigger strange, unexplained, ghostlike happenings. Only when fear and hatred disappear can things return to normal.

Rodgers, Mary. **Freaky Friday.** Har-Row 1972.

Annabel does not think she has enough freedom. So her mother fixes that by turning Annabel into her! Annabel is delighted to wake and find this out; but she doesn't know what's ahead for her, and she has a real surprise! Book World Children's Spring Book Festival Award; Christopher Award Children's Book Category.

Rosenberg, Sondra. **Are There Any More at Home Like You?** St Martin 1973.

Since Roberta is musical and looks like her aunt, a concert pianist who died young, Roberta's mother, the sister of that famous aunt, has been expecting Roberta to be that same person. The mother also has a weakness for sentimentalizing her relationship with that sister, forgetting all her own jealousy, the fights, the running away from home. With the visit of the elderly woman who raised the sisters, Roberta and her mother see the roles they have been playing. Roberta learns to trust herself and her own feelings, and the confidence pours into her music. She is more understanding with her own little sister, but tries to let her feelings show even if they aren't the most admirable kind.

Schulman, L. M., editor. **A Woman's Place.** Macmillan 1974.

The short stories in this anthology are about the price women pay when they refuse to take "woman's place," and the price they pay when they remain in it. Such powerful writers as Doris Lessing, Katherine Mansfield, Carson McCullers, and Jessamyn West examine the lives of women playing such roles as Southern belle, housewife, free spirit, careerist, and English spinster.

Spinner, Stephanie, editor. **Feminine Plural: Stories by Women about Growing Up.** Macmillan 1972.

This anthology of ten of the twentieth century's finest women writers focuses on woman as victim. She is seriously handicapped as she emerges from girlhood into the adult, masculine world, with its brutal rules for romance, virginity, marriage, talent, sexuality, race, and physical beauty.

Stolz, Mary. **Leap Before You Look.** Dell 1973.

Divorce is always a painful experience, and more so if one is not prepared for it. Jimmie Gavin isn't. Her mother is moody and intellectual, taken to spending most of her time alone. Her father is affectionate and easygoing, the direct opposite. Jimmie is so busy being fourteen, and with the problems of her friends, she doesn't see the growing antagonism between her parents. It is a shock when the Gavins announce they are going to get a divorce and Jimmie learns she will be living with her snobbish grandmother. A new friendship and a new awareness of life bring Jimmie and her father back together.

Sykes, Pamela. **Our Father!** Nelson 1970.

A family constantly on the move, a hotel in France, and a young girl's dreams—all add up to a summer that is far from ordinary. This story is written with warmth and humor.

Sykes, Pamela. **Phoebe's Family.** Nelson 1974.

A sequel to *Our Father,* this book tells more about the Devonish family and its four children, as they settle down into an English town after years abroad.

Symons, Geraldine. **Miss Rivers and Miss Bridges.** Macmillan 1971.

Atalanta and Pansy, two thirteen-year-old girls, are on holiday in England in the early 1900s. Free from a strict private girls' school, they seek adventure masquerading as suffragettes. The girls are determined to help women gain the vote even if they must "rot in jail" to get it done.

Sypher, Lucy J. **The Edge of Nowhere.** Atheneum 1972.

Lucy is small for her age and has never had a girl friend because no other girls her age live in her town, a small frontier settlement on the northern border of North Dakota. She moans that nothing exciting ever happens, but within months she and her family and community face a severe blizzard, a fire which destroys half the town, and later in the year, a tornado. Lucy emerges from a small timid child into a courageous, independent person, proving to herself that she has personal strength and resources she never imagined.

Terris, Susan. **Plague of Frogs.** Doubleday 1973.

Jo is disgusted by Marcella, the pregnant teenager her mother brings home one day. Marcella is fat, ignorant, and disfigured by a red birthmark which covers half her face. Jo calls her a "hillbilly" and adds to her misery by treating her like a live-in servant, laughing at her appearance and her superstitions. She is fascinated by her as well, and when

Marcella wants to go home, Jo arranges to go with her. In the small mountain town, Jo unwillingly identifies with Marcella as they confront her father, sister, and the townspeople. A violent scene with a raging father forces them to run away into the woods, which brings on Marcella's labor. Jo is terrified, and for the first time in her life her confidence is shaken. She is initiated into womanhood by the suffering, courage, and strength of Marcella as she gives birth.

Whitney, Thomas P., editor. **The Young Russians: A Collection of Stories about Them.** Macmillan 1972.

Ten stories of Russian youth by Russian authors have been collected from literary journals of Russia. These stories, for mature readers, include that of the boy who hopes to win the high jump and the girl he likes; of the boy who searches for the good luck stone with the hole in the center and then gives away his prize possession; of a honeymoon couple hiking in the woods who realize the pitfalls of marriage. One story tells a story of first love and how that memory never leaves; another, of scientists' efforts to keep their findings from the press.

Wilder, Laura Ingalls. **The First Four Years.** Har-Row 1971.

The final book in the "Little House" series, based on the author's early life on frontier homesteads in the nineteenth century. In this volume, Laura at nineteen, has married Almanzo Wilder, a farmer with a passion for beautiful horses, and has promised to try farming for four years. But she is so discouraged by her own family's long years of difficulty that she wants to try a more secure way of life. The Wilders have a child who fills their hardworking lives with joy. A second baby comes but soon dies. They survive sickness, storms, and the usual farming disasters, preserving their joy in family life.

Zolotow, Charlotte. **An Overpraised Season: Ten Stories of Youth.** Har-Row 1973.

Ten stories deal with the troubles and daily joys of teenage life. Each story explains a different facet of life for teenagers in their relations with other people. The excellent stories are written by a number of respected authors, including Doris Lessing and Kurt Vonnegut.

On growing up male

Aaron, Chester. **Better Than Laughter.** HarBraceJ 1972.

Running away from home is a long bicycle ride to the country dump for Sam and Allan. These young teenage brothers resent their parents' busy lives. At the dump, the boys climb a giant redwood tree. The ancient caretaker of the dump becomes their friend and helps them realize that they have to return home to face their problems.

Alcock, Gundrum. **Run, Westy, Run.** Lothrop 1966.

Westy's parents are working long hours to make a good income, and to save money, the family is crammed into an ugly, small apartment. Westy is constantly running away, and his repeated escapes are infuriating his parents and getting him into trouble with the police. His last escape finally brings him face to face with himself.

Benchley, Nathaniel. **Gone and Back.** Har-Row 1971.

As Obed's family careens across the country, heading West to take advantage of the Homestead Act, Obed becomes aware of his father's tendency to fail in whatever he attempts. He is enthusiastic and means well, but his plans are ill-laid and his impulsiveness leads to frequent mistakes. On the way West, another family makes their acquaintance, and Obed finds a real friend, a girl. The two confide their problems to each other and although not particularly romantically inclined, they experiment with sex. Obed gradually takes on more responsibility for family projects, even though his father is reluctant to have his authority undermined.

Blume, Judy. **Then Again, Maybe I Won't.** Bradbury Pr 1971.

This story tells frankly and warmly the adjustments that must be made by thirteen-year-old Tony in a single summer. He moves from the working class neighborhood in Jersey City where he grew up to a wealthy New York suburb, and begins to change from a boy into a young man.

Bonham, Frank. **Cool Cat.** Dell 1971.

Dogtown is a hard place to live—not enough jobs, not enough money, but a whole lot of drugs. Buddy is making it as a lifeguard, Little Pie as a police cadet. The others just drift along until they can get enough money to start a hauling business. But there's trouble with the Machete gang. The gang shoot out the tires of the truck and firebomb it. Little Pie retaliates by destroying the leader's car.

Bonham, Frank. **The Nitty Gritty.** Dell 1968.

Should he go to school today or earn a little money by shining shoes, Charlie Matthews wonders. When his favorite uncle comes to town, clever Charlie manages to earn almost two hundred dollars in two weeks in order to go into business with him. Charlie longs to escape the slum where his family lives.

Bonham, Frank. **Viva Chicano.** Dell 1970.

Keeny Duran is a victim of the slums, his family's instability, and most of all the system. He has been in trouble since age seven and has even been in juvenile prison. This story tells of his struggle to get right with himself and the system, but on his own terms.

Bragdon, Elspeth. **That Jud!** Viking Pr 1957.

Jud is an orphan who is a town "charge" of Spruce Point, Maine, a small fishing village. He doesn't seem to get much love and encouragement, and his great desire is to fix up a campsite on a nearby island where he can escape the critical villagers and live alone. He does build some tentative friendships with other people, but he is often hurt and disappointed. It takes nothing less than a grand heroic act to give him trust in himself and security in his relations with others.

Bragdon, Elspeth. **There Is a Tide.** Viking Pr 1964.

The young boy telling this story is a modern, articulate rebel who has failed in school and with his father. As a drastic attempt to get the father and son talking to each other, the school principal recommends that the two go off together to an isolated place which will eventually force them to come to terms with each other. What happens is not particularly dramatic or miraculous, but the boy's truthfulness about himself and his sensitivity to his father and other people around him make this an extremely interesting book.

Buck, Pearl S. **The Big Wave.** John Day 1973.

A tidal wave caused by volcanic eruption destroys a fishing village in Japan. Jiya watches in horror as his family and home disappear into the sea. The simplicity of this short story accentuates the starkness of the tragedy; there are no frills to soften the blow. But equally realistic is the way Jiya's grief is absorbed into his new life with the family of his friend. Child Study Association of America/Wel-Met Children's Book Award.

Byars, Betsy. **The 18th Emergency.** Avon 1974.

Marv Hammerman is the biggest kid in the sixth grade, and he is mean and tough. Why Mouse chooses to endanger his own life by taunting Marv is a question he asks himself as he shivers with fear waiting for the revenge which is sure to come. After days of dodging Marv by hiding and running, Mouse finally decides to end the suspense and "give himself up." The subsequent fight surprises both boys.

Byars, Betsy. **The Midnight Fox.** Viking Pr 1968.

Tom's parents are off to Europe for the summer and have arranged for him to stay on a farm with some cousins. The thought of all those animals, no TV, and farm chores horrifies Tom, who would much rather stay home and share literally fantastic adventures with his friend Pete. The visit starts out as badly as he had expected. Uneasy and bored, Tom spends many hours wandering through the fields trying to avoid any frightening animals. But he is stunned rather than frightened the first time he sees the black fox, because he has never before known anything so wild and beautiful.

Cassiday, Bruce. **The Wild One.** Pyramid Pubns 1969.

Rick Murdock is a kid with a problem. He has just had a fight with his girl Linda, he's in trouble at school, and the cops have their eye out for him after a mess with the outlaw motorcycle gang, the Scarlet Angels. Now he has to figure out how to keep his motorcycle without losing his cool.

Childress, Alice. **A Hero Ain't Nothing but a Sandwich.** Avon 1974.

Benjie tells the story, as he sees it, of why and how he takes to "fooling" a little with "the stuff." He shares with the reader the way he sees his mother, whom he loves dearly, her relationship with her

boyfriend, his grandmother, his friends, and his teacher
at school. At the same time, the reader is allowed
to hear the story from the other people's viewpoints.
Jane Addams Book Award.

Cleaver, Vera, and Bill Cleaver. **Grover.** Lippincott
1970.

Grover's mother is ill; she commits suicide. His
father dissolves into an unyielding grief. It isn't the
usual family story with understanding, comforting
adults standing by to shield and protect the children.
With the Cleavers' own unique style, they give us a
study of grief in a child's mind and how he works
through it even more adeptly than his father is able
to do. National Book Award.

Clymer, Eleanor. **Me and the Eggman.** Dutton 1972.

The eggman is an old farmer determined to remain independent even though his health is poor and money
is scarce. His plight is discovered by Donald, a
city boy with problems of his own, who stows away
in the eggman's truck to escape his own family. Living
a few days with the old man causes Donald to put
aside his own difficulties for a time and see life as
the eggman sees it. Donald is in the country for the
first time, and though he has always dreamed of a
freshly painted farm and clean animals, he never
realized the immense hard labor that is necessary to
maintain a farm. Easy to read.

Collier, James L. **Rock Star.** Schol Bk Serv 1974.

Tim is a musician whose guitar playing comes as
naturally to him as breathing. He is shy in most
situations, but when he is performing with his band,
he feels alive and confident. He can't understand
why his father ignores his talent and love for music,
and even discourages his playing. Things come to a
head when a flunking math grade and a local band
contest collide. After more misunderstandings Tim
heads for New York and the promise of some help
from a recording producer.

Cooper, Susan. **Dawn of Fear.** HarBraceJ 1970.

World War II has been going on for some time now,
and each family in the London suburb has its own
routine for air raids. Three boys live close together
and play together constantly, enjoying the excitement
of the air raids when they come, and not touched
by the war in any meaningful way. This week their

main enemy is the gang of kids who live on another street, and the two groups meet one afternoon to fight it out. This is the closest violence has come to their lives, and for the moment it silences them as they see the older boys fighting with great hate and know that soon those same boys will be in the real war.

Corcoran, Barbara. **All the Summer Voices.** Atheneum 1973.

This is a story about one important summer in the life of David, a fourteen-year-old boy. Since the family needs money, David's father decides to sell a horse that David has loved and cared for. The story follows David's desperate and, finally, successful efforts to save the horse. The plot moves fast and the story deals with a familiar problem: difficulties kids have communicating with their parents.

Cordell, Alexander. **The Traitor Within.** Nelson 1973.

Ling lives in a huge commune in Red China. He tries to take the place of his missing father and to be very brave, as he resists those people who call his father a traitor and as he fights the Taiwan forces. Ling's pet water buffalo is a loyal companion.

Courlander, Harold. **The Son of the Leopard.** Crown 1974.

In an African village, the people think the dead are reincarnated in the living. Each new baby born is told who he was in an earlier life. The witch doctor says one new baby was Solde Nebri, a former leader who killed many people. So when the boy is ten years old, he is thrown out of the village. He tries to perform good deeds but in his anger fulfills a strange prophecy that he will fail three times. He finally finds his true identity and receives a new name.

Davis, Verne T. **The Devil Cat Screamed.** Morrow 1966.

Ray McClung has many adventures living on a ranch and learning to be a cowboy, but always in the background is the deadly cougar which Ray has made his enemy. Ray knows that sooner or later he and the cougar must confront each other.

Donovan, John. **I'll Get There. It Better Be Worth the Trip.** Dell 1969.

Thirteen-year-old Davy Ross tells his story. Davy and

Fred, his dachshund pal, try to adjust to living in a New York apartment with an alcoholic mother, after his beloved grandmother dies. With insight and humor, Davy also tells about his new school, his new friends, and his success in sports.

Eyerly, Jeannette. **Radigan Cares.** Lippincott 1970.

When the story begins, Doug Radigan is a cool guy who cares about girls and his old car. He turns on to a lovely political campaign worker, and finds himself sweeping floors, ordering coffee, and ringing doorbells in order to be near her. Gradually he realizes he is beginning to share her sincere enthusiasm for the candidate, and even after this election he wants to continue to be involved in politics, helping to elect people who will struggle to solve the problems.

Fife, Dale. **Ride the Crooked Wind.** Coward 1973.

Po Threefeathers loves his Indian heritage. He wants to stay with his grandmother on the reservation and learn the way his people, the Paiutes, used to do things. When Po's grandmother becomes ill and has to go to the hospital, Po's uncle insists that he go to an Indian boarding school. Po hates his uncle and the school at first. He cannot understand why he has to learn the white man's ways like his uncle. Gradually Po learns that he must learn and accept the white man's ways and preserve his Indian heritage too.

Forman, James. **My Enemy, My Brother.** Schol Bk Serv 1972.

This is the story of a boy's journey to Israel after his release from a concentration camp at the end of World War II. There are flashbacks to his happy childhood in the Warsaw ghetto which disintegrated into the horror of Nazi occupation. The strength of the book is in the realism of the characters' reactions to their own suffering and to the events which draw them up and force decisions upon them, decisions clouded with compromises. The Arab cause is given a hearing along with differing political positions among the Israelis. Book World Children's Spring Book Festival Award.

Garst, Shannon. **The Golden Bird.** HM 1956.

Tara is a Mexican Indian whose tribe lives an isolated life subsisting on simple agriculture and on their skill at exceptionally fine crafts. On Tara's first trip to the

market in Mexico City, he is lost and hurt. Because
he knows no language but the dialect of his tribe, he
cannot communicate with the people who help him.
He doesn't know their name for his tribe and village,
and the only clue they have to his identity is the
painted water gourd which he has with him. During
Tara's long recuperation he learns Spanish and something about the world which exists outside of his
small village. By the time he is able to return home,
he knows he wants to help his people benefit from
modern medicine and technology while still preserving
their own traditions.

George, John, and Jean C. George. **Meph the Pet Skunk.**
Dutton 1952.

Rescued from a storm and placed under a summer
kitchen, Meph, a young skunk, becomes the pet of
young Will Light. Will, who tames Meph, feels frustrated by his unsuccessful attempts to persuade his
father to farm more scientifically.

Glasser, Barbara, and Ellen Blustein. **Bongo Bradley.**
Hawthorn 1973.

Bongo Bradley, a kid from Harlem, spends the summer with relatives in North Carolina. He learns a lot
about himself, his family, and his heritage as a black
person. Bongo also learns that his country cousin,
Vernon, knows a few things that life in the big city
can't teach. The plot contains some mystery, but the
novel is mainly interesting for its account of Bongo's
thoughts and feelings.

Greene, Constance C. **The Good-Luck Bogie Hat.** Dell
1974.

Ben buys sharp used clothes and prides himself on his
coolness until he falls for Penny, a snobbish kid from
boarding school. He loses his own identity trying to
please her until he is dumped. Charlie, his younger
brother who has always idolized him, watches all this
transformation and heartbreak with disbelief and dismay.

Guy, Philip A. **Black Horizon.** Exposition 1970.

Brought to an orphanage as an infant just after the
turn of the century, Johnny McBride has known no
other home. The overburdened Catholic sisters do
their best, but that is not enough for a youngster with
Johnny's spirit and inquiring mind. After a brutal

beating by a staff member and a talk with Sister Angela, the only person in the orphanage who understands him, Johnny takes an important step toward finding his way to individuality and retaining his belief in the goodness of life.

Hall, Lynn. **Sticks and Stones.** Dell 1972.

Moving out of the city into a small town is at first a novelty, but soon becomes lonely for a guy whose love of classical music is seen as strange. An army veteran returns to build an isolated cottage where he can write, and this too seems strange and unnatural to the townspeople. When the two meet, there is immediate understanding between them; they respect each other's talent and need each other's companionship. Soon rumors begin around the school and around the town that the two are homosexuals. The strain is almost more than the high school student can bear, and when he discovers that his older friend was discharged from the army because of homosexual behavior, he is horrified and scared that perhaps the rumors are true, that maybe he is a homosexual as well.

Hamilton, Dorothy. **Jason.** Herald Pr 1974.

Jason, a high school senior, decides that he should transfer to a vocational school. Although his father wants him to go to college, Jason knows that his aptitude and interests are in construction and electrical wiring. This and other problems facing teenagers—drugs, family illness—are met and worked out together by Jason, his family, and his friends.

Hamilton, Virginia. **M. C. Higgins, the Great.** Macmillan 1974.

While his parents work, M.C., who is thirteen years old and black, helps take care of the younger children. He steals off to play when he can and likes to sit atop a forty-foot pole so that he can survey his domain, the strip-mine-scarred mountain his family owns. M.C. dreams that the folklorist who visits them will offer his mother a fortune to leave the mountain and become a recording star. Then his family would be away from the danger of the slow-moving spoil heap which was left from strip mining. A girl who comes from "outside" helps M.C. realize that he can take the initiative to help mold his fate, right where he is. John Newbery Medal; National Book Award.

Hentoff, Nat. **I'm Really Dragged but Nothing Gets Me Down.** Dell 1968.

Jeremy Wolf, a high school senior, talks to his friends, his dad, and himself about all his problems. He does not want to go to war and kill. Should he refuse to sign up for the draft, or would a draft-counseling project be more useful than "getting lost in jail?" Written during the Vietnam War.

Hesse, Hermann. **Peter Camenzind.** Bantam 1975.

Setting out from the mountain village in Switzerland where he was raised, the young writer Peter Camenzind grows to manhood through his encounters with the world. He makes one great friend, falls in love several times, and then to escape from the anguish of unreturned love, turns to drink and the company of a circle of artists. Finally, Peter's love for the world leads him out of his restlessness toward the discovery of his true ideals.

Hinton, S. E. **The Outsiders.** Dell 1967.

After their parents die, the three Curtis brothers stay together in their home. They are poor and, therefore, "greasers." The youngest brother tells the story of constant fighting between Socs and Greasers, resulting directly in the death of one boy and indirectly in the destruction of several others.

Hinton, S. E. **That Was Then, This Is Now.** Dell 1971.

Gang wars, drugs, and everyday teenage existence in a slum neighborhood are part of this story. Mark and Bryon grow up together like brothers—close friends. They are very different, but they are good buddies. After Bryon falls in love with Cathy, their lives change.

Holland, Isabelle. **The Man without a Face.** Bantam 1973.

Charles feels trapped at home. His mother is preoccupied with collecting husbands. His obnoxious older sister and his fat, lonely younger sister are no fun to be with. While studying during the summer for boarding school entrance exams, in hopes of leaving home, Charles develops a disturbing relationship with his tutor, a disfigured, bitter, brilliant man. Longing to be near his teacher, Charles is afraid he may be a homosexual. One night, everything between them erupts, and Charles desperately needs to sort out his feelings.

Jackson, Jesse. **The Fourteenth Cadillac.** Doubleday 1972.

Stonewall Jackson is seventeen and lives in a black community in a small town in the 1920s. There is nothing particularly dismal about his life, but he is feeling crowded. Everyone is pressuring him to join the Baptist church and be "saved." His favorite aunt has died and no one is able to fill her place as a wise listener in his life. He isn't finishing high school and is on the lookout for a job. His best friend is working as a stable boy for race horses and Stonewall wants to be with him, travelling around the country; but his mother is convinced the life would ruin him morally and spiritually. It is a light, mostly fun book.

Johnson, Annabel, and Edgar Johnson. **Count Me Gone.** S&S 1968.

The values of the older generation just aren't for Rion. His older brother Doug's way of dissecting every emotion leaves him cold. He's a misfit at high school and in the sheltered suburb where he lives. He can't explain the car accident and the fist fight. Looking over the events of the past four days only raises questions—no answers. Why did his brother say that Shirli didn't exist and why did he tell the police that Rion belonged in a mental ward?

Johnston, William. **Love Is a Three Letter Word.** G&D 1970.

Marsh Wade, a student at Walt Whitman High School, constantly picks fights with Pete Dixon, his history teacher. He also seems to be in love with Pete's girl, Liz, a counselor. His father, Damon Wade, is leading a parent group against the sex education course. Alice, the student teacher, Mr. Kaufman, the principal, and Pete and Liz work together to solve these puzzling problems. This is one of several books based on the television series, *Room 222*.

Kerr, M. E. **If I Love You, Am I Trapped Forever?** Dell 1974.

Alan Bennett is very handsome and very cool. But things don't turn out the way they should his senior year. It starts with the publication of a weird newspaper that seems to have a strange effect on all the girls and ends with the loss of his girlfriend. The book takes an honest look at divorce, a boy's attraction to an older woman, and growing up, frustrations and all.

Kingman, Lee. **The Year of the Raccoon.** HM 1966.

Joe is the middle brother. He spends his time doing the gardening, tending wild animal pets, and watching TV, while his older brother spends hours at the piano and his nine-year-old younger brother is a scientific genius. Joe feels shapeless and ordinary. He can't even get good grades in school. His magnetic, successful father is threatening a boarding school in Scotland if Joe fails his subjects. A pet raccoon is getting older and wilder, and the family wants Joe to get rid of it. Then Joe discovers that he isn't the only one who feels inadequate beside his dynamic father.

Knowles, John. **Phineas.** Bantam 1969.

Each of this group of six short stories, by the author of *A Separate Peace,* concerns a young boy facing a difficult situation. Loneliness, fear of rejection, the need to excel are all examined. Each boy must learn to know and accept himself before others can.

Konigsburg, E. L. **(George).** Atheneum 1974.

This is a complex psychological story which is fascinating, but which requires some sophistication to understand. Ben is a brilliant child who is doing scientific work far beyond the average work of an eleven-year-old. He is also a multiple personality (explained by the psychiatrist in the book). A man named George lives in Ben's body, and these two are friends as well as enemies. Their struggle together is the core of the story.

Krumgold, Joseph. **Onion John.** Apollo Eds 1970.

Andy is caught between childhood and adulthood and between his friendship with an eccentric, kindly immigrant and his relationship with his "modern" father. Onion John is the immigrant who lives "somewhere in the fourteenth century" as Andy's father puts it. He is fascinating because of the simple way he lives and because of his superstitious belief in exorcism and alchemy. The town, led by Andy's father, tries to change Onion John's way of life and the result almost ends in tragedy. Andy isn't particularly rebellious, yet he does press his father to admit that he is stubbornly pressuring Andy into following a career in science which he had dreamed of for himself. Andy insists he should be free to choose his own career. John Newbery Medal.

Lee, Mildred. **The Skating Rink.** Dell 1970.

Constant friction with his father, rejection by his classmates, and a speech defect make Tuck Faraday's life miserable until he becomes friends with Pete Degley and his wife. Pete is building a roller skating rink billed as "Elysium on Wheels," and Tuck becomes the star on opening night after keeping it a secret that he has been learning how to skate.

Lewis, Elizabeth Foreman. **Young Fu of the Upper Yangtze.** Dell 1974.

Between World Wars, when soldiers, bandits and foreigners roam chaotic China, Young Fu and his widowed mother leave their unproductive farm to see whether survival may be easier in the big city of Chungking. There Young Fu, alive with curiosity, becomes a coppersmith's apprentice and a student to a wise scholar. Ed Young's ink drawings beautifully capture the colorful Chinese setting. John Newbery Medal.

MacKellar, William. **The Ghost of Grannoch Moor.** S&S 1975.

Who is the dog that haunts the moor? Davie is afraid it's Laddie, the young German shepherd he cared for but did not love. Laddie has run away and the whole town has tried to hunt him down, convinced he is the mysterious sheep killer. Davie wrestles with his conflicting feelings about his dog as he searches the moor to save Laddie from the traps and gain a second chance to earn his dog's love.

Maddock, Reginald. **The Pit.** Little 1966.

Butch Reece has a bad reputation and a questionable background, so when there's trouble at school, Reece gets the blame. A good picture of school life in England.

Madison, Arnold. **Think Wild!** HR&W 1968.

Frustrated by his father's refusal to let him drive the family car alone, Ted concentrates on fixing up Blue Monster, a wreck he and a friend bought at a junkyard. Everyday problems of cars and dating take a back seat, however, when student rioters rampage

Ted's suburb and a right-wing group lashes out at all teenagers. Ted matures through his first confrontation with bigotry and violence and he and his father come to a new understanding.

Madison, Winifred. **Max's Wonderful Delicatessen.** Little 1972.

Max graduates from high school with his future (like his past) already mapped out by loving parents. But he decides to try a life independent of his parents' plans, as a sculptor of junk. The climax comes when he accidentally wrecks a $10,000 car, and must somehow turn the demolished remains into a thing of beauty. He manages it with a little help from some friends.

Mazer, Harry. **Guy Lenny.** Dell 1972.

Guy has all the problems most twelve-year-olds have and then some. His girl likes an older boy, a tough who has a way of causing many problems. Guy has lived the past seven years with his father, but now Emily is taking his father away and destroying their way of life. His mother has come back and wants him to live with her at his father's request. Guy feels he is being bought, bounced around, and that everyone is a cheat and a liar.

McNeer, May. **Stranger in the Pines.** HM 1971.

Adam Quinn, a runaway apprentice, is full of hatred for his grandfather, who made him an apprentice at eight because he couldn't stand the sight of the boy. Adam now is fifteen, crippled by his smoldering hatred, and full of aggression. When he knocks down his master in a fit of rage, he believes he has killed him, so his wild flight is haunted by the threat of a hangman's rope if he is caught. He seeks refuge in the Pine Barrens of New Jersey with a black herb doctor and his wife. Gradually he grows strong enough to reveal his past and make some responsible decisions for the future.

Morey, Walt. **Angry Waters.** Dutton 1969.

Dan, at fifteen, never has had a real home. His only friends in the city were a gang of petty thieves who involved him in a holdup. Because of his background, the judge offers to allow him a year's probation as a farm worker. Dan is stunned by the wet emptiness of the countryside. He is alternately afraid and bored by the new situation. The man he works for is efficient, strong, and fair, but not a warm person. Dan feels he must somehow prove himself. The birth of a calf changes his feelings about the farm. He feels closer and less alone. Just as he is settling down, the young thieves from his gang escape from prison and come to him for help.

Morgan, Alison. **Pete.** Har-Row 1973.

Pete is an ordinary Welsh schoolboy who finds himself in a difficult situation at school. To escape, he decides to travel alone to his father, a technician on a construction job far away on a Scottish island. Pete is robbed and mugged on the trip and a gentle young family living in a parked railway car take him in. He manages to earn enough money to continue his journey, and once he reaches his father, he is surprised by the life he leads. For the first time, Pete feels that maybe he can get to know the man.

Neufeld, John. **Edgar Allan.** S G Phillips 1968.

A book that examines, through the story of "E. A.," the relationships between a ten-year-old Michael and his father, between a mother and father, between sisters and brothers. It further probes the feelings of all of the members of a family as they adjust to the possible adoption of a newcomer, Edgar Allan, who is black, three years old, and eager. This is Michael's story of how the problems and concerns surrounding the acceptance of Edgar Allan are worked out. Michael further shares with the reader his concerns about how a boy works out the problems of reconciling adults' behavior with what they *say* is right.

Neville, Emily. **It's Like This, Cat.** Har-Row 1963.

This sensitive novel about a boy growing up in New York City with his stray cat offers an excellent picture of the city and its people. John Newbery Medal.

North, Sterling. **Rascal.** Dutton 1963.

This true, warm account tells of an eleven-year-old boy, his raccoon Rascal, and their problems with his family and friends in a period during and after World War I. Lewis Carroll Shelf Award; Dorothy Canfield Fisher Children's Book Award.

O'Hara, Mary. **Green Grass of Wyoming.** Dell 1974.

In this story, Ken McLaughlin, the main character in two previous novels by Mary O'Hara, has to deal with an outlaw stallion. Ken recaptures the stallion after a series of adventures in which his fiancée nearly freezes to death. The adventure theme is complicated by romance and by Ken's efforts to become a mature, self-reliant young man.

O'Hara, Mary. **My Friend Flicka.** Dell 1973.

Ken McLaughlin, the main character in the story, is a daydreamer, more interested in horses than in his schoolwork. When his father acquires a wild colt, Ken begs to be allowed to keep and raise it. His father is reluctant but finally approves. Ken manages to train the horse, although both horse and boy come near death in the process.

O'Hara, Mary. **Thunderhead.** Dell 1973.

Thunderhead is an ugly, wild colt; he's fast and strong, but undependable. Ken McLaughlin is anxious for a colt he can train for racing so that he can help out his parents, who are in financial difficulty with their ranch. Ken tries to train Thunderhead and partly succeeds.

Peck, Robert Newton. **A Day No Pigs Would Die.** Dell 1972.

A moving story about Robert Newton Peck, a Vermont boy who, in the course of the story, becomes a man. The usual problems of his age are helped by an understanding family and friends. The book is a New England rendition of the Waltons. Each chapter encompasses one episode in Robert's life. The characters are so well portrayed that you begin to feel you know them as people. Characters' language may offend some readers.

Peyton, K. M. **Pennington's Last Term.** T Y Crowell 1971.

Pennington seems to function best in revolt. He is a complex person: outwardly a thug with no conscience. But how, then, to explain his expertise as athlete and pianist? He is loyal to certain friends, but has adversaries who seem to deserve all he gives them. Pennington discovers that he does have a certain pride in work well done—his music. He has suffered through exercises on the piano as though they were punishments handed down by those in authority. Now he sees that he actually might be playing for himself as well. If you like this, continue with *The Beethoven Medal*.

Phipson, Joan. **Cross Currents.** HarBraceJ 1966.

Through accidents and misunderstanding, Jim and Charlie are alone, sailing up the coast of Australia. Jim is seventeen, smart, but a failure in school, and now, against his family's wishes, wants to quit school and get a job away from home. Charlie, his skinny younger cousin, knows nothing about sailing, but is devoted to Jim. They rescue a drifting family and the man tries to tell Jim to reconsider his decision. Charlie is torn between his devotion to Jim and the strong conviction that Jim is making the wrong choice and should return to school.

Richard, Adrienne. **Pistol.** Little 1965.

Billy Catlett, from a small town in Montana, spends his fourteenth summer working with cowboys as a horse wrangler. He feels that he has found a perfect life. Then comes the Depression, and with it a series of problems which force Billy to face the harsh realities of life and to take the difficult giant step from childhood to manhood.

Ropner, Pamela. **The House of the Bittern.** Coward 1967.

Richard has always felt at home on the London streets, and has never given the countryside much thought. An invitation to his uncle's farm changes all that; he almost immediately feels a great love for the land. However, he gets caught in the middle of a struggle between two fanatical old men: one who wants to exploit the land for money, and the other who wants to rescue and preserve every living thing. When their fanaticism ends in violence and death, Richard realizes he must find a realistic, workable solution to saving the land from callous real estate developers.

Sachs, Marilyn. **Marv.** Dell 1972.

Marv's home life is dominated by a brilliant but nasty older sister who is never satisfied with her family. Marv wants desperately to find some way to please her, but it seems impossible. He is also a failure in school, overlooked by teachers as slow; but actually he is usually distracted by his elaborate plans for building projects. He is a natural mechanic, always building, fixing, and dreaming of new things to build and fix. Unfortunately his sister doesn't like anything he makes.

Sanford, David E. **My Village, My World.** Crown 1969.

Nikos has always expected to spend his life working on the family farm and someday to inherit the land for himself and his children. This is the order of things in his small Greek village, and no one questions it. Nikos enjoys school and his teacher believes he should consider going away to the university to learn a profession—something few people in the village have done before. It seems a hopeless dream, even after a wealthy man agrees to give Nikos the money for school, because the family relies on his labor and would have a difficult struggle farming without him.

Saroyan, William. **The Human Comedy.** Dell 1973.

Homer Macauley is a part-time student and a part-time telegraph messenger. His story is one of small adventures—trying to beat his archrival in a track meet, getting his younger brother out of trouble—but these adventures are not the point of the story. The story is really about understanding the everyday, commonplace things that go on, seeing them as part of the "human comedy," the sort-of-funny, sort-of-sad experience everyone has.

Schmidt, Kurt. **Annapolis Misfit.** Crown 1974.

"I used to think a man was a guy who could drink hard stuff, swear good, and be a big deal with the women," Charlie Hammel, fourth classman at Annapolis, says. Charlie changes his attitude about what it means to be a man, as well as his attitude about what life at Annapolis is really like.

Shore, June Lewis. **What's the Matter with Wakefield.** Abingdon 1974.

Christmas vacation is a bore if you no longer believe in Santa Claus and you're too young to go to adult parties or have a flyrod. Wakefield feels that he is a part of an in-between age. He spends his class's money on a new flyrod and then has to pay the money back. But nothing goes right. His grandmother doesn't send the ten dollars she usually does. Wakefield learns a lot about responsibility and about people.

Snyder, Zilpha K. **Eyes in the Fishbowl.** Atheneum 1972.

Alcott-Simpson's is a fantastic department store until a certain girl appears. Only Dion knows who and what she is and why she is there. There is also the problem of Dion's father, who never has a regular job. He gives music lessons, but is so easygoing that he takes day-old doughnuts instead of cash for payment. Dion wishes his father had more backbone— until Alcott-Simpson's closes.

Sommerfelt, Aimeé. **The White Bungalow.** Hale 1963.

Lalu's decision is similar to the one in *My Village, My World.* However, the conditions are even worse in India, where Lalu lives, than they are in Greece. He has an opportunity to leave home to study medicine at a university, but if he does so, he must leave his family who desperately need his help. The decision is not an easy one; each alternative has advantages and disadvantages which must be considered.

Southall, Ivan. **Josh.** Macmillan 1972.

Josh is an intense young poet who goes to visit his wise though domineering great aunt in a small rural village. His thoughts are recorded as they come, and they mostly come with strong emotions. It is difficult to always understand why he gets so very upset about seemingly ordinary situations, but the writing is excellent in capturing Josh's extraordinary sensitivity.

Stolz, Mary. **Lands End.** Har-Row 1973.

This book is about a twelve-year-old boy, Joshua, who lives on one of the Florida Keys. He is very talkative, and gets upset easily at parents and friends. Then he meets the Arthurs, who accept him immediately as though he were a member of their family. They live simply and are very poor. After a hurricane, Joshua realizes that the Arthurs have changed his life in a strange way. The book is very well written.

Swarthout, Glendon. **Bless the Beasts and Children.** S&S 1970.

The Box Canyon Boys' Camp in Arizona advertised, "Send us a boy and we'll send you a cowboy." But they never bargained for the Bedwetters, the nail-biting, thumb-sucking misfits. They set out on a mission to prove themselves, led by Cotton, and it turns out to be an eerie and frightening experience. Through their experience, we may learn something about our own lives.

Taylor, Theodore. **The Maldonado Miracle.** Doubleday 1973.

Jose isn't sure what to expect in California. He certainly hates the trip crossing the Mexican border and sneaking illegally into the States to join his father at a camp for migrant workers. He really wants to stay in Mexico, living simply by the sea and continuing to paint. But his father doesn't think much of artists, and although a silent man, he is domineering and used to getting his own way.

Terris, Susan. **The Drowning Boy.** Doubleday 1972.

Jason is a bumbler whose father is a competitive, successful man. In fact, the father is so aggressive and irritating, Jason uses his own inadequacies as one way to hurt his father. His mother is a vague woman defeated by the power struggles and no help at all to Jason. This summer, Jason is getting involved with a young family who are taking care of an autistic child, a six-year-old who is almost totally withdrawn. For the first time, Jason is the stronger half of a relationship, but even the progress the two make together fails. Things are so desperate, Jason even considers suicide.

Treffinger, Carolyn. **Li Lun, Lad of Courage.** Abingdon 1947.

When Li Lun refuses to go to sea on his man-making voyage, his angry father gives him seven rice grains to plant on the mountain. He cannot return until he brings back a harvest of seven times as much rice. No islander has ever grown rice before.

van Iterson, Siny R. **Pulga.** Morrow 1971.

For most of his fifteen years, Pulga roamed the slum streets of Bogotá, Colombia. Roused from his apathy by the experiences he has while working as a truck driver's helper, Pulga feels the first glimmers of self-respect. This adventure tale turns into one of self-discovery. Mildred L. Batchelder Award.

Viereck, Phillip. **The Summer I Was Lost.** John Day 1965.

This hero has always been somewhat less than adequate in school athletics, preferring fishing and hiking to aggressive team sports. One summer he is sent to a camp and gets lost in the mountains. For several days he is alone with little food, and through ingenuity he finds his way back to civilization, even catching some tasty fish with a paper clip to stave off hunger. The experience is important as proof to himself that he is capable of accomplishing more than he could have ever guessed possible; and he is the kind of kid who can use the extra confidence. Dorothy Canfield Fisher Children's Book Award.

Wellman, Alice. **Time of Fearful Night.** Putnam 1970.

Buale is an African who must decide whether to leave his country to study medicine or to return to his tribe to help his family. Colonial brutality has kept his people isolated from the benefits of modern civilization, but Buale is able to see their needs clearly because he has spent his teenage years with an American doctor helping as a medical technician. He knows how much medical care can mean to his tribe, but he also feels an immediate responsibility to stay home, helping his family and the girl he loves.

Wersba, Barbara. **Run Softly, Go Fast.** Bantam 1972.

Davy is nineteen and living with a terrific girl in the East Village. They love each other deeply, but something is eroding their happiness. Davy hates himself for hurting her and for being unable to make any real commitment to her; and so he turns to the unresolved relationships in his family trying to find some answers. He knows that he is obsessed by a hatred for his father, a hatred which grew from bitter disappointment that his father wasn't the hero he had believed him to be.

Whitney, Thomas P., editor. **The Young Russians: A Collection of Stories about Them.** Macmillan 1972.

Ten stories of Russian youth by Russian authors have been collected from literary journals of Russia. These stories, for mature readers, include that of the boy who hopes to win the high jump and the girl he likes; of the boy who searches for the good luck stone with the hole in the center and then gives away his prize possession; of a honeymoon couple hiking in the woods who realize the pitfalls of marriage. One story tells a story of first love and how that memory never leaves; another, of scientists' efforts to keep their findings from the press.

Wier, Ester. **The Loner.** McKay 1963.

A nameless orphan boy has survived as long as he can remember by "looking out for himself." All he knows is the life of a migrant worker, shifting, working, moving on. This is the story of his learning what it means to belong, to depend on others emotionally as well as materially. Stunned by a tragic accident, he drifts northward and is found hungry and freezing to death by a sheepdog and a shepherd. "Boss," the shepherd, is a woman able to give him a home and a name, but who finds it difficult to give him the affection he is starved for. David fights for her approval and is able to win it through courage and his own awakening ability to love and care about others.

Wier, Ester. **The Wind Chasers.** McKay 1967.

The story begins with a father and his four sons heading for a barren stretch of land in Arizona where the father is determined to force his boys to settle down and stick it out. For the next few years the boys are left on their own to try to come to terms with their new surroundings. Each boy has special problems, but the father persists in a stubborn attitude offering no help in easing the adjustment.

Wojciechowska, Maia. **Don't Play Dead Before You Have To.** Har-Row 1970.

Byron's ideas about life and himself change, through his friendship with the child for whom he babysits and through insights gained on his job at a home for the aged.

Wojciechowska, Maia. **Shadow of a Bull.** Atheneum 1973.

This award-winning novel is about Manolo Olivar, the son of a great Spanish bullfighter. Well-meaning friends and townspeople expect Manolo to follow in his father's footsteps. Confused, frightened, but wanting to prove himself, Manolo learns to recognize his limitations and conquer his fears. John Newbery Medal.

Wojciechowska, Maia. **Tuned Out.** Har-Row 1968.

When Kevin comes home from his first year at college, his younger brother notices the change right away.

Kevin is tense and withdrawn, and too thin. He tells
his brother he has been living alone all year, staying
"stoned" smoking marijuana day after day. Several
times he had taken LSD and now he wants to take
another "trip" to try to discover himself. The next
LSD experience revives a recurring nightmare and
Kevin collapses in mental agony. His brother is
frightened and calls for an ambulance which whisks
Kevin away to a mental hospital. His brother feels
guilty about the betrayal and hates the psychiatrist
who insinuates that Kevin must be mentally disturbed.
After the effects of the LSD have worn off, Kevin is
relieved to be in a hospital getting help.

Zindel, Paul. **I Never Loved Your Mind.** Har-Row 1970.
A dropout, Dewey Daniels works in inhalation therapy
at a local hospital. Yvette Goethals, also a dropout,
works at the same place. This novel puts these oddly-
matched teenagers together in a funny, sad, frustrating story of love and loss. Their problems are similar,
but their methods of attack are very different. This
love story is told from the boy's point of view and does
not necessarily end happily—or does it? The lives of
teenagers are more realistic for this handling.

Zolotow, Charlotte. **An Overpraised Season: Ten Stories
of Youth.** Har-Row 1973.
Ten stories deal with the troubles and daily joys of
teenage life. Each story explains a different facet of
life for teenagers in their relations with other people.
The excellent stories are written by a number of respected authors, including Doris Lessing and Kurt
Vonnegut.

On solving a mystery

Aiken, Joan. **Died on a Rainy Sunday.** HR&W 1972.
Jane, forced to take a London job to meet debts,
leaves her daughter Caroline with the McGregors, a
surly, uncooperative couple. Jane feels the McGregors
may have a hold over her husband, Grant, and terror-
stricken hours lie ahead of Jane and Caroline.

Aiken, Joan. **The Green Flash.** Dell 1973.
This is a collection of tales of horror, suspense, and
fantasy. For example, "Mrs. Considine" is a tale about
a girl whose nightmares appear to come true, and "The

Dreamers" is about a husband who murders his wife and doesn't get caught.

Allen, Judy. **The Spring on the Mountain.** FS&G 1973.

Peter, Michael, and Emma, brought together for a holiday in a small English village, meet a strange old lady who tells them about the mysterious mountain that towers over the village. Despite warnings, the children decide to climb the mountain themselves. Filled with fear and a sense of the supernatural, the children find the magic spring at the summit of the mountain.

Antoncich, Betty. **The Mystery of the Chinatown Pearls.** McKay 1965.

Awkward Marcy Adams wants to learn about poise, charm, and self-confidence. When she finds that she has a glamorous "double," she little dreams that her "great impersonation" will involve her with FBI agents, desperate criminals, and romance.

Arthur, Ruth M. **A Candle in Her Room.** Atheneum 1972.

When her father inherits a large sum of money, Melissa Mansell, along with the rest of her family, moves out of London to a 300-year-old house on the coast of Wales. Trouble begins when Melissa's youngest sister discovers an ancient, beautifully carved doll in the attic of the old house. The three sisters, Melissa, Judith, and Briony, have never been close, and the doll mysteriously causes tension among them to become even greater. The novel is made up of four stories—two told by Melissa, one told by Judith's daughter, and one told by Judith's granddaughter— and covers the loves and misfortunes that take place over a period of forty years.

Benedict, Stewart H., editor. **The Crime Solvers: 13 Classic Detective Stories.** Dell 1966.

An anthology of mysteries by well-known authors such as Agatha Christie, Arthur Conan Doyle, and Edgar Allan Poe.

Bennett, Jay. **The Deadly Gift.** Hawthorn 1969.

Finding $10,000 can cause many problems. Where did it come from? What should be done with it? John-Tom, a Mohawk Indian living in New York City, must make the decision, a decision that could change his life. He must also deal with Carey, a man without scruples, who tells John-Tom, "People have been murdered for a lot less. A whole lot less." On the other hand, $10,000 could do a lot for John-Tom's people and maybe mean college for himself.

Bennett, Jay. **Deathman, Do Not Follow Me.** Hawthorn 1968.

For a school assignment, Danny has to see the new Van Gogh painting at the Brooklyn Museum and write a paper about it. The first time Danny looks at the painting, he sees it through the eyes of his friend George Cheever and feels its fierce angry triumph. The next time he knows it's a fake—there is no feeling in this painting. Unfortunately, Danny's small discovery endangers his life.

Bennett, Jay. **Shadows Offstage.** Nelson 1974.

Peter Kowalski, feeling that the death of his sister, actress Cinderella Wharton, might not have been suicide, tries to find an explanation in her past.

Bosley, Jo Ann. **The Strangest Summer.** Blair 1970.

Pat Merriman and Toni D'Alessandro have never heard of each other nor of their distant relative Helena Constantine until surprise telegrams bring Pat and Toni together for a summer filled with excitement and intrigue, on an island in the Florida Keys.

Bower, Louise, and Ethel Tigue. **The Secret of Willow Coulee.** Abingdon Pr 1966.

Benjy Cheney gets a job as a paper carrier along the Mississippi. Although he gets to know Captain Van, Cap'n Hank and other interesting river people, he runs into trouble with a gang called the Barracudas. Benjy's sense of duty and loyalty helps him save his friends and family from the evil plot of the Barracudas.

Butterworth, W. E. **The Narc.** Four Winds 1972.

Dan Morton, a youthful-looking graduate of the police academy, is assigned as an undercover narcotics agent at the local high school. His job is to trace the source of heroin purchases among students.

Carlson, Dale. **The Mountain of Truth.** Atheneum 1973.

Ten children have mysteriously disappeared from the international summer camp in futuristic Tibet, and their parents are climbing the Himalayas to look for them. Peter, who returned safely, is expected to guide the expedition. He knows where his brother, Michael, and the other children are hidden, but he must prevent the adults from reaching them and learning their secret.

Chance, Stephen. **Septimus and the Danedyke Mystery.** Nelson 1971.

The Danedyke Cup, an ancient relic, causes problems for Septimus Treloar, a country parson who was on the police force for thirty years. Villainous ghosts in the church are hunted down by Septimus and his dog.

Chance, Stephen. **Septimus and the Minster Ghost Mystery.** Nelson 1972.

Septimus Treloar, a retired police inspector who is now a country parson, investigates unearthly organ music and bloodcurdling screams at the Minster. This book tells of the further adventures of Septimus, introduced in *Septimus and the Danedyke Mystery.*

Clewes, Dorothy. **Storm over Innish.** Nelson 1973.

This Irish tale centers around a mysterious young man with amnesia and broken bones. It tells of his struggle to remember and heal with the help of a girl. A background of family conflict and gun-smuggling enlivens the story.

Cobalt, Martin. **Pool of Swallows.** Nelson 1972.

Martin Babbacombe, a thirteen-year-old farm boy, sees the Swallows, three pools on the farm, suddenly rise to engulf and drown the family's cows. Ghosts run through the house, all the farm animals leave in a straight line, and the ancestral curse of the family comes true.

Corcoran, Barbara. **The Winds of Time.** Atheneum 1974.

When Gail's mother is hospitalized, the social worker puts Gail in the care of Uncle Chad. Gail doesn't trust her uncle, and as they journey to his house, she and her cat escape into the woods, where they are cared for by a strange family living in a spooky old house.

Curry, Jane Louise. **The Ice Ghosts Mystery.** Antheneum 1972.

Professor Bird disappears in a crevasse in Austria, and his family—Mrs. Bird, Oriole, Perry and Mab—fly to Austria themselves to try to unravel the mystery surrounding Mr. Bird's disappearance. The fam-

ily soon becomes aware of a sinister plot that could
end the world as we know it.

Dickinson, Susan, compiler. **The Drugged Cornet and
Other Mystery Stories.** Dutton 1973.

This collection of fifteen classic and contemporary
mystery stories ranges from the quietly strange to
the totally unexplainable. No weapon can be found
for an unsolved murder, a prison escapee masquerades
as a Lord Bishop, a girl carries a strange suitcase onto
a train, sixty-eight-year-old Miss Gertrude vanishes
without a trace, and a sundial solves a mystery.

Divine, David. **The Stolen Seasons.** T Y Crowell 1970.

Two British children and their American friend, pretending to be barbarians, set out to prove they can get
across ancient Hadrian's Wall without being seen.
Additional suspense is created when a valuable dish
disappears from an archaeological dig and the children, despite remarkable odds, determine to recover it.

Divine, David. **The Three Red Flares.** T Y Crowell
1972.

Peter, Mig, and their American friend Clint find the
oldest map in England, revealing the location of an
ancient cathedral. Since the sea now covers the ruins,
Peter, Mig, and Clint decide to scuba dive. When
three strangers arrive on the scene, the excitement
turns to danger for the three.

Emery, Anne. **Mystery of the Opal Ring.** Westminster
1967.

Paula Page takes a summer job on Lake Geneva, Wisconsin. The presence of college boys and girls promises romance and friendship, but instead there is a
stolen heirloom and a threatening note.

Farmer, Penelope. **A Castle of Bone.** Atheneum 1973.

Four children, Hugh, Anna, Penn and Jean, get a
secondhand cupboard, and strange things begin to
happen. When anything is put into the cupboard, it
turns into its original state. When a pigskin wallet is
put inside, a pig comes out! Hugh has the cupboard
in his room, and he has nightly dreams. The adventure truly begins when young Penn falls into the
cupboard by accident and turns into a baby. Then
the children have the task of entering the cupboard
to find a way to return Penn to his normal state. They
learn about themselves and find the castle of bone.

Finlay, Winifred. **Danger at Black Dyke.** S G Phillips 1968.

Three young boys, who have formed a secret society in Northumberland, offer Bud Riley, an American, a place to hide when he seems to be followed by some sinister characters. Edgar Allen Poe Award.

Fitzgerald, John D. **Private Eye.** Nelson 1974.

Wally Stone, a ten-year-old boy who has a skill for finding things, forms a private detective business. He solves several cases during the course of the story.

Furman, A. L. **Haunted Stories.** S&S 1965.

A mysterious, invisible boat, the spirit of a recently dead old woman, and the ghost on the silver horse carrying an ax are some of the eerie subjects in this collection of seven short stories. In each case, young people use their wit and courage to solve the mystery.

Garfield, Leon. **The Strange Affair of Adelaide Harris.** Pantheon 1971.

Adelaide Harris has a way of affecting many lives— and she is only a baby. The tale begins when Adelaide's brother decides to leave her in a field where she might be suckled by a she-wolf, just like the Roman infants in ancient history. But Adelaide is found by Tizzy and Ralph, two young lovers, who take her away. The story becomes tangled and funny as people at the Academy and in town get involved.

Hallstead, William F. **Ghost Plane of Blackwater.** Har-BraceJ 1974.

Youth and inexperience combine to cause Greg Stewart many troubles as an agricultural pilot. Neither, however, causes as much trouble as his search to help his friend Roy prove his innocence in a long-ago plane crash. As their search for the downed plane narrows, both men realize that more than nature opposes their success. Tense adventure in the air and on the ground make this an exciting mystery to solve.

Hamilton, Virginia. **The House of Dies Drear.** Macmillan 1970.

Thomas Small and his family are leaving the South to move to a small town in Ohio where his father will teach history. They all think they are lucky to have found a large house for rent, a house which once was a part of the Underground Railroad for escaping slaves. The house has secret tunnels, walls, hiding places; it has weird sounds and some say it is haunted by the ghosts of Dies Drear, the abolitionist, and the two escaped slaves who were murdered with him. Thomas and his father are determined to search out the facts about the house, but they are frightened soon by evidence that the evil in the house is not supernatural, but caused by real men who want to scare them away. Edgar Allen Poe Award.

Hersey, John. **The Child Buyer.** Bantam 1961.

A small town in America becomes the scene of confusion and horror when an unknown man arrives and, in the name of a mysterious patriotic organization, tries to buy a young boy. The organization's plan is to scientifically change gifted children into thinking machines, but no one seems to know the real reason or the mastermind behind these plans.

Jordan, Hope Dahle. **The Fortune Cake.** Lothrop 1972.

Jenny's parents leave for a short trip to Europe and Jenny is handed over to her aunt for safekeeping, even though she is seventeen. Jenny's father, a judge, is afraid there may be danger threatening because one of the criminals he sent to jail has recently escaped. You can guess how the plot continues, out there in the isolated summer cottage, knowing there is a criminal near, but not knowing which person is guilty. Finally Jenny and her young, retarded cousin Dawn are kidnapped as hostages, their lives dependent on Jenny's ability to outwit their kidnapper.

L'Amour, Louis. **The Californios.** Bantam 1974.

If Sean Mulkerin is to save his family's ranch, he knows he will have to find his way to some gold his father discovered long ago. Since his father is dead, Sean has to rely on Old Juan, the mysterious Indian whom all the other Californios fear and respect, to lead him to the gold. His search for the treasure leads him to remote parts of the California hills, where Sean has to confront not only the men who pursued him but also the "old ones" that Juan seems to know.

MacKellar, William. **The Ghost of Grannoch Moor.** S&S 1975.

Who is the dog that haunts the moor? Davie is afraid it's Laddie, the young German shepherd he cared for but did not love. Laddie has run away and the whole town has tried to hunt him down, convinced he is the mysterious sheep killer. Davie wrestles with his conflicting feelings about his dog as he searches the moor to save Laddie from the traps and gain a second chance to earn his dog's love.

McGraw, Eloise Jarvis. **Greensleeves.** HarBraceJ 1968.

Shannon Lightley feels she doesn't belong anywhere—not in Europe with her parents or in her "native" America. Uncle Frosty, a prominent Portland lawyer and friend of her father's, rescues her from her despair by asking for help in finding out about the beneficiaries of a very unusual will that is being contested. After changing her appearance, Shannon lives among these people for an entire summer. On her own for the first time in her life, Shannon discovers who she is and what she wants to do about her future.

McLaughlin, Lorrie. **The Cinnamon Hill Mystery.** T Y Crowell 1967.

The teenage girls of a family are annoyed and bored when they hear that a distant cousin is coming to visit them in the country. Little do they dream that William will unearth a mystery and upset the whole town.

Nixon, Joan Lowery. **The Mysterious Red Tape Gang.** Putnam 1974.

Mike, Linda Jean, and the rest of their gang decide to take care of some community problems without going through the usual "red tape." When the gang boards up a dangerous abandoned house, they find themselves threatened by some tough-looking men who are involved in stealing auto parts.

Parker, Richard. **A Time to Choose.** Har-Row 1973.

A glimpse of a world other than theirs is shared by Stephen and Mary, and they must answer their questions themselves. This novel is set in England and deals with typical teenage problems which are solved in a most unusual way.

Peyton, K. M. **A Pattern of Roses.** T Y Crowell 1973.

Tim Ingram, a sixteen-year-old boy recovering from glandular fever, moves with his family to an old English country house. A small tin box patterned with roses is found in the chimney, and its contents spark the adventure. T.R.I. are the initials of a boy Tim's age, Tom Inskip, who died in 1910, but left remarkable drawings in the tin box. Tim knows he is much like Tom and is aided in his search for more about Tom's life by Rebecca, a girl who is remarkably like Netty, Tom Inskip's friend from the past. The solution to the puzzle of Tom's life and death gives Tim answers to problems in his own life, about his parents and his future work.

Platt, Kin. **Mystery of the Witch Who Wouldn't.** Dell 1969.

Twelve-year-old Steve, his English bulldog Sinbad, and his friend Minerva Landry meet a white witch by the name of Aurelia Hepburn in Mucker's Swamp. The tale becomes involved as black magicians attempt to learn a scientist's secret invention.

Platt, Kin. **Sinbad and Me.** Dell 1966.

A determined boy, Charlie, and his fearless dog, Sinbad, stick their noses into a million-dollar eighteenth-century mystery and come out with a million regrets. Edgar Allen Poe Award.

Reuter, Carol. **The Secret of the Rocks.** McKay 1967.

Mysterious behavior on an archaeological expedition, missing family jewels, a romantic Italian setting— these are some of the elements of a summer of suspense and romance for young Rachel Porter.

Reynolds, Marjorie. **The Cabin on Ghostly Pond.** Har-Row 1962.

Lonely twelve-year-old Jo Shaw, feeling rejected by his divorced parents, spends the summer with his grandparents. Not only does he solve the mystery of a ghostly visitor, but he comes to the aid of an escapee from a nearby reform school.

Robinson, Jean. **The Secret Life of T. K. Dearing.** Seabury 1973.

A story about a bunch of boys who find some things missing from their clubhouse. When they blame Potato Tom, the "hermit" in the area, they are caught in a puzzling mystery which involves them with Potato Tom and the police.

Roueché, Berton. **Feral.** Har-Row 1974.

A stray cat becomes the focus of a tale of horror and fear in this chilling novel. Dumped by tourists and living in the wild, cats breed in a remote section of Long Island until they are formidable in number. They eliminate their natural food supply of birds and small mammals and must turn to larger game for survival. Jack and Amy Bishop become a central part of the novel, which builds to a terrifying climax, then tapers to a surprising anticlimax.

Sachs, Marilyn. **The Truth about Mary Rose.** Dell 1974.

Mary Rose was named after another Mary Rose who was just eleven when she died in a fire, saving her brother's life and many other people's as well. The present Mary Rose is a happy girl with a lot of energy and imagination, and when her family moves back to New York, her interest in the first Mary Rose consumes this energy. She finds some of her things, and through conversations and eavesdropping on other people's conversations, she learns the truth about what Mary Rose was really like. She is stunned at first, but also for the first time begins to understand just how complicated human personalities can be.

Severn, David. **The Girl in the Grove.** Har-Row 1974.

This suspenseful story about fifteen-year-old Jonquil (Jon) Darley, who moves with her mother to the English countryside, is charged with mystery when the Darleys befriend the Hunters. Jon and Paul Hunter do not get along well. Their troubles begin when Jon meets a mysterious girl, Laura, in the woods—only to discover that Laura is actually the ghost of Laura Seccombe, a young girl killed in a fall from her horse in the late 19th century! This book has adventure, humor, and romance!

Shecter, Ben. **The Whistling Whirligig.** Har-Row 1974.

Josh Newman, alone for the holidays at Cragsmoor Military Academy, shares Christmas with his history teacher, Mr. Wicker, a stray dog named Oliver, and the ghost of a slave boy named Matthew.

Smith, Beatrice S. **Don't Mention Moon to Me.** Nelson 1974.

Holly Woodworth, who is traveling in Europe, gets involved with Emily Fortsaker, who is smuggling moondust. Holly ends up being followed by Ross Belanca, an FBI agent, and Frank Hoffman, a scientist, who are racing each other to get the moondust.

Smith, Emma. **No Way of Telling.** Atheneum 1972.

This is a tight suspense novel, set in an isolated Welsh cottage which is further cut off by a fierce blizzard. Amy and her grandmother find themselves dependent on their courage and wits for survival. One difficulty is determining who is good and who is evil among the strangers who seek refuge in their cottage during the story, hence the title, "no way of telling." They know that someone has to be lying, and they sense the threat of danger in the tension, likely to explode at any moment.

Snyder, Zilpha K. **Eyes in the Fishbowl.** Atheneum 1972.

Alcott-Simpson's is a fantastic department store until a certain girl appears. Only Dion knows who and what she is and why she is there. There is also the problem of Dion's father, who never has a regular job. He gives music lessons, but is so easygoing that he takes day-old doughnuts instead of cash for payment. Dion wishes his father had more backbone—until Alcott-Simpson's closes.

Snyder, Zilpha K. **The Headless Cupid.** Atheneum 1971.

How would you react if the twelve-year-old stepsister you've been waiting to meet turned out to be a fancier of the occult who dresses in crazy-looking costumes and has a crow for a Familiar? Eleven-year-old David Stanley faces this dilemma after his dad marries again. Amanda catches the four young Stanleys up in a fantastic round of initiations and seances. Before long, she proclaims that the headless statue of a cupid, on the stairway of the old mansion, proves the house has been haunted by a poltergeist. But is the noisy ghost real or just Amanda? International Board on Books for Young People Honor List.

Snyder, Zilpha K. **The Truth about Stone Hollow.** Atheneum 1974.

Two children explore a canyon believed by the townspeople to be haunted and evil. The boy is new in town, and his ideas are new to Amy. He says that he sees people in Stone Hollow and events which took place in the past. Amy doesn't know what to think. She believes he is telling the truth as he understands it, but she is not sure what the truth really means.

Stevenson, Robert Louis. **Dr. Jekyll and Mr. Hyde.** S&S 1972.

The eminent Dr. Jekyll has another side to his character, but it is not suspected that he has another personality and identity, that it is he who becomes a fiendish prowler in the night, a cruel murderer. Written in the 1880s, this is the first best-selling story of the split personality.

Storey, Margaret. **The Family Tree.** Nelson 1973.

A mild tension builds up as Kate, a lonely orphan, unravels the history of her family. After being sent to live with her cousin Lawrence, a gruff but sensitive man, she explores his large, foreboding house. She befriends a mysterious boy, and together they examine the attic's treasure of old letters and photographs— clues to the puzzle of Kate's place in the family tree.

Sykes, Pamela. **Mirror of Danger.** Nelson 1973.

Lucy, after living a quiet life with Aunt Olive, goes to live with a noisy family of distant relatives. Feeling extremely lonely, Lucy is only too glad to make friends with Alice. But who is Alice anyway? Lucy lives through some terrifying days before finding the answer to that question.

Thiele, Colin. **Fire in the Stone.** Har-Row 1974.

Fourteen-year-old Ernie Ryan, working a mine in Australia, discovers opal. Someone robs his claim, but Ernie and his Aboriginal friend Willie Winowie set out to find the thief.

Windsor, Patricia. **Something's Waiting for You, Baker D.** Har-Row 1974.

In this mystery for mature readers, Baker D. knows something is after him. He names the something Slynacks, not knowing who or what they are. Mary the Hulk, who makes following people a compulsive hobby, follows Baker and his kidnappers from New York to Sawtruck, Maine, where the two of them make some startling discoveries.

York, Carol Beach. **Dead Man's Cat.** Nelson 1972.

Michael and Queenie, through the "help" of a dead man's cat, solve the mystery of a valuable lost stamp collection.

Young, Miriam. **A Witch's Garden.** Atheneum 1973.

A garden of Wolfbane, hemlock and other poisonous plants? Is Mrs. Mathews a witch? It is a childish whim of Jenny's to put a curse on the committee. But members of the club became ill one after the other. Mrs. Mathews is so strange, using the tombstone as a table top, having that garden and a pet rat, but as Jenny reasons there are good witches and bad witches, if they exist at all.

THE PAST

On living in America

Baker, Betty. **A Stranger and Afraid.** Macmillan 1972.

Although the Indians of the Cicuye pueblo treat the Wichita Indian boy, Sopete, and his brother Zabe well after taking the boys captive in a raid on their village, Sopete yearns to escape and return to his family's lodge on the plains. He is worried that Zabe, younger than he, has become too attached to the ordered life of the pueblo Indians. Then word comes that "strangers riding monsters," Spanish conquistadores, have attacked a nearby Zuni pueblo. Sopete gets his chance to return home, not by escaping but as a guide for the Spanish.

Benedict, Rex. **Good Luck Arizona Man.** Pantheon 1972.

"Here on Apache wings of truth begins my tale." Arizona Slim, a boy known to Apaches as Good Luck Arizona Man, is curious about his own beginnings and some rumored Apache gold. He and his horse, Moon Dance, have many adventures, in which they meet El Lobo, Sheriff Missing Toe, Head Toter, and gangs of outlaws and bandits. Arizona Slim has a daring ride in an attempt to outlive the Apache curse on the gold.

Benedict, Rex. **Last Stand at Goodbye Gulch.** Pantheon 1974.

A young man, Territory Gore, sets out to help a dying man in Goodbye Gulch. He meets Cherokee Waters, a part-Indian girl, who is looking for the same dying man to clear her father of a crime. They find Goodbye Gulch, a strange community of outlaws from the Southwest, and encounter marshals and others who want to capture the outlaws for ransom or bounty.

Benner, Judith A. **Lone Star Rebel.** Blair 1971.

Counterfeiters cheat Rob and his brother when they
sell their Texas cattle to the Confederacy. The mystery is finally solved after fourteen-year-old Rob joins
the staff of Colonel Lawrence Sullivan Ross as a cour-
ier and orderly. Rob saves the colonel's life in a Civil
War skirmish, sees action in several battles, and discovers the counterfeiters' hideout.

Bourne, Miriam Anne. **Nelly Custis' Diary.** Coward
1974.

Nelly Custis, step-granddaughter of George Washington, our first president, kept a diary. She began it in
1789 at the age of 10, and continued until after General Washington's death in 1801. She was then 22.
Through the eyes of a young girl growing up, the
reader learns of General Washington's adventures of
traveling back and forth to the nation's three early
capitals (New York City, Philadelphia, and Washington, D.C.), what children studied in school, their games
and activities, the concerns General Washington had
as president for two terms, and the adventures of
living at Mount Vernon, Washington's 8,000-acre plantation in Virginia.

Collier, James L., and Christopher Collier. **My Brother
Sam Is Dead.** Four Winds 1974.

Behind our cherished traditions of Minutemen and
the American Revolution is a sometimes bitter reality
of conflicting loyalties and families torn apart. Tim,
second son of the tavern-keeper's family in a Massachusetts Tory town, tells the story of what happens
after Sam, his sixteen-year-old brother, joins the Continental Army in the early days of the war. It involves not only adventure and suspense, but the day-
to-day struggle, harsh ironies, and meaningless deaths
that are part of all wars. In later life, Tim asks,
"Might there have been another way to freedom?"
John Newbery Medal.

Dahlstedt, Marden. **Shadow of the Lighthouse.** Coward
1974.

Jane's father is a lighthouse keeper. Although Jane
loves exploring the lonely island, her mother thinks
her time will be better spent studying and learning the
serving and cooking skills a young lady should know.
The conflict reaches a crisis point and forces both
Jane and her mother to try to understand each other.

Field, Rachel. **Calico Bush.** Dell 1973.

The story of a twelve-year-old French convent girl who migrates to America. After her grandmother and uncle die during the strenuous voyage, a family on board the ship has to be responsible for her. She is called a "bound-out girl." She will remain with that family until she is eighteen. Marguerite loves her new life in the new country.

Fitzgerald, John D. **Brave Buffalo Fighter.** Independence Pr 1973.

This story is based on the diary of Susan Parker, who traveled by wagon train from St. Joseph, Missouri, to Ft. Laramie. Indian fights, illness, and frustration plague the family's trip. Her brother Jerry's bravery earns him the Indian name of Brave Buffalo Fighter. That name carries a responsibility that no one on the wagon train wants to face, and sets the stage for a moving climax.

Fletcher, Inglis. **The Scotswoman.** Bantam 1974.

Flora MacDonald and her Scottish clan have supported Bonnie Prince Charlie in his rebellion against the English in 1745. The failure of their uprising leads to economic troubles and political harassment. Flora, her husband Allan, and other clan members decide to leave the Isle of Skye and make an adventurous voyage to North Carolina to find a better life. Instead, they are met with political turmoil and danger in a colony rebelling against England.

Forbes, Esther. **Johnny Tremain.** Dell 1973.

Johnny Tremain's dreams of becoming a noted silversmith are dashed when his right hand is severely burned and crippled for life. Because of this, he seeks a new way of life which leads him into the intrigue and adventure of the Boston Tea Party and the American Revolution against England. John Newbery Medal.

Forman, James. **The Cow Neck Rebels.** FS&G 1969.

This war story (or anti-war story to be more exact) is set during the American Revolution. What is now Long Island, New York, was then a rural area populated by a mixture of patriots, British sympathizers, and people just out for gain any way possible. Bruce and his brother Malcolm follow their fanatical grandfather into battle, urged on by his hatred of the Brit-

ish and his stirring tales of Scottish battles of the
past, particularly the Scottish defeat at Culloden.
But the boys soon discover there is not much glory
in warfare, and the horror of the suffering sends
Bruce back home to reconsider his own position in the
madness.

Gillett, Mary. **Bugles at the Border**. Blair 1968.

Bart McLeod is twelve years old when the North Carolina settlers send a resolution declaring their freedom
from England to the 1775 Continental Congress. Bart's
story—his training to be a doctor, his personal fight
with a young Tory neighbor—is told against an authentic background of Revolutionary War battles.

Hamilton, Dorothy. **Jim Musco**. Herald Pr 1972.

Jim Musco doesn't completely understand why he and
his father and mother are shunned by the other Delaware Indians. But Jim knows he likes working for Mr.
Reese on his farm. When Mr. Reese gives Jim and
his mother the little cabin that had been the Reese's
first home when they settled in Indiana, Jim is determined to stay. But there is talk that his tribe plans
to carry him off when they move west, because they
will need young men to be hunters and warriors in
their new home.

Hanna, Mary Carr. **Cassie and Ike**. Blair 1973.

This story deals with family life and the happenings
in the village and country of Quaker America of the
nineteenth century. The main character, Cassie, is a
new school teacher. She experiences many conflicts
as she tries to reconcile her feeling that a person
should strive to be happy and think her own thoughts
with the teaching of her church—the Society of
Friends—which believes she should form no opinions
of her own.

Harris, Christie. **Raven's Cry**. Atheneum 1966.

This is the story of the Haidas, the Lords of the Northwest Coast of America, a proud and cultured people
whose art has come to be admired throughout the
world. It is the story of how they lived before the
coming of the white man and how their culture declined and almost disappeared after the white man
settled British Columbia and the Queen Charlotte
Islands. The story is told through the eyes of three
generations of Haida Eagle Chiefs.

Haynes, Betsy. **Cowslip.** Nelson 1973.

This story of Cowslip, a thirteen-year-old black girl, begins in 1861, as she waits on an auction block to be sold as a slave once again. On the new plantation on the Mississippi River, she becomes a nursemaid to Colonel Sprague's children. The reader learns about the laws of slavery, the physical and mental shackling of the slaves, and their methods of self-defense. Life among the other slaves teaches Cowslip that she is a human being with dignity, who can learn to read and write and might someday be free. The Underground Railroad, an organization of blacks and whites dedicated to the freeing of all slaves, figures in the story.

Henry, Marguerite. **Mustang: Wild Spirit of the West.** Rand 1966.

Based on fact, this engrossing story tells of Wild Horse Annie Johnston, who carried her plea all the way from the country courthouse to the White House in an effort to save the wild mustangs of the West from extermination.

Hickman, Janet. **The Valley of the Shadow.** Macmillan 1974.

This novel is based on historical records of Moravian missionaries, who taught Christian doctrine to Indian tribes in early America. Through the eyes of a thirteen-year-old boy, we see their pilgrimage to find safe and neutral land for a group of Delaware Indian converts. The story explores the boy's difficulty in communicating with his father and in understanding why white men (Long Knives) trained in Christian ways like the Moravians, treat Indians so cruelly. Differences in tribal customs are pictured.

Hunt, Irene. **Across Five Aprils.** G&D 1965.

Jethro is too young to fight in the Civil War, and so he stays home, watching his older brothers go off to separate armies, watching his parents deteriorate with grief and suffering, watching the neighbors turn into violent gangs bent on vengeance. All those long five years, Jethro does the work of a man on the family farm and tries to make some sense of the madness around him.

Johnson, Dorothy M. **A Man Called Horse and Other Stories.** Ballantine 1970.

Realistic presentations of Indians and whites on the

Minnesota-Montana frontier. Original title: *Indian Country*.

Jones, Weyman B. **Edge of Two Worlds.** Dial 1968.

A young boy is the only survivor of an ambush on a wagon train. In his attempt to find his way back to civilization he becomes involved with an old Indian who is on a journey to Mexico. Through this friendship, understanding grows. Western Heritage Juvenile Book Award.

Koob, Theodora J. **Hear a Different Drummer.** Lippincott 1968.

A fast-paced story of a bondservant who runs away from his master and whose journeys take him through frontier country and involve him in the French and Indian War.

Lawson, John. **The Spring Rider.** T Y Crowell 1968.

The present meets the past as brother and sister, Jacob and Gray, meet people who fought in the Civil War. Jacob gets involved in the battle along with a young Union soldier Hannibal, General Jackson, and Colonel Turner Asby. Gray is loved by Hannibal, who faces choices about war and about sacrificing Gray. The legendary Spring Rider, famous and mysterious, watches over the people and works for peace. Boston Globe-Horn Book Award.

Lester, Julius. **Long Journey Home.** Dial 1972.

Drawing on historical references to black slaves and their experiences, Julius Lester has created characters who could well have existed as slaves in the South of the 1880s. In these six stories we meet Rambler and his music; Ben, the "perfect" slave; Louis, the runaway; Bob Lemmons, who has a way with wild horses; Jake and Mandy, a husband and wife separated by slavery; and a group of slaves who walk from their masters and into the sea. Through these individuals, a piece of black history is recreated. National Book Award Honor.

Meltzer, Milton. **Underground Man.** Bradbury Pr 1972.

The story of a young, white farm boy who leaves his upstate New York home during the period when America was divided into free states and slave states. Josh Bowen hopes to find a life of his own. After a chance meeting with a runaway slave on a raft on the Ohio river, Josh spends the years between 1835 and 1861 helping slaves escape from the state of Kentucky. The story depicts slave trading and experiences of escaping slaves, as well as Josh's life in prison, after he is convicted of helping slaves escape.

Miller, Albert G. **Mark Twain in Love.** HarBraceJ 1973.

Mark Twain's courtship of Livy Langdon was a colorful and interesting period in the writer's life. Mark Twain's humor and nonconforming behavior and Livy's understanding, encouragement and loyalty to Twain are described well in this fictionalized biography.

Montgomery, Jean. **The Wrath of Coyote.** Morrow 1968.

Kotola, chief of the Miwok people, was just a boy when the Spanish first came to the region around San Francisco Bay. As chief, he led the futile conflict against the white men, and lived his last years under Mexican rule.

O'Dell, Scott. **The King's Fifth.** Dell 1973.

While he is imprisoned and awaiting trial, Esteban writes a journal of his explorations as a mapmaker with Coronado in 1540 along the Pacific Coast. Young Esteban confesses that he is guilty of not giving the King of Spain his fifth of a large quantity of gold which the young man and his party discovered.

O'Dell, Scott. **Sing Down the Moon.** Dell 1970.

A fourteen-year-old Navaho Indian girl tells how Spanish slavers capture her and her friend. Following the brave girls' escape and return to their tribe, the Navahos are forced to march three hundred miles to Fort Sumner. Bright Morning tells the story of Navaho life, customs, and hardships in 1863.

Richter, Conrad. **The Fields.** Knopf 1946.

This second novel of Conrad Richter's trilogy (including *The Trees* and *The Town*) is the story of Sayward Luckett's growth as a woman and her constant struggle with the wilderness.

Richter, Conrad. **The Town.** Knopf 1950.

In this third novel about the Luckett family, Sayward lives to see the transition of her family and her friends, American pioneers, from the ways of wilderness to the ways of civilization. *The Trees* began the story of the Luckett family and *The Fields* continued it. Pulitzer Prize.

Richter, Conrad. **The Trees.** Knopf 1940.

A portrait of frontier life, this novel introduces the Luckett family and tells the story of the transition of American pioneers from the ways of the wilderness to the ways of civilization. This is the first of three novels about the characters introduced here; the others are *The Fields* and *The Town.*

Schellie, Don. **Me, Cholay and Co. Apache Warriors.** Four Winds 1973.

When the lieutenant puts seventeen-year-old Joshua Thane in charge of a young Apache prisoner, no one realizes that the boys will become good friends. Together they rescue the Apache's little sister from a Papago tribe, which had massacred 125 Apache women and children.

Speare, Elizabeth George. **Calico Captive.** Dell 1957.

The members of the Johnson family are driven out of their home by the Indians and forced to march for days through the wilderness to Montreal, where they are sold to the French. The Indians are kind and hold up the trek for several days when Mrs. Johnson gives birth to a baby during the march.

Speare, Elizabeth George. **The Witch of Blackbird Pond.** Dell 1973.

After the death of her uncle, Kit is forced to leave the life of ease in tropical Barbados and to seek out her only relative who is an aunt she has never met. The aunt and her family are seventeenth century New England Puritans. Kit's ideas and habits are no more welcome than her willful nature. She survives hardships, hatred, and an epidemic to prove herself and win a new life. International Board on Books for Young People Honor List; John Newbery Medal.

Steele, William O. **The Wilderness Tattoo: A Narrative of Juan Ortiz.** HarBraceJ 1972.

Juan Ortiz is left behind on the beach by his Spanish countrymen in 1528, captured and tortured by the fierce Timucuan Indians of Florida. He is saved by the chief's daughter, Acuera, who helps him escape to a neighboring village where he is treated not as a slave but as a friend. Juan, who wonders if he will ever see his homeland again, is adopted into the tribe and learns the Indians' ways.

Summers, Mark W. **A Student Cartoonist's View of Great Figures in American History.** S&S 1972.

A book of caricatures which gives a fresh perspective on the people who made the American past. America's heroes and heroines are revealed as human beings with the strengths and weaknesses we all possess. History comes alive, through the eyes of a witty student.

Vidal, Gore. **Burr.** Bantam 1974.

Aaron Burr is famous as our nation's third vice president and for his duel with Alexander Hamilton. Here he is presented as a charming and intelligent man, and this biography sheds a different light on other famous men who surround him. Characters and story line follow history; conversations and motives are fictional.

Walsh, Jill Paton. **Toolmaker.** Seabury 1973.

Ra is skillful in toolmaking. His flint axes and spearheads are admired by the other men in his tribe. They propose a new idea. If Ra will make their tools and weapons, they will furnish his food. Ra stays home from the daily hunting and makes tools.

Wechter, Nell Wise. **Betsy Dowdy's Ride.** Blair 1960.

Courageous Betsy, according to the old storytellers, swam and rode her Banker pony at night through swift tides and the Great Dismal Swamp to get help for the North Carolina patriots in their fight against the British soldiers. Her life on the Outer Banks during the American Revolution makes an interesting story as Betsy and her father work together salvaging goods from shipwrecks.

Weik, Mary Hays. **The Scarlet Thread.** Atheneum 1968.

In this book, young actors and actresses will find five colorful scripts to choose from when it comes time for their schools' one-act plays. The author has written plays set in ancient Greece, medieval Europe, Renaissance Italy, Eighteenth Century France, and pre-Civil War America. Each play is in the theatrical tradition of its period—commedia dell'arte, minstrel show, etc.

Wellman, Manly Wade. **Settlement of Shocco: Adventures in Colonial Carolina.** Blair 1963.

Edward and Abigail Jones, with their five children, come to Shocco Creek in the Carolinas to establish a farm home and raise their family. Life is good but money is scarce. The pioneers often have trouble paying ground rents to their English landlords. When a dishonest rent collector tries to claim the family land, young James Jones fights for their rights.

West, Jessamyn. **Except for Me and Thee.** Avon 1970.

Jess and Eliza Birdwell are young lovers with a frontier to conquer. Eliza is a preacher woman, and as they move west their Quaker faith is put to many tests. They face war, rebellion, and racial intolerance. These same characters appear in an earlier novel, *The Friendly Persuasion.*

Wick, Gorden E. **Saints in Buckskins.** Exposition 1974.

Sage Wick and his friend Little Finch, a Ute Indian, find the mysterious Picture Rock Mine and its lost treasure of gold and silver. They also discover the secret of the mine's blue-veined quartz, which makes people invisible. Sage and Little Finch use their gold and the power of the blue-veined quartz to help people and uphold law and order in Southern Colorado. Because of their generosity and good deeds, they become known as the "Saints in Buckskins."

Wilder, Laura Ingalls. **The Long Winter.** Har-Row 1953.

The first of the blizzards hits in October, and one after another they continue throughout the winter. The prairie town on the frontier where the Ingalls live is running low on food and fuel. The trains can't get through with more supplies, and the Ingalls have only seed grain for food. All winter they huddle around their small stove burning twisted straw for warmth and grinding the grain in a coffee grinder to mix with water for bread.

Witheridge, Elizabeth. **And What of You, Josephine Charlotte?** Atheneum 1969.

Josephine Charlotte was named after the Empress of France, but in fact she is a slave on a Maryland farm. Fortunately her life so far has been cushioned with the love of her grandmother and the special love shared between her and the daughter of the master, Sarah. Circumstances are changing, however, as Sarah's marriage approaches and Jo doesn't know what will happen when Sarah leaves home. For the first time, her position as a slave is threatening and frightening. She hears talk of selling some slaves for money to pay for the wedding, and she realizes that she could be sold, now that she is no longer sheltered by Sarah's presence in the household.

On living in other parts of the world

Aiken, Joan. Midnight Is a Place. Viking Pr 1974.

When Midnight Court castle burns, Sir Randolph Grimsby dies in the fire and his two young wards have no place to live in the hostile town. The children survive by working in the great carpet factory, by escaping death, and by fleeing through the filth of the underground sewers.

Aitmatov, Chingiz. The White Ship. Crown 1972.

A grim, but somehow lyrical story of a boy's life in a bleak Russian landscape. This sensitive boy escapes the stark cruelty of his daily life by dreaming of animals—of the Horned Mother Deer goddess of his tribe, and of the swimming fish he longs to become. *The White Ship* is a modern folk tale. It is simply written but examines mature emotions.

Alexander, Lloyd. The Marvelous Misadventures of Sebastian. S&S 1970.

Sebastian loses his job as fourth fiddler in the court because of an accident which causes great embarrassment to the Baron. This starts a chain of events in which Sebastian is crowned by a runaway princess, becomes a circus fiddler, gets a magic fiddle, is helped by a stray cat, and has many other adventures—or misadventures! National Book Award.

Andrews, J. S. Cargo for a King. Dutton 1973.

A sea story of pirates and small cargo ships on the Irish Sea in the thirteenth century. Rag, a Norman, becomes captain of a trading vessel after the death of his father. King John of England hears about Rag's bravery in dealing with the pirates and orders him to deliver a cargo of beer to his castle.

Andrews, J. S. The Man from the Sea. Dutton 1971.

A stranger named Hadra with bronze axe-heads and knife-blades comes to a fishing village on the shore of what 3,600 years later is Donaghadee Sound in Northern Ireland. He guides some of the children in a search across the sea for the village men.

Buck, Pearl S. The Good Earth. PB 1968.

The epic story of a poor farmer and his family in nineteenth century China and of their rise in fortune.

Wang Lung, a young man at the beginning of the book, buys a piece of land. He and his wife O-Lan struggle through years of wars and famine to build their farm and to become important and independent. Just as they seem to achieve these goals, their lives are complicated by events that threaten their values and relationships. Wang Lung takes a young concubine to live in his household, and his sons attempt to change the family's way of life.

Buck, Pearl S. **A House Divided.** PB 1975.

Yuan, the young son of a large farming family in China, becomes exposed to books and develops a great love of learning that eventually causes him to leave behind his family, his country, and the ways of his ancestors. *A House Divided* concludes the story begun in *The Good Earth* and *Sons*, with Yuan's search for a way to end the ignorance and poverty of his people. He goes to America to study and while there encounters new ideas, customs, and faiths. When he returns to China, his way of looking at his home has changed, and he must find a way to combine his background with the modern way of life.

Buck, Pearl S. **Sons.** PB 1975.

In *Sons,* the sequel to *The Good Earth,* Wang Lung's three sons divide their father's land and fortunes and pursue their own separate dreams. Wang the Eldest and the second son, Wang the Merchant, establish families of their own, while the youngest son, Wang the Tiger, becomes a soldier and sets out to conquer as much territory as he can. These three sons have children of their own, who are just as determined to live their own lives regardless of their father's wishes.

Burroughs, Edgar Rice. **The Eternal Savage.** Ace Bks 1972.

A visit to Africa, a twist in time, and Victoria Custer enters a Stone Age adventure. With her is the mighty warrior Nu. Their lives are threatened by the prehistoric life surrounding them. Emotions and senses are attacked in their strange encounters. Can time again be twisted to release its captives?

Burroughs, Edgar Rice. **The Lad and the Lion.** Ace Bks 1974.

From a royal court to a derelict steamer to an African

nation, a young man finds his greatest friend is a giant lion. A series of adventures brings Michael from youth to maturity and eventual love. A parallel story details the intrigue occurring in the country from which the young prince fled. Together, they provide a clear picture of the contrast between civilization and the law of the wild.

Burroughs, Edgar Rice. **The Outlaw of Torn.** Ace Bks 1973.

In the year 1243, a kidnapping occurs. Prince Richard, three-year-old son of the King of England, is abducted. Some twelve years later a terror arises among the English. A treacherous highwayman, seemingly French born, roams the land robbing and plundering. He is Norman of Torn, and his victims are the evil and the powerful rich. The conclusion is expected, but very well handled.

Chauncy, Nan. **Hunted in Their Own Land.** Seabury 1973.

The Toogee people are happy on Tasmania, their island home south of Australia. Then a "whale with wings" (a sailing ship) finds their island, and the Toogee see white men take their food, chop down their tall trees, and finally drive them from their homes.

Chute, Marchette. **The Innocent Wayfaring.** Dutton 1955.

Anne Richmond runs away from an English convent with a monkey to find a group of entertainers. From June 23 to June 26, 1370, she visits a fair, an ale house and a caste with a young man, Nick, during a journey to her parents' home.

Clark, Mavis T. **Blue above the Trees.** Meredith Corp 1968.

An English family emigrate to Queensland, Australia, in the 1880s and begin clearing a farm from the vast forest wilderness filled with dingoes, koalas, and lyre birds. The family is a large one, each member is different and there is constant conflict. The major source of trouble is the fact that some of the family want to conquer the land and others want to treasure it and protect it. The author manages to relate the mystery and vastness of the forest which today no longer even exists.

Coatsworth, Elizabeth. **The Cat Who Went to Heaven.**
Macmillan 1967.

A three-colored cat brings good luck to a Japanese
artist who is working on a picture for the temple of
the Great Buddha. John Newbery Medal.

Conway, Helene. **The End Is the Beginning.** Follett
1972.

This historical novel is set in the year 1690, when the
Catholic Irish were struggling against their English
Protestant overlords. Thirteen-year-old Owen Bourke
is too young to ride off to battle with his father. But
when his father does not return, Owen finds himself
the man of the family. Many adventures follow Owen's
discovery of a deed to lands in the colony of Maryland
that will be rightfully his if he can keep the deed in
his possession. They involve the "rapparees," outlawed
veterans of the campaigns against the English, who
lived in hiding in the wild Irish hills.

Coolidge, Olivia. **The King of Men.** HM 1966.

Vividly imagined adventures of the youth who as-
cended the Mycenaean throne as King of Men are recounted against a background of chariot races, a bear
hunt, a human sacrifice, and the interference of the
Olympian gods.

Cordell, Alexander. **The Traitor Within.** Nelson 1973.

Ling lives in a huge commune in Red China. He tries
to take the place of his missing father and to be very
brave, as he resists those people who call his father
a traitor and as he fights the Taiwan forces. Ling's
pet water buffalo is a loyal companion.

Crossley-Holland, Kevin. **The Sea Stranger.** Seabury
1973.

This is a story of the year 653, before Christianity had
come to the East Saxons. From his favorite spot on
the beach, Wulf sees in the distance a rowboat with a
man in it. He is Cedd, a Northumbrian missionary,
who brings Christianity to the East Saxons. Cedd,
with his monks, builds a cathedral.

Dickens, Charles. **A Christmas Carol.** Atheneum 1966.

Merry Christmas? "Bah . . . Humbug . . . If I
could work my will . . . every idiot who goes about
with 'Merry Christmas' on his lips should be boiled
in his own pudding, and buried with a stake of holly
through his heart." Almost everyone knows—from

reading this book or seeing the story on television—
that Old Scrooge comes to regret his unkind words.
But it's always fun to turn back to this British classic
and see again the ghosts of Christmas past, present,
and future, and to experience with Scrooge the rediscovery of what the Christmas season is all about.

Forman, James. **Ring the Judas Bell.** FS&G 1965.

In the Greek Civil War, a priest's son and daughter
are kidnapped with other village children by the Communists and forced to march to Albania to be held as
hostages. The boy is a pacifist and his sister is committed to survival at any cost. Throughout their ordeal
they occasionally doubt their own beliefs. The sister
admires the boy's kindness and humanity, and he admires her reason and strength.

Graves, Robert. **The Siege and Fall of Troy.** Dell 1973.

This story of the war between the Trojans and the
Greeks links together episodes from ancient greek
epics. It begins with the founding of Troy and ends
with the victory of the Greeks in the Trojan War. Included are stories of many gods and humans: Zeus,
Achilles, Ajax, Helen, Odysseus, Agamemnon and
Hector.

Greaves, Margaret. **Stone of Terror.** Har-Row 1972.

In the seventeenth century fifteen-year-old Philip Hoskyn comes from England to join his grandfather on
the island of Serq. Philip meets the witch and priestess
of the haunting stone and falls in love with Marie, the
niece of the priestess, whom he has to save from her
aunt's strange powers.

Greenleaf, Margery. **Dirk: A Story of the Struggle for
Freedom in Holland, 1572–1574.** Follett 1971.

Sixteen-year-old Dirk has seen most of his family
perish at the hands of the Spanish masters of the
Netherlands in the sixteenth century. All that is left
is the chance to serve William, Prince of Orange, in
his never-ceasing efforts to unite the Dutch people to
fight for their land and their liberties. One further
hope sustains Dirk: that of finding his sister alive.

Harnett, Cynthia. **The Writing on the Hearth.** Viking
Pr 1973.

The author lives in an English medieval thatched cottage in the area which is the setting for this book. This
story of a boy of the fifteenth century is enriched by

descriptions of the area, Oxford University, and London of that time. Witchcraft, royalty, and political intrigue surround Stephen's life as a clerk to the earl of Suffolk.

Haugaard, Erik Christian. **The Little Fishes.** HM 1967.

Guido is a little "fish" among many other little fish caught in Italy during World War II. He is homeless, groveling for food, hiding from bombs, alone, and afraid. Somehow he joins up with a girl and her younger brother and the three wander through Italy, in search of a corner where they can be safe and free from hunger. This is a desperate story of survival. Book World Children's Spring Book Festival Award, Boston Globe-Horn Book Award, Jane Addams Book Award.

Haugaard, Erik Christian. **The Rider and His Horse.** HM 1968.

At Masada a band of Jews resolve to stand against the Roman army in 73 AD. All over Israel people are suffering after an abortive attempt to drive the Romans out of their country. People are starving; crucifixions line the waysides in an effort to frighten people into submission. At an impregnable desert fortress, a group of people refuse to surrender. When their defeat is inevitable, they decide to kill themselves, even their women and children, rather than give in. A fourteen-year-old boy, who is a witness, is allowed to survive the mass suicide so that he can tell the story.

Hodge, Jane A. **Watch the Wall, My Darling.** Doubleday 1966.

During the Napoleonic Wars a young American visits her family's home in Sussex. Spies, smugglers, and romance involving her mysterious cousin, Ross, follow.

Hoover, H. M. **The Lion's Cub.** Four Winds 1974.

Jemal-Edin is the son of a warrior fighting against the Russians. In the Wars of the Caucasus (1800–1859), Russia was determined to conquer the mountains and to open a route to India. After he is captured, Jemal-Edin is reared in the palace and becomes a loyal Russian.

Huffaker, Clair. **The Cowboy and the Cossack.** S&S 1973.

The year is 1880 and the place is Siberia, where fifteen cowboys from Montana and fifteen Russian cossacks must learn to coexist during a 4,000-mile cattle drive. They soon learn that they haven't time for the instant hatred each feels for the other. There are worse problems, such as wolf packs, tigers, flash floods, wars, and an entire Tartar army.

Hunter, Mollie. **The 13th Member.** Har-Row 1971.

Set in sixteenth century Scotland, this story of witchcraft is based on records of a plot to murder King James I. Adam Lawrie, a servant boy, follows Gilly Duncan, the kitchenmaid, one night and sees the Devil himself! Adam and Gilly, a self-confessed witch, help to expose the plot against the king.

Kimmel, Eric A. **The Tartar's Sword.** Coward 1974.

Hrisha, a Ukranian serf in 1623, kills his master to avenge his father and then sets out to join the Cossacks. He is idealistic and feels the famous Cossacks are fighting for freedom. He finds out they fight for many reasons, and even comes to admire their enemies, the Tartars. Hrisha has many experiences and realizes more about his own personal freedom.

Kingman, Lee. **Escape from the Evil Prophecy.** HM 1973.

Ketil and Thordis, brother and sister, go to live at the hall of foster parents, a common custom in eleventh century Iceland. Their foster parents have a son, Orm, believed to be under a spell. Orm's mother, who believes in the heathen gods, has a vision that the spell can be broken. Halldor, the foster father and chieftain, is a new Christian. Murder and fighting result.

Linevski, A. (translator Maria Polushkin). **An Old Tale Carved Out of Stone.** Crown 1973.

Seventeen-year-old Liok is forced to become a man and a shaman (similar to Indian witch doctor) without a guide. His tribe represents primitive society banded together for survival against a cruel world. Superstitions and traditional legend form the basis for their lives. Survival is a struggle in a world where nature and human nature work against the individual.

Lloyd, Norris. **The Village That Allah Forgot: A Story of Modern Tunisia.** Hastings 1973.

Food and jobs are scarce in the tiny, backward Tunisian village in which Ali lives. After his father is killed by French guns, Ali works for independence and a better life for himself and his village. Allah sends good things.

Lofts, Norah. **The Maude Reed Tale.** Dell 1972.

In fifteenth century England, girls from good families were sent to great castles to learn to be ladies. Maude Reed wants to be a wool merchant, not a lady. This is the story of how she became both.

Lovett, Margaret. **Jonathan.** Dutton 1972.

Fourteen-year-old Jonathan leads a family of orphaned children and a homeless handicapped child to employment: first in a pottery, then in a mill and in a mine with dangerous working conditions, and finally in a mill owned by a man who is working to improve conditions for children in England about 1815.

Marks, J. M. **Ayo Gurkha!** Nelson 1971.

The title means "The Gurkha comes!" the battle cry of the Gurkha Rifles of Nepal. Fourteen-year-old Aitahang Limbu lies about his age to become a recruit. He would save his pay to buy land. He would avenge the death of his best friend by going after One-Eye, the bandit.

Ottley, Reginald. **The War on William Street.** Nelson 1973.

A story of Australian youth during the Depression is the basis of this book. It centers around three boys from wide-ranging backgrounds, involved in gang warfare in Sydney, Australia, of the thirties. The author describes the lifestyle of the well-off and the poor, and the way boys from three backgrounds can get along.

Paterson, Katherine. **The Sign of the Chrysanthemum.** T Y Crowell 1973.

Thirteen-year-old Muna, a Japanese boy, buries his dead mother and is free now to hunt for the father he has never seen. He has two clues: his father was a samurai and he had a chrysanthemum tattooed on his left shoulder. Muna stows away on a boat to the capital. The first person he meets on his adventure is a pirate.

Rosenfeld, Semyon E. (translator Miriam Morton). **The First Song.** Doubleday 1968.

This story of a Russian boy is set in Odessa at the beginning of this century. It tells of his efforts to obtain a musical education, his experiences at work and in revolutionary activities.

Roth, Arthur. **The Iceberg Hermit.** Four Winds 1974.

Seventeen-year-old Allan Gordon is a sailor on a whaling ship that crashes into an iceberg in 1757. Old stories tell how Allan lives with a polar bear which he trains as a cub, then finds a tribe of Viking descendants during seven years marooned in the Arctic.

Sonnleitner, A. T. (translator Anthea Bell). **The Cave Children.** S G Phillips 1971.

In this book with a long-ago setting, two young children hide in the woods with their grandmother, who is accused of being a witch. After their grandmother dies, they learn to survive. They find shelter in a cave and food in the forest; they invent tools, and clothe themselves with animal skins.

Speare, Elizabeth George. **The Bronze Bow.** HM 1972.

We are all familiar to some extent with the life of Jesus as told in the New Testament. This book gives us an interesting view of that life as it tells the story of a young Galilean named Daniel whose family has been destroyed by Roman soldiers occupying his homeland. Daniel's hatred for the Romans has taken him to the Galilean hills where he has joined a band of guerilla revolutionaries. When he hears Jesus speak, Daniel thinks he must be a new political leader, the one capable of leading them in their revolt against Rome. John Newbery Medal, International Board on Books for Young People Honor List.

Sutcliff, Rosemary. **Heather, Oak and Olive.** Dutton 1972.

Three separate stories about courage take place in Wales, Rome, and Greece, the three countries represented by heather, oak and olive. In "The Chief's Daughter," Dara, a ten-year-old chief's daughter, helps a young twelve-year-old Irish captive escape before his sacrifice and endangers her own life. In "A Circlet of Oak Leaves," Aracos allows the other men to think he has won the highest award for bravery, the circlet of oak leaves. Both Aracos and the men have a surprise in store when a young Medic visits him at night. Two boys in "A Crown of Wild Olive" are from enemy countries but become good friends and learn something about victory at the ancient Olympic games.

Sutcliff, Rosemary. **Warrior Scarlet.** Walck 1958.

Drem has a crippled arm: how can he ever become a warrior and earn the right to wear the scarlet cloth that is reserved for men of his tribe? This story provides an accurate view of life and customs in Bronze Age Britain.

T'ieh-Yün, Liu (translator Harold Shadick). **The Travels of Lao Ts'an.** Cornell U Pr 1952.

This classic Chinese novel tells of Lao Ts'an, who has studied much poetry, but has never passed the examinations to get a degree. Fortunately he meets a Taoist priest who teaches him some cures. So, being glib-tongued, he travels wherever the rivers and roads lead. He has many adventures, curing people and dispensing quick-witted advice wherever he goes.

Treffinger, Carolyn. **Li Lun, Lad of Courage.** Abingdon 1947.

When Li Lun refuses to go to sea on his man-making voyage, his angry father gives him seven rice grains to plant on the mountain. He cannot return until he brings back a harvest of seven times as much rice. No islander has ever grown rice before.

Turner, Philip. **Devil's Nob.** Nelson 1973.

Taffy, an apprentice carpenter at a slate quarry in England, goes fishing when he can. Often he gives the fish to his beloved Sarah, who tries to support a sick father and her brothers and sisters. Taffy bets a week's wages on a race between an engine and a horse.

Vernon, Louise A. **Ink on His Fingers.** Herald Pr 1972.

This is a story of the struggle to print the first Bible with movable type. Gutenberg wants to make printing an art and to print a Bible as beautiful as those copied by the monks. To do this, Gutenberg needs money, time, loyal workers, and faith in God. Twelve-year-old Hans wants to help.

Watson, Sally. **Linnet.** Dutton 1971.

Fourteen-year-old Linnet runs away from home and accepts hospitality from a handsome stranger who is really king of London's underworld and teaches children to be thieves. She discovers a plot to overthrow Queen Elizabeth and put Catholic Mary, Queen of Scots, on the throne of England.

Weik, Mary Hays. **The Scarlet Thread.** Atheneum 1968.

In this book, young actors and actresses will find five colorful scripts to choose from when it comes time for their schools' one-act plays. The author has written plays set in ancient Greece, medieval Europe, Renaissance Italy, Eighteenth Century France, and pre-Civil War America. Each play is in the theatrical tradition of its period—commedia dell'arte, minstrel show, etc.

Weir, Rosemary. **The Three Red Herrings.** Nelson 1972.

A delightful story of a family in Victorian England. Fourteen-year-old Eva Herring brings her eleven-year-old ballet-dancing sister Midge, her nine-year-old science and math genius brother Willie, and herself through hard times after her theatrical father dies.

Wheeler, Thomas Gerald. **All Men Tall.** S G Phillips 1969.

This is a story of the English court in the Middle Ages—an age of intrigue and treachery. Thomeline, a fifteen-year-old orphan, escapes from London and joins the household of Hugh the Armourer. The history of the discovery of gunpowder is woven into the story.

Wheeler, Thomas Gerald. **A Fanfare for the Stalwart.** S G Phillips 1967.

Alain Dieudonne is appointed trumpeter to Napoleon's Imperial Guard. In 1812, his regiment advances toward Moscow. When Alain is injured, he is left behind stranded. He is joined by two refugees, Annette, the daughter of a French officer, and her governess, in a bitterly cold march across Russia and Poland.

Willard, Barbara. **The Cold Wind Blowing.** Dutton 1972.

When his uncle, a priest, is murdered in the robbery of an English monastery, Piers Medley brings home a strange girl. This story of joy and tragedy tells how the tumult that took place after King Henry VIII declared himself head of church and state affected family life in the countryside.

Willard, Barbara. **The Iron Lily.** Dutton 1973.

A story of Tudor England. When Lilias is fifteen years old, she discovers that she does not belong in the family with whom she lives. She has a crested ring and a record of her baptism to indicate which family in this Iron Country is hers. She becomes the owner of two iron foundries and eventually finds her father.

Willard, Barbara. **The Sprig of Broom.** Dutton 1972.

Medley Plashet, a boy in sixteenth century England, wonders about the many mysteries surrounding his father when he leaves Medley and his mother in a cottage in the forest. His mother is killed because she is suspected of being a witch. Wanting to go marry an aristocratic girl, Medley traces his father and learns the secret.

Williams, Ursula Moray. **Jockin the Jester.** Nelson 1973.

In this tale of adventure and intrigue set in medieval England at the time of the plague, the author writes of the trials and tribulations of a boy, thin and sullen, who becomes a court jester in a manor house—loved and loving children, animals, and anyone—in a time of hate and cruelty to man and beast.

THE FUTURE

On imagining the world of tomorrow

Allison, Leonard, Leonard Jenkin, and Robert Perrault, editors. **Survival Printout: Science Fact, Science Fiction.** Random 1973.

Here is a collection of science fiction stories about evolution/identity, earth probabilities, ecosystems cellular and solar, and time-space travel by such famous fiction writers as Arthur C. Clarke and Robert Heinlein. There are also factual science articles about communications satellites, exploding stars, and the possibility of direct contact among galactic civilizations.

Anderson, Poul. **Brain Wave.** Ballantine 1954.

A sudden mental surge which raises the intellectual capacity of both man and animal indicates a new age which will change all destinies. This is the premise of this novel, which examines vast world changes and recounts the intimate human story of a few individuals.

Anthony, Piers. **Race against Time.** Hawthorn 1973.

John Smith senses that he is being watched secretly, but until he discovers the African girl, Ala, he does not realize why. He and Ala are two of only six racially pure beings. Their adventures in contacting the other four, determining the reason for their existence, and coming to terms with their needs and the goals of the Standard beings make exciting reading. The novel examines the meaning of freedom and reality.

Asimov, Isaac. **Asimov's Mysteries.** Dell 1968.

Fourteen stories by Isaac Asimov make up this book. Each is based in science fiction, but each also has a mystery interwoven with it. The techniques used in the stories, as well as their solutions, make for interesting reading.

Avallone, Michael. **Beneath the Planet of the Apes.** Bantam 1970.

Two men, Taylor and Brent, find themselves catapulted from the twentieth century to another time— Earth thousands of years from now. Apes, acting and talking just like men, rule the planet and worship "the Great Bomb," bringer of life and death. Waiflike Nova, one of the mute, barbaric humans left on the planet all but destroyed by atomic war, accompanies each of these men on their nightmarish adventures toward an exciting and surprising climax.

Brackett, Leigh. **The Halfling and Other Stories.** Ace Bks 1973.

The seven stories in this volume contain all the ingredients of science fiction. Mystery and murder at an interplanetary carnival, shadows that devour men, and attempts to civilize savage planets are among the themes of the stories.

Bradbury, Ray. **Farenheit 451.** Ballantine 1953.

Farenheit 451 is the temperature at which book paper catches fire and burns. It is also a group of firemen, of which Guy Montag is one. In this book the firemen don't put out fires; they start them. Books aren't allowed to be owned or read. Books must be destroyed by fire. Guy becomes curious about what's in these books, but knows he can only read them at the risk of his own life.

Bradbury, Ray. **The October Country.** Ballantine 1972.

Nineteen stories by Ray Bradbury make up this volume and show the diversity of the author's style. Bradbury's stories deal with people as we know them, caught up in fantastic and unreal situations.

Brunner, John. **Stand on Zanzibar.** Ballantine 1968.

This giant book encompasses a world of intelligent computers, psychedelics, political assassination, superstitions, scientists and near-hysterical masses. Two individuals are picked out for close observation. They are Norman Niblock House and his roommate Donald. One works for the General Technic Corporation and the other is programmed as an assassin.

Burroughs, Edgar Rice. **Carson of Venus.** Ace Bks 1973.

Carson Napier and his love, Duare, attempt to reenter her homeland. This means sure death for Carson, as Duare's father has vowed to kill him. Many other dangers lie before them prior to this threat, however. Futuristic life on Venus is shown to be very dangerous.

Burroughs, Edgar Rice. **Escape on Venus.** Ace Bks 1974.

Because of her love for Carson Napier, Duare is sentenced to die. Her rescue by Carson and the dangers they face in seeking to survive the many terrors of Venus make an action-filled tale.

Burroughs, Edgar Rice. **The Lost Continent.** Ace Bks 1973.

This adventure story is set in a period when European countries are but memories of the ancients in Pan America. Circumstances force Jefferson Turck to go beyond Longitude 30 West to visit these forgotten countries. His visit leads to many encounters and a meeting with Victory.

Burroughs, Edgar Rice. **Lost on Venus.** Ace Bks 1973.

On Venus, Carson Napier encounters near-death time and again. His great love for Duare, princess of Kooaad, causes him to attempt her rescue from the bird-like creatures who abduct her. Her confession of love for him compels Carson to fight for survival against great odds.

Burroughs, Edgar Rice. **The Moon Maid.** Ace Bks 1974.

In the year 2025, the spaceship Barsoom leaves Earth for Mars. A treacherous crew member causes a forced landing on the moon. An unknown world is discovered and Julian the fifth becomes involved in war. He is successful in winning the love of the Princess of Layeth, The Moon Maid. Many adventures befall them before they attempt to return to Earth.

Burroughs, Edgar Rice. **The Moon Men.** Ace Bks 1974.

Two separate novels of descendents of one line make up this book. Both novels deal with Julians, the ninth in *The Moon Men* and the twentieth in *The Red*

Hawk. In both tales, a lunar force has control of most of Earth and the remaining natives are nearly overcome. Both novels describe great adventure, and the latter brings the entire exploit full circle.

Burroughs, Edgar Rice. **The Wizard of Venus & Pirate Blood.** Ace Bks 1973.

Two separate stories make up this book. The first provides further adventures of Carson Napier on Venus, as he combats evil forces using magic to enslave people. The second story is earth-bound and deals with modern-day piracy. It includes many adventures and some emotional scenes.

Carlson, Dale. **The Mountain of Truth.** Atheneum 1973.

Ten children have mysteriously disappeared from the international summer camp in futuristic Tibet, and their parents are climbing the Himalayas to look for them. Peter, who returned safely, is expected to guide the expedition. He knows where his brother, Michael, and the other children are hidden, but he must prevent the adults from reaching them and learning their secret.

Carr, Terry, editor. **Worlds Near and Far: Nine Stories of Science Fiction and Fantasy.** Nelson 1974.

New ways of seeing the world, now and in the future, are presented in these nine stories of science fiction, ghosts, and fantasy. A mutant horse must get along without three legs; space explorers find creatures that seem to be supernatural demons; a solution to the population problem comes 350 years in the future; aliens from space visit Earth in the future to find a surprise; and new kinds of ghosts appear in *Hamlet.*

Christopher, John. **Beyond the Burning Lands.** Macmillan 1971.

An England from the past has emerged in a future time after devastating wars and earthquakes. A future prince is kept in hiding and his half-brother rules in his absence. The novel concerns Luke's life in hiding and the terrible events which draw him back to Winchester. Death and murder surround and threaten Luke until he is accepted as high prince.

Christopher, John. **The City of Gold and Lead.** Macmillan 1967.

Within the fearsome city of the Tripods, Will and

Fritz wear false caps and become servants of the Masters in an attempt to discover their secrets. A story of bravery and danger, this novel continues the adventures of John Christopher's earlier novel, *The White Mountains*.

Christopher, John. **The Lotus Caves.** Macmillan 1969.

In a future time, life on the moon is well regulated. Men must live within a self-sufficient Bubble. Their adventure is marred when they become trapped in a series of caves where a plantlike superintelligence begins to take over their brains. Escape is their only chance of salvation, and the novel focuses on this attempt.

Christopher, John. **The Pool of Fire.** Macmillan 1968.

An attack on the Tripods and the cities of the Masters is waged by the Uncapped. Will and his friends help overcome the tyranny of the Tripods to attempt a world of peace. Problems interfere with peace, however, and further work must be done to unify all men.

Christopher, John. **The Prince in Waiting.** Macmillan 1970.

In a future time which resembles medieval history, Luke is transformed from a carefree youth to the prince who will succeed to the throne. His lot becomes unhappy as rage and fear plague the people. His life is spared only by a secret escape to a sanctuary, where he must wait until he can come to power.

Christopher, John. **The Sword of the Spirits.** Macmillan 1972.

On becoming Prince of Winchester, Luke is enmeshed in a deception of the Seers, who plan a scientific renewal. Many plots imperil Luke and bring Winchester and the civilized world to disaster. Luke can only flee for salvation to other lands, where his adventures are many.

Christopher, John. **The White Mountains.** Macmillan 1967.

In a future time which resembles the medieval period of history, youths of fourteen are capped to become docile servants of the Tripods, a machine-like domineering race. Three boys decide to flee this ritual, and the novel covers their flight, their pursuit by the Tripods, and their eventual salvation.

Clarke, Arthur C. **Against the Fall of Night.** Pyramid Pubns 1960.

It is one billion years from now, and mankind has achieved all of the goals we are seeking today. There is peace and leisure; culture is flourishing. Why, then, is Alvin dissatisfied, frightened for mankind? His city, Diaspar, has everything anyone needs. No one has even left the city for millions of years. The records he has studied say that if anyone leaves the city, the "Invaders" will come again. But Alvin knows that as it is, curiosity and ambition have died. He must do something, and so he begins his adventure into the unknown.

Clarke, Arthur C. **Childhood's End.** Ballantine 1974.

The overlords have been sent to Earth from their star NGS S49672, to prepare mankind for a gradual change that will mark the end of homo sapiens. Much of the book deals with the developments that take place on earth, from the time of the overlords' arrival to their eventual departure. Only one human is ever able to enter the evolutionary world of the overlords.

Clarke, Arthur C. **Earthlight.** Ballantine 1955.

Sadler, a secret agent, visits the moon. In these future times the moon is as easy to reach from Earth as a foreign country is from America now. Civilization on the Moon and Mars is developing, but still depends on Earth for resources. Earth, however, puts a very special price on these resources because of her jealousy of the newly colonized planets. This leads to a tense and dangerous situation.

Clark, Arthur C. **Expedition to Earth.** Ballantine 1953.

This book is a collection of eleven science fiction short stories. Some tell of expeditions to Earth from distant worlds, when Earth is no longer recognizable. Some are about space exploration and encounters in space. These stories are complete with advanced worlds, space vehicles, and space weaponry.

Delany, Samuel R. **Babel-17.** Ace Bks 1973.

When the language expert Rydra Wong is asked to decipher the strange language, Babel-17, used by the invaders in the interstellar war, she becomes the target of their attack. Her interstellar ship is sabotaged and all aboard are in danger. This and other perils provide excitement in the search for the meaning of the strange language.

Delany, Samuel R. **The Einstein Intersection.** Ace Bks 1971.

Love and adventure in a far future world, aliens entering human bodies, and travel across a lush planet are components of this novel. The intersection, in time, of the Einsteinian and alien universes precipitates the adventures of Lobey. This novel juggles the basic concepts of time and space to provide an engrossing story.

Del Rey, Lester. **Prisoners of Space.** Westminster 1968.

In this novel, Dave Harmon and Jane Larkin, the first two children to be born on the moon, face all the problems of adapting to a life alien to the earth. Their search of the moon uncovers some strange creatures and some subterranean tunnels.

Elwood, Roger, editor. **And Now Walk Gently through the Fire and Other Science Fiction Stories.** Chilton 1972.

This collection of ten stories mixes biochemistry and religion—technical details and the mystical reverence of the occult. The stories which have not been previously published were gathered by the editor because of their similar themes.

Elwood, Roger, editor. **Children of Infinity: Original Science Fiction Stories for Young Readers.** Watts 1973.

Each of the ten stories in this anthology deals with a young person of the future. Intriguing, frightening, and sad situations surround the characters in each of the stories. Emotionalism runs high.

Elwood, Roger, editor. **Continuum 1.** Putnam 1974.

This is the first of a four-book series of anthologies of which two have been published at this writing. The eight authors represented in *Continuum 1* will carry their science fiction stories forward through the other anthologies.

Elwood, Roger, editor. **Continuum 2.** Putnam 1974.

A sequel to *Continuum 1,* this anthology continues the same eight stories begun in the previous volume. The same approaches are evident and the central themes and characters are carried forward.

Elwood, Roger, editor. **Crisis: Ten Original Stories of Science Fiction.** Nelson 1974.

The characters in these ten science fiction stories all face crises of one kind or another. In "The Boy Who Brought Love," eleven-year-old Serov of the planet Crucis Two proves to a tyrant that love can destroy. A young couple goes to live on another planet, Star World, where Lora Lee dies and returns to life again. Deke runs away to join the other children to learn to be a ruthless hunter in "Mommies and Daddies." Nostalgia is against the law in "The Proust Syndrome," and a scientist is a victim.

Elwood, Roger, editor. **The Learning Maze and Other Science Fiction.** Messner 1974.

This collection contains science fiction stories about life in the future and fantastic things that happen in the present. One story is about a woman who travels through time. Another tells of a flying saucer that lands on the earth. Many of the main characters are young people.

Elwood, Roger, editor. **The Many Worlds of Poul Anderson.** Chilton 1974.

This is a collection of works by and about Poul Anderson. Eight stories by the author are included as well as two analyses written about the author. Together their selections provide a complete portrayal of the author and his broad range of abilities. His works encompass the humorous to the heartbreaking, but all are excellent science fiction fare.

Elwood, Roger, editor. **The Other Side of Tomorrow: Original Science Fiction Stories about Young People of the Future.** Random 1973.

Nine popular science fiction writers tell about the future from the point of view of its young people. The characters are tested to find their correct, computerized place in society. They are fed "Biskies" to control them. In another story, they escape to begin communes on a new planet. They face many real problems too—hunger, mechanization, overpopulation, war.

Elwood, Roger, editor. **Survival from Infinity: Original Science Fiction Stories for Young Readers.** Watts 1974.

The eight selections in this science fiction anthology

are all original, all feature young persons in the central roles, and all are based on the theme of survival. The different kinds of survival create interest and conflict within the stories.

Engdahl, Sylvia Louise. **Beyond the Tomorrow Mountains.** Atheneum 1973.

A continuation of a previous book, *This Star Shall Abide,* this novel continues the story of Noren, who rose from villager to Scholar. Now holding the secret of the Machines which support life on his planet, he is overcome by despair about the future of his planet and people. Finally, involved in a desperate crisis, Noren learns the secret of survival, although another has to explain his discovery to him.

Engdahl, Sylvia Louise. **Enchantress from the Stars.** Atheneum 1970.

The time of this story is undetermined, but different levels of people exist. A girl from a highly advanced race becomes involved in a medieval situation with a woodcutter's son. Combat against misunderstanding and a dragon unites the two, but also marks their separation. The novel deals with the misunderstanding too little information can cause.

Engdahl, Sylvia Louise. **The Far Side of Evil.** Atheneum 1971.

Assigned to the planet Toris, Elana is to be an observer of its Critical Stafe—that time when people know enough about nuclear power to destroy themselves but not enough about self-control to keep from doing it. Another agent fumbles, disaster results, and only Elana can remedy the damage. Many severe trails must be overcome, and the chances of failure and death are great.

Engdahl, Sylvia Louise. **Journey between Worlds.** Atheneum 1970.

In a time when space travel is relatively common, Melinda Ashley has no real desire to go to Mars. Her father urges her to accompany him, however, and her feelings begin to cause problems. Critical of the Mars colonization project, Melinda creates enemies. Her only friend is Alex, and when her father is accidentally killed on Mars, Alex becomes much more to her. This novel explores a new concept of prejudice.

Engdahl, Sylvia Louise. **This Star Shall Abide.** Atheneum 1972.

Rebellion by a villager is the central focus of this
novel. Noren, by his position, is restricted by the
higher level Technicians and the highest level Scholars.
His rebellion against their policies is a heresy and in
discovering the punishment of heretics, Noren finds
that his future can be more exciting and less certain
then he planned. This is the first of two books
dealing with Noren. Christopher Award Children's
Book Category.

Haldeman, Joe, compiler. **Cosmic Laughter: An Anthology of Humorous Science Fiction.** HR&W 1974.

A collection of nine science fiction stories, in which
humor is the unifying thread. There are unusual and
intriguing characters and even more unusual machines.
Despite the humor, the stories revolve around serious
topics.

Harrison, Harry, and Brian W. Aldiss, editors. **Best SF
73.** Putnam 1974.

Nineteen selections from various sources and authors
make up this collection of science fiction works, centering on life in the future.

Heinlein, Robert A. **Between Planets.** Ace Bks 1971.

Rebellion in an interplanetary federation and a non-
citizen are the chief elements in this story of the future.
Disregard of the rights of the individual causes Venus
to rebel and push Don into a decision on his al-
legiance.

Heinlein, Robert A. **Red Planet.** Ace Bks 1971.

Exploration of Mars is the next item in the U. S. space
race. The previously unexplored planet holds many
unusual and surprising adventures for the first explorers of its surface.

Heinlein, Robert A. **Rocket Ship Galileo.** Scribner 1947.

This book preceded the American space program by
a decade but tells in great detail a story very similar
to the actual moon landings. It is a novel made more
exciting by its close similarity to the actual events of
recent history.

Heinlein, Robert A. **The Rolling Stones.** Scribner 1952.

Humor in space is present in this account of the seven

members of the Luna family. They are an intriguing group, and their adventures provide entertainment for the reader. The story combines excitement with humor.

Heinlein, Robert A. **Space Cadet.** Scribner 1948.

In 2075, several young men from the space academy become members of the Solar Patrol. Their adventures lead to a realistic story of what interplanetary communication may mean.

Heinlein, Robert A. **The Star Beast.** Ace Bks 1975.

Smuggled to Earth as a small pet, Lummox gradually outgrows an elephant in size. The problem of Lummox becomes galactic in scope. Lummox, despite its size, is a very appealing and lovable creature.

Heinlein, Robert A. **Time for the Stars.** Ace Bks 1971.

The use of telepathy to transmit messages between Earth and the stars is explored in this story. The exploding population on earth has made it necessary to look for habitable sites among the stars.

Heinlein, Robert A. **The Worlds of Robert A. Heinlein.** Ace Bks 1972.

An introduction and five stories by the author comprise an exciting collection of science fiction by one of its best known writers. From the predictions in the introduction through the adventure in his stories, this author holds the reader's attention.

Herbert, Frank. **Dune.** Ace Bks 1974.

Many different plots are interwoven in this lengthy novel. Dune is a desert-like planet where a treacherous plot is unfolding which could encompass more worlds and lives than expected. It is also the site where a savior could arise to aid people ready for a bloody revolt.

Herbert, Frank. **Under Pressure.** Ballantine 1974.

In the twenty-first century, an oil shortage causes the United States to take oil from underwater deposits in enemy territory. Tugs loading the oil disappear, and an investigation is launched. This novel becomes a spy story set in a war of the future. It deals with many problems growing more real every day.

Herbert, Frank, **The Worlds of Frank Herbert.** Ace Bks 1971.

Nine stories by Frank Herbert are included in this volume. They deal with varied topics, but science fiction and its inhabitants are part of each one. Humor, treachery, and dangerous happenings abound.

Hoover, H. M. **Children of Morrow.** Four Winds 1973.

It's long after the Great Destruction. Tia and Rabbit have always been different from the others in the village. They see visions of a strange place called The Sea and a tall, graceful woman named Ashira. They are in great danger from the Major who rules the village, and when Rabbit accidentally kills a village official trying to protect Tia, they are forced to flee. In their journey through the wilderness, they are guided telepathically by Ashira, and when they finally reach The Sea after many adventures, they learn the secret of the children of Morrow.

Hoyle, Fred, and Geoffrey Hoyle. **Into Deepest Space.** Har-Row 1974.

A lengthy space trip involves Dr. Dick Warboys and his three extraterrestrial friends who encounter the hated Yela. Adventure and intriguing scientific detail fill this tale of space travel. Capture by the Yela spaceship and a return to earth figure in the story. One question lingers, however. Is it really earth?

Jackson, Jacqueline, and William Perlmutter. **The Endless Pavement.** Seabury 1973.

In the time when wheels have replaced legs and concrete covers the earth, Josette lives happily in her Home-a-rolla—until a thought enters her mind and she sees a tree. This entertaining fantasy has appeal for readers of all ages.

Johannesson, Olaf. **The Tale of the Big Computer: A Vision.** Coward 1968.

Not truly science fiction and yet not quite pure science, this tale records a life in the future with all events and details based on the development, use, and consequences of the computer as a force in the world of man.

Knight, Damon, editor. **Orbit 12.** Putnam 1973.

The fourteen stories in this anthology are all original science fiction by both new and already prominent authors. These well-written stories deal with monsters, mysterious lands, and nonhuman beings.

Lanier, Sterling E. **Hiero's Journey.** Chilton 1973.

The hunt for a secret which can save the remains of human civilization is the theme for this fantasy. The hunter is Hiero, who has powers and skills but faces unknown dangers in his search. Romance becomes a part of his search when he discovers a girl. Adventures, terrors, and discoveries crowd this story.

Le Guin, Ursula K. **The Left Hand of Darkness.** Ace Bks 1969.

In this intergalactic world, the planet Gethen has been overlooked. Now an envoy is sent onto its ice-covered surface to establish diplomatic relations. The people of Gethen, also known as Winter, have the capacity to be either male or female. This adds a very interesting aspect on the nature of love. The envoy must experience much in trying to bring the planet into the confederacy.

Leiber, Fritz. **Swords against Death.** Ace Bks 1970.

This series of ten short stories tells of the adventures of Fafhrd and the Gray Mouser. The loss of their first loves leads them into a quest and a series of adventures.

Leiber, Fritz. **Swords against Wizardry.** Ace Bks 1968.

From an encounter with a sorceress and near-death to further quests in the terrifying land of Quarmall, this book relates the adventures of Fafhrd and the Gray Mouser in four short stories.

Leiber, Fritz. **Swords and Deviltry.** Ace Bks 1970.

A series of four short stories which begin an epic of two legendary heroes. Each story leads to the further development of their relationship.

Leiber, Fritz. **The Swords of Lankhmar.** Ace Bks 1968.

This novel completes the saga of the two heroes Fafhrd and the Gray Mouser. Neither is the most honorable of men, but each is very human. The adventure and intrigue of the pair continue in this novel.

Leiber, Fritz. **You're All Alone.** Ace Bks 1972.

This is a collection of three stories by the same

author. The major story deals with a world of imitation people. Each story embodies the best of science fiction.

McCaffrey, Anne. **Dragonquest.** Ballantine 1973.

In this novel, dragons fight against the threat to their land of Pern, bearing dragon-riders who fight with them. The union of dragon and riders creates strength for fighting, but anger between riders weakens dragons as well. These great beasts are usually regarded as the enemy, but here the dragon is heroic.

Mendelsohn, Felix, Jr. **Superbaby.** Nash Pub 1969.

In the year 2009, Alan Corvallis is born after being carefully constructed in the laboratory. Physically he is perfect, but he has no conscience.

Niven, Larry. **Ringworld.** Ballantine 1970.

This lengthy novel carries people into a fantastically conceived, scientifically logical world. But there is a question of their purpose for being there, and even sanity is questioned. The entire world created in this novel is mysterious and intriguing.

Niven, Larry, and John Brunner (with Jack Vance). **Three Trips in Time and Space: Original Novellas of Science Fiction.** Dell 1973.

These three short novels by different authors center on the idea that man can transport himself from place to place on the earth's surface instantly as well as anywhere in time.

Norton, Andre. **Android at Arms.** Ace Bks 1973.

An android, a double for the rightful Emperor of Inyanga, creates a world of unreality which is beleaguered by energies both internally and externally. Andas Kastor is kept in a mind lock, unable to salvage his empire. He must fight in the duplicate world all the evils which drew both worlds near disaster.

Norton, Andre. **The Beast Master.** Ace Bks 1972.

Only Hosteen Storm, a Navajo Indian, survives the destruction of his planet by the Xiks. In his isolation, he trains animals and establishes very strong relations with them, and they become his team. With his team, he joins the settlers of another planet, Arzor, as a scout. There he find the Xiks, outlaws, and an unknown race. A novel filled with action.

Norton, Andre. **Breed to Come.** Ace Bks 1973.

This novel offers the reader a new point of view. The primary race considered is feline, though far different from the cats we know. They have developed into very intelligent beings. The demons are men, and their return to the planet causes much trouble for the cat tribes. Conflict rages until a climax is reached.

Norton, Andre. **Catseye.** Ace Bks 1971.

Life in the city of Tikil bears many similarities to our own. An interplanetary space shop provides a temporary job for Troy Horan, and he discovers an ability to hold communication with some of the animals imported for sale. This leads to his discovery of a plot to upset the peace of the Confederation. Troy flees Tikil to the safety of a dead underground city, then helps to combat the threat and reinstate an equality among the people of the planet.

Norton, Andre. **The Crystal Gryphon.** Atheneum 1972.

An ancient curse, a kingdom, a betrothed bride, and an invasion are the ingredients to this exciting tale of Kerovan and his intended, Joisan. Their marriage arranged in youth, the two communicate, but never meet until a desperate effort to save their people leads them to the outer edges of their world. With many similarities to a medieval tale, this novel adds the mystery of science fiction.

Norton, Andre. **Dark Piper.** Ace Bks 1974.

A small group of survivors is left on the planet Beltane following its destruction in the aftermath of a global war. These few survivors are trapped underground, and their battle to the surface contains terror, despair, and tragedy. Their eventual success leaves them even more vulnerable to the possible hostilities of their planet.

Norton, Andre. **Daybreak—2250 A.D.** Ace Bks 1952.

As a mutant with special abilities, Fors is not accepted by the Puma Clan. To prove himself, he and the great cat, Lura, venture into the Plains where the wreckage of the civilization of the Old Ones lies. Decaying cities, unknown races, lizard beings, and, most terrible, the Beast Thing await him. Arskane also waits. True brotherhood among all humankind becomes the eventual goal of the adventurer.

Norton, Andre. **The Defiant Agents.** Ace Bks 1972.

In future time, both the U.S. and U.S.S.R. send colonists who have regressed to periods of their past to a distant planet. The warrior Apaches and the Mongol hordes share conflicts with each other, the hostile nature of the planet, and an even more dangerous force from beyond the stars. The action on Topaz creates an exciting story.

Norton, Andre. **Exiles of the Stars.** Viking Pr 1971.

The trade ship Lydis agrees to carry Forerunner treasure out of the civil war on Thoth, only to make a forced landing on the planet Sekhmet. There, terrors await the traders and strange beings attempt to take over the bodies of Krip Vorlund and the others. The power of Esper and the cunning of the Thassa, Maelen, heighten the adventure.

Norton, Andre. **Galactic Derelict.** Ace Bks 1959.

During an attempt to transfer an alien spaceship from a past time to the present, an involuntary galactic tour is begun. Travis Fox, an Apache, Ross Murdock, and Dr. Gordon Ashe hurtle through many different times and encounter many unusual beings and events. Strange winged men and the weasel creatures add to the excitement of their journey. Their adventures lead, finally, to a safe return to earth.

Norton, Andre. **High Sorcery.** Ace Bks 1971.

A series of five short stories which delve into the techniques of future existence. Each story centers on a particular character whose abilities, physical or mental, promote the action of the plot. The plots hinge on the fears and the desires of men.

Norton, Andre. **Ice Crown.** Ace Bks 1971.

On the closed planet Clio, Roane and the Princess Ludorica explore for the greatest Forerunner treasure of all—the Ice Crown. As an outsider, Roane is in constant danger of discovery, since her kind is banned. Princess Ludorica is being sought by those who would destroy the monarchy and its royal line. Together, the girls encounter hostile territory and persons in the search.

Norton, Andre. **Judgement on Janus.** Ace Bks 1973.

As a slave on Janus, Naill Renfro is receptive to transformation. He becomes a changeling to Ayyar of Iftean, child of an ancient race. As Iftin, he and other changelings fight to regenerate the ancient race and to combat the settlers who attempt to overtake Janus. Underlying the action is an intriguing concept of transmission.

Norton, Andre. **Key Out of Time.** Ace Bks 1973.

The sea planet Hawaika is without civilization. But two Time Agents explore its past and are plunged into the conflict which must have been the struggle that destroyed all civilization on the planet. Murdock and Ashe help battle the alien forces to a conclusion both know.

Norton, Andre. **The Last Planet.** Ace Bks 1974.

Stellar Patrol ship Starfire crashes while mapping galactic borders and plunges its crew, both humans and nonhumans, into strange adventures on an uncharted planet. The planet is fertile and can sustain life, but a serious problem of discipline threatens the crew. A deserted city yields other castaways, and decisions have to be made about the future course of their lives.

Norton, Andre. **Lord of Thunder.** Ace Bks 1971.

The natives of Arzor leave their homes across the planet to regather in the unfamiliar and uncharted Peaks. Hosteen Storm is the one dispatched to uncover the reason for this migration. His discovery of a fabulous underground world and a plot by the natives against the off-worlders set up the action of the novel.

Norton, Andre. **Moon of Three Rings.** Viking Pr 1966.

Transformed from his human body into the form of an animal, Krip Vorlund retains his soul, but must exist as an animal. The sorceress Maelen has transformed him as a protection against those who wish Krip harm. Together they share adventure and encounter danger until Maelen's powers are almost spent. Krip Vorlund will live again, but under another form, until he can be reinstated in his own body.

Norton, Andre. **Night of Masks.** Ace Bks 1973.

Not only homeless from the war, but disfigured as well, Nik Kolherne agrees to participate in a kidnapping in exchange for facial surgery. A unique sort of crime takes place and then a reversal occurs when the criminal must become the savior of the person kidnapped. Unusual terrors build throughout the story to create a hero from a criminal.

Norton, Andre. **Operation Time Search.** HarBraceJ 1967.

Have you ever wondered whether Atlantis could have existed? The scientists in this book invent a time machine for bringing back films of the past, but accidentally Ray Osborne, newspaper photographer, walks into the path of the time beam. He is knocked right into the middle of a war between the Atlanteans and the Murians.

Norton, Andre. **Ordeal in Otherwhere.** Ace Bks 1973.

To escape imprisonment on the planet Demeter, Charis Nordholm becomes a cloth buyer on the planet of Warlock. The mysterious dream power of the Wyverns of Warlock is opened to her. The curl-cat Tsstu becomes her ally as does Shann Lantee, a member of a patrol party. Trying to establish a treaty with the Wyvern witches causes a power struggle.

Norton, Andre. **Plague Ship.** Ace Bks 1972.

Treachery has planted a plague on board the Solar Queen, an intergalactic trade ship. Not only can she not return to her home base, Terra, she is ordered to be destroyed on sight for fear of creating an interplanetary epidemic. Her crew must attempt to save themselves without jeopardizing the rest of the world. Tense and exciting moments fill the story.

Norton, Andre. **Postmarked the Stars.** Ace Bks 1971.

Treachery aboard a freetrader marks the first of a series of nightmare plots in this novel. Dane Thorson is kidnapped and another substituted for him to begin the mystery surrounding the strange cargo the Solar Queen carries. An intergalactic plot is uncovered and Thorson and his crew become the center of its activity.

Norton, Andre. **Quest Crosstime.** Ace Bks 1972.

Blake Walker is a very important link in the salvation of the civilization of the planet Vroom. Not of that planet, and with none of the mind power of its citizens, he is, nevertheless, destined to save it. Time travel, real versus imaginary enemies, hallucinations, and many other exciting events fill the novel.

Norton, Andre. **Sargasso of Space.** Ace Bks 1971.

Buying a newly discovered planet at a cosmic auction launches Dane Thorson and the crew of the Solar Queen into strange adventure. The planet Limbo is a graveyard of wrecked space ships with no signs of life. The discovery of the danger the planet holds, a criminal race, and a dangerous Forerunner installation set the novel up for adventure.

Norton, Andre. **Sea Seige.** Ace Bks 1971.

Isolated on a tiny island after an atomic attack has silenced the rest of the world, Griff Gunston and others must face a new terror. Vivid descriptions of undersea life and action enhance this story of a new sort of intelligence operating from the ocean floor. The story becomes more interesting because its time is the not-too-distant future.

Norton, Andre. **Secret of the Lost Race.** Ace Bks 1972.

Suddenly singled out among the many citizens of the galaxy, Joktar is afraid and flees to the Constellation of Fenris. There, among the refugees of the universe, he waits for whatever is to happen. His past, obscured to him by a mental block, holds the key to the search. Other refugees on Fenris rise to his aid when forces descend to take him. An interesting story of loneliness and misunderstanding among men.

Norton, Andre. **Shadow Hawk.** Ace Bks 1972.

Based on the struggles of the Egyptians to drive out their Hyksos conquerors, the novel takes place some two thousand years before the birth of Christ. The Shadow Hawk is the figure who spurs the action on and aids the two young princes who are the heroes of the battle.

Norton, Andre. **The Sioux Spacemen.** Ace Bks 1974.

The blood of the Sioux Indians flows in the veins of Kade Whitehawk, who must use his heritage to help others gain their freedom. As a rebel to many ideas of the Space Service, Kade overthrows their beliefs when he finds the Ikkinni on the planet Klor. Their defiance of the overmen who tyrannize and enslave them makes him realize that he must help.

Norton, Andre. **Sorceress of the Witch World.** Ace Bks 1972.

Kaththena, the witch, seeks to confirm her destiny. Her powers are weak, but their strength is increasing.

She is separated from the brothers with whom she has shared much. Held captive by stronger powers, she becomes seeress of a strange race as she tries to find freedom. Many adventures, high and low magic, and wizardry enliven this novel.

Norton, Andre. **Star Born.** Ace Bks 1971.

Interstellar travel has not touched the planet Astra in many years. The unexpected arrival of Raf Kurbi's spaceship awakens memories for the remaining members of an earth colony and many dangers from the inhuman fiends who are terrorizing them. Mind thought, mermen, and mutant life fill this book with adventure. Dalgard and Raf share many experiences before the spaceship is freed to leave Astra.

Norton, Andre. **Star Gate.** Ace Bks 1974.

The Star Lords are a searching group going from Gorth to Gorth seeking a place to settle. When Kincar s'Rud follows them he finds that Gorths differ greatly. People who look like friends are actually enemies, and other personalities of himself will fight for control of his body. The Star Lords will offer aid where they can throughout alternate universes and Kincar will truly become one of them.

Norton, Andre. **Star Guard.** Ace Bks 1973.

In a future time, Earthmen are enslaved to serve as mercenaries of Central Control. Kana Karr is one of these, but on a routine visit to another planet he becomes involved in a plot of the Venturi to return humankind to the role of power. The action of the novel concerns this intergalactic struggle. Kana must not only battle the beings of Central Control, but must change the thinking of Earthmen who have been enslaved for decades.

Norton, Andre. **Star Hunter and Voodoo Planet.** Ace Bks 1968.

Two short novels of adventure make up this volume. Both deal with the unique powers of the mind. One concerns a transfer of brain patterns giving an individual unknown powers, and the other develops the conflict between the rational and the hypnotic.

Norton, Andre. **Storm over Warlock.** Ace Bks 1973.

Shann Lantee is left alone and weaponless on the planet Warlock. The Throg force which destroyed the other members of the Terran survey team become his dangerous enemies. Finally receiving assistance from the witches of Wyvern and a new survey team, Lantee oversees the control of the Throg race to the benefit of the other races.

Norton, Andre. **Three Against the Witch World.** Ace Bks 1972.

In an effort to regain some of their decreasing powers, the witches of Estcarp seize the young Kaththea, who has special powers. Her two brothers plan for her rescue, but a place of safety must be found for their defense. Every power of the witches will be turned against them as outcasts. Together, the three share one power over the witches and it can be their salvation.

Norton, Andre. **The Time Traders.** Ace Bks 1974.

In the last quarter of the twentieth century, Ross Murdock is given the choice of a sentence with the Rehabilitation Service or a volunteer assignment with a government project. Volunteering, Ross discovers that the life he has known does little to prepare him for research in several levels of time. Travel among different eras of history and the many events which befall him make Ross realize that life has a purpose for him after all.

Norton, Andre. **Uncharted Stars.** Ace Bks 1972.

A search for the source of a gem from outer space leads Murdoc Jern and his mutant cat, Eet, through space and time. Finding the star map will provide the route to determining the secret of the gem and the origin of Eet. Eet's destiny is also discovered and provides a surprising finish to the story.

Norton, Andre. **Victory on Janus.** Ace Bks 1973.

A battle for survival against the powerful force of evil is the central struggle in the story. The Iftins of Janus are being slaughtered, and only the death of THAT, which directs this slaughter, can save them. A fast-paced plot of survival against great odds, with assistance beyond human comprehension.

Norton, Andre. **Web of the Witch World.** Ace Bks 1972.

Safety can never come to Simon Tregarth and his wife, Jaelithe, until those beings from Kolder are conquered. To be conquered, though, Tregarth must allow great danger to befall himself and Jaelithe. With the powers he has and those of this witch-wife, Tregarth fights against the forces of Kolder.

Norton, Andre. **Witch World.** Ace Bks 1974.

As a hunted man, Simon Tregarth must give himself up to the destiny of the Siefe Perilous. It will judge him and deliver him up to a world where his mind can be at ease. His destiny is to be the witch world, and his human background does little to prepare him for the power of the witches of Estcarp.

Norton, Andre. **The X Factor.** Ace Bks 1972.

Not feeling a part of his home, Diskan Fentress steals a spaceship and lands on the unexplored planet Mimir. There he meets the creatures called Brothers-In-Fur with whom he feels a strong relationship. His life has new meaning and his visit to his former home convinces him that the Brothers-In-Fur have much to offer.

Norton, Andre. **Year of the Unicorn.** Ace Bks 1974.

The mystery of the Were-Riders is untangled by Gillan, one of the thirteen brides paid as a settlement for the conquest of the Hounds of Alizon. Gilland is able to see beyond the illusion of the Were-Riders to the mysteries and dangers of their past. Her adventures coupled with those of Herrel, a half-Were, create an engrossing story.

Norton, Andre. **The Zero Stone.** Ace Bks 1969.

Murdoc Jern searches for the origin of the strange stone left to him by his foster father. Accompanied by Eet, a feline mutant with extrasensory perception powers, Murdoc becomes the target of various forces because he possesses the stone. He is led to the planet of the apelike sniffers where he faces further threats from the Patrol and the Thieves' Guild.

Norton, Andre, and Ernestine Donaldy, editors. **Gates to Tomorrow: An Introduction to Science Fiction.** Atheneum 1973.

One interesting aspect of this collection of stories is that they were tested in tenth grade classes and approved by the students before being included in the book. The twelve stories are by different authors and involve different ideas, but all share the fascination of science fiction.

Nourse, Alan E. **PSI High and Others.** McKay 1967.
Three related stories of the Galactic Watchers and
their concern with the planet Earth. The stories concern man's ability to handle his increased life-span,
to deal with extrasensory powers, and to communicate
with an alien intelligent race.

Page, Thomas. **The Hephaestus Plague.** Bantam 1973.
In this science fiction tale, Parmiter, believing that a
previously unknown breed of beetle-like insects is
highly intelligent, finds a way to breed them while
scientists try to destroy the insects before they destroy
the earth.

Panshin, Alexei. **Rite of Passage.** Ace Bks 1968.
Years after the destruction of Earth, young Mia
Havers is approaching the age of testing. Life exists
only in the huge starships and at age fourteen, children
must prove their worth. They are placed in the wilds
of a colony world to either live or die by their own
devices and thus prove themselves. This is the time
Mia is approaching.

Pesek, Ludek. **The Earth Is Near.** Bradbury Pr 1970.
This novel recounts the story of the first expedition to
Mars. Told by one of the survivors of Project Alpha,
it recounts the excitement, the terror, and the mental
and physical challenges of such an expedition. Translated from the German, this story retains all the drama
of the original.

Pohl, Carol, and Frederik Pohl, editors. **Science Fiction:
The Great Years.** Ace Bks 1973.
Seven stories by different authors make up this science
fiction anthology. Some reflect futuristic images of
current or past actions and others focus on humor or
horror.

Pohl, Frederik, editor. **Nightmare Age.** Ballantine 1970.
Thirteen stories: thirteen tomorrows we may be building today, if technology continues unchecked and af-
fluence progresses unabated. The authors speculate on
the future and show how we are building a fragmented
society, a long, hot lifetime of urban conflict. They
predict the eco-catastrophes awaiting us under the
curse of plenty, disasters so unexpected and bizarre
as to make mere war and famine look ordinary and
commonplace.

Rienow, Leona T., and Robert Rienow. **The Year of the Last Eagle.** Ballantine 1970.

It is the year 1989—the Bicentennial of the Establishment of the American Republic. There is only one thing missing—our National Emblem. This is a realistic story, with hair-raising probabilities about the world of the future.

Silverberg, Robert. **Beyond Control.** Dell 1972.

In these seven science fiction stories, the editor has gathered serious and light plots dealing with some of the dangers of advanced scientific experimentation. The stories are primarily meant to entertain and amuse, but they also suggest dangers in scientific discovery.

Silverberg, Robert, editor. **Infinite Jests: The Lighter Side of Science Fiction.** Chilton 1974.

Eleven stories by as many authors provide the antidote to the sometimes too-serious theme of science fiction. The humor may be grim, but it is present in each of these stories. The tales range from the future to the past and prove that in science fiction, as in our world, laughter ranges near to tears.

Silverberg, Ribert. **Mind to Mind: Nine Stories of Science Fiction.** Dell 1971.

The nine stories in this collection are centered around a theme of mental telepathy and other unusual mental powers. In various ways, each author has utilized his science fiction skill to deal with a very real problem, that of communication. In these cases, it is mind-to-mind communication.

Silverberg, Robert, editor. **The Science Fiction Bestiary.** Dell 1971.

A mozart bird, a six-legged hurkle, blue giraffes, gnurrs, and hokes all inhabit these nine science fiction stories. Each author has used his imagination to create a spectacularly unusual creature fit to live in the science fiction world of each story. All types of stories are included, but each was chosen for its creatures.

Sladek, John, **The Müller-Fokker Effect.** S&S 1973.

In this humorous novel Bob Shairp, a technical writer and dreamer, becomes the guinea pig for an army experiment. His personality is transferred to computer tapes. Shortly after this process, however, a computer accident wipes out his body, and only his computer tapes remain! Must he remain on tape forever, or can he be "reconstituted"?

Smith, Cordelia Titcomb. **Great Science Fiction Stories.** Dell 1964.

Eleven stories of science fiction from early to modern authors make up this collection. From Jules Verne to Robert Heinlein, these stories contain satire, humor, and mystery, but all involve science in its many forms.

Sturgeon, Theodore. **More Than Human.** Ballantine 1971.

Winner of the International Fantasy Award, this story deals with the world's first anti-gravity device and its effect upon certain members of society: Lone the Idiot, who builds it; Gerry, who tries to steal it; Janie, the Twins, and Baby who are caught in the middle.

Vance, Jack. **The Dragon Masters.** Ace Bks 1973.

Joaz Banbeck prepares his war dragons for combat against the Basics. The effects of genetic experimentation on both Basics and man has left each side with fierce competitors in this war. Its outcome could determine the future of the race of man on the planet.

Van Vogt, A. E. **The Weapon Shops of Isher.** Ace Bks 1973.

In current time, on a parallel planet, strange weapon shops appear and disappear to sell a variety of guns. Police and the army of Isher cannot gain entry to the shops. The story chronicles the lives of several characters who are associated with the weapon shops in opposition to the totalitarian rule of Isher. An interesting approach to explaining underground activities on any planet is developed here.

Verne, Jules. **Tigers and Traitors.** Assoc Bk 1959.

The vision of Jules Verne has created a steam elephant pulling luxurious houses on wheels through the deep Indian jungles. This, with a tiger hunt, a white goddess, and rampaging elephants, creates an exciting novel written years before such technical wonders were developed.

Wilhelm, Kate, editor. **Nebula Award Stories, No. 9.** Har-Row 1974.

How do his surroundings—a mental ward of the future—look to a boy who's had the two halves of his brain separated? Why do human beings fear and revere snakes? What happens when a robot and its creator share a psychosis? These are just a few of the questions Nebula Award winners ask and answer.

Zelazny, Roger. **The Dream Master.** Ace Bks 1973.

Life in the next century may hold unexpected dangers such as control by the dream master. He has perfected a technique for entering men's minds to experience their thoughts and manipulate their lives. Sleep may offer the chance for him to enter any mind. This novel presents a rather frightening look at what may await mankind.

Zelazny, Roger. **This Immortal.** Ace Bks 1973.

A partially destroyed Earth faces complete destruction from the star Vega. A mysterious hero, Conrad Nimikos, provides a focus for conflict. His past unfolds to play a major part in determining Earth's salvation.

On traveling in space

Ballou, Arthur W. **Marooned in Orbit.** Little 1968.

Astronaut Ike Sanborn, major in the U.S. Air Force, is given the task of rescuing two men marooned in a tiny spacecraft orbiting the moon.

Blish, James. **Star Trek 11.** Bantam 1975.

Six stories follow the starship Enterprise and its crew, led by the self-assured and adventurous Captain Kirk and his friend Mr. Spock, who is only part earthling and whose special powers rescue Kirk from numerous dangers. Along the way, the starship encounters men of other planets, people from other times, in incidents that are sometimes suspenseful, sometimes humorous, but always full of surprises.

Blish, James. **Welcome to Mars.** Putnam 1968.

Seventeen-year-old Dolph Haertel is disappointed when the space program fails to put men on Mars. Dolph constructs his own spaceship, rockets to and crashes on Mars, and learns to adapt to an alien civilization.

Boulle, Pierre. **Planet of the Apes.** Vanguard 1963.

Placed well into the future, this story is concerned with the unusual experiences of Ulysse Merou, who is stranded on the planet Soror. Soror, a planet much like our own, is controlled by a population of intelligent but cruel apes. The human inhabitants of Soror do not speak or think and are hunted as wild game by the apes. Ulysse is captured for scientific experimentation and fights for his freedom.

Burroughs, Edgar Rice. **Beyond the Farthest Star.** Ace Bks 1973.

Transported from death on earth, the man Tangor lives on the planet Poloda. In that futuristic world much terror is caused by the evil Kapars. Adventure in a world beyond fills this novel.

Burroughs, Edgar Rice. **The Moon Maid.** Ace Bks 1974.

In the year 2025, a spaceship Barsoom leaves Earth for Mars. A treacherous crew member causes a forced landing on the moon. An unknown world is discovered and Julian the Fifth becomes involved in war. He is successful in winning the love of the Princess of Layeth, the Moon Maid. Many adventures befall them before they attempt to return to Earth.

Burroughs, Edgar Rice. **The Moon Men.** Ace Bks 1974.

Two separate novels of descendents of one line make up this book. Both novels deal with Julians, the Ninth in *The Moon Men* and the Twentieth in *The Red Hawk.* In both tales, a lunar force has control of most of Earth and the remaining natives are nearly overcome. Both novels describe great adventure, and the latter brings the entire exploit full circle.

Clarke, Arthur C. **Earthlight.** Ballantine 1955.

Sadler, a secret agent, visits the moon. In these future times the moon is as easy to reach from earth as a foreign country is from America now. Civilization on the moon and Mars is developing, but still depends on Earth for resources. Earth, however, puts a very special price on these resources because of her jealousy of the newly colonized planets. This leads to a tense and dangerous situation.

Clarke, Arthur C. **Expedition to Earth.** Ballantine 1953.

This book is a collection of eleven science fiction short stories. Some tell of expeditions to Earth from distant worlds, when Earth is no longer recognizable. Some are about space exploration and encounters in space. These stories are complete with advanced worlds, space vehicles, and space weaponry.

Clarke, Arthur C. **Rendezvous with Rama.** HarBraceJ 1973.

The new celestial body that appears in the outer reaches of the solar system in 2130, believed at first to be an asteroid and named Rama, soon proves to be a vast cylindrical spacecraft over thirty miles long. When Commander Bill Norton and his crew land on Rama and make their way into its hollow interior, they find a self-contained world. It seems a dead world at first, though not without its perils, and these perils intensify when Rama proves to be, in its own way, very much alive. Science Fiction Writers of America Nebula Award.

Delany, Samuel R. **Babel-17.** Ace Bks 1973.

When the language expert Rydra Wong is asked to decipher the strange language, Babel-17, used by the invaders in the interstellar war, she becomes the target of their attack. Her interstellar ship is sabotaged and all aboard are in danger. This and other perils provide excitement in the search for the meaning of the strange language.

Engdahl, Sylvia Louise. **Enchantress from the Stars.** Atheneum 1970.

The time of this story is undetermined, but different levels of people exist. A girl from a highly advanced race becomes involved in a medieval situation with a woodcutter's son. Combat against misunderstanding and a dragon unites the two, but also marks their separation. The novel deals with the misunderstanding too little information can cause.

Fisk, Nicholas. **Trillions.** Pantheon 1971.

The Trillions come from outer space—by the trillions. They look like tiny jewels. Mina uses them to decorate herself, but Scott and Ben and their Mentor, Icarus, want to communicate with them and find out why the Trillions have invaded the earth.

Foster, Alan Dean. **Star Trek—Log One.** Ballantine 1974.

Captain Kirk and his famous crew explore the cold, hostile frontier of outer space: Spock goes back in time to save the life of his childhood self; the Enterprise is invaded by an intelligent creature of pure energy that needs a "body"; Kirk and his crew save a planet from being "eaten" by a gigantic living cloud

in this, the first of a series of Star Trek books, based
on the television series.

Lightner, A. M. **Gods or Demons?** Four Winds 1973.

When the time machine that Eli has invented is
accidentally activated, he, his brother Tom, and their
friend Sadie find themselves in a strange, barren landscape—the earth tens of thousands of years ago. The
time machine is damaged, and while Eli tries to fix
it, Tom and Sadie set out in search of food and water
without weapons to defend themselves in this hostile,
primitive world. They soon discover that there are
"people," but not just one race of primitive men.
There are three, including a group of highly developed
alien space travelers who are conducting experiments
on the earth men.

Norton, Andre. **Dark Piper.** Ace Bks 1974.

A small group of survivors is left on the planet Beltane
following its destruction in the aftermath of a global
war. These few survivors are trapped underground,
and their battle to the surface contains terror, despair,
and tragedy. Their eventual success leaves them even
more vulnerable to the possible hostilities of their
planet.

Norton, Andre. **Dread Companion.** Ace Bks 1972.

This book tells of the adventure of Kilda c' Rhyn in the
space-time year 2405. Kilda learns that one of the
two children she has been hired to care for is under
the power of a being from another world, far different
from her own. Kilda and the children are eventually
trapped in this bizarre other world of grotesque and
deadly creatures and must muster all of their strength
and wit to survive.

Norton, Andre. **Galactic Derelict.** Ace Bks 1959.

During an attempt to transfer an alien spaceship from
a past time to the present, an involuntary galactic tour
is begun. Travis Fox, an Apache, Ross Murock, and
Dr. Gordon Ashe hurtle through many different times
and encounter many unusual beings and events.
Strange winged men and the weasel creatures add to
the excitement of their journey. Their adventures lead,
finally, to a safe return to earth.

Norton, Andre. **The Last Planet.** Ace Bks 1974.

Stellar Patrol ship Starfire crashes while mapping

galactic borders and plunges its crew, both humans and nonhumans, into strange adventures on an uncharted planet. The planet is fertile and can sustain life, but a serious problem of discipline threatens the crew. A deserted city yields other castaways, and decisions have to be made about the future course of their lives.

Norton, Andre. **Quest Crosstime.** Ace Bks 1972.

Blake Walker is a very important link in the salvation of the civilization of the planet Vroom. Not of that planet, and with none of the mind power of its citizens, he is, nevertheless, destined to save it. Time travel, real versus imaginary enemies, hallucinations, and many other exciting events fill the novel.

Norton, Andre. **Star Born.** Ace Bks 1971.

Interstellar travel has not touched the planet Astra in many years. The unexpected arrival of Raf Kurbi's spaceship awakens memories for the remaining members of an earth colony and many dangers from the inhuman fiends who are terrorizing them. Mind thought, mermen, and mutant life fill this book with adventure. Dalgard and Raf share many experiences before the spaceship is freed to leave Astra.

Panshin, Alexei. **Rite of Passage.** Ace Bks 1968.

Years after the destruction of Earth, young Mia Havers is approaching the age of testing. Life exists only in the huge starships and at age fourteen, children must prove their worth. They are placed in the wilds of a colony world to either live or die by their own devices and thus prove themselves. This is the time Mia is approaching.

OF ALL TIME, OF NO TIME

On fantasy

Adams, Richard. **Watership Down.** Macmillan 1972.

It is the best of all rabbit worlds until Fiver has a vision of the destruction of their home. The runt of the litter, Fiver has no future in the rabbit warren, which is governed by the Owsla. Fiver's brother Hazel has always protected him. They have to talk to the Chief Rabbit about "the vision," but are sure he won't listen to them. So begins the fantastic saga of a maverick band of wild rabbits searching for a better way of life—a new, more humane, home. Carnegie Medal.

Alexander, Lloyd. **The Foundling and Other Tales of Prydain.** HR&W 1973.

The enchanted land of Prydain is the subject of all six stories in this book. Strong-willed Princess Angharad, Menwy the harper who defies the Death-Lord, bad-tempered Doli of the Fair Folk, and Kadwyr, the rascal crow, all play their parts. Each chapter tells about a person who has been wronged in some way and each offers ideas about human behavior.

Behn, Harry. **The Faraway Lurs.** Avon 1963.

Visiting the Danish countryside where his mother had grown up, the author of this novel learned of the discovery, years before, of an ancient grave. Inside was the still-preserved body of a young girl who had lived three thousand years ago. This is the story of the life that girl might have lived in that older world, a story of two enemy peoples, the Sun People and the Forest People, and of the man that the girl Heather loves, but is forbidden to love.

Bradbury, Ray. **The Illustrated Man.** Bantam 1952.

While walking through the Wisconsin countryside, the narrator meets a mysterious and troubled man whose body is covered with elaborate tattoos, except for one blank spot on his shoulder. The pictures on his body tell different stories, which make up the book, but the final frightening story to appear before the narrator's eyes turns out to predict his own future.

Burroughs, Edgar Rice. **At the Earth's Core.** Ace Bks 1972.

A machine which bores into the earth's crust carries Davis Innes five hundred miles down to the subterranean world of Pellucidar. It is a world of inverted evolution, where a gorilla-like race enslaves a near-human race. A beautiful slave girl becomes the concern of Innes, and together they help reverse the situation. They plan to return to the earth's surface together.

Burroughs, Edgar Rice. **The Land That Time Forgot.** Ace Bks 1973.

Having had his ship sunk by a German U-boat and finally comandeering that very U-boat, Bowen Tyler and the girl he rescued sail into the strange land of

Caprona. Treachery within his crew, attacks by primitive people, and the capture of the beautiful Lys plague the small party. Tyler leaves the group to seek Lys and encounters the terrible hatchet-men. All hope of rescue seems futile.

Burroughs, Edgar Rice. **Out of Time's Abyss.** Ace Bks 1973.

Stranded on the mysterious Caspak, Bradley and his small band of men go in search of other men. They encounter the terrible, flying Weiroos, who take Bradley captive. He escapes from their skull city with a beautiful girl. Their adventures in returning to her land make up the rest of the story.

Burroughs, Edgar Rice. **Pellucidar.** Ace Bks 1972.

David, Emperor of Pellucidar, uses the great burrowing machine to again penetrate the earth's crust and return to the land of unending sun. He seeks the beautiful Dian and his former companion Perry, and to reestablish the federation begun on his first visit. Again the Mahars are his opponents as he tries to establish a civilization using earth's twentieth-century skills.

Burroughs, Edgar Rice. **The People That Time Forgot.** Ace Bks 1973.

Tom Billings enters the unkown Caprona to seek Bowen Tyler and Lys LaRue. Into the impenetrable territory called Caspak, he flies a small hydroplane, which is attacked and downed by a prehistoric form of pterodactyl. His discovery by the beautiful Ajor and their subsequent adventures in seeking the lost Americans comprise the remainder of the novel.

Byars, Betsy. **The Winged Colt of Casa Mia.** Viking Pr 1973.

Charles comes, serious and bookish, from boarding schools to visit his Uncle Coot, a former movie stunt man, in Texas. They have trouble understanding one another until a strange colt is born. The colt has wings! This strange colt not only takes them on an adventure but brings the boy and his uncle closer together.

Cameron, Eleanor. **The Court of the Stone Children.** Dutton 1973.

Nina has recently moved from Nevada to an apartment in San Francisco, and she is lonely in the large city. Her desire to be a museum curator takes her to a large French museum. There she meets a strange, beautiful girl, Dominique, whom no one else can see, and finds that the stone children come to life for her. The museum was once a family home in France during Napoleon's rule, and Nina has a part to play in solving a murder from the past. Her adventures also include a famous painting and setting right a new manuscript about these stone children. National Book Award.

Carr, Terry, editor. **Into the Unknown: Eleven Tales of Imagination.** Nelson 1973.

These fantasy-reality stories are meant to make you feel uneasy, puzzle you, and make you laugh. Outstanding writers such as Ray Bradbury, Robert Silverberg, and Jorge Borges tell of a strange child who refuses to grow older, a man who gets more than he bargains for in a used car, and the way "chance" came into the world. What if you had a chance to relive your life, or find that you suddenly have disappeared, or discover your dog can talk, or find a drowned giant washed up on the beach? All these unrealities are found in the stories.

Carr, Terry, editor. **Worlds Near and Far: Nine Stories of Science Fiction and Fantasy.** Nelson 1974.

New ways of seeing the world, now and in the future, are presented in these nine stories of science fiction, ghosts, and fantasy. A mutant horse must get along without three legs; space explorers find creatures that seem to be supernatural demons; a solution to the population problem comes 350 years in the future; aliens from space visit Earth in the future to find a surprise; and new kinds of ghosts appear in *Hamlet*.

Cooper, Susan. **The Dark Is Rising.** Antheneum 1974.

Will Stanton has an unusual eleventh birthday. First, the animals on the farm behave strangely when he walks by; then a neighbor gives him an unusual iron sign. Will discovers there are two forces in the world: the Light and the Dark. He is the last of the Old Ones, immortals who keep the world from the forces of the Dark, the evil. This job takes Will and the Old Ones through many adventures which include the collection of the six signs, the kidnapping of Will's sister, and a furious snowstorm. Boston Globe-Horn Book Award.

Crayder, Dorothy. **The Pluperfect of Love.** Atheneum 1971.

Zena, a girl of the 1920s, different in every way from her family in the past, is trying to find a true love. One day, after dreaming of finding her love at the famous New York Plaza Hotel, she leaves Central Park and meets Jabez, a matchmaker. Jabez, with failure in his past, wants to prove through Zena his best matchmaking skills. Zena goes through many experiences before she meets a strange, "unknightable" young man, and reality.

Del Rey, Lester. **Tunnel through Time.** Westminster 1966.

After Doc Tom fails to return from a scientific expedition to study life in the past, his son Pete and a friend Bob enter the time machine in search of him.

Dickson, Gordon R., and Ben Bova. **Gremlins Go Home.** St Martin 1974.

A boy and his dog become involved in intrigue with gremlins looking for a means of returning to their home planet. Rolf Gunnarson helps the gremlins plan to stow away on a Mars-bound rocket. This fantasy-adventure helps many individuals become better aware of themselves and their situations. It has humor and a serious concern for life.

Elwood, Roger, editor. **Crisis: Ten Original Stories of Science Fiction.** Nelson 1974.

The characters in these ten science fiction stories all face crises of one kind or another. In "The Boy Who Brought Love," eleven-year-old Serov of the planet Crucis Two proves to a tyrant that love can destroy. A young couple goes to live on another planet, Star World, where Lora Lee dies and returns to life again. Deke runs away to join the other children to learn to be a ruthless hunter in "Mommies and Daddies." Nostalgia is against the law in "The Proust Syndrome," and a scientist is a victim.

Farmer, Penelope. **A Castle of Bone.** Atheneum 1973.

Four children, Hugh, Anna, Penn and Jean, get a secondhand cupboard, and strange things begin to happen. When anything is put into the cupboard, it turns into its original state. When a pigskin wallet is put inside, a pig comes out! Hugh has the cupboard in his room, and he has nightly dreams. The adventure truly begins when young Penn falls into the cupboard by accident and turns into a baby. Then the children have the task of entering the cupboard to find a way to return Penn to his normal state. They learn things about themselves and find the castle of bone.

Fisk, Nicholas. **Grinny: A Novel of Science Fiction.** Nelson 1973.

Who was Great-Aunt Emma? This story, in the form of a diary kept by Tim, tells of her unexpected coming and her frightful ending. Beth and Tim cannot convince their parents about this old lady, so along with their friend Mac, they have to prove the truth by themselves. Maybe it is her strange grin that gives them their first clue.

George, John, and Jean C. George. **Vison, the Mink.** Dutton 1949.

Vison is a sly mink who rules the area along the Muddy Branch in Maryland. With the help of a friend, Sam, Vison escapes from the hunters' traps. As he grows older and slower, he sees a threat to his "kingdom," a younger mink, so Vison challenges the younger animal. With beautiful drawings the book describes dramatically the life of a mink.

Haining, Peter, editor. **The Monster Makers: Creators and Creations of Fantasy and Horror.** Taplinger 1974.

Eighteen short stories all center around monster-makers and their creations. Such contributors as Edgar Allan Poe, H. G. Wells, Ray Bradbury, Isaac Asimov, and Ambrose Bierce write about such matters as robots roaming about, dead bodies receiving life again, puppets coming to life, demons, golems, and monsters of all varieties.

Harris, Rosemary. **The Moon in the Cloud.** Macmillan 1969.

This is the story of Reuben, a poor musician who travels to Egypt to get a royal cat and two lions for the ark, so that Ham will save him and his wife from the flood.

Heinlein, Robert A. **Have Space Suit—Will Travel.** Ace Bks 1971.

With his own spacesuit, Kip Russell is able to realize his dream of going to the moon. He also gets to see Pluto, a planet of Vega, and the Lesser Magellanic

Cloud. Mother Thing is his guide through these adventures. The story has humor as well as excitement.

Hieatt, Constance. **The Minstrel Knight.** T Y Crowell 1974.

Sir Orfeo, a traveling knight, comes to King Arthur's Camelot and charms everyone with his ability to sing on the harp. He sings of meeting his own wife, Lady Etain, in an enchanted forest. When the news arrives that his wife is imprisoned, he begins his long quest for her. His adventures take him through the Magic Woods, the Court of the Dead, and many other places. The legend is similar to that of the Greek Orpheus, who must search the underworld for his beautiful Eurydice.

Hoban, Russell. **The Sea-Thing Child.** Har-Row 1972.

The main character in this fantasy, the Sea-Thing Child, is born in the sea and washed up on the shore on a clear day. He is only scale and feathers. He remains frightened until he meets fiddler-crab who has no bow to play his fiddle. "The child" soon learns to build stone igloos and befriends an albatross and and eel. A sensitive and gentle story.

Key, Alexander. **Escape to Witch Mountain.** S&S 1973.

Tony and Tia have lost their memory, but are aware that they possess some supernatural powers. Soon, however, they find themselves chased by men who want to use their powers for evil purposes. With the help of Father O'Day, they escape their enemies and return to their real home.

Lawrence, Louise. **The Power of Stars: A Story of Suspense.** Har-Row 1972.

A frightening novel of a young girl who is controlled by other powers. The one person who realizes the danger that Jane carries cannot make others understand. Suspense builds as Jimmy tries to explain to the others the serious threat of Jane's accident, but the greatest threat may be to him.

Lefebure, Molly. **The Loona Baloona.** Nelson 1974.

Cat astronauts plan an expedition to the moon, and two opposing teams pursue the same goal. The writer has very cleverly poked fun at the space program and at pompous people. If you like cats and love to laugh, you'll like this "moon" trip.

Le Guin, Ursula K. **Planet of Exile.** Ace Bks 1974.

The farborns and the natives of Eltanin have shared the planet for years, but have remained separate. But the terrible winter of the tenth year causes changes. Hordes of ravaging barbarians called Gaals and the weird, frightening snowghouls come to prey on the wintering people. The hilf girl, Rolery, and the human man, Agat, are to wed and show the way to a new life.

Le Guin, Ursula K. **A Wizard of Earthsea.** Ace Bks 1973.

In the world of Earthsea, there is an island called Gont, the home of many wizards. From this island, the wizard Ged moves among the islands and oceans of Earthsea, striving to understand all there is to know. An adventure story set in a world where magic carries the importance that science does in our world. Boston Globe-Horn Book Award.

L'Engle, Madeleine. **A Wind in the Door.** Dell 1973.

The illness of her young brother propels Meg Murry and Calvin O'Keefe into an inner spectrum of time and space to seek a cure. The cure may be for the world as well as for Charles Wallace. In their attempt to help, the youngsters meet many fantastic beings and have a brush with death.

L'Engle, Madeleine. **A Wrinkle in Time.** Dell 1962.

Three very atypical youngsters find themselves transferred from their typical lives into another dimension of time. Meg Murry, her younger brother Charles Wallace, and Calvin O'Keefe meet many challenges in seeking to overcome the all-powerful IT, which holds possession first of Meg's father and then of her younger brother. Activities far beyond the natural world create exciting adventure and intriguing mystery. John Newbery Medal.

Levin, Betty. **The Zoo Conspiracy.** Hastings 1973.

Tuatara Benjamin, loris Jerry, platypus Ernest, and other zoo animals want to find and get rid of a mysterious new addition to the zoo. They are afraid this 250-million-year-old specimen will get all the attention. Lena, a mean, bubble-gum-chewing girl, first tells them of this new addition and then helps them plot against it. The zoo animals don't expect the reaction of this new specimen, and learn something about themselves in their own reactions during the adventure.

Mayne, William. **Earthfasts.** Dutton 1967.

Nellie Jack John, a boy in the infantry over two hundred years ago, comes through a dark tunnel into the twentieth century. He was looking for King Arthur and his treasures under a huge fortress which had crumbled years ago. Two boys, Keith and David, try to find an explanation to this strange phenomenon when they run into King Arthur himself, a ghost, and many strange adventures.

Mayne, William. **A Game of Dark.** Dutton 1971.

Donald Jackson, a boy in England, leads a dull life at school and at home. His father is an invalid and his mother is narrow-minded. But Donald finds he can be transported into some other kind of world where he serves Breakbone, lord of a village. In this new medieval world, he finds plenty of adventure—especially fighting a giant worm. But in each world, he must always "come home to himself."

McKenzie, Ellen Kindt. **Drujienna's Harp.** Dutton 1971.

A. Crane's Curio Shop contains fascinating objects—especially a harp whose strings look as if they go through the ceiling and two round glass bottles with an odd bubble in the blue one. The bottles, made by a Yugoslavian in the 900s, have a strange legend attached to them. When Duncan and his sister, Tha, try to touch the bubble, they are transported into a strange land of T'Pahl and drawn into the legend. They encounter the forbidden lore, the curse, the prophecies, the imprisoned Eldordo, the Lodzati, Great Jadido, the Know-Nothings, Eshone and Acheron. Tha has a part to play in the awaiting of the people of T'Pahl for the playing of Drujienna's harp.

Norton, Andre. **Dragon Magic.** T Y Crowell 1972.

Four American boys find that a mysterious, dusty puzzle takes them each on an adventure backwards in time. Each boy (from African, Chinese, Scandinavian, and Welsh backgrounds) learns about his own heritage through a famous dragon legend. When the puzzle disappears, they wonder if that is the way it was meant to be—that they work the puzzle only once.

Norton, Andre. **Lavender-Green Magic.** T Y Crowell 1974.

Holly, Judy, and Crock must leave Boston when their father is reported missing in Vietnam and live with their grandparents at a rural place called Dimsdale. Since the children are black, they experience difficult adjustments to the new school and town. They feel compelled to explore the garden, where their adventure begins. They are taken back to colonial days where a feud is going on between two witches of good and evil. The ancient curse on Dimsdale brings the threat of disaster to everyone.

Phipson, Joan. **The Way Home.** Atheneum 1973.

As Richard, Prudence, and Prudence's little brother Peter are driving through the Australian countryside, the car in which they are riding is swept off the road by a flash flood. This incident begins a series of incredible adventures that take them far back in time, to the Ice Age, and far ahead into the future. Through all this, they are guided and protected by some mysterious force, which Prudence and Peter accept but which Richard refuses to believe in.

Silverberg, Barbara, editor. **Phoenix Feathers: A Collection of Mythical Monsters.** Dutton 1973.

Seven mythical monsters are described in this book, which gives the sources for stories about each one. Included are the griffin, the kraken, the dragon, the unicorn, the roc, the basilisk, and the phoenix. Sources include old novels, histories, modern-day adventures, children's books, and magazines. Each monster has its own unique history.

Skurzynski, Gloria. **The Remarkable Journey of Gustavus Bell.** Abingdon 1973.

The unusual story of a boy stricken with the halving disease. He repeatedly shrinks to half his size and encounters various beings and events in the process. A humorous approach gives the book appeal to the younger reader.

Swahn, Sven Christer. **The Island through the Gate.** Macmillan 1973.

Carried out to sea on an air mattress, a young boy drifts to a strange island called Oberour. Michael meets two island children and has many mystifying experiences. He finally meets the island hermit,

Gorven, and manages a dramatic escape. Excitement, danger, and fear make this a lively story.

Vonnegut, Kurt, Jr. **Cat's Cradle.** Dell 1970.

Atomic scientists, ugly Americans, midgets, Caribbean dictators, Bokononism, the end of the world. What do all these things have in common? They are all subjects in this fantasy (or is it?) by Kurt Vonnegut, Jr. A wild imagination mixes with a humorous story, to make you wonder if there isn't some reality hidden there after all!

Warburg, Sandol Stoddard. **On the Way Home.** HM 1973.

A boy awakens in a frozen wasteland to find a Bear guarding him. He and the Bear try to find a warmer land, and this is the struggle they make together. Some of their adventures include a battle with the Great Ice Worm, getting out of the Monkey King's castle, meeting the boy's exact duplicate, Twain, finding Sabrina, who rewards them, and being save from the Frog King by the Great Blue Heron.

Williams, Jay. **The Hero from Otherwhere.** Dell 1972.

Jesse Rosen and Rich Dennison, enemies from first meeting, become possessors of the greatest gift of man through a series of other-worldly adventures. Called into a parallel time, they can be the only saviors of the people of Givyliath from the mighty wolf Fenris, a symbol of all evil.

Williams, Ursula Moray. **Castle Merlin.** Nelson 1972.

Susie arrives at Castle Merlin, an English castle once famous for its hawks, for a holiday. She finds Bryan, who can read the Book of Merlins, and between them they discover their ability to meet with people from the past. People and objects disappear, and Susie has a frightening encounter. Through it, she learns more about herself and others.

Wrightson, Patricia. **The Nargun and the Stars.** Atheneum 1974.

Simon Brent is orphaned when a car crash kills his parents. He is sent off to Wongadilla in northern Australia to live with relatives who have a very different life-style. This lonely boy wanders the lonely countryside and finds the harmless elves and creatures such as Potkoorok, Turongs, Nyols, and finally the monster Nargun. This dangerous monster moves only at night, has moved eight hundred miles, and now is approaching Wongadilla. Simon keeps the monster a secret until he kills a sheep, but then the family must use their ingenuity and strength to fight the monster.

Yolen, Jane, editor. **Zoo 2000: Twelve Stories of Science Fiction and Fantasy Beasts.** Seabury 1973.

All twelve science fiction stories center around animals of the future. The tales include a bear with three eyes, wolfmen, a talking lemming, a mouse with a human brain, giant moths that threaten the world, dragons bred from alligators, a catlike being from another planet, and in the last story, the most dangerous animal of all—the "king of the beasts."

On folklore and legend

Arnott, Kathleen. **African Myths and Legends.** Walck 1963.

This addition to the Oxford Myths and Legends series tells thirty-four dramatic tales from many lands in Africa. We learn, for instance, why the dog is man's friend and why the crab has no head.

Baker, Betty. **At the Center of the World.** Macmillan 1973.

This is the story of the creation of the world as told in the legends of the Pima and Papago Indians of southern Arizona and northern Mexico. It tells how Earth Magician made the world and the first people with the help of Buzzard, and how Coyote caused a great flood that destroyed the first people. It is also the story of how Eetoi created new people and protected them from the killing pot and eagle man. Later Eetoi's people rebelled against him in the First War.

Baumann, Hans. **The Stolen Fire: Legends of Heroes and Rebels from Around the World.** Pantheon 1974.

These twenty-seven tales are legends of heroes and rebels from around the world. Each person uses intellect and strength to meet some foe. In the Polynesian legend, "The Stolen Fire," Maui tricks the giant into giving him fire for mortals. "The Flute Player," from South America, tells of warriors who will not fight the boa constrictor who swallows everything. But

the flute player takes food and a knife, is swallowed
by the boa constrictor, and cuts it away, piece by
piece, until he comes to the monster's heart. This is
why boa constrictors no longer eat human beings; they
don't want to get stomachaches. Tardanak of Siberia
outwits the seven-headed Yelbeggen and saves his life;
African Leutsi sets a trial to determine which of three
men is the greatest hero; and Nana Miriam of Nigeria,
a beautiful daughter with magical powers, finally con-
quers the hippopotamus monster.

Buck, Pearl S., editor. **Fairy Tales of the Orient.** S&S
1965.

If you are curious about China, Japan, India, Russia,
or Persia, this is a rich collection of fairy tales and
legends that will transport you to these magic lands.
Appealing illustrations.

Burland, C. A. **Gods and Heroes of War.** Putnam 1974.

War has been considered both disastrous and splendid
by the ancients. Many people have had their gods
and semi-divine heroes of war: Grecian Achilles, "Blue
Hummingbird on the Left" or Huitzilopochtli of the
Aztecs, Babylonian Bel Marduk, Viking Thor Red-
beard, and Hammer Thrower, and the heroes of the
Bronze Age. These gods and heroes still live deep in
our unconscious minds, and their stories are collected
here.

Creel, J. Luke. **Folk Tales of Liberia.** Denison 1969.

The Liberian people and animals are the subjects of
these folktales. A spider and a firefly join together
to steal food in a great famine; a servant trades places
with an unsuspecting princess; a dreaded loso gets a
beautiful girl for his wife by trickery. These folktales
appear in their original form and show the flavor and
mood of Africa.

Feldmann, Susan, editor. **The Storytelling Stone: Myths
and Tales of the American Indians.** Dell 1965.

A collection of myths and folktales of the American
Indian. The stories tell of how the earth was formed
and how mankind came to be, about the theft of fire,
the flood, and how the Indians' unique cultures came to
be. Also included are tales of mythological heroes and
supernatural journeys. The short, readable tales, which
resemble Aesop's fables, show the value structures of
the tribes.

Garfield, Leon, and Edward Blishen. **The God Beneath the Sea.** Pantheon 1971.

Many Greek legends are told in one continuous story divided into three parts: the making of the gods, the making of men, and gods and men. The stories begin with Hephaestus, first son of Zeus, being thrown from heaven because of his ugliness and end with Hephaestus being helped back to Olympus by his brother, Hermes. Also, at the end, the mortal son of Hermes writes to his daughter about the building of Troy and hopes his grandson, Odysseus, might visit it.

Gates, Doris, **Two Queens of Heaven: Aphrodite and Demeter.** Viking Pr 1974.

Aphrodite, goddess of love, and Demeter, goddess of fertility, touched the lives of both gods and mortals. Eight stories about Aphrodite include her love for two mortal youths, her power to make a statue come alive, her help to a young man eager to win a race for love, her jealous treatment of a beautiful rival, the love tragedies of a girl who sets a signal at a wrong time, and two lovers who meet in a tomb. The last story is of Demeter, sister of Zeus, who showed men how to work the earth. However, when her daughter is kidnapped, she punishes the earth until her daughter is returned.

Ghidalia, Vic, and Roger Elwood. **Beware the Beasts.** Macfadden 1971.

Legends are based on superstition and should be taken lightly—or should they? Ask the old cotter and his wife who made the mistake of killing cats in "The Cats of Ulthar." Ask the vicar who ignored the warnings and opened the forbidden tomb in "Here, Daemos!" Ask Défago about "The Wendigo." Here are ten short stories about legends and those who dared to explore and defy them.

Graves, Robert. **Greek Gods and Heroes.** Dell 1973.

The twelve most important gods and goddesses of Greece were called the Olympians and lived upon Mount Olympus where they quarreled and interfered in the lives of other gods and humans. Twenty-seven separate short chapters tell of gods and heroes. Among those included are: lovely Persephone captured by the god of the underworld, Hades; the barber who told that Midas had long, hairy ears like an ass; the winged horse Pegasus, who carried Bellerophon in his adventures; Theseus, who outsmarted King Minos with a ball of twine; the unbelievable labors of Hercules, who then let himself be burned to death.

Hieatt, Constance. **The Minstrel Knight.** T Y Crowell 1974.

Sir Orfeo, a traveling knight, comes to King Arthur's Camelot and charms everyone with his ability to sing on the harp. He sings of meeting his own wife, Lady Etain, in an enchanted forest. When the news arrives that his wife is imprisoned, he begins his long quest for her. His adventures take him through the Magic Woods, the Court of the Dead, and many other places. The legend is similar to that of the Greek Orpheus, who must search the underworld for his beautiful Eurydice.

Hodges, Elizabeth Jamison. **A Song for Gilgamesh.** Atheneum 1971.

Adaba is a potter and poet in ancient Sumer. When he discovers the art of writing through his business visits to the temple, he wants to learn. When he does, however, he is accused of stealing temple magic, and his adventures begin. He escapes violence and goes on a mission for the queen with Gilgamesh. The story is made even more exciting by the fact that history recognizes the Sumerians as the first known to develop a system of writing and a primitive democracy. They are also responsible for the first great folk epic, *The Epic of Gilgamesh.*

Hodges, Margaret. **The Other World: Myths of the Celts.** FS&G 1973.

Margaret Hodges retells ten Celtic myths full of mighty heroes who are aided by the gods of the Other World. These include four children who are turned into swans by their stepmother; Cuchulain, whose neck could not be touched by an ax; the monster of the loch, who could sink boats and carried off the king's daughter; three tales of the famous King Arthur, and others. The Celts were known for their "fire," which means they abandoned themselves to joy, grief, bravery, or battle. All these can be found in the ten myths.

Jones, Hettie. **Longhouse Winter: Iroquois Transformation Tales.** HR&W 1972.

The Iroquois Indians of the northeast were great story

tellers. But they only told the tales and legends of
their people during the long, cold winters sitting around
the fire in the longhouse. The stories in this book are
called transformation stories because the hero of the
story is changed in some way, like the young chief who
becomes a robin, the princess who becomes a fish so
she can live with her lover, the evil dancers who become rattlesnakes, and the animals of the forest who
bring a hunter back to life.

Le Guin, Ursula K. **The Tombs of Atuan.** Atheneum
1974.

When Tenar is only six years old, she is offered by the
people of Atuan as a high priestess to the Powers of
the Earth. This means she is taken from her home
and put in the Place of the Tombs. She is to grow
there and receive a new name, Arha, the Eaten One.
In the darkness of her new life, she learns her own
cruelty. It isn't until the young wizard comes that
she is forced to choose between that darkness and a
new light, a new power. A broken ring is part of that
solution. National Book Award.

Lynch, Patricia. **Knights of God: Tales and Legends of
the Irish Saints.** HR&W 1969.

These stories of the lives of Ciaran, Patrick, Enda,
Brigid, Brendan, Columcille, Kevan, and Lawrence
O'Toole are a blend of history and legend, revealing
a great deal about early Ireland and her people.

Matson, Emerson N., editor. **Longhouse Legends.** Nelson 1968.

This collection of the myths and legends of the Indians of the Pacific Northwest includes the stories of
the star children and of Princess Ko, who became the
bride of the son of the great spirit of the sea to save
her people from starvation. There are tales of the
supernatural and witchcraft and stories that the Indians used to teach children important lessons, such
as not killing animals except for food.

McKenzie, Ellen Kindt. **Drujienna's Harp.** Dutton 1971.

A. Crane's Curio Shop contains fascinating objects—
especially a harp whose strings look as if they go
through the ceiling and two round glass bottles with
an odd bubble in the blue one. The bottles, made by
a Yugoslavian in the 900s, have a strange legend attached to them. When Duncan and his sister, Tha,

try to touch the bubble, they are transported into a strange land of T'Pahl and drawn into the legend. They encounter the forbidden lore, the curse, the prophecies, the imprisoned Eldordo, the Lodzati, Great Jadido, the Know-Nothings, Eshone and Acheron. Tha has a part to play in the awaiting of the people of T'Pahl for the playing of Drujienna's harp.

Mercatante, Anthony S. **Zoo of the Gods.** Har-Row 1974.
This book of myths in which animals have major roles is both informative and fun to read.

Norton, Andre. **Dragon Magic.** T Y Crowell 1972.
Four American boys find that a mysterious, dusty puzzle takes them each on an adventure backwards in time. Each boy (from African, Chinese, Scandinavian, and Welsh backgrounds) learns about his own heritage through a famous dragon legend. When the puzzle disappears, they wonder if that is the way it was meant to be—that they work the puzzle only once.

Norton, Andre. **Here Abide Monsters.** Atheneum 1973.
From a typical country road, Nick, Linda, and her dog Lung are suddenly transported to another time—the Avalon of Arthurian legend. Realizing that they are trapped in this other time, they meet many others like themselves and learn of the dangers which surround them. The story covers their struggles and adventures as they strive to decide whether to follow the believers or unbelievers.

Norton, Andre. **Huon of the Horn.** Ace Bks 1951.
Huon, Duke of Bordeaux, is betrayed in Charlemagne's court and must fulfill an almost impossible task to be allowed to return to France. Befriended by Oberon, the Elf King, and with a few magical gifts, Huon achieves his goal. This novel picks up a part of the Charlemagne Saga not usually retold through translation.

Reed, A. W. **Myths and Legends of Australia.** Taplinger 1973.
These fifty-five legends are evenly divided among creation myths, hero stories, and legends of animals, birds, sun, moon, stars, river, lake, and shore. Some stories, such as that of a tribe punished by crawling, include terror. Others are happy, such as the story of the sun-goddess who created light-heartedly. Some are

humorous, among them, the tale of a man who spied on his wife, only to find spines growing on his skin.

Schiller, Barbara. **Hrafkel's Saga.** Seabury 1972.

The saga takes place in Viking Iceland, and is about Hrafkel, a chieftain who rules an entire valley and is the most powerful chieftain for a time. Hrafkel rules with a strong arm, and kills a shepherd boy for disobeying him. Hrafkel is then surprised and angered when he is taken to court for his crime.

Singer, Jane, and Kurt Singer. **Folk Tales of Mexico.** Denison 1969.

Ten popular Mexican folktales tell of people and places important in the Mexican heritage. A simple potter meets the president; two lovers become mountains that stand side by side; a leader is turned into a rare cactus; a Zapotec shows his wisdom through foolishness; an unselfish Mongolian princess has great influence on Mexico; and gods create the earth.

Suhl, Yuri. **The Merrymaker.** Four Winds 1975.

Among Eastern European Jewish families, the merrymaker enlivens wedding celebrations and brings good fortune to those who invite him to dinner. This short, delightful story gives the reader an excellent picture of customs and folklore of this ethnic group. The tale is not only informative but written with simplicity and charm.

Sutcliff, Rosemary. **Beowulf.** Dutton 1962.

The Old English epic of Beowulf is retold in modern language. Denmark is terrorized by the monster Grendel, the Night Stalker, who has already killed thirty of King Hrothgar's noblest men. Beowulf, a warrior of Geatland, sails for Denmark to do battle with Grendel and his monster, the monster Sea Woman. Even after Beowulf returns to Geatland and becomes king, he must fight the Fire-Drake, from whom he receives his fatal wound.

Whedbee, Charles Harry. **Legends of the Outer Banks and Tar Heel Tidewater.** Blair 1971.

The Outer Banks, territory along the coast of North Carolina, have many legends connected with them. These eighteen legends include such subjects as strange, healing water; a white doe transformed into human form; the Arabian Quork who challenged God;

strange lights on the water, said to lead to Black-
beard's treasure; Miss Mabe, a witch who told children's fortunes; and the strange happenings to a crew-
less ship marooned on Diamond Shoals. The heroes
are both admirable and whimsical, and the legends
tell much about the kinds of people who live in this
coastal region.

Whitney, Alex. **Stiff Ears: Animal Folktales of the North
American Indian.** Walck 1974.

The American Indians were great story tellers. They
used folktales both to entertain and to teach. These
animal folktales of the Hopi, Chippewa, Iroquois, Chi-
nook, Pawnee, and Cherokee Indians teach such valuable lessons as the importance of listening to one's
elders because of their experience and wisdom, and
of never giving up.

On magic and the supernatural

Allan, Mabel Esther. **A Chill in the Lane.** Nelson 1974.

Lyd, the adopted daughter of the Allbrights, feels a
strange foreboding chill in the lane by their vacation
cottage. Lyd and Saul, the young son of a fisherman,
have to search the past for answers.

Arthur, Ruth M. **The Autumn People.** Atheneum 1974.

Karasay—the old-timers call it the Island of the
Witches. It was here that Romily William's great-
grandmother met Rodger Graham, a mysterious young
man who practiced witchcraft in a cave not far from
his parents' home. Rodger cast an evil influence on
Romily's family that is not broken until Romily visits
the island on a summer vacation. While at Karasay,
Romily comes to know the Autumn People, ghosts of
the family and friends of Romily's great-grandmother.
Rodger's influence is ended when Romily meets her
future husband—a descendant of the man her great-
grandmother had loved.

Bradbury, Ray. **The Halloween Tree.** Bantam 1974.

The Feast of Samhain. The Day of the Dead. El Dia
de Muerte. Halloween. We—secure in the twentieth
century—forget what it means. We forget the ancient
terror, the fear that when the sun goes down it may
disappear forever. For us the skeleton suits and masks
are just part of a silly game. But a visit to a weird

old mansion, a trip back into time, and a bargain with Death make nine boys in this book relearn the age-old fears. This book plays tricks on you. One scene flows into the next like patterns in a kaleidoscope. Readers who can keep up with the changing patterns will understand what the boys learn at the Halloween Tree.

Burroughs, Edgar Rice. **The Monster Men.** Ace Bks 1972.

A quick glance at a lovely lady sends Townsend J. Harper, Jr. on a strange adventure. He is led into a world of subhuman beings and is changed into such a creature, but continues his pursuit of the lovely lady.

Carr, Terry, editor. **Into the Unknown: Eleven Tales of Imagination.** Nelson 1973.

These fantasy-reality stories are meant to make you feel uneasy, puzzle you, and make you laugh. Outstanding writers such as Ray Bradbury, Robert Silverberg, and Jorge Borges tell of a strange child who refuses to grow older, a man who gets more than he bargains for in a used car, and the way "chance" came into the world. What if you had a chance to relive your life, or find that you suddenly have disappeared, or discover your dog can talk, or find a drowned giant washed up on the beach? All these unrealities are found in the stories.

Clapp, Patricia. **Jane-Emily.** Dell 1969.

Young Jane Canfield and her Aunt Louisa spend the summer in a large dark mansion. At first "Emily" appears to be just a figment of Jane's imagination. Later Louisa begins to wonder if Emily is indeed a creature of the supernatural.

Cobalt, Martin. **Pool of Swallows.** Nelson 1972.

Martin Babbacombe, a thirteen-year-old farm boy, sees the Swallows, three pools on the farm, suddenly rise to engulf and drown the family's cows. Ghosts run through the house, all the farm animals leave in a straight line, and the ancestral curse of the family comes true.

Cooper, Susan. **Greenwitch.** Atheneum 1974.

Simon, Jane, and Barney come to Trewissick in England with their Great-Uncle Merry. They meet a strange boy, Will Stanton, who has mysterious powers. Together they hunt for the golden Celtic grail which has mysteriously disappeared from the museum. With magic and counter-magic, the war between the Light and the Dark goes on. The Dark has taken the grail and is gathering more power to overthrow the Light. Finally the Greenwitch appears from the sea. She has wild magic and a gift to give to Jane, who had made the only wish which wasn't self-serving. *Greenwitch* is the third book of the sequence called *The Dark Is Rising*.

Dickinson, Susan, editor. **The Usurping Ghost and Other Encounters and Experiences.** Dutton 1971.

For one's "ghostly pleasure" these nineteen stories range from the nineteenth century to modern times and are divided into actual "encounters" and "experiences." The stories are varied enough to include the old West, haunted mansions, a fun fair, old English churchyards, Hawaii, a computer in Scotland, and a feared red room.

Dickson, Gordon R., and Ben Bova. **Gremlins Go Home.** St Martin 1974.

A boy and his dog become involved in intrigue with gremlins looking for a means of returning to their home planet. Rolf Gunnarson helps the gremlins plan to stow away on a Mars-bound rocket. This fantasy-adventure helps many individuals become better aware of themselves and their situations. It has humor and a serious concern for life.

Fisk, Nicholas. **Grinny: A Novel of Science Fiction.** Nelson 1973.

Who was Great-Aunt Emma? This story, in the form of a diary kept by Tim, tells of her unexpected coming and her frightful ending. Beth and Tim cannot convince their parents about this old lady, so along with their friend Mac, they have to prove the truth by themselves. Maybe it is her strange grin that gives them their first clue.

Greaves, Margaret. **Stone of Terror.** Har-Row 1972.

In the seventeenth century fifteen-year-old Philip Hoskyn comes from England to join his grandfather on the island of Serq. Philip meets the witch and priestess of the haunting stone and falls in love with Marie, the niece of the priestess, whom he has to save from her aunt's strange powers.

Haining, Peter, editor. **The Monster Makers: Creators and Creations of Fantasy and Horror.** Taplinger 1974.

Eighteen short stories all center around monstermakers and their creations. Such contributors as Edgar Allan Poe, H. G. Wells, Ray Bradbury, Isaac Asimov, and Ambrose Bierce write about such matters as robots roaming about, dead bodies receiving life again, puppets coming to life, demons, golems, and monsters of all varieties.

Heinlein, Robert A. **Have Space Suit—Will Travel.** Ace Bks 1971.

With his own spacesuit, Kip Russell is able to realize his dream of going to the moon. He also gets to see Pluto, a planet of Vega, and the Lesser Magellanic Cloud. Mother Thing is his guide through these adventures. The story has humor as well as excitement.

Hunter, Mollie. **The 13th Member.** Har-Row 1971.

Set in sixteenth century Scotland, this story of witchcraft is based on records of a plot to murder King James I. Adam Lawrie, a servant boy, follows Gilly Duncan, the kitchenmaid, one night and sees the Devil himself! Adam and Gilly, a self-confessed witch, help to expose the plot against the king.

Lawrence, Louise. **The Power of Stars: A Story of Suspense.** Har-Row 1972.

A frightening novel of a young girl who is controlled by other powers. The one person who realizes the danger that Jane carries cannot make others understand. Suspense builds as Jimmy tries to explain to the others the serious threat of Jane's accident, but the greatest threat may be to him.

Le Guin, Ursula K. **The Farthest Shore.** Atheneum 1973.

Arren, prince of Enlad, brings bad news to the land of Roke, Isle of the Wise, where magic is taught. In Enlad, magic has lost all powers; wizardry is no longer effective. Ged, Archmage of Roke, has heard such stories from other lands, and it is time to meet this trouble. Arren and Ged set out on an amazing adventure that will test the ancient prophecies of Earthsea. National Book Award.

Le Guin, Ursula K. **Planet of Exile.** Ace Bks 1974.

The farborns and the natives of Eltanin have shared

the planet for years, but have remained separate. But the terrible winter of the tenth year causes changes. Hordes of ravaging barbarians called Gaals and the weird, frightening snowghouls come to prey on the wintering people. The hilf girl, Rolery, and the human man, Agat, are to wed and show the way to a new life.

Le Guin, Ursula K. **The Tombs of Atuan.** Atheneum 1974.

When Tenar is only six years old, she is offered by the people of Atuan as a high priestess to the Powers of the Earth. This means she is taken from her home and put in the Place of the Tombs. She is to grow there and receive a new name, Arha, the Eaten One. In the darkness of her new life, she learns her own cruelty. It isn't until the young wizard comes that she is forced to choose between that darkness and a new light, a new power. A broken ring is part of that solution. National Book Award.

Le Guin, Ursula K. **A Wizard of Earthsea.** Ace Bks 1973.

In the world of Earthsea, there is an island called Gont, the home of many wizards. From this island, the wizard Ged moves among the islands and oceans of Earthsea, striving to understand all there is to know. An adventure story set in a world where magic carries the importance that science does in our world. Boston Globe-Horn Book Award.

Leiber, Fritz. **The Big Time.** Ace Bk 1961.

Outside of life, a war is being waged over the structure of both past and future. Spiders and snakes are the combatants, and a place called the Place is the scene of the action of this story. It concerns a small group of beings from all times, who must exist together for a frightening period. Personality clashes and an atomic bomb scare add to their predicament.

L'Engle, Madeleine. **A Wind in the Door.** Dell 1973.

The illness of her young brother propels Meg Murry and Calvin O'Keefe into an inner spectrum of time and space to seek a cure. The cure may be for the world as well as for Charles Wallace. In their attempt to help, the youngsters meet many fantastic beings and have a brush with death.

L'Engle, Madeleine. **A Wrinkle in Time.** Dell 1962.

Three very atypical youngsters find themselves transferred from their typical lives into another dimension
of time. Meg Murry, her younger brother Charles
Wallace, and Calvin O'Keefe meet many challenges in
seeking to overcome the all-powerful IT, which holds
possession first of Meg's father and then of her younger
brother. Activities far beyond the natural world create
exciting adventure and intriguing mystery. John Newbery Medal.

Leodhas, Sorche Nic. **XII Great Black Cats: And Other
Eerie Scottish Tales.** Dutton 1971.

Ten tales of the supernatural, ghosts, hauntings, and
strange happenings in Scotland fill this book. Some
of the eerie events include cats pursuing a man in the
late hours, ghosts needing a place to haunt, an old
lady putting a curse on the king, an honest ghost
wanting to return something borrowed, and a lass told
to watch a dead man.

Luckhardt, Mildred Corell, editor. **Spooky Tales about
Witches, Ghosts, Goblins, Demons and Such.** Abingdon 1972.

These spooky tales, folktales, and poems are collected
in four divisions: other beings, mortals, ghosts, and
Halloween. Well-known and little-known selections
come from England, Czechoslovakia, Canada, Liberia,
Hawaii, and Ireland, as well as the early and present
United States. The stories include travelers forced to
dance to death; the Ponaturi or evil spirits of Hawaii,
who keep the people inside; a doctor who hears strange
nightly footsteps in a haunted house; a ghost who
guards gold in a sawmill in North Carolina; the Halloween that brought a bull in a hayloft; and the woman
who must break the spell of the witches with horns
on their foreheads.

Manley, Seon, and Gogo Lewis, editors. **Shapes of the
Supernatural.** Doubleday 1969.

Twenty tales by well-known masters of the supernatural are collected in this book, including stories of
banshees and werewolves.

Matson, Emerson N., editor. **Longhouse Legends.** Nelson 1968.

This collection of the myths and legends of the Indians
of the Pacific Northwest includes the stories of the

star children and of Princess Ko, who became the bride of the son of the great spirit of the sea to save her people from starvation. There are tales of the supernatural and witchcraft and stories that the Indians used to teach children important lessons, such as not killing animals except for food.

Norton, Andre. **Here Abide Monsters.** Atheneum 1973.

From a typical country road, Nick, Linda, and her dog Lung are suddenly transported to another time— the Avalon of Arthurian legend. Realizing that they are trapped in this other time, they meet many others like themselves and learn of the dangers which surround them. The story covers their struggles and adventures as they strive to decide whether to follow the believers or nonbelievers.

Norton, Andre, compiler. **Small Shadows Creep.** Dutton 1974.

This is an anthology of stories about young ghosts that wandered long ago. For example, there are the ghostly schoolgirls that come to play with little lonely Monica, and then there is faithful Jenny Dove who, even after death, waits for her lover to return home from the war.

Poole, Josephine. **The Visitor: A Story of Suspense.** Har-Row 1972.

Only Harry Longshaw seems to notice the strangeness of Mr. Bogle, Harry's new tutor. Mr. Bogle has never been to Fury Wood before, yet he knows the inscription above the fireplace. Also he seems to have a strange power over the villagers, but nobody listens to Harry until it is almost too late.

Severn, David. **The Girl in the Grove.** Har-Row 1974.

This suspenseful story about fifteen-year-old Jonquil (Jon) Darley, who moves with her mother to the English countryside, is charged with mystery when the Darleys befriend the Hunters. Jon and Paul Hunter do not get along well. Their troubles begin when Jon meets a mysterious girl, Laura, in the woods— only to discover that Laura is actually the ghost of Laura Seccombe, a young girl killed in a fall from her horse in the late 19th century! This book has adventure, humor, and romance!

Snyder, Zilpha K. **The Headless Cupid.** Atheneum 1971.

How would you react if the twelve-year-old stepsister

you've been waiting to meet turned out to be a fancier of the occult who dresses in crazy-looking costumes and has a crow for a Familiar? Eleven-year-old David Stanley faces this dilemma after his dad marries again. Amanda catches the four young Stanleys up in a fantastic round of initiations and seances. Before long, she proclaims that the headless statue of a cupid, on the stairway of the old mansion, proves the house has been haunted by a poltergeist. But is the noisy ghost real or just Amanda? International Board on Books for Young People Honor List.

Spicer, Dorothy. **The Humming Top.** S G Phillips 1968.
Orphan Dorcas Gray goes into a trance when she spins the mysterious top that she was clutching when she was found by the orphanage. Dorcas, usually unaware of what happens when she spins the top, appears to have an uncanny way of seeing into people's lives and of predicting future events.

Swahn, Sven Christer. **The Island through the Gate.** Macmillan 1973.
Carried out to sea on an air mattress, a young boy drifts to a strange island called Oberour. Michael meets two island children and has many mystifying experiences. He finally meets the island hermit, Gorven, and manages a dramatic escape. Excitement, danger, and fear make this a lively story.

Sykes, Pamela. **Mirror of Danger.** Nelson 1973.
Lucy, after living a quiet life with Aunt Olive, goes to live with a noisy family of distant relatives. Feeling extremely lonely, Lucy is only too glad to make friends with Alice. But who is Alice anyway? Lucy lives through some terrifying days before finding the answer to that question.

Van Vogt, A. E. **The Silkie.** Ace Bks 1973.
Silkies are able to move through water, space, or land and have the ability to read minds. The major portion of the novel centers on Nat Cemp, who is a Silkie. He faces confrontation with an anti-human alien posing as his son. The novel provides an entertaining view of a very unexpected type of life-form.

Van Vogt, A. E. **The Universe Maker.** Ace Bks 1973.
From an automobile accident in which a young woman is killed, to a point in the future when many people

live in space, Morton Cargill makes the full cycle. Pursued by the shadows, then becoming one of them, Cargill discovers many things about himself. This novel provides a fascinating glimpse into the realm of the supernatural.

Williams, Jay. **The Hero from Otherwhere.** Dell 1972.

Jesse Rosen and Rich Dennison, enemies from the first meeting, become possessors of the greatest gift of man through a series of other-worldly adventures. Called into a parallel time, they can be the only saviors of the people of Givyliath from the mighty wolf Fenris, a symbol of all evil.

Williams, Ursula Moray. **Castle Merlin.** Nelson 1972.

Susie arrives at Castle Merlin, an English castle once famous for its hawks, for a holiday. She finds Bryan, who can read the Book of Merlins, and between them they discover their ability to meet with people from the past. People and objects disappear, and Susie has a frightening encounter. Through it, she learns more about herself and others.

Windham, Kathryn Tucker. **Jeffrey Introduces 13 More Southern Ghosts.** Strode 1971.

This collection of ghost lore relates the tales of thirteen ghosts throughout the South. The mystery and romance of each story will appeal to those who enjoy the supernatural.

Zelazny, Roger. **The Dream Master.** Ace Bks 1973.

Life in the next century may hold unexpected dangers such as control by the dream master. He has perfected a technique for entering men's minds to experience their thoughts and manipulate their lives. Sleep may offer the chance for him to enter any mind. This novel presents a rather frightening look at what may await mankind.

NONFICTION

More and more people are reading nonfiction today. One reason for that surely is that there are more and more fine books available. Name a topic you're interested in and probably you can find a book that will tell you about it.

Many of the books in this section are biographies or autobiographies; for convenience, both are listed in the category, "Biography." To make the life stories of people you want to read about easier to find, we have grouped these books into seven subcategories. The remainder of the nonfiction section is arranged according to the topic or subject matter dealt with in the book.

A sure way to get interested in some of the books listed in this section is to read through the titles. The titles, themselves, can make you aware of interests you didn't even know you had!

ANIMALS

Adamson, Joy. **The Spotted Sphinx.** HarBraceJ 1969.

Pippa is an eight-month-old cheetah who is given to the author. Mrs. Adamson cares for her and finally restores her to her natural habitat.

Alexander, Lloyd. **My Five Tigers.** Dutton 1973.

Lloyd Alexander describes his five pet tigers: an alley cat named Rabbit; the actor, Heathcliff; a half-Siamese called David; copper-eyed Solomon; and popularity-seeking Moira. The personalities and influences of each tiger over Alexander are clearly and imaginatively shown.

Amory, Cleveland. **Man Kind?** Har-Row 1974.

After reading this powerful book, you will love animals more and be stunned by the incredible war mankind has waged on wildlife. Many species have already been slaughtered to extinction. The author makes a convincing case against trappers and hunters who maim and torture animals.

Bailey, Jane H. **The Sea Otter's Struggle.** Follett 1973.

Sea otters lead a life of high drama. The small mammal has had to cope with starvation, animal competition, predators, and human enemies. The threat to his existence has moved a considerable number of people to work to insure the sea otter's survival. This book encompasses many of the known facts concerning one of the earth's most fascinating creatures and contains many black and white photographs.

Colby, Constance Taber. **A Skunk in the House.** Lippincott 1973.

The story of what happens to the Colby family when they acquire a skunk from a pet shop. The skunk, Secret, is soon running the household according to his own routine. The Colby family shares many hilarious adventures with Secret, who never really adjusts to the lifestyle of a household pet.

Durden, Kent. **Gifts of an Eagle.** Bantam 1974.

The story begins with the Durdens capturing a wild eaglet from its nest. At first, Lady is merely a research project but after sixteen years Lady occupies a place in the family's home and heart. Lady becomes actress, mother, and daughter during her stay. It is only after she finds a mate that she leaves the Durden family.

Fox, Michael. **Sundance Coyote.** Coward 1974.

Sundance is a coyote living in eastern New Mexico and northwestern Texas and often persecuted by man. The author describes the behavior and mind of the coyote, his relationship to other animals and the semi-arid environment, and his bond with an Indian boy. Through the story the reader is helped to understand the basic laws of nature and the interrelationship of everything in nature.

Fox, Michael. **The Wolf.** Coward 1973.

Through the life of Shadow, a wolf, and her cubs the reader learns the part a wolf plays in preserving a balance of nature in the wilderness. Christopher Award Children's Book Category.

Gardner, Richard. **The Baboon.** Macmillan 1972.

This book describes the life-style of different kinds of baboons. It identifies their eating habits, ways of communicating, and the surroundings in which they live.

The book also points out that humans and baboons are similar.

Gray, Robert. **Children of the Ark: The Rescue of the World's Vanishing Wildlife.** Schol Bk Serv 1974.

Over a thousand species of wildlife are threatened with extinction. This is the story of how active conservationists are attempting to solve the problem.

Jenkins, Alan C. **Wild Life in Danger.** St Martin 1973.

About wildlife conservation, this book discusses such topics as extinct animals, the balance of nature, the place of zoos and parks in conservation, and various methods currently being used for wildlife conservation. Many photographs are included.

Leslie, Robert Franklin. **The Bears and I: Raising Three Cubs in the North Woods.** Dutton 1968.

Robert Leslie vividly tells his humorous and exciting experiences of raising three orphaned bear cubs in the Canadian wilderness. Leaving college temporarily because of lack of money, Robert goes to Babine Lake to pan for gold. There a foster mother bear gives Robert three bears to look after. During the three years Robert spends in this remote area he and the bears live, play, and work together.

McClung, Robert M. **Lost Wild America: The Story of Our Extinct and Vanishing Wildlife.** Morrow 1969.

This survey of rare and extinct wildlife traces the history of conservation in the U.S. and discusses over seventy-five species now in danger of extinction.

McCoy, J. J. **Saving Our Wildlife.** CCPr Macmillan 1970.

Wildlife communities are being destroyed. Wildlife is one of our most valuable natural resources. The author tells how we can save our animals and birds by establishing ways that men and wildlife can live together. For example, man can change hunting laws and outlaw the use of certain chemicals.

McCoy, J. J. **Wild Enemies.** Hawthorn 1974.

Wild enemies or natural resources? J. J. McCoy explores this question and examines the habits and struggles for survival of predators such as wolves, coyotes, bears, mountain lions, and hawks. He describes the function of these animals in the environment and recalls some of the legends surrounding them. He discusses man's relationship to wild animals, and some conservation efforts to save them.

McHugh, Tom. **The Time of the Buffalo.** Knopf 1972.

Everything you ever wanted to know about the exciting animal of the Great Plains, the buffalo, has been gathered into one book by the man who filmed *The Vanishing Prairie.* The author reaches back into prehistory and follows the buffalo through the time when entire Indian cultures of the plains revolved around it. He gives a close-up view of behavior of buffaloes within the herd, from their battles to their playful moments. White settlers reacted to the buffalo first with awe, then with an eye for plunder, almost wiping out the herds and destroying the Indian cultures. The author's photographs and many reproductions of early drawings enrich this book. Western Writers of America Spur Award.

Murphy, Robert. **A Heritage Restored: America's Wildlife Refuges.** Dutton 1971.

This book describes in words and beautiful photographs the wildlife of our country and the areas where the animals and birds live. In Part I the author tells what happened in the past to the animals and birds and the importance of bird migration in conservation. In Part II he describes refuges representative of the five major regions of our national system of wildlife refuges: Northwest; Southwest; Midcontinent and the Pothole Country; Southeast; and the Northeast. Included are a map of the National Wildlife Refuge System and a foreword by Stewart L. Udall.

Osmond, Edward. **Animals of Central Asia.** Abelard 1968.

Strange and interesting animals inhabit this remote and forbidding area. The author, who is an art historian and illustrator, provides much information, not only on the animals, but also on the people of Central Asia who are dependent on them for their needs. Superb illustrations.

Osteen, Phyllis. **Bears around the World.** Coward 1966.

This comprehensive book describes bears by size, includes some information about the history of bears and bears in folklore, and gives information about their lives and behavior.

Prince, J. H. **Animals in the Night: Senses in Action after Dark.** Nelson 1971.

The author describes how animals use their eyes, ears, senses of taste, touch, and smell to get food, find their mates, and protect themselves. Diagrams and photographs are interesting and helpful.

Rappaport, Eva. **Banner Forward: The Pictorial Biography of a Guide Dog.** Dutton 1969.

This book tells the story of Banner, a golden retriever trained as a guide dog for the blind, and her relationships with people: Jesse, the boy who raises her; Scott, the man who trains her; and June, the blind woman who loves and cares for Banner and depends on her.

Ricciuti, Edward R. **To the Brink of Extinction.** Har-Row 1974.

An extremely scientific coverage of seven species of wild animals that have been threatened by extinction, this book discusses the factors which hinder the survival of the species. Each chapter includes the origin of the species, the habitat, feeding habits, and breeding habits of the species. The author suggests what humans can do to combat wild animal extinction.

Rood, Ronald. **Loon in My Bathtub.** Greene 1974.

The author's hobby of "collecting" wild critters—whether it's caring for those that have run afoul of man's ways, or getting to know others in their own surroundings—is a wonderfully rewarding one. This is a delightful book about the animals and plants that share this land with us.

Russell, Franklin. **The Sea Has Wings.** Dutton 1973.

Franklin Russell believes the sea birds along the northeastern coast of North America are "the most dramatic of all winged creatures." Studying the terns, puffins, gulls, gannets, and other birds, he describes with many details their habits and territories. In one hundred photographs Les Line has "captured" the birds in action.

Schaller, George B., and Millicent E. Selsam. **The Tiger, Its Life in the Wild.** Har-Row 1969.

The tiger—its food, family, social life, language, living habits, behavior—is the subject of this beautiful book.

Scott, Jack Denton. **Loggerhead Turtle: Survivor from the Sea.** Putnam 1974.

This picture essay records the birth of the loggerhead turtle off the coast of Florida. This animal has remained unchanged for 150 million years but is now an endangered species.

Scott, Jack Denton. **Speaking Wildly.** PB 1971.

Traveling all over the world, Jack Scott has come in contact with a wide range of animals, from the peacock to the skunk to the lion. (Have you ever heard of the baboon who became a railroad switchman?) This is a collection of adventures with twenty-five different animals, some amusing and some frightening, but all exciting.

Silverberg, Robert. **Forgotten by Time: A Book of Living Fossils.** T Y Crowell 1966.

Although living things change with time, some—like the okapi, aardvark, platypus, penguin, wombat, and anteater—have survived with little change. A fascinating account of the discoveries of these "living fossils."

Simon, Hilda. **Snakes: The Facts and the Folklore.** Viking Pr 1973.

This book tells myths, anecdotes, and scientific facts about snakes. Along with colored illustrations, the author presents many of the world's snakes, describing their habits and personalities. Also included is a guide for the care and feeding of pet snakes and a checklist for identification of snakes found in North America.

Smith, Howard G. **Tracking the Unearthly Creatures of Marsh and Pond.** Abingdon 1972.

Not all strange and bizarre creatures live in remote corners of the universe or in novels of the future. Some inhabit the most ordinary ponds and streams of America, and they include beetles that attack and kill frogs and small fish; worms that can grow two heads, two tails, or divide in half; and many others, better known, that have interesting life-styles. The book includes "tracking guides" for each species—where to look and what to look for—and directions for building a wild pond aquarium. Christopher Award Children's Book Category.

Stephen, David, editor. **Dogs.** Putnam 1973.

This book has colored pictures and vivid word descriptions of all the best-loved breeds of dogs. Included also are the origins of the dog, common characteristics, the many uses of the domestic dog, and a study of the wild canids such as jackals and foxes.

Wellman, Alice. **Africa's Animals: Creatures of a Struggling Land.** Putnam 1974.

This book has three parts: Part I describes Africa—its past and present, with geographical facts, animal stories of ancient days, and details of the widespread extermination of animals in the years 1500-1950. Part II describes animals in various areas—the thornbush, rain forest, plains, swamps, highlanus, and open bushwood lands. Part III tells how Africa is trying to preserve areas.

Wilkes, Paul. **Fitzgo: The Wild Dog of Central Park.** Lippincott 1973.

Fitzgo, the wild dog of New York's Central Park, was first noticed by the author and his wife because of his amazing independence. The writer tells how an old gentleman finally wins Fitzgo's trust. When he can no longer keep the dog, Fitzgo goes to live with the Wilkeses in Brooklyn.

BIOGRAPHY

Adventurers

Gannon, Robert. **Great Survival Adventures.** Random 1973.

Nine persons tell in their own words their experiences of suddenly trying to stay alive: Gary Beeman trapped in the desert; John Walsh surviving the rapids in the Surinam River in South America; Charles Stover marooned on an ice cap; Jean-Pierre Hallet driving two hundred miles for help after his right hand was blown off by dynamite; Scott Seegers struggling in the icy Potomac River; Nicholas Clinch climbing the giant mountain, Mashebrum, in the Himalayas; John Fairfax roaming alone across the Atlantic Ocean; Helen Klaben surviving a plane crash in the Yukon wilderness; Arthur Ray Hawkins being ejected from a plane traveling faster than the speed of sound.

Gerson, Noel B. **Passage to the West: The Great Voyages of Henry Hudson.** Messner 1968.

Hudson's four voyages are interestingly presented, showing Hudson's personality, his relationships with men like John Smith and Sir Walter Raleigh, and the results of his discoveries.

Graham, Alberta Powell. **Lafayette: Friend of America.** Abingdon 1952.

This book tells the story of Lafayette's life, first as a wealthy, young Frenchman, trained in the military, who risks his life and gives his own money voluntarily to fight for the colonies' freedom in the American Revolution; later, as a military and political leader in France during its revolu·on, and finally as a hero returning to a growing America.

Graham, Robin Lee. **Dove.** Bantam 1974.

Robin was sixteen when he left the marina in his small sailboat to travel around the world. It took 33,000 lonely miles and five years for his incredible voyage. On the way, he passed from boyhood to adulthood, and he talks about love, loneliness, fate, various lands and people, sailing. In the South Pacific he met another American, Patti, and they knew that they were special together, but both felt that Robin should finish his journey to satisfy something in himself. And so Patti met him when possible at several ports, and as Robin's loneliness almost overwhelmed him, she would be there to encourage him. This is a special, special story, particularly since it is a true one.

Harris, Sherwood. **Great Flying Adventures.** Random 1973.

This book relates the true stories of aviators who had narrow escapes in flying.

Hogg, Garry. **They Did It the Hard Way: Seven Astounding Adventures.** Pantheon 1973.

Seven courageous persons go on dangerous journeys in the twentieth century, without using modern mechanical equipment: Douglas Mawson travels in Antarctica; William P. Thesiger, in the Arabian desert; Peter Fleming, in the Brazilian jungle. Dervla Murphy Wheeling wheels her way from Ireland to India; John Hillaby walks across Kenya in search of Lake Rudolf; Andre Mîgot journeys from Kunming in China's Yünnan Province to Koko Nor in Chinghai Province, bandit country; and Laurens vander Post surveys in Nyasaland. Each person shows initiative, faith, and endurance in reaching his or her goal.

Jackson, W. H. (with Ethel Dassow). **Handloggers.** Alaska Northwest 1974.

William H. "Handlogger" Jackson tells his adventure tale of handlogging in the Alaskan wilderness, beginning in the early twentieth century. The book describes the forty-three years William Jackson and his wife Ruth braved the dangers and appreciated the beauty of the area.

Proenneke, Richard (editor Sam Keith). **One Man's Wilderness: An Alaskan Odyssey.** Alaska Northwest 1973.

From the diary of Richard Proenneke, who lived in the Alaskan wilderness for eighteen months, Sam Keith, a friend, compiled this book. Richard Proenneke's exquisite photographs and his graphic day-by-day account of his adventures reveal his sensitivity to and appreciation for all forms of nature.

Robertson, Dougal. **Survive the Savage Sea.** Bantam 1974.

When the Robertson family decides to take a pleasure cruise on the schooner "Lucette," they have no idea what is going to happen before they complete that trip. The "Lucette" is attacked by killer whales, and all six of the family have to survive on a small raft and lifeboat. With a lot of determination, very little fresh water, and ten days' supply of food, they try to find land. They learn many techniques of survival.

Steele, William O. **The Old Wilderness Road: An American Journey.** HarBraceJ 1968.

This is the story of the Old Wilderness Road, but especially, the story of the four men who made the road in Virginia: Thomas Walker, Daniel Boone, Elisha Wallen, and John Filson. The author has used journals and other contemporary sources for his book, and supplemented it with maps.

Wilkinson, Burke, editor. **Cry Sabotage!** Bradbury Pr 1972.

Here are twenty-seven true stories about acts of sab-

otage. Most of them take place in the twentieth
century; they range from the sinking of the *U.S.S.
Maine* (which led to United States' declaration of war
on Spain in 1898) to more recent acts of sabotage,
such as those in the Vietnam War.

Wilkinson, Burke, editor. **Cry Spy!** Bradbury Pr 1969.

Every major country has secret agents operating during
war and peacetime. Here are the stories of over two
dozen twentieth-century spies and their techniques.
The characters include the well-known Mata Hari and
the unknown German "sleeper spies" in World War I
Britain. There are also stories about the infamous
Soviet espionage ring that stole the secret plans for the
atomic bomb.

American leaders

Alvarez, Joseph A. **Vice-Presidents of Destiny.** Putnam
1969.

An account of the lives and achievements of the eight
U.S. vice-presidents who, as a result of Presidents'
deaths, became our leaders.

Archer, Jules. **Front Line General: Douglas MacArthur.**
Messner 1963.

Douglas MacArthur was a boy genius inspired by his
father, a career military man, and by his mother,
who convinced him he was going to be the greatest
MacArthur. His life at West Point, his work as a
military aide to President Theodore Roosevelt and
later as Army Chief of Staff are described in this book.
Included also is the controversy occurring after the end
of the war in the Pacific, when, as Head of the Occupation Forces, MacArthur was reluctant to heed the
authority of the President of the U.S.

Archer, Jules. **The Unpopular Ones.** Macmillan 1968.

The lives of several Americans whose ideas were unpopular in their day are described. John Peter Zenger,
Thomas Paine, Horace Greeley, Henry David Thoreau,
Amelia Bloomer, Eugene Debs, Woodrow Wilson, Margaret Sanger, Robert Oppenheimer, J. William Fulbright, Ann Royal, Joseph Palmer, Jonathan Walker,
and Bethenia Owens.

Armstrong, William H. **The Education of Abraham
Lincoln.** Coward 1974.

In this historical biography, the world of Lincoln is

recreated. The influences of Lincoln's life are described—the various kinds of schools with the different teaching methods, such as the "blab school" and Caleb Hazel's school; the philosophy of listening to learn; the books Lincoln read; and the superstitions of the period.

Brookter, Marie (with Jean Curtis). **Here I Am, Take My Hand.** Har-Row 1974.

Marie Brookter, born in Louisiana to a poor black family, was the only one of the twelve children to be educated beyond high school. In her childhood, she feared white people. Her cousin Lester interested her in civil rights work and politics for black people. After Lester was shot for trying to register to vote, Marie dedicated herself to the black cause. She worked in five presidential campaigns, including those for John F. Kennedy, Lyndon B. Johnson, and George McGovern. The black TV shows she has worked on have received several Emmys. She is a true communicator between black and white views.

Buckmaster, Henrietta. **Women Who Shaped History.** Macmillan 1966.

To change prisons, medicine, education, slavery, and religion, women pioneers fought at least one common enemy—the inferior status nineteenth-century America assigned to females. This book tells about six heroines every student of American history should know: Dorothea Dix, Prudence Crandall, Elizabeth Cady Stanton, Elizabeth Blackwell, Harriet Tubman, Mary Baker Eddy. They accomplished their work in spite of limited opportunities.

Burt, Olive W. **First Woman Editor: Sarah J. Hale.** Messner 1960.

This biography tells how Sarah Hale, as editor of the first magazine for women, promoted women's rights, encouraged the development of machines to make housework lighter, and crusaded for the preservation and building of national monuments.

Burt, Olive W. **Physician to the World: Esther Pohl Lovejoy.** Messner 1973.

Determined to become a doctor, Esther Pohl Lovejoy hid bones under a pile of ladies' underwear in the store where she worked, bringing them out to study when no one was looking. Esther's work as a doctor and as director of the American Hospital Service took her to many parts of the world.

Cook, Fred J. **The Demagogues.** Macmillan 1972.

The book discusses first "What is a demagogue?" then the causes and effects of demagoguery. People and events of various periods in U.S. history are described: the Salem witch-hunt and Samuel Parris; the Civil War, with William Lloyd Garrison and William Lowndes Yancy; the attack on Catholics by Lyman Beecher, Samuel F. B. Morse, and Anna Carroll; the modern period, with Huey Long, Father Coughlin, and Joseph McCarthy.

Davis, Daniel S. **Marcus Garvey.** Watts 1972.

Marcus Garvey, born in Jamaica and descended from escaped slaves, spent his life pursuing a dream of improving the lives of black people and inspiring them to return to Africa to set up an independent nation. Arriving in the U.S. in 1916, he developed his idea of a Universal Negro Improvement Association, starting a weekly newspaper to promote racial pride and self-help among impoverished blacks. He launched a steamship company financed by stock holdings of black people. Financial mismanagement ruined the steamship line and brought Garvey a prison term. Though he did not live to see independent nations spring up in Africa, his ideas influenced such organizations as today's Black Muslims, with their emphasis on business enterprise and black pride.

Davis, Daniel S. **Mr. Black Labor: The Story of A. Philip Randolph, Father of the Civil Rights Movement.** Dutton 1972.

Asa Philip Randolph, son of a southern minister, learned early of the injustices the blacks suffered and the courage needed to bring them racial freedom, social justice, and economic equality. This biography tells how, as a young man, Randolph went to New York for an education, accepted socialism as a way to help the blacks, started a newspaper, *The Messenger*, and worked at many jobs. He brought blacks into the labor movement in the twenties and thirties and organized the civil rights movement in spite of powerful opposition.

Epstein, Perle. **Individuals All.** CCPr Macmillan 1972.

Seven Americans, all nonconformists, are described:

poets Emily Dickinson and Walt Whitman; Henry David Thoreau, the writer and philosopher; Isadora Duncan, the dancer; Thomas Merton, a Trappist monk, poet, philosopher, mystic, and peace advocate; Dick Gregory, comedian and social critic; and the Brook Farm Commune, a group that tried to create a Utopia in the nineteenth century. The contributions of each to society and quotations from each individual are stressed.

Faber, Doris. **Oh, Lizzie! The Life of Elizabeth Cady Stanton.** Archway 1974.

Elizabeth Cady Stanton, one of the first leaders of the women's rights movement in America, began her campaign for equal rights as a child, hoping desperately to please her father as much as her dead brother had. Through her determination, she was allowed to enter an almost exclusively boys' school, and became dedicated to spreading the philosophy of equal rights to women of every class. Only years after her death was the Nineteenth Amendment to the Constitution passed.

Fleming, Alice. **The Senator from Maine: Margaret Chase Smith.** T Y Crowell 1969.

Mrs. Smith was drawn to politics as the wife of a congressman; ultimately she became the only woman to serve in both houses of the United States Congress.

Fleming, Thomas. **Benjamin Franklin.** Schol Bk Serv 1972.

The long life of Benjamin Franklin is the subject of this book. It also includes much information about Franklin's family: his son William who became governor of New Jersey and remained loyal to the king of England during the American Revolution, his wife, his daughter, and his grandson. Franklin retired from business at forty-two, and dedicated the rest of his life to science and to his country.

Gibson, William. **American Primitive.** Bantam 1974.

The actual words of Abigail and John Adams are taken from their diaries and letters and arranged as a play. John is absent from home for years serving the new country during the revolution and the writing of the Constitution. Abigail runs the farm and the family.

Gilfond, Henry. **Heroines of America.** Fleet 1970.

The lives of thirty-four courageous American women of the eighteenth, nineteenth, and twentieth centuries are described briefly. The hardships and contributions of the following women are highlighted: Elizabeth Blackwell, Clara Barton, Jane Addams, Lillian Wald, Harriet Tubman, Sojourner Truth, Mary McLeod Bethune, Helen Keller, Margaret Sanger, Eleanor Roosevelt, Amelia Earhart, Mildred Didrickson Zaharias, Margaret Chase Smith, Shirley Chisholm, Phillis Wheatley, Julia Ward Howe, Harriet Beecher Stowe, Pearl Buck, Rachel Carson, Maude Adams, Ethel Barrymore, Minnie Fisk, Katharine Cornell, Marian Anderson, Georgia O'Keefe, Margaret Bourke-White, Marie Mitchell, and Coretta King.

Graham, Shirley. **Booker T. Washington.** Messner 1955.

The life story of the pioneering black educator, Booker T. Washington. The experiences and struggles of black families emerging from slavery are portrayed through the story of Washington's family. Booker T. was the first in his family to go to school. The book shares his insight into the importance of books, learning, schooling, education.

Graves, Charles P. **Eleanor Roosevelt.** Dell 1968.

This is a clear, concise, easy-to-read biography of Eleanor Roosevelt, beginning with her youth and telling of her marriage to Franklin Roosevelt, who later became President, and her later years.

Green, Margaret. **Defender of the Constitution: Andrew Johnson.** Messner 1962.

Born into poverty in North Carolina the son of uneducated parents, Johnson learned tailoring at the age of twelve, taught himself to read, and became a student of American history. Moving into Tennessee, he succeeded as a tailor and was elected to state and national political offices. He championed the cause of the poor and the working people and defended the Constitution. Upholding his beliefs, he withstood a trial of impeachment and preserved the Union.

Green, Margaret. **President of the Confederacy: Jefferson Davis.** Messner 1963.

The book gives the life story of Jefferson Davis. A soldier, congressman, secretary of war, and senator

loyal to the South, he showed outstanding courage
and ability in establishing a confederate government
in perilous times and raising an army that fought
heroically.

Gridley, Marion E. **American Indian Women.** Hawthorn
1974.

This book contains the stories of eighteen prominent
Indian women who made significant contributions to
their people and their country. Included are such
women as Sacajawea, guide for the Lewis and Clark
Expedition, and Susan La Flesch Picotte, the first
Indian woman physician.

Hamilton, Virginia. **W. E. B. DuBois: A Biography.**
T Y Crowell 1972.

This is the story of W. E. B. DuBois' life and development as a black leader. His adherence to the
principle of black separatism brought him in conflict
even with other black leaders. His conflict with what
he considered the "Uncle Tomism" of Booker T.
Washington is thoroughly explored and explained.

Haskins, Jim. **Ralph Bunche: A Political Analysis.**
Hawthorn 1974.

The life of Ralph Bunche, who rose above poverty
and racial discrimination to succeed in school as a
scholar and athlete, and as an American leader in
the United Nations and winner of the Nobel Peace
Prize. This book describes the life of a modest,
intelligent, unselfish, kind, and hardworking American
statesman.

Hawke, David Freeman. **Paine.** Har-Row 1974.

Thomas Paine was a fierce lover of liberty and contributed his genius to both America and France
during their revolutions. A man with several countries
and no country, Paine was exiled from England for
writing *The Rights of Man*. This is a colorful and
thorough biography.

Ipsen, D. C. **Eye of the Whirlwind: The Story of John
Scopes.** A-W 1973.

This book is more than the story of a Kentucky boy,
son of a railroad mechanic, who grew up in Illinois,
graduated from the University of Kentucky, became a
teacher in Dayton, Tennessee, and later an oil geologist. The book tells the dramatic story of the teacher

who was the center of the Tennessee Evolution Trial,
with William Jennings Bryan and Clarence Darrow
battling to determine whether a teacher "could teach
any theory that denies the story of the Divine Creation
of man as taught in the Bible and teach instead that
man had descended from a lower order of animals."

Johnson, Dorothy M. **Warrior for a Lost Nation: A
Biography of Sitting Bull.** Westminster 1969.

The Sioux boy called Slow became Sitting Bull,
eloquent leader and great warrior of the Plains Indians,
in their hopeless struggle against the encroaching
white man.

Kane, Joseph Nathan. **Facts about the Presidents.** PB
1968.

Vital statistics, important career dates, election information, and significant national and international
events for each president from George Washington to
Lyndon Johnson are presented in itemized form.

Khan, Lurey. **One Day, Levin . . . He Be Free.** Dutton
1972.

William Still was a fearless fighter for slaves running
away from the South. Son of Levin Still, who had
bought his freedom, and a mother who had run away,
William Still became the executive secretary of Philadelphia's Anti-Slavery Society. He kept accurate and
detailed records of runaway slaves and took an active
leadership role in the Underground Railroad. From
his records he published in 1872 *The Underground
Railroad.* From that book came this biography and
history, which includes Levin's work and the letters,
newspaper clippings, and records related to the slave
problem.

Lader, Lawrence, and Milton Meltzer. **Margaret Sanger:
Pioneer of Birth Control.** Dell 1974.

From her girlhood in the early 1900s, Margaret Sanger
was aware of and sensitive to the miseries of people
in the slums of New York. This biography tells
how, with courage and intelligence, she sought ways to
aid these people. For fifty years she crusaded for
Planned Parenthood throughout the world.

Leipold, L. Edmond. **Famous American Teachers.** Denison 1972.

This book tells the stories of ten American men

and women teachers who influenced other people's lives through their courage—in overcoming obstacles of racial prejudice, lack of money, and physical handicaps—and introduced new and unpopular ideas: William McGuffey, author of pioneer readers; Booker T. Washington, founder of Tuskegee Institute; Horace Mann, founder of the American public education system; Emma Hart Willard, founder of the first women's college; Mary Lyon, founder of Mount Holyoke College for Women; Martha Berry, founder of a school in the Georgia hills; John Dewey, a believer in experiment in the classroom; James Bryant Conant, advocate of individual freedom; Mary McLeod Bethune, founder of the Daytona (Florida) Educational and Industrial Training School for Negro Girls later known as Bethune-Cookman College; and Anne Sullivan Macy, Helen Keller's teacher.

Leipold, L. Edmond. **Famous American Women.** Denison 1967.

The book presents the life stories of ten women who contributed to America's growth and greatness, from the American Revolution to the twentieth century: Willa Cather, writer; Molly Pitcher, heroine of the American Revolution; Susan B. Anthony, suffragette leader; Sacajawea, Indian guide to the Lewis and Clark Expedition; Martha Washington, wife of the General and President of U.S.; Elizabeth Peabody, founder of kindergartens in the U.S.; Emily Dickinson, poet; Clara Barton, founder of the American Red Cross; Emma Lazarus, writer; Amelia Earhart, aviatrix; and Dolly Madison, wife of a U.S. President and heroine of the White House.

Levine, Israel E. **Young Man in the White House: John Fitzgerald Kennedy.** Messner 1964.

John F. Kennedy's life story shows a hard-working man, courageous, concerned about others, and determined to help them. The book describes his family and its influence, his schooling, his experiences in World War II, and his political career.

Lomask, Milton. **This Slender Reed: A Life of James K. Polk.** FS&G 1966.

From his humble origins on a Tennessee frontier farm to his position as eleventh president of the United States, James Knox Polk gave a life of service and hard work to his country. This is the story of his life.

Martin. Ralph G. **President from Missouri: Harry S Truman.** Messner 1973.

This is the story of a man who is shown as a loyal, cocky, outspoken, tough, honest, and courageous leader. The book describes Harry S Truman's early years in rural Missouri, his years in service in World War I, his struggle in a clothing store in Kansas City, his rise in politics, and his achievements as a leader of our country.

Myers, Elisabeth P. **Madam Secretary: Frances Perkins.** Messner 1972.

After devoting most of her life to improving conditions for working women, Frances Perkins was appointed Secretary of Labor in President Franklin Roosevelt's administration—the first woman cabinet member in the history of the U.S. This biography tells how her design for labor programs helped to pull the country out of the Depression.

Oakley, Mary Ann B. **Elizabeth Cady Stanton.** Feminist Pr 1972.

A biography of Elizabeth Cady Stanton, the first American to suggest in public that women should have the vote. She wrote the "Declaration of Sentiments" for the Seneca Falls convention of 1848; it began, "We hold these truths to be self-evident, that all men and women are created equal."

O'Connor, Richard. **Sitting Bull: War Chief of the Sioux.** McGraw 1968.

Sitting Bull is one of the most famous Indian tribal chiefs and warriors. This story tells of his concerns, his struggles, his strategies for battle, as he tries to keep the Sioux tribes from losing their land and their heritage to the white man.

Orrmont, Arthur. **The Amazing Alexander Hamilton.** Messner 1964.

This book relates the life of Alexander Hamilton from his early years in the Dutch West Indies. It describes his college days in the American colonies, his influence as a brilliant orator and aide to George Washington, his heroic action in the American Revolution, his leadership in ratifying the Constitution, his founding of the fiscal system of our government and finally, his death in a duel by a political opponent, Aaron Burr.

Ortiz, Victoria. **Sojourner Truth: A Self-Made Woman.** Lippincott 1974.

Sojourner Truth, a slave born in North Carolina in 1797, preached about slavery, women's rights, and Christianity. This biography tells how she eventually went to Washington, D.C., where President Lincoln gave her an important role as counselor to freed slaves living in the city.

Powell, Adam Clayton, Jr. **Adam by Adam.** Dial 1971.

Adam Clayton Powell, Jr., tells the story of his rise in politics and reveals many equally colorful details of his personal life. We see him as the carefully reared only son, a student at Colgate, a Harlem minister and fiery leader, and a member of the U.S. House of Representatives. He also tells his side of his expulsion from Congress. Finally he presents his outlook for the future of black America.

Shulman, Alix. **To the Barricades: The Anarchist Life of Emma Goldman.** T Y Crowell 1971.

Emma Goldman emigrated to the U.S. from Russia in 1885. Spurred on by the death of the anarchists accused of inciting Chicago's Haymarket Riot, she decided to dedicate her life to fighting for anarchism. This biography describes how Emma was arrested many times for exercising her freedom of speech by lecturing on anarchism and the revolt of women, and was finally stripped of her U.S. citizenship and deported to Russia in 1919.

Suhl, Yuri. **Eloquent Crusader: Ernestine Rose.** Messner 1970.

In 1836, it took Ernestine Rose five months of trudging through the snow and knocking on doors to obtain five signatures on a petition for the Married Woman's Property Bill. Undaunted by this beginning, Ernestine Rose devoted her life to obtain rights for women and freedom for slaves.

Swados, Harvey. **Standing Up for the People: The Life and Work of Estes Kefauver.** Dutton 1972.

Estes Kefauver was a sensitive, gentle boy who grew up to be a fearless senator from Tennessee. This biography tells how he used obstacles as stepping stones to success and fought for the little man of all races. He led investigations of big business monopolies, the drug industry, and underworld crime. He sup-

ported the Tennessee Valley Authority, school de-
segregation, and civil rights.

Vestal, Stanley. **Sitting Bull: Champion of the Sioux.**
U of Okla Pr 1972.

Begins with the boy-volunteer called "Slow" and ends
with great chief's death because he refused to be captured. Picture of a wise, independent, and very human
man. Walter Stanley Campbell, whose pseudonym is
Stanley Vestal, has written widely about the West; he
researched records and interviewed friends and family
of Sitting Bull. Vestal is sympathetic to his subject.
The Gallup *Book List,* an Indian publication, called
this book a "stirring account of the death throes of a
mighty nation and its leader who became known as
the man who killed Custer."

Yates, Elizabeth. **Prudence Crandall: Woman of Courage.** Dutton 1955.

Running a boarding school for girls in the 1800s wasn't
easy, but Prudence Crandall found it was even harder
when the school was for black girls. Nothing stopped
her, however, not even broken windows and being
thrown in jail.

Athletes

Axthelm, Pete. **The City Game.** PB 1971.

This is the New York Knicks' story, personifying basketball at its best. New York loves the game, from
the young children in the streets to the national championship team. Big stars like Willis Reed, Walt Frazier, Dave DeBusschere, and others take part in some
exciting and important games. We begin to understand the mystique of "the city game."

Brennan, Joe. **Duke Kahanamoku: Hawaii's Golden
Man.** Hogarth 1973.

This is the story of Duke Kahanamoku, a legend in
his own time—Olympic gold medal swimmer, champion surfer, actor in the silent movies, and Sheriff of
Honolulu. Young surfers will especially enjoy pictures
of the Duke with his gigantic surfboard.

Butler, Hal. **Sports Heroes Who Wouldn't Quit.** Messner
1973.

A collection of short biographical sketches about sports
heroes who had handicaps of different kinds or were

members of minority groups. They include Jackie Robinson, Johnny Unitas, Gertrude Ederle, and Pete Gray, a one-armed outfielder. These are stories of people who succeeded against great odds.

Gibson, Bob (with Phil Pepe). **From Ghetto to Glory: The Story of Bob Gibson.** Popular Lib 1969.

This is Bob Gibson's life story. He writes about all the things that stood in the way of his becoming a great pitcher: being poor, being sickly, and being black. He also tells about some of the most important games he pitched and some of the best batters he faced.

Gutman, Bill. **New Breed Heroes in Pro Baseball.** Messner 1974.

All twelve of these superstars are highly individualistic. Yet the author shows us what players like Nolan Ryan, Johnny Bench, and Vida Blue have in common. They are men who worked hard to overcome hardships and personal tragedy to become stars.

Gutman, Bill. **New Breed Heroes of Pro Football.** Messner 1973.

Here are brief sketches of the lives of twelve pro football superheroes. Included in the sketches are descriptions of the players' most outstanding football games. The author tries to show how each player has added new excitement to the game of football.

Hano, Arnold. **Roberto Clemente: Batting King.** Dell 1973.

Roberto Clemente overcame racial prejudice to become a great baseball player. His talent and hard work helped him to make three thousand hits. The book describes his career and his projects to help other people have happier and more successful lives.

Hirshberg, Al. **Henry Aaron: Quiet Superstar.** Putnam 1969.

This book details the life of Hank Aaron, who was born in a ghetto in Mobile, Alabama, and pursued a career in baseball.

King, Billie Jean, and Kim Chapin. **Billie Jean.** Har-Row 1974.

Billie Jean King tells of her active tennis life, from receiving her first tennis racquet to becoming the number one female tennis player in the world. She describes the difficulties and pressures of the game and the practice necessary to become a champion. Billie Jean talks about tennis from her point of view as a pro.

Leipold, L. Edmond. **Famous American Athletes.** Denison 1969.

The lives of eight men and two women athletes are described. Each famous athlete had obstacles to overcome. Using his or her special abilities and working hard, each person excelled in one sport: Bob Feller, baseball pitcher; Joe Louis, boxer; "Babe" Ruth, baseball hitter; Bill Tilden, tennis player; Johnny Weissmuller, swimmer; Bobby Jones, golfer; Bob Mathias, decathlon winner and all-around outstanding athlete; Carol Heiss Jenkins, ice skater; Jack Dempsey, boxer; and Shirley Garms, bowler.

Libby, Bill. **Heroes of the Heisman Trophy.** Hawthorn 1973.

This book gives the history of the Heisman Trophy, a brief account of many of the thirty-eight winners and runners-up, with high points in their football careers, and comments of sports writers and broadcasters. Heisman Trophy voting results from 1935 through 1972 are listed.

Libby, Bill. **O. J.: The Story of Football's Fabulous O. J. Simpson.** Putnam 1974.

Rising from a San Francisco ghetto O. J. Simpson became the star of a national championship football team at the University of Southern California and the winner of the Heisman Trophy and the National Football League's Player of the Year Award. This book describes O. J.'s experiences in his many games.

Libby, Bill. **Parnelli: A Story of Auto Racing.** Dutton 1969.

The story of the 1963 Indianapolis 500 winner is presented here for racing enthusiasts.

Liss, Howard. **Hockey's Greatest All-Stars.** Hawthorn 1972.

Howard Liss selects twelve hockey stars and places them on two teams. He describes these players from their beginnings in hockey through their professional careers and their most exciting experiences in hockey.

On the first team are Gordie Howe, Bobby Hull, Jean
Beliveau, Eddie Shore, Doug Harvey, and Terry Saw-
chuk. For the second team the author picks Maurice
"Rockett" Richard, Ted Lindsay, Stan Mikita, Bobby
Orr, Leonard Patrick, "Red" Kelly, and Jacques Plante.

Morris, Jeannie. **Brian Piccolo: A Short Season.** Dell
1972.

This book is written in part by Brian Piccolo, the football star, and was finished after his death by Jeannie
Morris, the wife of Brian Piccolo's friend, Johnnie
Morris. The career and character of the football
player who died at twenty-six from cancer are described. His fighting spirit on the football field and
in the hospital and his genuine concern for others
are shown in this biography.

Palmer, Arnold (with William Barry Furlong). **Go for
Broke!** S&S 1973.

Arnold Palmer tells about his whole life in golf: hardships, fame, personal traits, great tournaments, and
hints about the game. His philosophy in golf is to
win by thinking boldly and taking chances. He gives
the thoughts and ideas that come to him while actually playing golf, and how he overcame his problems
and difficulties.

Pepe, Phil. **Stand Tall: The Lew Alcindor Story.** G&D
1970.

Anyone who is seven feet one-and-three-eighths inches
tall is bound to cause a sensation. But when that person also plays basketball, leads UCLA to three consecutive national championships, and goes pro for the
astounding amount of one and a quarter million dollars, only to take the Rookie of the Year award—well,
that is a sensation. But there is another side to this
famous black athlete, a side proud to be black, proud
of his African heritage, and concerned with the role
of blacks in America today.

Peters, Alexander. **Heroes of the Major Leagues.** Random 1967.

The book consists of brief biographies of Frank Robinson, Roberto Clemente, Sandy Koufax, Harmon
Killebrew, Juan Marichal, Hank Aaron, Al Kaline,
Tony Oliva, Joe Torre, Brooks Robinson. Good
photographs.

Plimpton, George. **One for the Record.** Har-Row 1974.

This book describes what Hank Aaron went through as he was nearing Babe Ruth's home run record. The book tells of attempts on Aaron's life as he neared the record. It also tells of opposing pitchers' feelings about Aaron.

Robinson, Jackie (with Alfred Duckett). **I Never Had It Made.** Fawcett World 1974.

Jackie Robinson was the first black player in major league baseball. He had fame, money, awards, and yet he still felt like a black man in a white world. Here is the Jackie Robinson story as Jackie Robinson sees it. Not only a baseball story, it is also the story of great courage and determination, of a man who wanted something better for himself and his people. Coretta Scott King Award.

Wagenheim, Kal. **Clemente!** WSP 1974.

Roberto Clemente was a major league baseball star known to millions. But there was much more. Kal Wagenheim traces Clemente's life, from his childhood in Puerto Rico to his extraordinary career with the Pittsburgh Pirates. But the thing we'll all remember most is his tragic death in a plane crash while traveling to Nicaragua to help the earthquake victims.

Williams, Billy (with Rick Simon). **Iron Man.** Childrens 1970.

Billy Williams Day was one of the biggest thrills of Billy Williams' life. It made him think back on how he became what he was, a major league baseball star. He reflects on the racial prejudice he met in his baseball career, the excitement of getting into the minor leagues, and the thrill of knowing he had made it in the majors. Information on the life of a professional athlete is provided.

Scientists

Bigland, Eileen. **Madame Curie.** S G Phillips 1957.

This biography of Eve Curie includes her childhood, her life as a student in Paris, her fame after discovering radium, and her contributions during World War I. Madame Curie was not only a scientist but also an ardent Polish patriot, a devoted wife and mother, and a citizen of France. She experienced discrimination because of her sex and her place of birth.

Boesen, Victor. **William P. Lear: From High School Dropout to Space Age Inventor.** Hawthorn 1974.

This life story of Bill Lear shows the family friction in his boyhood, his early interest in wireless and electricity, his improvisations, his leaving school and inventing new devices such as the first automobile radio, a number of aircraft navigational aids, the Lear jet, and the experimental steam-turbine-powered automobile.

Briggs, Peter. **Men in the Sea.** S&S 1968.

This book gives short biographies of nine men who made important contributions to the scientific study of the seas. It describes many of the now-famous experiments which first allowed man to live for days at hundreds of feet below the ocean's surface. The importance of the oceans is clearly shown, as well as their potential for future exploration and development.

Crawford, Deborah. **Lise Meitner, Atomic Pioneer.** Crown 1969.

In 1906 few women were atomic scientists; Lise, however, became the scientist whose part in the discovery of nuclear fission helped bring about the atomic bomb.

Esterer, Arnulf K. **Discoverer of X-Ray: Wilhelm Conrad Roentgen.** Messner 1968.

Roentgen discovered this short-wave ray, which provided an invaluable tool for medicine, laboratory research, art, and industry. In 1901 he was awarded the Nobel Prize for this achievement.

Garst, Shannon, and Warren Garst. **Ernest Thompson Seton: Naturalist.** Messner 1959.

The life of Ernest Thompson Seton, who overcame many obstacles to become an outstanding naturalist, writer, illustrator, painter of wild life, and organizer of the Woodcraft Indians, later known as the Boy Scouts of America. He struggled against the opposition of his father to his selecting a career as a naturalist; against lack of money for publishing his animal stories, and eventually against blindness, after he had started selling his stories.

Glines, Carroll V. **Jimmy Doolittle: Daredevil Aviator and Scientist.** Macmillan 1972.

This story presents Doolittle's adventurous and colorful

life, from his birth in 1896 through his entire career as one of the earliest aviators and one of the first persons earning a doctorate in aeronautical engineering. As a stunt-speed aviator, he won many trophies. In World War II he served as commander of the Tokyo Raiders and commander-in-chief of the Air Forces in North Africa and of the Eighth Air Force in the Normandy invasion.

Halacy, Dan. **Charles Babbage: Father of the Computer.** Macmillan 1970.

Charles Babbage is pictured as a tireless worker during his eighty years. Although he was the father of the computer, his continuous attacks on many persons, from governmental leaders to organ grinders, kept him from further developing and receiving credit for the computer.

Hoyt, Mary Finch. **American Women of the Space Age.** Atheneum 1969.

This book tells the stories of the many women who have helped to advance the exploration of outer space through their study of gravity, fuels, noise, and aerodynamics.

McKown, Robin. **Giant of the Atom: Ernest Rutherford.** Messner 1962.

Ernest Rutherford has led the world in major discoveries about the atom and radioactivity. This book tells about his early life in a large New Zealand family, his education in England, his experiments, discoveries, and honors, and his work with other eminent scientists.

Siedel, Frank, and James M. Siedel. **Pioneers in Science.** HM 1968.

The lives of forty-eight important scientific figures are presented in portraits that illustrate scientific development over 2,000 years.

Squire, C. B. **Heroes of Conservation.** Fleet 1973.

Using the life stories of the men most involved in America's conservation efforts, Squire tells the goals and accomplishments of yesterday's and today's conservation movement. The author shows us the personal struggles of these men in their efforts to save the environment.

Sterling, Philip. **Sea and Earth: The Life of Rachel Carson.** Dell 1974.

The life of a famous twentieth-century biologist and writer. Rachel Carson was determined to succeed in college although she had little money for an education. She was recognized early for her writing ability, her sensitivity to nature and concern for ecology. Pursuing science as a career, she combined her literary talent with her scientific findings to awaken the world to the widespread destruction of the natural environment. Christopher Award Children's Book Category.

Stoiko, Michael. **Pioneers of Rocketry.** Hawthorn 1974.

Five men who pioneered in rocketry are described— William Congreve of England, who developed in the early nineteenth century the first barrage rockets; Konstantin Tsiolkovsky of Russia, who furthered the principle of jet propulsion; Robert Esnault-Pelterie of France, who designed a liquid-propellant rocket engine; Robert Goddard of the United States, who was the first to prove a rocket would work in a vacuum; Hermann Oberth of Germany, who designed a rocket combustion chamber and cone nozzle. Included are a history of rockets and ideas about the future of rocketry.

Sullivan, Navin. **Pioneer Astronomers.** Atheneum 1964.

This book tells the progress man has made through the years in exploring the universe. The contributions of pioneer astronomers show how each man helped the others after him make new discoveries. The work of these astronomers is described: Copernicus, Kepler, Galileo, Newton, Herschel, Bessel, Adams, Leverrier, Frainhofer and Kirchoff, Huggins, Shapley and Hertzsprung, Hubble, Jansky and Reber, and Smith and Baade.

World figures

Apsler, Alfred. **Vive de Gaulle: The Story of Charles de Gaulle.** Messner 1973.

Even as a young man, de Gaulle was an idealist with a great love for his country, France. This biography tells how he worked courageously to be a leader, first in military positions in World Wars I and II, later as head of the Provisional Government after World War

II, and finally as prime minister and president of the Fifth Republic.

Archer, Jules. **African Firebrand: Kenyatta of Kenya.** Messner 1969.

The book describes the rise and work of an influential leader in the new Africa. Jomo Kenyatta, as an African shepherd boy, respected tribal tradition. As a student in England, he prepared himself to help the people of Kenya. As a patriot, he returned to his country to bring it together after the colonial government had failed.

Archer, Jules. **Ho Chi Minh: Legend of Hanoi.** CCPR Macmillan 1971.

Son of a revolutionary Indochinese, Ho Chi Minh grew up a dedicated communist always fighting for an independent Vietnam. This book describes Ho's life, from his peasant boyhood to jobs as a galley hand on a French ship, a pastry cook in London, a waiter in New York. It tells how he finally became the most powerful man in North Vietnam.

Archer, Jules. **Red Rebel: Tito of Yugoslavia.** Messner 1968.

This biography of Tito shows how poverty and injustices in his life led him to communism. It describes Tito's life as a prisoner of the Russians in World War I, his heroic leadership of Yugoslavian troops—ill-equipped and ill-fed—against the Nazis in World War II, and his courageous and independent action of establishing a socialist and communist state independent of Russia.

Archer, Jules. **Trotsky: World Revolutionary.** Messner 1973.

This book describes the rise of Trotsky, an intelligent, arrogant, stubborn man with a vision of a United States of Soviet Republics. It shows Trotsky's leadership in the 1905 and 1917 revolutions in Russia, his battle with Stalin, and his exile.

Bigland, Eileen. **Helen Keller.** S G Phillips 1967.

Before she was two years old, Helen Keller was left blind and deaf from a mysterious illness. This biography tells how, with the help of a teacher, Anne Sullivan, Helen overcame her handicaps and devoted her life to helping others who were blind and deaf.

Carlson, Dale. **The Beggar King of China.** Atheneum 1971.

When Chu Yuan-chang buries his parents and brother, who starved to death, he decides that China must be rid of its Mongol rulers. First he enters a monastery to get an education; then he joins the Red Turbans, the rebel bandits. Finally, in 1368, he becomes the Beggar King, Emperor of All China and founder of the Ming dynasty.

Carlson, Dale. **Warlord of the Genji.** Atheneum 1970.

The Fujiwaras ruled Japan for two centuries with the loyalty of two warrior clans, the Heike and the Genji, who finally turned against each other. Yoshitsune, a young boy, heir to leadership of the Genji, is imprisoned in a monastery without knowing his real identity. When this story begins, his clansmen are helping Yoshitsune escape to lead the Genji's return to power.

Colver, Anne. **Florence Nightingale.** Dell 1966.

The story of Florence Nightingale, whose lifetime dream was to make the world better. She did her part by helping in the Crimean War as a nurse and by starting a nursing school for girls.

de Trevino, Elizabeth Borton. **Juarez: Man of Law.** FS&G 1974.

The story of Mexico's nineteenth-century folk hero. Juarez, a full-blooded Indian, born in 1806, began life as a shepherd boy with an ambition to go to school. He managed to become a law student and worked his way up in politics, becoming a deputy to the Mexican Congress. After opposing the dictator Santa Anna, Juarez was exiled, and took part in a successful plot to overthrow Santa Anna in favor of constitutional government. He became president in 1861. When the French invaded Mexico and put Maximilian on the throne, Juarez led the resistance. Throughout his career, he worked to rid Mexico of feudal injustices.

Graff, Stewart, and Polly Anne Graff. **Helen Keller.** Dell 1966.

An account of how Helen Keller, deaf and blind, learned to speak, read, and write with the help of her teacher, Anne Sullivan. After college, Miss Keller went on speaking tours around the world specifically working for schools for blind children.

Harmelink, Barbara. **Florence Nightingale: Founder of Modern Nursing.** Watts 1969.

When Florence Nightingale became interested in nursing, her family rejected her. This biography tells of the accomplishments of this nineteenth-century British woman who pioneered in aiding the poor, sick, and wounded.

Keating, Bern. **Chaka, King of the Zulus.** Putnam 1968.

Chaka was born a nobody in southern Africa in 1787 and as a boy, wandered with his disgraced mother from village to village. He grew up to be a military genius who became a mighty king and made the Zulus great and powerful.

Lamb, Beatrice Pitney. **The Nehrus of India: Three Generations of Leadership.** Macmillan 1967.

This book relates the life stories of three courageous and determined Nehrus—the grandfather Motilal; the son Jawaharlal; and the granddaughter Indira Gandhi. It traces the influence of the three on India after it became independent of England.

Ludwig, Emil (translators Eden Paul and Cedar Paul). **Napoleon.** PB 1973.

By combining military genius with political intrigue, Napoleon rose from his birth on the impoverished island of Corsica in 1769 to become Emperor of France. Focusing on the intelligence and egotism which gave Napoleon his power over others, the author retells the political intrigues, love affairs, and battles of the Nile, Moscow, and Waterloo which ended in Napoleon's exile and death on the island of St. Helena in 1821.

Mann, Peggy. **Golda: The Life of Israel's Prime Minister.** Coward 1971.

A biography of Golda Meir—her early years in Russia, her school years in Milwaukee, her move to Palestine with her husband, Morris Myerson, her home life with her children, her government work. It is also the story of the Jews during this century and the history of the nation of Israel.

McNeer, May, and Lynd Ward. **Armed with Courage.** Abingdon 1957.

This book recounts the lives of seven selfless persons who had dreams to help others and the courage to

make the dreams come true: Florence Nightingale;
Father Damien; George Washington Carver; Jane Addams; Wilfred Grenfell; Mahatma Gandhi; and Albert
Schweitzer.

Morris, Terry. **Shalom, Golda.** Hawthorn 1971.

This biography of Golda Meir takes her from her childhood home in Russia to her position as prime minister
of Israel. Even before Golda and her husband leave
the United States to live in a kibbutz in Palestine,
Golda has become effective in public speaking, a talent
that leads her into many positions with the government
of the new state of Israel.

Noble, Iris. **Israel's Golda Meir: Pioneer to Prime Minister.** Messner 1974.

Golda Meir left the United States to work on a farm
in an underdeveloped country that later became Israel.
Golda did whatever she could for Israel: smuggling
Jews into the country, participating in hunger protests,
rallying support for Israel on speaking engagements in
the United States. She served Israel in many governmental positions, including that of prime minister.

Nolan, Jeannette C. **Florence Nightingale.** Messner
1947.

Dying British soldiers in the Crimea stirred Florence
Nightingale to lead a group of nurses to Scutari in
1854. Following the war, she worked continuously for
reform in health and sanitation for England. Her
Nightingale Training School for nurses became the
blueprint for nursing schools throughout the world.

Paine, Albert Bigelow. **The Girl in White Armor.** Macmillan 1967.

Using authentic records, Albert B. Paine presents the
story of the courageous medieval French leader, Joan
of Arc, from her early childhood when she heard
voices, to her search for a king to lead France against
English invaders, her imprisonment, torture, excommunication as a heretic, her trial and execution.

Reed, Gwendolyn. **The Beginnings.** Atheneum 1971.

In this collective biography are stories of the childhoods of these famous men: Benvenuto Cellini,
Michael de Montaigne, Johann Dietz, William Hutton,
Francois Rene de Chateaubriand, Samuel Langhorne
Clemens, Tomas O'Crohan, and Alfred Kazin.

Yolen, Jane. **Friend: The Story of George Fox and the Quakers.** Seabury 1972.

George Fox was the founder of a religious group called Quakers. This story of his life tells how he was often imprisoned because of his beliefs. His belief in the Inner Light present in everyone led to a Quaker belief in equality of sexes and nationalities. Fox refused to join Cromwell's army, to take oaths, to remove his hat to authority. The book describes his two-year visit to America in 1671.

Zweig, Stefan. **Marie Antoinette.** S&S 1972.

Marie Antoinette was a notorious figure in eighteenth century France. She was married to Louis XVI of France to improve the Austrian-French alliance, and was somewhat unpopular on this basis alone. But as the seeds of the French Revolution grew, the queen was forced into a more dominant role because of the inactivity of her husband. Though several powerful people charged she was immoral, Marie Antoinette was a source of courage and unity to the royal family. The situation worsened steadily for her, ending with the guillotine in 1793. This is a fascinating study of one of the most famous women in history.

Writers

Archer, Jules. **Fighting Journalist: Horace Greeley.** Messner 1966.

This book tells of Horace Greeley's rise from printer's devil to big city editor who influenced nearly every aspect of American life.

Baker, Carlos. **Ernest Hemingway: A Life Story.** Bantam 1970.

From his birth in Illinois to his death by his own hand at the age of sixty-one, Ernest Hemingway was a complex and unpredictable man. Having been severely wounded in World War I, he took up journalism as a war correspondent and worked hard at his own writing. The immorality of war, his fascination with the Spanish Civil War, and his own personal sorrows, such as the loss of his wife and child through divorce, all find their way into his powerful novels. Through reading the story of his life, we can begin to understand the man who wrote such classics as *For Whom the Bell*

Tolls, The Sun Also Rises, and *The Old Man and the Sea.* More than fifty photographs.

Banning, Evelyn I. **Helen Hunt Jackson.** Vanguard 1973.

The story shows the courage, individuality, creativeness, and humanitarianism of Helen Fiske Hunt Jackson. Born in Amherst, Massachusetts, the daughter of a professor, she early felt grief in the loss of her mother and in the deaths of her husband and later two sons. To relieve her sorrow she wrote. After she became aware of the tragedy of the Ponce Indian tribe in Nebraska, she devoted her energy to Indian problems, writing *A Century of Dishonor* and *Ramona.*

Block, Irvin. **The Lives of Pearl Buck: A Tale of China and America.** T Y Crowell 1973.

As the daughter of a missionary in China, Pearl Buck adopted the language, customs, and life style of the Chinese. Her upbringing gave her material for her novels, which brought her the Pulitzer Prize and the Nobel Peace Prize for literature.

Brooks, Gwendolyn. **Report from Part One: An Autobiography.** Broadside 1972.

The autobiography of Gwendolyn Brooks, a Pulitzer Prize-winning poet, tells of her struggle to become accepted as a black poet. Twenty-three pages of photographs are included.

Carroll, Sara Newton. **The Search: A Biography of Leo Tolstoy.** Har-Row 1973.

This story of the famous Russian author of *War and Peace,* Leo Tolstoy, is rich in information about Russian customs and history in the nineteenth century. Tolstoy's long career as a writer, his efforts to help the serfs, and his ideas of nonviolence are part of a lifelong search for perfection.

Conn, Frances G. **Ida Tarbell, Muckraker.** Nelson 1972.

The life of a crusading journalist. Born in her grandfather's log cabin in the oil-producing area of Pennsylvania, Ida Tarbell early saw the miseries of economic depression, the effects of a standard oil monopoly on independent oil men such as her father, and the discrimination against women after the passage of the

Fourteenth Amendment to the Constitution. After graduation from college, she became a head mistress at Poland College in Ohio, a member of the staff of the magazine *Chautauquan,* a biographer and historian of Lincoln's life and period, and a journalist with *McClure's* magazine, exposing corruption.

Daughtery, James. **Henry David Thoreau: A Man for Our Times.** Viking Pr 1967.

James Daughtery has collected and illustrated several short selections by Thoreau, one of America's great nineteenth-century writers and individualists. Many of the selections were written during Thoreau's year in the woods near Walden Pond.

de Angeli, Marguerite. **Butter at the Old Price.** Doubleday 1971.

A lively account of a life full of interesting events and people. Marguerite de Angeli tells of the particular places and personalities that inspired her many popular children's books. Her first book was published in 1935, and since then she has written many award-winning stories. The qualities she has been honored for are the same ones that infuse this book—honesty, curiosity, humor, an underlying sense of values, and above all, genuine warmth.

Garst, Shannon. **Jack London: Magnet for Adventure.** Messner 1944.

This biography tells how Jack London's struggle for money, from childhood through his adult life, and his love of adventure led him to seek his fortune on the waterfront and in the gold fields in California, Canada, and Alaska, in Hawaii, Australia, the South Sea Islands, and China. This book describes his adventures, his struggles, and his failures.

Greene, Graham. **A Sort of Life.** S&S 1971.

This is the autobiography of a famous British writer, Graham Greene. He was the son of a schoolmaster, and in his early teens made several clumsy suicide attempts. Psychoanalysis followed, but did not resolve whatever was bothering him, because while at Oxford University he played Russian roulette with a loaded revolver on six separate occasions! Involvement with the secret service began a lifelong interest in the realities of espionage.

Greenfeld, Howard. **Gertrude Stein: A Biography.** Crown 1973.

The biography of an innovative American writer, who moved to Paris after college in 1903 and lived there the rest of her life. Her magnetic personality drew a generation of famous writers and artists to her studio as visitors. Among them were Pablo Picasso, Henri Matisse, and F. Scott Fitzgerald.

Hansberry, Lorraine (editor Robert Nemiroff). **To Be Young, Gifted and Black: Lorraine Hansberry in Her Own Words.** P-H 1969.

Letters, journals, speeches, interviews, and scenes from her plays have been compiled by the late Lorraine Hansberry's husband to give the reader an insight into the black experience and the creative process.

Harlow, Alvin F. **Joel Chandler Harris: Plantation Story Teller.** Messner 1941.

The story of a shy newspaper man, Joel Chandler Harris, who became famous when he published the fables of talking animals he had heard as a boy.

Hodge, Jane Aiken. **Only a Novel: The Double Life of Jane Austen.** Fawcett World 1973.

How can a nineteenth-century lady have a double life? Jane Austen was loved by her family as a kindly spinster aunt. They never guessed at her depth and talent as a writer, and she herself, at the mercy of her publishers, never made much money from her work. There are many mysteries surrounding this two-sided life, but Mrs. Hodge has researched her letters, books, and family memoirs to reconstruct the surprising and often sad life of a great writer.

Hodges, C. Walter. **Shakespeare and the Players.** Coward 1970.

Hodges briefly sketches the life and writings of William Shakespeare, England's great poet and playwright. He also compares the Globe Theatre, where many of Shakespeare's plays were first produced—along with others of the time—and describes the players, audiences, and performances in the sixteenth century. Illustrated by the author; revised edition.

Kane, Harnett T. **Young Mark Twain and the Mississippi.** Random 1966.

Kane writes of his book "in the broad sense, this is a

true story—of a boy and a river and a uniquely picturesque era in American history."

Kelen, Emery. **Mr. Nonsense: A Life of Edward Lear.** Nelson 1973.

Edward Lear, the twentieth child in an English family, rose above the problems of being ugly and often ill, of being rejected by his mother, and of being poor to achieve fame as a painter of birds and a writer of humorous verses. This biography includes some of Lear's verses.

Leighton, Margaret. **Shelley's Mary: A Life of Mary Godwin Shelley.** FS&G 1973.

This is the story of Mary Shelley, probably best known for her book *Frankenstein.* The author tells of Mary's childhood and her disturbed and disturbing stepsister Clara, and concentrates on Mary's life with the poet Percy Bysshe Shelley. The reader learns of the loss of Mary's children, Shelley's early death by drowning, and Mary's lifetime efforts to have his work recognized and appreciated.

MacBride, Roger Lea, editor. **West from Home: Letters of Laura Ingalls Wilder, San Francisco, 1915.** HarRow 1974.

Laura Ingalls Wilder went to San Francisco by train to visit her daughter Rose in 1915. She wrote her husband long letters telling him about the Panama-Pacific International Exposition. These letters have been compiled into a book that gives a rich picture, not only of the Laura of the "Little House" books but of San Francisco in 1915.

Manley, Seon, and Susan Belcher. **O, Those Extraordinary Women! or the Joys of Literary Lib!** Chilton 1972.

This book consists of short biographies of European and American female writers. Included also are excerpts from their work, plus numerous pictures. National Book Award.

Meltzer, Milton. **Langston Hughes: A Biography.** T Y Crowell 1968.

Sensitive portrait of a black poet from his birth in Kansas City to acceptance by Afro-Americans as poet laureate of his people. National Book Award.

Proudfit, Isabel. **The Treasure Hunter: The Story of Robert Louis Stevenson.** Messner 1939.

This story of Robert Louis Stevenson's life describes his childhood, his university days, his experiences in France and California where he sought improved health, and finally his settling in Samoa.

Rhodehamel, Josephine DeWitt, and Raymond Francis Wood. **Ina Coolbrith: Librarian and Laureate of California.** Brigham 1973.

Ina Coolbrith, a librarian and poet laureate of California, once said her poetry would be her biography, so many excerpts from her poetry are included in this story of her life.

Richter, Hans Peter (translator Edite Kroll). **I Was There.** Dell 1973.

The author, Hans Richter, joined the "brown shirts" (Hitler Youth) when he was nine years old. He tells the story of his life as a young boy in Germany during the time of Adolph Hitler. At the beginning of World War II, Hans and two good friends served together in the Hitler Youth; later, they enlisted together in the German infantry.

Rogers, W. G. **Carl Sandburg, Yes: Poet, Historian, Novelist, Songster.** HarBraceJ 1970.

The biographer tells the experiences of Carl Sandburg—from his birth in Galesburg, Illinois, to his death in North Carolina—and introduces the people who influenced Sandburg in his career. Included are many excerpts from Sandburg's own prose and poetry.

Shafter, Toby. **Edna St. Vincent Millay: America's Best-Loved Poet.** Messner 1957.

Edna St. Vincent Millay—she preferred to be called "Vincent"—grew up in a family of three daughters with an absent father. Although living almost at the poverty level, Vincent's childhood was happy enough, and, when she reached high school, her poetry was already receiving notice. This biography recounts how she grew up to become America's best-loved poet.

Squire, Elizabeth D. **Heroes of Journalism.** Fleet 1973.

Heroes of Journalism is the story of men and women who have defended freedom of the press in America. Journalists such as Benjamin Franklin, Daniel Craig,

Joseph Pulitzer, Margaret Bourke-White, and Edward R. Murrow struggled to bring the news speedily and truthfully to the people. The book also tells why the journalist's job is exciting and important.

Thurber, James. **My Life and Hard Times.** Har-Row 1973.

We go back with James Thurber to the midwestern town of his youth, and he tells us some of the most humorous and poignant events: the night the bed fell, the night the ghost got in, the day the dam broke, and others. Through the humor we see ourselves and realize that we are all quite vulnerable and quite human.

Tobin, Richard L., editor. **The Golden Age: The Saturday Review 50th Anniversary Reader.** Bantam 1974.

Celebrating its first half century, *The Saturday Review of Literature* presents this fabulous collection of articles which have appeared in the magazine. Early reviews of some great novels, biographical sketches of famous writers, articles by Eleanor Roosevelt, Norman Cousins, Albert Schweitzer, and Robert F. Kennedy, and, finally, a short humor section are included.

Wilson, Ellen. **They Named Me Gertrude Stein.** FS&G 1973.

Gertrude Stein was raised in California, went to Radcliffe College, attended medical school, and then lived in Europe as a respected novelist, art collector, and philosopher. Her brother Leo and best friend Alice B. Toklas are important figures in this biography.

Wood, James Playsted. **Emily Elizabeth Dickinson: A Portrait.** Nelson 1972.

Emily Dickinson, the poet, is still respected and well known for her ability to express thoughts and feelings shared by everyone. The author of this biography uses first-hand accounts to tell of Emily Dickinson's early life and of her later years when she hid from the public.

Wood, James Playsted. **Spunkwater, Spunkwater: A Life of Mark Twain.** Pantheon 1968.

America's great humorist is introduced through several amusing anecdotes. Twain's life, his feelings, and his works are described in detail. Included are several photographs of Twain with his family and friends.

Wright, Richard. **Black Boy: A Record of Childhood and Youth.** Har-Row 1969.

This autobiography of a great black author is really a look at any black boy growing up in the South. Richard Wright was hated or pitied by the whites for his color; he was resented and scorned by the blacks for trying to find something better. His poverty, fear, and hatred led him to lie, steal, drink, and even torture and kill animals. His experiences give him, and us, insight into attitudes and their effects.

Other

Alderman, Clifford Lindsey. **The Royal Opposition: The British Generals in the American Revolution.** Macmillan 1970.

The colorful stories of the British High Command in the American Revolution: Sir Guy Carleton, John Burgoyne, Sir William Howe, Thomas Gage, Sir Henry Clinton, and Earl Cornwallis.

Ardizzone, Edward. **The Young Ardizzone: An Autobiographical Fragment.** Macmillan 1971.

A well-known illustrator of children's books, Ardizzone intimately tells of his life in England sharing the excitement of the times in the early twentieth century and the problems of growing up in a family from whom the father often was away. Ardizzone's sketches created for the book are delightful.

Bailey, Pearl. **The Raw Pearl.** PB 1972.

Pearl Bailey, famous black entertainer and actress, started out in show business as a child in an amateur show, then became a chorus girl, and worked her way up to the Upper East Side, the wealthy section of New York City. She talks about what being black meant—or didn't mean—about her career, her life with her husband Louis Bellson, the great drummer, and the ups and downs of a life in show business.

Bailey, Pearl. **Talking to Myself.** PB 1973.

The famous black singer shares with us her views on contemporary life. Her rich experiences, described in her autobiography *The Raw Pearl*, have contributed to her ideas on the state of the nation, the American family, the entertainment world, and the perils of fame.

Often funny, and always compassionate, Pearl explores life's themes of birth, death, hate, and love.

Baker, Rachel. **America's First Trained Nurse.** Messner 1959.

Linda Richards, the first American to graduate from nursing school, can be credited with the establishment of Massachusetts General Nursing School and the first school of nursing in Japan, the development of patient progress charts, and the preparation of nurses for work with the mentally ill.

Bates, Daisy. **The Passing of the Aborigines: A Lifetime Spent Among the Natives of Australia.** PB 1973.

In the early 1900s, Daisy Bates, who has worked for a London journalist, travels to Australia to investigate tribal conditions among the aborigines. Learning that these ancient, primitive people are slowly disappearing, she decides to stay. Gradually she gains the respect and affection of the natives and is allowed to be present at ceremonies that no woman had seen before. Living over thirty-five years in the desert wilderness, she is exposed to their rituals of initiation, their habits of cannibalism, their courtesy as well as their savage warring instincts.

Beam, Phillip C. **Winslow Homer at Prout's Neck.** Little 1966.

In this informative and often amusing biography, Beam captures the essence of Winslow Homer—the charming but rather eccentric man in love with nature—as well as the great American artist who valued expression of ideas in his paintings. The book stresses Homer's most productive years (1883–1910), those spent at Prout's Neck, Maine. Illustrated with ninety-two paintings and photographs.

Berkowitz, Freda Pastor. **Unfinished Symphony and Other Stories of Men and Music.** Atheneum 1963.

Fifty-three stories of how the world's great pieces of music received their popular names. Also included are sixteen biographies of musicians that show how music theory developed in the last 250 years.

Berry, James. **Heroin Was My Best Friend.** CCPr Macmillan 1971.

This book reveals actual conversations the author had

with seven young ex-addicts who began using drugs in
their teens, and with an addict's mother. Each ex-
addict explains why he took drugs as well as the reasons for quitting. Some smoked pot. Others popped
pills. But Donny took heroin—up to twenty bags a
day.

Blackburn, Joyce. **Martha Berry: A Biography.** Lippincott 1968.

This book tells how, despite many obstacles, Martha
Berry devoted her life to providing an education for
boys and girls who would never have had one without
her.

Boom, Corrie Ten (with John Sherrill and Elizabeth
Sherrill). **The Hiding Place.** G K Hall 1973.

Corrie Ten Boom describes her experiences as a Dutch
girl growing up during the Nazi invasion of Holland.
As devout Christians her family risked their lives and
fortune to hide Jewish people. Her accounts of her life
in Nazi camps show the terrible conditions and treatment of prisoners and the strong faith Corrie had to
survive.

Bourdeaux, Michael. **The Evidence That Convicted Aida
Skripnikova.** D C Cook 1973.

Aida Skripnikova, a Russian Christian, stood up for
her religion in spite of persecution. Some Christians
in Russia were jailed for their religious convictions.

Carpozi, George, Jr. **The Johnny Cash Story.** Pyramid
Pubns 1970.

The road to success was not an easy one for Johnny
Cash, popular country singer. He grew up on a farm
in Arkansas during the Depression and began singing
at an early age, but after his first years of popularity,
a narcotics problem and the breakup of his first
marriage almost ruined his career. It wasn't until
later in the sixties that he experienced changes in his
life that began to bring him new success.

Clark, Dorothy, Jane Dahl, and Lois Gonzenbach. **Look
at Me, Please Look at Me.** D C Cook 1973.

This is the story of two women who dedicate themselves to helping the mentally handicapped. At first
they are shocked and repulsed by the sight of the
children. Through many of their stories and ex-

periences, the reader sees these women learning to accept the children and discovers what hidden beautiful qualities the handicapped can have.

Crane, Louise. **Ms. Africa: Profiles of Modern African Women.** Lippincott 1973.

Louise Crane, born in the Belgian Congo of missionary parents, writes profiles of successful African women of today. Whether a judge, singer, or physician, each woman has struggled to overcome difficulties and achieve equality and recognition.

Crary, Margaret. **Susette La Flesche: Voice of the Omaha Indians.** Hawthorn 1973.

A biography of Susette La Flesche, who traveled to meetings all over the United States telling people about the Omaha and Ponca tribes, their hardships, and their plans for the future.

Crawford, Deborah. **Four Women in a Violent Time.** Crown 1970.

Mary Dyer, Deborah Moody, Anne Hutchinson, and Penelope Van Princes were heroines of the 1640s in early America. Each woman was courageous and resourceful in her own way, contributing to the growth of the new land.

Davis, Sammy, Jr. (editors Jane Boyar and Burt Boyar). **Yes, I Can: The Story of Sammy Davis, Jr.** FS&G 1965.

The famous singer, dancer, and show business personality recounts his life story, beginning with his lean childhood, on the road in the thirties with his family's vaudeville act. He describes his struggle toward the American Dream of success and fortune—made tougher because of being black. Davis tells how achieving fame turned him into "a Jekyll and Hyde character," losing touch with his audience and hating himself, and the soul-searching he had to do to change and become human again.

De Leeuw, Adele. **Civil War Nurse: Mary Ann Bickerdyke.** Messner 1973.

Throughout the Civil War, Mary Ann Bickerdyke defied doctors' orders, doing instead what she felt was right for "her boys." Sometimes she even had to take supplies that were not hers to use.

De Leeuw, Adele. **Edith Cavelle: Nurse, Spy, Heroine.**
Putnam 1968.

Edith Cavelle gave up a teaching career to become a
nurse in the London slums; ultimately she returned to
Belgium where, after a heroic nursing career, she was
executed for spying during the First World War.

Donovan, Frank. **The Women in Their Lives.** Dodd
1966.

The author tells of the characters, personalities, appearances, and influences of the women involved with
Franklin, Washington, Adams, Jefferson, Hamilton,
and Madison. Quotes from letters and diaries add to
the reality of the book and give it a personal touch.

Edmonds, I. G. **The Magic Man: The Life of Robert
Houdin.** Nelson 1972.

The Frenchman Robert Houdin was the father of
modern magic. This book describes his rise as a
master of illusion. By performing the difficult trick
of catching a bullet in his teeth, Houdin convinced a
group of Arab magicians that he was truly a magician
and stopped a war between France and Algeria. The
author adds an illustrated chapter, "The Secrets of
Robert Houdin Revealed."

Fabe, Maxene. **Beauty Millionaire: The Life of Helena
Rubinstein.** T Y Crowell 1972.

A biography of Helena Rubinstein, a poor little girl
from Poland, who was the first to recognize that quality
cosmetics could be mass-produced and attractively
marketed. For seventy years, Helena Rubinstein, a
tiny lady who never took time to use her own products,
was the queen of the beauty industry.

Fraser, Amy Stewart. **The Hills of Home.** Routledge &
Kegan 1973.

A true account of life in a small glen in Scotland
during the late 1800s and early 1900s, this book includes comments on the laws, religious beliefs, and
morals of Amy Stewart Fraser's community.

Furneaux, Rupert. **The World's Most Intriguing True
Mysteries.** Arc Bks 1969.

Thirty-three true-life unsolved mysteries are recounted,
some involving famous personalities. The evidence is
examined carefully, the mysteries are speculated upon,

and—where possible—new light is shed on the previously unexplainable.

Garfield, Leon (with David Proctor). **Child O'War.** HR&W 1972.

The *Memoir of Sir J. T. Lee,* written in 1836, is the source of this story about a boy who joins the British Navy at the age of five and a half. He sees victory with Lord Nelson at the Battle of the Nile. Historical notes about the years following the French Revolution and Napoleon's activities precede each chapter.

Glendinning, Victoria. **A Suppressed Cry: Life and Death of a Quaker Daughter.** Routledge & Kegan 1969.

Winnie Seebohm, an ancestor of the author, left enough of her notebooks and letters to give us a portrait of a courageous woman's struggle to keep herself from being "suppressed" in Victorian England. Encouraged by the scholarly traditions of her Quaker family, Winnie gave up the decorative role of middle-class "lady" and went to Cambridge to study history.

Gregory, Susan. **Hey, White Girl.** Lancer 1970.

Susan and her family decide to move to the South Side of Chicago in 1967 as a part of a mission project to understand life in the ghetto. She is the only white girl in a black high school. At first she is frightened and ill at ease, knowing that she is the different one. Soon she begins to make friends and to feel as though she belongs. The vitality, spontaneity, and "soul" of the black community amazes her after her experiences in middle class "up-tight" schools. She bases this account on a diary which she kept that year, and her narrative is full of detailed impressions, feelings, characterizations, and events.

Guidry, Sister Mary Gabriella. **The Southern Negro Nun: An Autobiography.** Exposition 1974.

Devoted to improving the spiritual and educational condition of the Negro, Sister Mary Gabriella Guidry has been a Negro nun since 1935. She tells of an early period in British Honduras, and her work and education in the southern United States.

Harnan, Terry. **African Rhythm—American Dance.** Knopf 1974.

This is the biography of Katherine Dunham, a black

woman who traveled to the Caribbean to bring back black tribal dances for American audiences. She became a famous dancer and choreographer.

Harris, Eleanor Van Buskirk. **The Ship That Never Returned.** Chris Mass 1973.

Stephen Harris was an officer on the *Pueblo,* a U.S. Naval vessel that was captured by the North Korean military. His mother tells her side of the story—the agonizing eleven months she spent waiting for and working toward her son's release.

Hautzig, Esther. **The Endless Steppe: Growing Up in Siberia.** T Y Crowell 1968.

In June 1941, Esther Rudomin's family was placed under arrest in Poland and taken to Siberia, which was to be their home for five years. Esther recounts how her family had to struggle for everyday things like food, clothing, and shelter. Throughout it all, she learned strength, love, and humor. Jane Addams Book Award. Lewis Carroll Shelf Award. National Book Award Honor.

Hayes, Helen, and Sanford Dody. **On Reflection: An Autobiography.** Lanewood 1969.

In her introduction, this celebrated actress writes, "We play many parts in this world and I want you to know them all." Her book tells the story of a colorful, energetic life on and off the stage.

Houston, Jeanne Wakatsuki, and James D. Houston. **Farewell to Manzanar.** Bantam 1974.

When Japanese planes bombed Pearl Harbor, Jeanne Wakatsuki was seven years old. To her and her family, this event was far less real than the daily business of living in southern California, where her father was a commercial fisherman. In most ways, Jeanne and her family were much like any other Americans of the early 1940s. But their physical appearance and family background caused them to be labeled enemy. As such, they were forced to leave their home and most of their possessions; they were moved eventually to what was virtually a prison camp. In the book Jeanne tells of life in the camp and—on being released at the end of the war—of her attempt to be accepted in white society.

Jackson, Jesse, editor. **Make a Joyful Noise unto the**

Lord: The Life of Mahalia Jackson. T Y Crowell 1974.

Mahalia Jackson rose from laundry woman to queen of gospel singers. This biography also tells how she worked with Dr. Martin Luther King, Jr., for equal rights for black people.

Jones, Hettie. **Big Star Fallin' Mama.** Viking Pr 1974.

This is the story of five black women and black music. Included are the biographies of Ma Rainey, Bessie Smith, Mahalia Jackson, Billie Holiday, and Aretha Franklin. The author tells each woman's feelings about her music and about being a black woman.

Kelen, Emery. **Fantastic Tales, Strange Animals, Riddles, Jests, and Prophecies of Leonardo Da Vinci.** Nelson 1971.

This is a book of stories, riddles, jests, and puzzles that the artist Leonardo Da Vinci used to entertain the court of Ludovico Sforza, in Milan in the fifteenth century. The book is filled with Da Vinci's drawings.

Kennerly, Karen. **The Slave Who Bought His Freedom: Equiano's Story.** Dutton 1971.

In the eighteenth century, Olaudah Equiano was stolen from his Ibo tribe in West Africa and was sold to black masters. Equiano describes his experiences with both black and white masters, his trip on a slave ship, his life in England, America, and the West Indies, and his desire and struggle to learn to read and write.

Killilea, Marie. **Karen.** P-H 1962.

Karen, a child with cerebral palsy, brings love and inspiration to her family. With courage and determination she proves to herself and others that she can do anything—walk, talk, read, and write. Marie Killilea, the mother and author of the book, shares the devotion of the family in helping Karen.

Knox, Jack. **Riverman.** Abingdon 1971.

"Wet Willie" Bate was nicknamed for the time he jumped into the Mississippi River to rescue a deckhand who fell overboard. Willie tells about his life rafting and steamboating up and down the big river. Pen and ink sketches by the author show the river and the different kinds of boats.

Kosterina, Nina (translator Mirra Ginsburg). **The Diary of Nina Kosterina.** Crown 1968.

Nina Kosterina began a diary when she was fifteen and

living in Moscow. Her diary ends days before her death on the front, fighting the Germans, in 1941. Nina was a rebellious teenager, but she was loyal, loving, and sometimes confused and lonely as well.

Krueger, Starry. **The Whole Works: Autobiography of a Young American Couple.** Random 1973.

Tape-recorded interviews tell the story of Bruce and Gail Erickson, twenty-one and nineteen, who grow up in Michigan, marry, and move to California, where they live in a migrant labor camp. The book is a picture of two people who do temporary farm work.

Kunhardt, Philip B., Jr. **My Father's House.** Random 1970.

Every boy who has enjoyed a summer's day fishing with his father, or climbing a mountain with him, or just plain talking and being together will understand what the author felt for his father. In 1963 Philip Kunhardt's father died of a heart attack. His warmth and strength stayed with his son and made Philip remember what his mother had once said, "Everything you've said or done makes a difference on other people's lives, so that long after death you live in the world in a different form." This is the story of a father, a son, and a whole family growing together.

Leipold, L. Edmond. **Famous American Artists.** Denison 1969.

The lives of ten men and women artists are described. These artists of the eighteenth, nineteenth, and twentieth centuries are James Whistler, artist and etcher; Benjamin West, known as father of American art; Gilbert Stuart, portrait painter of George Washington and other famous Americans; Arthur Davies, a wandering artist; Grant Wood, an Iowa artist; Mary Cassatt, often called America's greatest woman artist; Charles Willson Peale, painter in residence during the American Revolution; George Caleb Bingham, painter of the early West; Winslow Homer, painter of the sea; and John Singer Sargent, portrait painter.

Levit, Rose. **Ellen: A Short Life Long Remembered.** Bantam 1974.

Ellen is fifteen when she finds she has cancer and a short time to live. The true-life account, written by her mother, includes many letters and poems composed by Ellen. Her friends and family are helpful and comforting as she goes through many mental and physical hardships. Even though she must live life fully in a short while, she is able to help friends and her own family in their troubles.

Lindeman, Bard. **The Twins Who Found Each Other.** PB 1971.

Tony Milasi and Roger Brooks are identical twins. Each one grew up without ever seeing the other. Separated as infants, they were raised in completely different environments—one Catholic in New York, the other Jewish in Miami. A freak case of mistaken identity by a busboy initiated a chain of events that eventually brought these two brothers together at the age of twenty-four. The uncanny similarities in the physical, psychological, emotional, and even habitual traits of these two men have been the subject of study for geneticists, psychologists, and other scientists.

Loud, Pat (with Nora Johnson). **Pat Loud: A Woman's Story.** Coward 1974.

The Loud family agreed to have their home life filmed for public television. This is the story behind what we all saw on that series: the break-up of a marriage, the oldest son's homosexuality, and the other things that caused this family to become instant celebrities. Pat Loud, woman, mother, and wife, explains in this book what she feels we never saw on TV.

Matchette, Katherine E. **Walk Safe through the Jungle.** Herald Pr 1974.

This is the story of Hans, an orphaned German boy, who came to America in 1908 at the age of fourteen and worked in a glass factory. At fifteen, he felt called to be a missionary. He completed high school and college in Asbury, Kentucky, married and went to the Dutch East Indies as a missionary.

McKown, Robin. **Heroic Nurses.** Putnam 1966.

Here are twelve biographical sketches of famous nurses including Jeanne Mance, Florence Nightingale, Clara Barton, Elizabeth Kenny, and Mary Breckinridge, as well as some less famous ones. This book is good background reading on the nursing profession and gives the reader insight into the lives and times of these women.

Mersand, Joseph, editor. **Great American Short Biographies.** Dell 1966.

Twenty stories of distinguished American women and men in the arts—literature, music, painting, the dance—in science, and in public life: Roger Williams, George Washington, Thomas Jefferson, Paul Revere, Daniel Webster, Washington Irving, Stephen Foster, Louis Agassiz, Emily Dickinson, Mark Twain, Thomas Alva Edison, Charles Copeland, Grant Wood, Carl Sandburg, the Wright Brothers, Marian Anderson, Agnes De Mille, and Henry David Thoreau.

Noble, Iris. **Cameras and Courage: Margaret Bourke-White.** Messner 1973.

"Face your fears; then do something" was the life-time motto of professional photographer Margaret Bourke-White. Margaret photographed such things as the pouring of molten steel and a bombing mission in World War II. Even when she was stricken with a rare disease, her enthusiasm and courage never left her.

Noble, Iris. **Emmeline and Her Daughters: The Pankhurst Suffragettes.** Messner 1971.

Spurred on by her late husband's words—"scratch their eyes out"—Emmeline Pankhurst and her daughters did all they possibly could to help win the women of England the right to vote.

Noble, Iris. **First Woman Ambulance Surgeon: Emily Barringer.** Messner 1962.

A biography of Emily Barringer, the first woman intern in a public hospital. Although she was first in the competitive examinations for two hospitals, she was not placed in either one. Finally she got a place as intern at Gouverneur Hospital in New York City. There, although she was discriminated against because of her sex, she became a gynecologist.

Noble, Iris. **Nurse Around the World.** Messner 1964.

After coming to the rescue of earthquake victims in Italy, Alice Fitzgerald served at the front lines in France during World War I. This biography also describes her later pioneering efforts to set up nursing schools in the Phillipines and Siam.

Northup, Solomon. **In Chains to Louisiana: Solomon Northup's Story.** Dutton 1971.

Solomon Northup was born a free man in New York

state. His father was a freed slave. Solomon was successful as a carpenter, farmer, and bargeman. One day, however, he was tricked by two men who promised him an excellent job opportunity if he would go with them to other areas of the U.S. Instead of getting a job, he was sold into slavery and held for twelve years. Finally he returned home and wrote his story.

Parlin, John. **Amelia Earhart.** Dell 1972.

Amelia Earhart's dream was to be the first woman to fly across the Atlantic Ocean alone. This biography tells how she made her dream come true.

Pitrone, Jean Maddern. **Trailblazer: Negro Nurse in the American Red Cross.** HarBraceJ 1969.

A biography of Frances Reed Elliott, the first black nurse in the American Red Cross. Her early ambition to become a nurse was finally fulfilled when she completed her training, at the age of thirty-one.

Reiss, Johanna. **The Upstairs Room.** T Y Crowell 1972.

Because they were Jewish, Annie and her sister Sini had to leave their family when the Germans attacked Holland in 1941. Until the war was over, Annie and Sini hid in the upstairs room of a remote farmhouse of the Oosterveld family. This book tells of their experiences. Charles & Bertie G. Schwartz Award; Jane Addams Book Award Honor.

Richter, Hans Peter (translator Edite Kroll). **Friedrich.** Dell 1973.

The Nazis made life for Jews in Germany full of sorrow and danger. Hans Richter, the author, tells about his best friend, Friedrich, a Jewish boy who lived upstairs. Friedrich and his loving family were robbed of their jobs, their home, and their lives by Hitler's government. Mildred L. Batchelder Award.

Rigert, Joe. **All Together: An Unusual American Family.** Har-Row 1974.

A family of eight children, seven of them adopted, presents many trials, especially if many races are represented. The discrimination of race relations and of how people react to an interracial family are very meaningful and thought-provoking.

Rockwell, Anne. **Glass, Stones and Crown.** Atheneum 1968.

This is the story of Abbé Suger and the building of

St. Denis church and the French nation. The author
tells how the monk, Abbé Suger, with his cleverness,
diplomacy, and great devotion, helped rebuild the historical St. Denis church. She tells how he and the
carpenters, glassmakers, sculptors, and masons worked
hard to develop the Gothic style of architecture, known
for its pointed arches, rib-vaulted walls, and beautiful
stained glass windows.

Rogers, W. G. **Mightier Than the Sword: Cartoon, Cari-
cature, Social Comment.** HarBraceJ 1969.

Mightier Than the Sword reveals brief life histories
and achievements of scores of cartoonists and anima-
tion artists who lived as far back as 1527. The book
explains many cartoons and shows their effect on society.

Rollins, Charlemae Hill. **Famous Negro Entertainers of
Stage, Screen, and TV.** Dodd 1967.

Biographical sketches of sixteen black entertainers.
Among those included are Harry Belafonte, Lena
Horne, Duke Ellington, and Louis Armstrong.

Rushmore, Robert. **Fanny Kemble.** CCPr Macmillan
1970.

The life story of Fanny Kemble, an English actress
married to a wealthy American plantation owner.
Appalled at the conditions of slavery, she divorced
her husband and returned to England, where she wrote
a journal containing her reactions to slavery. Fearing
Britain would support the South in the Civil War, she
published the journal. Britain shifted its support to the
Union. Many persons believe Fanny Kemble's journal
influenced Britain's leaders.

Scheibel, Barbara. **Tops in Pops Music.** Pendulum Pr
1970.

Over 250 pop music stars and groups are here, each
with a photo, short biography, and a list of outstanding
achievements. There are even addresses given, where
you can write to your favorites.

Schulman, Arnold. **Baba.** PB 1973.

Every year pilgrims flock to see Baba, the Hindu
holy man who cures all ills, creates objects out of
thin air, and performs other miracles. Arnold Schulman, screenwriter and playwright, went to India to

see Baba. He was amazed by this mystic figure and came away unable to explain what he had witnessed.

Scott, John Anthony. **Fanny Kemble's America.** T Y Crowell 1973.

When the great Shakespearean actress, Fanny Kemble, came to the U.S.A. and married a Philadelphia man, she was shocked to find that he owned a large Georgia slave plantation. Morally against slavery, Fanny kept factual accounts of her year on the plantation, including horrors she witnessed. Fanny's views on slavery greatly differed from those of her husband, and their marriage ended in divorce.

Shapiro, Irwin. **Yankee Thunder: The Legendary Life of Davy Crockett.** Messner 1944.

In this legendary account, Davy Crockett is presented as a hunter, backwoodsman, congressman, and traveler to the South Seas. His unusual size, his animal pets—the buffalo Mississip, the bear Death Hug, and the Cape Cod Sea Sarpint—are described in this book.

Sine, Jerry (with Gene Klinger). **Son of This Land.** Childrens 1970.

White Beaver, a small Indian boy, helped his parents earn a living by demonstrating Indian dances. He worked hard at getting an education, but was pulled into World War II. When he returned, he found jobs hard to get. He began by doing paste-up work for a large firm, but soon became a commercial artist and improved so much that a prestigious advertising agency hired him. When he married and started a family, he knew his hard work had been rewarded. Information about work as a commercial artist is given.

Standerford, Betsy (with R. Conrad Stein). **No Hablo Inglés.** Childrens 1970.

Vincente (Betsy) Standerford grew up in New Mexico in a primitive village, speaking only Spanish, full of superstition, and yet curious about the world. When her family moved to Colorado, she was frightened by the city and teased by her classmates. When her father tried to marry her off to a stranger, she left home and eventually found an employer who understood her fright and self-consciousness. She married and moved to Chicago, where she became a personnel manager, helping others like herself find themselves and their places in life. Information on work as a personnel manager is provided.

Tibble, Anne. **Greenhorn: A Twentieth-Century Childhood.** Routledge & Kegan 1973.

The author spent her childhood as a coachman's daughter on a wealthy estate in Yorkshire, England. The life of a young girl growing up in the country during the early twentieth century is full of friends, excitement, fresh air, and good times. A delightful book for mature readers.

Trapp, Maria Augusta. **The Sound of Music: The Story of the Trapp Family Singers.** Dell 1966.

Maria Augusta Trapp tells the true story of leaving an Austrian convent to become a governess for a baron's seven children. Winning the love of the family, she later becomes the wife of the baron. In the aftermath of the war and depression, Maria helps the family to support themselves by singing and touring the world.

Van Voris, Jacqueline. **Constance de Markievicz: In the Cause of Ireland.** Feminist Pr 1972.

This is the story of Constance de Markievicz, who lost her wealth and beauty fighting for the liberation of Ireland and of women. In 1922 she wrote, "The question of votes for women, with the bigger thing, freedom for women and opening of the professions to women, has been one of the things that I have worked for and given my influence and time to procuring all my life. . . ."

Viscott, David S. **The Making of a Psychiatrist.** Fawcett World 1974.

What does it really take to become a psychiatrist? The author describes his experiences, from student to practicing psychiatrist. He relates his fears, frustrations, the long hours on the job, and the uncertainties on and off the job. This is a good insight, especially for anyone interested in psychiatry as a profession.

Wayne, Kyra Petrovskaya. **Shurik: A Story of the Siege of Leningrad.** G&D 1972.

The author was a young Russian actress in Leningrad when World War II began. As her city was threatened, she became a nurse for a time during the siege of Leningrad, and this is the story of that time in her life. Toward the beginning of the bombing, she finds a ten-year-old orphan named Shurik, and she feels a responsibility to take care of him. There is constant bombing and the Nazis have cut off all supplies of food, fuel, and medicine. The people starve and die, but the strength of the survivors includes a capacity to share the little they have even in this time of desperation.

Williams, Eric, editor. **The Will to Be Free: Great Escape Stories.** Nelson 1971.

Eleven persons tell their true and varied stories of escape from captivity, either in a prison or in a country. Each person is escaping from oppression of an enemy or a government using force.

Williams, Frances Leigh. **Plantation Patriot: A Biography of Eliza Lucas Pinckney.** HarBraceJ 1967.

Largely set in pre-Revolutionary America, this authenticated biography of Eliza Lucas Pinckney reveals much about the uncertainties experienced and courage required by those living on the colonial plantations of the South.

Yates, Elizabeth. **Amos Fortune: Free Man.** Dell 1971.

This is the true story of an African slave, Amos Fortune, who in 1725 at the age of fifteen was captured and brought to Massachusetts. Sold at auction, he lived as a slave until sixty years of age, when he purchased his freedom. He saved his money to purchase the freedom of other slaves. As a tanner, Christian, and citizen of Jeffrey, Massachusetts, he was a respected member of the community. Book World Children's Spring Book Festival Award. John Newbery Medal.

FINE ARTS

Alden, Carella. **Sunrise Island: A Story of Japan and Its Arts.** Parents 1971.

Myths and legends exploring the birth and history of Japan begin this trip into a culture completely different from our own. There are dozens of pictures showing the art of Japan, as well as some photographs of old and modern Japanese buildings. Old Japanese customs and traditions, some of which are still observed today, are explained.

Ardizzone, Edward. **The Young Ardizzone: An Auto-biographical Fragment.** Macmillan 1971.

A well-known illustrator of children's books, Ardizzone intimately tells of his life in England sharing the excitement of the times in the early twentieth century and the problems of growing up in a family from whom the father often was away. Ardizzone's sketches created for the book are delightful.

Beam, Phillip C. **Winslow Homer at Prout's Neck.** Little 1972.

In this informative and often amusing biography, Beam captures the essence of Winslow Homer—the charming but rather eccentric man in love with nature—as well as the great American artist who valued expression of ideas in his paintings. The book stresses Homer's most productive years (1883-1910), those spent at Prout's Neck, Maine. Illustrated with ninety-two paintings and photographs.

Berkowitz, Freda Pastor. **Unfinished Symphony and Other Stories of Men and Music.** Atheneum 1963.

Fifty-three stories of how the world's great pieces of music received their popular names. Also included are sixteen biographies of musicians that show how music theory developed in the last 250 years.

Bierhorst, John, arranger. **Songs of the Chippewa.** FS&G 1974.

A collection of traditional songs of the Chippewa Indians. They include ritual chants, dream songs, medicine charms, and lullabies with easy arrangements for piano and guitar.

Casty, Alan. **The Dramatic Art of the Film.** Har-Row 1971.

A primer on film, the art form of man plus machine. Without once losing sight of man as the central subject of art, Casty shows how the unique techniques of photography and editing can reveal dramatic profundities of human experience denied to theater.

Deschin, Jacob. **Photography in Your Future.** Macmillan 1965.

Readers interested in a career in photography will find here the steps which can be followed in preparing for photography-related jobs. Thirty-four areas of specialization are described in detail.

Fabe, Maxene. **Beauty Millionaire: The Life of Helena Rubinstein.** T Y Crowell 1972.

A biography of Helena Rubinstein, a poor little girl from Poland, who was the first to recognize that quality cosmetics could be mass-produced and attractively marketed. For seventy years, Helena Rubinstein, a tiny lady who never took time to use her own products, was the queen of the beauty industry.

Fenin, George N., and William K. Everson. **The Western: From Silents to the Seventies.** Grossman 1973.

One hero known worldwide is the cowboy in the tall white hat; one art form that has grown out of the very soul of America, her myths and her history, is the Western. Beginning with "The Great Train Robbery," that famous silent movie of 1903, this book follows the development of the Western. Generously illustrated with movie shots.

Harnan, Terry. **African Rhythm—American Dance.** Knopf 1974.

This is the biography of Katherine Dunham, a black woman who traveled to the Caribbean to bring back black tribal dances for American audiences. She became a famous dancer and choreographer.

Hemphill, Paul. **The Nashville Sound: Bright Lights and Country Music.** S&S 1970.

Following country music performers and fans through the United States, the author has written what amounts to a story of life in America, a history of some of its people—hillbillies, truck drivers, the down-and-outs, and the up-and-coming. The music that has its capital in Nashville, Tennessee, is also big business, and the author takes us behind the scenes to meet the singers and operators.

Hodenfield, Chris. **Rock '71.** Pyramid Pubns 1970.

Every type of group on the rock scene is explored and questioned, from Janis Joplin to Elvis Presley, from the Beatles to Blood, Sweat & Tears. What do they think? Why are they successful? What's it like to be a rock musician? A center section of photography shows some of the most popular stars performing and relaxing.

Hunt, Kari, and Douglas Hunt. **Pantomime: The Silent Theater.** Atheneum 1964.

Cavemen may have been the first pantomimists when

they re-enacted hunts for one another. This book tells how pantomime became an art in Greece, Rome, England, China, in the silent movies, and on TV today. Good photographs of Marcel Marceau and other great mimes.

Jackson, Jesse. **Make a Joyful Noise unto the Lord: The Life of Mahalia Jackson.** T Y Crowell 1974.

Mahalia Jackson rose from laundry woman to queen of gospel singers. This biography also tells how she worked with Dr. Martin Luther King, Jr., for equal rights for black people.

Jacobs, Susan. **On Stage: The Making of a Broadway Play.** Knopf 1972.

The magic of a Broadway play begins with the playwright, who writes and rewrites. Then comes the search for an agent and producer. The author skillfully interviews these people as well as the director, the actors, and the technicians. This book follows the play *Johnny No-Trump* from its writing to its closing.

Jones, Hettie. **Big Star Fallin' Mama.** Viking Pr 1974.

This is the story of five black women and black music. Included are the biographies of Ma Rainey, Bessie Smith, Mahalia Jackson, Billie Holiday, and Aretha Franklin. The author tells each woman's feelings about her music and about being a black woman.

Kauffmann, Stanley. **Figures of Light: Film Criticism and Comment.** Har-Row 1971.

Stanley Kauffmann's book is a valuable document in two senses. First, it gives detailed analyses of many important films, both American and foreign, of the late sixties. Second, in discussing the themes and values, implicit and explicit, which pervade these films, the author pictures a time in the recent past that future historians of American culture will undoubtedly see as a watershed.

Kauffmann, Stanley. **Living Images: Film Criticism and Comment.** Har-Row 1974.

If you enjoyed *Fiddler on the Roof, Cabaret, The Exorcist,* and movies in general, you'll also enjoy comparing your reactions to Stanley Kauffmann's. This book is a collection of his reviews of recent movies. An exacting critic, Kauffmann also includes several essays showing relationships between threatre and film, and also between foreign and domestic cinema.

Kelen, Emery. **Fantastic Tales, Strange Animals, Riddles, Jests, and Prophecies of Leonardo Da Vinci.** Nelson 1971.

This is a book of stories, riddles, jests, and puzzles that the artist Leondardo Da Vinci used to entertain the court of Ludovico Sforza, in Milan in the fifteenth century. The book is filled with Da Vinci's drawings.

Larson, Rodger (with Ellen Meade). **Young Filmmakers.** Dutton 1969.

A documentary about a grandmother called Bubby. A fantasy about an invisible boy. Animated vegetables. These are some of the movies by young filmmakers that will make you want to try your own hand at the camera. The authors will help you script, shoot, edit, and even distribute your film.

Leipold, L. Edmond. **Famous American Artists.** Denison 1969.

The lives of ten men and women artists are described. These artists of the eighteenth, ninetheeth, and twentieth centures are James Whistler, artist and etcher; Benjamin West, known as father of American art; Gilbert Stuart, portrait painter of George Washington and other famous Americans; Arthur Davies, a wandering artist; Grant Wood, an Iowa artist; Mary Cassett, often called America's greatest woman artist; Charles Willson Peale, painter in residence during the American Revolution; George Caleb Bingham, painter of the early West; Winslow Homer, painter of the sea; and John Singer Sargent, portrait painter.

Price, Christine. **Made in Ancient Egypt.** Dutton 1969.

Combining history and art, Christine Price has described the 1,500 years of Egypt's greatest culture, beginning with 3100 B.C. Included are a time chart of the dynasties of Ancient Egypt, a map of Egypt and the ancient Near East, and a list of books for further reading. Beautiful photographs and drawings also help the reader understand the life of the ancient Egyptians through their arts.

Price, Christine. **Made in Ancient Greece.** Dutton 1967.

Christine Price describes the diverse forms of art of the ancient Greek people and thus shows their life during different periods of their history. Beautiful drawings and photographs appear throughout the book. A map of "the world of the Greeks" and a reference list of additional books for reading are included.

Price, Christine. **Made in the Middle Ages.** Dutton 1961.

The author has divided this book on craftsmen of the Middle Ages into two parts: "Things Made for the Castle" and "Things Made for the Church." Included in Part I are descriptions of armor, weapons, clothing, jewels, sports, pastimes, tapestries, furniture, tableware, books, diptychs, and reliquaries. In Part II are embroidery, wood carving, painting, treasures of the church, and books. Many interesting illustrations are included, as well as a map showing places mentioned.

Price, Christine. **Made in the Renaissance: Arts and Crafts of the Age of Exploration.** Dutton 1963.

Christine Price describes in words and pictures the craftsmen of the Renaissance and their works—the printers of books, weavers of cloth, designers of nautical and musical instruments, carvers of furniture, makers of maps, goblets, and tableware, jewelry, and bibelots.

Price, Christine. **Made in West Africa.** Dutton 1975.

This book explores West African arts of the past and present. The wooden masks of the Yoruba people have always been more than showpieces, as the author's description of a present-day village ceremony reveals. The arts of West Africa are an integral part of the spiritual and everyday lives of the people. Illustrated with 160 black and white photographs.

Price, Christine. **The Story of Moslem Art.** Dutton 1964.

In the seventh century, the Arabs started a conquest of India, the Atlantic Coast of Africa, Spain, Portugal, and France. In addition, they controlled the craftsmen and artists of Egypt, Syria, Greece, and Persia. These arts under the domination of the Arabs came to be known as Moslem Art. This book describes in words and beautiful drawings these various kinds of art.

Richards, Stanley, editor. **Ten Great Musicals of the American Theatre.** Chilton 1973.

Theatre fans will enjoy this book, which includes the text and lyrics for the following musicals: *Of Thee I Sing, Porgy and Bess, One Touch of Venus, Briga-*

doon, Kiss Me, Kate, West Side Story, Fiddler on the Roof, Gypsy, 1776, and *Company.*

Rublowsky, John. **Music in America.** Macmillan 1967.

Jazz, folk, and rock and roll music are just a few of the types of music dealt with in this history of music in America. The author tells of the development of these various forms of music, covering everything from psalm-singing to the electronic music of John Cage. He discusses influence of slavery, religion, and ethnic groups on American music.

Ruskin, Ariane (editor Howard Smith). **Nineteenth Century Art.** McGraw 1973.

A well-organized survey of nineteenth century European and American art and artists. Descriptions of the lives, personalities, and influence of the major artists. Many illustrations in full color.

Scheuer, Steven H., editor. **Movies on TV.** Bantam 1974.

This is a listing of the movies shown on TV, including brief plot descriptions, names of stars, and ratings.

Shaw, Arnold. **The Rock Revolution: What's Happening in Today's Music.** Macmillan 1969.

An informative book on the teenage rebellion that conquered the "good music" of earlier eras. It thoroughly covers the history of rock from its birth through the '60s. B.B. King, Muddy Waters, Elvis Presley, Bob Dylan, the Beatles, Rolling Stones, and James Brown are only a few of the many artists covered.

Streatfeild, Noel. **The First Book of the Opera.** Watts 1967.

A useful introduction to opera—its history, production, performers. Numerous illustrations.

Titcomb, Margaret. **The Ancient Hawaiians: How They Clothed Themselves.** Hogarth 1973.

Much Hawaiian ritual and art was once centered on making tapa, the cloth whose patterns and textures today's machines cannot reproduce. As the women pounded the bark of mauke, the cloth-plant, they evolved music and a message system. Photographs shows, vaudeville, the follies, showboats, Broadway, and ing fine designs on the tapa boards.

Wehrum, Victoria. **The American Theatre.** Watts 1974.

This book will open the reader's eyes to the richness and variety of theater in America. Resourceful actors gave plays even when they were banned. The author describes indoor theaters, outdoor theaters, minstrel shows, vaudeville, the follies, showboats, Broadway, and off-Broadway. She also tells about great plays and actors and actresses who have become legends.

Whiteford, Andrew Hunter. **North American Indian Arts.** Western 1970.

This handy little book has numerous pictures in color of designs and objects made by North American Indians: pottery, baskets, textiles, skinwork, woodwork, stonework, metal work, etc. Brief descriptions of the objects or designs accompany the pictures. The author is a professor of anthropology and director of the Logan Museum of Anthropology. Many of the illustrated examples come from the Logan Museum, but extensive use has also been made of collections in the Field Museum of Natural History of Chicago and the Milwaukee Public Museum.

Zaidenberg, Arthur. **How To Draw Flowers, Fruit, and Vegetables.** Abelard 1964.

While flowers, fruit, and vegetables can "hold a pose," they have a vitality and freshness that the artist must capture. This book gives basic shapes but urges the young artist to see for himself and not just make copies.

GOVERNMENT

Alterman, Hyman. **Counting People: The Census in History.** HarBraceJ 1969.

About census-taking, this book discusses methods used to count people, why people have been counted, and what age groups or social groups are chosen for a census. Also included are the problems that confront census takers and the ways these problems have been overcome over the years.

Arm, Walter. **The Policeman: An Inside Look at His Role in Modern Society.** Dutton 1969.

Describes the role of the policeman in today's society. To help the reader understand today's policeman, the author gives a history of police, discusses the growth of crime, describes the police organization, and tells the steps a person takes to become a policeman. Details about the jobs of detectives and other police specialists are given, and "problem cops" are discussed.

Deming, Richard. **Man Against Man: Civil Law at Work.** Dell 1974.

Civil law and how it works in America is the subject of this book. The author begins with the origins of civil law and traces the law through the highly complex system of civil law of today. The different levels of the civil courts, from federal courts down to small county and city courts, are explained.

Deming, Richard. **Men and Society: Criminal Law at Work.** Dell 1974.

How does law work? Deming tries to explain our system of criminal law and our court procedures in terms anyone may understand. Descriptions of actions and procedures are given from time of arrest through preliminary hearing, arraignment, trial, post-trial, and appeal.

Goettel, Elinor. **America's Wars—Why?** Messner 1972.

The author traces America's wars from the American Revolution through Vietnam. She looks into the reasons for America's involvement in each of the wars and also gives her personal comments about the effects of war on our country.

Gutman, Judith Mara. **Is America Used Up?** Grossman 1973.

Judith Gutman takes a critical look at America, from the early 1900s to the present, she uses photographs to portray people's lack of interest in our society.

Klapper, Ivan. **What Your Congressman Does.** Sterling 1968.

A history of the United States Senate as well as the work of a typical senator are explained in detail in this well-illustrated book.

Liston, Robert A. **Who Shall Pay? Taxes and Tax Reform in America.** Messner 1972.

This book deals with the tax structure of the United States today and suggests how it might be reformed. The author discusses how to keep taxes low and still remedy such problems as pollution, urban blight, mass transit, inadequate housing, poor education, and social inequality.

Meltzer, Milton. **The Right to Remain Silent.** Har-BraceJ 1972.

This book deals with what the Fifth Amendment of the U.S. Constitution means. It traces through history the different methods of getting information which conflicted with the idea in this amendment, such as inquisition and torture. Abhorrence of these methods influenced the Congress of the U.S. to adopt the Fifth Amendment, stating the individual's right to remain silent to protect himself.

The New York Times, Staff of. **The End of a Presidency.** Bantam 1974.

The resignation of Richard M. Nixon from the presidency of the United States is documented by the staff of *The New York Times.* A pictorial history, a chronological history, and editorials about the event are included. The text of Nixon's letter of resignation and incriminating documents are presented.

Paradis, Adrian A. **Economics in Action Today.** Messner 1967.

This book deals primarily with economic systems around the world. It tells how money is circulated through society, why we pay taxes, and how the American economy has developed during the past two centuries.

Paradis, Adrian A. **Inflation in Action.** Messner 1974.

The author defines inflation, gives some historical background, tells whom inflation hits, and suggests ways inflation can be controlled.

Paradis, Adrian A. **International Trade in Action.** Messner 1973.

This book gives a very broad, simplified view of all aspects of international trade. Trading is traced from the ancient simple bartering to today's complex systems of trade.

The People's Bicentennial Commission. **Voices of the American Revolution.** Bantam 1975.

This book traces the American Revolution from its beginning to the final separation of the colonies from England. Many little-known facts are revealed. The last half of the book contains thoughts and quotations of participants in the Revolution. Included also are biographical sketches.

Sanderlin, George. **A Hoop to the Barrel: The Making of the American Constitution.** Coward 1974.

This book clearly outlines the questions and problems that faced the men who met in convention to write the U.S. Constitution. The answers, personalities, confrontations, and compromises that ensued are shown through many first-hand accounts.

Stevens, Leonard A. **Salute: The Case of the Bible versus the Flag.** Coward 1973.

Between World War I and World War II, many young Jehovah's Witnesses were expelled from school because they refused to salute the flag. This book traces this question of personal liberty as stated in the First Amendment through the courts to the Supreme Court.

Strouse, Jean. **Up Against the Law: The Legal Rights of People Under 21.** NAL 1970.

A clearly written explanation of the legal rights of young adults. Recent court decisions are reviewed and historical perspective is presented in a lively fashion.

Switzer, Ellen. **There Ought to Be a Law: How Laws Are Made and Work.** Atheneum 1972.

This book answers several questions: Why do we have laws? How are laws made? Who makes laws? What happens when someone breaks the law? The author explains in detail individual liberties and the laws we have in this country to insure that every person gets "his or her rights."

Thum, Gladys, and Marcella Thum. **The Persuaders: Propaganda in War and Peace.** Atheneum 1972.

This book explains how propaganda is and has been used to control people. Propaganda is used in wartime, but is also used in advertising, politics, and many other aspects of American life.

Walton, Richard J. **Canada and the U.S.A.** Parents 1972.

Beginning with a chronological history of conflicts between French and English settlers, this book traces the course of Canada through the War of 1812 to the present day. It tells in depth of the assassination of Deputy Premier Pierre Laporte. The final chapter discusses American investment in Canada and its effects.

Weingast, David E. **We Elect a President.** Messner 1973.

Filled with anecdotes and references to presidents in our history, this lively account examines the duties and the responsibilities of a president and discusses the qualities demanded of a successful candidate. Revised edition.

Wood, James Playsted. **New Hampshire.** Nelson 1973.

One of the Colonial Histories series, this book tells of the early history of New Hampshire. Many biographical sketches are included, and photographs and drawings are numerous. A guide to historical sites, plus a listing of important dates in the history of New Hampshire, are at the back of the book. Other books in the series include *Colonial Maryland* by Ann Finlayson, and *Colonial Virginia* by Harold Gill, Jr., and Ann Finlayson.

HEALTH

Ebon, Martin. **Which Vitamins Do You Need?** Bantam 1974.

A handbook of information about seventeen vitamins. It deals with such topics as preserving vitamins in fresh fruits and vegetables, the U.S. Food and Drug Administration's attitudes about vitamins and minerals, better health through nutrition, loss of vitamins and trace minerals in processing and preservation of food, vitamin preparations as dietary supplements and as therapeutic agents, and malnutrition and hunger in the United States. Includes charts.

Flender, Harold. **We Were Hooked.** Fawcett World 1973.

The author interviewed hundreds of young people in twenty-five drug treatment centers from California to Connecticut. He selected thirteen of them, ages 15 to 27, to tell their stories of how and why they got into drugs, the problems related to drugs, and how they kicked the addiction.

Hyde, Margaret O. **Mind Drugs.** PB 1973.

There are many questions asked about drugs and

their effects today. Some of the most common questions are answered in this book. What effects do different drugs have on the user? Which drugs can harm your health? Which are addictive? There is a glossary of drug slang and, perhaps most important of all, a section offering suggestions on where to get help.

Johnson, Eric W. **V D** Bantam 1974.

Information about venereal disease, given largely through questions and answers. The book tells people what to look for if they suspect that they have a venereal disease and where to go for treatment. Details about the free hot line anyone can call for advice.

Johnson, Eric W. **Get Smart: V.D.** Bantam 1973.

This factual book furnishes answers to questions young people ask about V.D.—how people catch V.D., the symptoms, the tests to find out whether a person has it, and where to secure free treatment.

Navarra, John Gabriel. **Drugs and Man.** Doubleday 1973.

Lots of questions about drugs are answered here by Dr. Navarra, including the *beneficial* uses to which drugs can be put. They can save lives—and destroy them. The author discusses everything from LSD to heroin to cigarettes; he describes the treatment available to those addicted to drugs, many of whom are between nine and twenty-five years old. Well illustrated.

Roebling, Karl. **Is There Healing Power?** D C Cook 1971.

Karl Roebling describes his personal experiences while visiting with faith healers and attending healing services. The author gives accounts of apparent healings.

Sgroi, Suzanne M. **V D: A Doctor's Answers.** HarBraceJ 1974.

This book informs the reader of the symptoms of V.D., the progress of the disease, the methods used to cure V.D. At the end of the book is a state-by-state listing of V.D. clinics throughout the United States.

Stricker, George, and Fred Weiss. **Kicking It.** Pyramid Pubns 1971.

Through words and pictures this book conveys the setbacks, struggles, and victories of the young people who find hope and help in Topic House. It is a story of drug abusers and drug addicts in distress and contains interviews with nine of the residents, who reveal how they kicked the habit and found new hope.

Woodburn, John H. **Know Your Skin.** Putnam 1967.

A book which answers some fundamental questions about a part of us we take for granted: our skin. What things affect the skin? What causes rashes and disfigurations of the skin?

HISTORY

American

Adoff, Arnold. **Black on Black.** Macmillan 1968.

Blacks speak out on blacks through a series of speeches, letters, excerpts from books, personal interviews, and exhortations. Authors such as Dick Gregory, Malcolm X, Langston Hughes, and Martin Luther King are represented.

Alderman, Clifford Lindsey. **The Royal Opposition: The British Generals in the American Revolution.** CCPr Macmillan 1970.

The colorful stories of the British High Command in the American Revolution: Sir Guy Carleton, John Burgoyne, Sir William Howe, Thomas Gage, Sir Henry Clinton, and Earl Cornwallis.

Alvarez, Joseph A. **From Reconstruction to Revolution: The Blacks' Struggle for Equality.** Atheneum 1971.

Even though, according to the Declaration of Independence, all men are created equal, the black person in America has had to struggle for equality, an ideal he has yet to achieve. Many different leaders and groups have come out of and shaped this struggle toward the goal of equal opportunity and equal rights for black people in the U.S. *From Reconstruction to Revolution* traces the development of the status of blacks from slavery to the present.

Alvarez, Joseph A. **Vice-Presidents of Destiny.** Putnam 1969.

An account of the lives and achievements of the eight U. S. vice-presidents who, as a result of Presidents' deaths, became our leaders.

Archer, Jules. **Front Line General: Douglas MacArthur.** Messner 1963.

Douglas MacArthur was a boy genius inspired by his father, a career military man, and by his mother, who convinced him he was going to be the greatest Mac-Arthur. His life at West Point, his work as a military aide to President Theodore Roosevelt and later as Army Chief of Staff are described in this book. In-cluded also is the controversy occurring after the end of the war in the Pacific, when, as Head of the Occu-pation Forces, MacArthur was reluctant to heed the authority of the President of the U.S.

Archer, Jules. **The Unpopular Ones.** CCPr Macmillan 1968.

The lives of several Americans whose ideas were un-popular in their day are described: John Peter Zenger, Thomas Paine, Horace Greeley, Henry David Thoreau, Amelia Bloomer, Eugene Debs, Woodrow Wilson, Margaret Sanger, Robert Oppenheimer, J. William Fulbright, Ann Royal, Joseph Palmer, Jonathan Walker, and Bethenia Owens.

Armstrong, William H. **The Education of Abraham Lincoln.** Coward 1974.

In this historical biography, the world of Lincoln is recreated. The influences of Lincoln's life are de-scribed—the various kinds of schools with the different teaching methods, such as the "blab school" and Caleb Hazel's school; the philosophy of listening to learn; the books Lincoln read; and the superstitions of the period.

Asimov, Isaac. **The Birth of the United States.** HM 1974.

This book describes the period in American history when the Americans and British were battling one another, from the Treaty of Paris in 1763 through the American Revolution and the War of 1812. Historical figures come alive in anecdotes and events are drama-tized.

Baldwin, Gordon C. **How the Indians Really Lived.** Putnam 1967.

This comprehensive but very readable description of the nine areas of Indian culture north of Mexico in-cludes information about food, homes, clothing, hair styles, social units, recreation, warfare, religion, and many other aspects of Indian life.

Berger, Raoul. **Impeachment: The Constitutional Problems.** Bantam 1974.

This book, written by a Harvard Law School Fellow, is a study of the historical foundations, the scope, and applications of impeachment proceedings in our government. The impeachment of President Andrew Johnson is thoroughly reviewed. The author asks many important questions about the limitations of the power of impeachment.

Bronson, William. **The Earth Shook, the Sky Burned.** PB 1971.

San Francisco was a bustling, growing metropolis before the morning of April 18, 1906, when earthquakes devastated the city. When he heard the first rumbling, the police commissioner looked up Washington Street and saw the whole street rising toward him like the waves of the ocean. The earthquake was followed by four days of fire and destruction. The author describes in great detail the panic of the citizens and the drama of the town's recovery, and has included a large number of photographs taken at the time of the catastrophe.

Brown, Dee. **Bury My Heart at Wounded Knee: An Indian History of the American West.** Bantam 1972.

This is the story of the white man's invasion of Indian lands in the 1800s, and of his broken promises to the tribes. The author shows how, little by little, whites destroyed the Indians' land and way of life; he views Indian attacks on whites as retaliation. The book helps readers see American history from the Indian viewpoint, even using Indian names for white leaders. General Custer is Long Hair; Kit Carson is Rope Thrower. When possible, the story is told in the words of Indians who were involved in the events.

Buckmaster, Henrietta. **Women Who Shaped History.** CCPr Macmillan 1966.

To change prisons, medicine, education, slavery, and religion, women pioneers fought at least one common enemy—the inferior status nineteenth-century America assigned to females. This book tells about six heroines every student of American history should know: Dorothea Dix, Prudence Crandall, Elizabeth Cady Stanton, Elizabeth Blackwell, Harriet Tubman, Mary Baker Eddy. They accomplished their work in spite of limited opportunities.

Burt, Jesse, and Robert B. Ferguson. **Indians of the Southeast: Then and Now.** Abingdon 1973.

This is the story of the Indians of the Southeastern United States: the Seminoles, Cherokees, Creeks, Choctaws, and Chickasaws. It tells how these Indians lived, highlights some of their great leaders such as Osceola, Tecumseh, and Sequoyah, and describes their conflict with the white man. It also tells how these Indians live today and how they are trying to keep their rich culture and traditions alive.

Callan, Eileen T. **A Hardy Race of Men: America's Early Indians.** HarBraceJ 1970.

This is the story of the early Indians who crossed the Bering Strait thousands of years ago from Asia and spread southward throughout America. It tells of the early Stone Age cultures such as the Clovis and Folsom people, and of the rise of the first Indian civilization. Among the Indian cultures described are those of the mysterious mound-building Hopewell of Ohio, who planned great cities for the dead, and the Iroquois of New York, who formed a confederacy and created the first democracy in America.

Capps, Benjamin, and the editors of Time-Life Books. **The Indians.** Time-Life 1973.

This is the story of the horse Indians: the Apache, Comanche, Cheyenne, Dakota, Crow, Shoshoni, Blackfoot, and Kiowa of the western plains, deserts and mountains. It tells how these tribes lived, about their religious beliefs and customs, and about their conflict with the white man who invaded their lands—the battles and massacres like Little Bighorn and Sand Creek and the peace treaties which were broken again and again as the white man pushed further west.

Cavanah, Frances. **Freedom Encyclopedia: American Liberties in the Making.** Rand 1968.

Brief articles arranged alphabetically give accurate information on events, ideas, documents, organizations, landmarks, and men, contemporary as well as historical, who have contributed to American freedom.

Clagett, John. **These Hallowed Grounds.** Hawthorn 1968.

The author has visited several of the best known battlefield parks and historic sites which are under the care of the Department of Interior. In chronological order, he describes the events they commemorate.

Collier, Peter. **When Shall They Rest? The Cherokee's Long Struggle with America.** HR&W 1973.

This book traces the struggle of the Cherokee Indians, from colonial times to today. Mainly about the fight of the Cherokees for land, the book contains descriptions of such events as "The Trail of Tears," the forced march of the Cherokees from their eastern homeland to the Oklahoma Territory.

Cook, Fred J. **The Demagogues.** Macmillan 1972.

The book discusses first "What is a demagogue?" then the causes and effects of demagoguery. People and events of various periods in U.S. history are described: the Salem witch-hunt and Samuel Parris; the Civil War, with William Lloyd Garrison and William Lowndes Yancy; the attack on Catholics by Lyman Beecher, Samuel F. B. Morse, and Anna Carroll; the modern period, with Huey Long, Father Coughlin, and Joseph McCarthy.

Coolidge, Olivia. **Women's Rights: The Suffrage Movement in America, 1848–1920.** Dutton 1973.

The fight for the ratification of the Nineteenth Amendment granting American women the right to vote began in 1848 with the Women's Rights Convention in Seneca Falls, New York, and continued until 1920. This book tells about the courageous leadership of such women as Susan B. Anthony, Alice Paul, and Carrie Catt. To win the vote, women picketed, lobbied, paraded, and went to jail.

Crawford, Deborah. **Four Women in A Violent Time.** Crown 1970.

Mary Dyer, Deborah Moody, Anne Hutchinson, and Penelope Van Princes were heroines of the 1640s in early America. Each woman was courageous and resourceful in her own way, contributing to the growth of the new land.

Davis, Daniel S. **Struggle for Freedom: The History of Black Americans.** HarBraceJ 1972.

This book provides a different look at American history. It presents American history from the point of view of generations of oppressed blacks who were rarely allowed to partake in any "American Dream."

For these Americans whose African heritage was lost in the "hell ships" of the slave trade, and whose American heritage has been lost through generations of enslavement and degradation, this book's purpose is to retell their forgotten pasts. It begins with ancient African history and continues through the treacherous years of slave trade and the cruelties of plantation bondage. Lastly, it recounts the hundred years since the Civil War, during which countless black men and women have struggled for their long-neglected rights as free Americans.

Day, A. Grove. **Kamehameha, First King of Hawaii.** Hogarth 1973.

This pamphlet gives a concise history of Hawaii at the time of King Kamehameha I, the mighty warrior who united the islands by conquest. Numerous illustrations include photographs of battle sites and portraits of such legendary figures as Captain James Cook and High Chief Kanina.

Deloria, Vine, Jr. **Custer Died for Your Sins: An Indian Manifesto.** Avon 1970.

A Sioux Indian and former executive director of the National Congress of American Indians clearly defines Indian values and their clashes with those of the whites. Documents past mistreatment of Indians by the United States government, church groups, and anthropologists; criticism of the political, social, and religious forces which perpetuate the stereotyping of his people. Description of tribal organization and what its values offer to modern society.

Donovan, Frank. **The Women in Their Lives.** Dodd 1966.

The author tells of the characters, personalities, appearances, and influences of the women involved with Franklin, Washington, Adams, Jefferson, Hamilton, and Madison. Quotes from letters and diaries add to the reality of the book and give it a personal touch.

Eiseman, Alberta. **From Many Lands.** Atheneum 1970.

A history of the immigrants who came from all over the world to settle in America and shape the nation. The book tells how these immigrants gave laws, culture, and language to America. It gives the reader an idea of what it was like to be an immigrant in the past and what it is like to be a newcomer to America today.

Epstein, Perle. **Individuals All.** CCPr Macmillan 1972.

Seven Americans, all nonconformists, are described:
poets Emily Dickinson and Walt Whitman; Henry
David Thoreau, the writer and philosopher; Isadora
Duncan, the dancer; Thomas Merton, a Trappist
monk, poet, philosopher, mystic and peace advocate;
Dick Gregory, comedian and social critic; and the
Brook Farm Commune, a group that tried to create
a Utopia in the nineteenth century. The contributions of each to society and quotations from each individual are stressed.

Fulks, Bryan. **Black Struggle: A History of the Negro
in America.** Dell 1969.

Fulks writes of the conflicts, burdens, and problems
blacks in America have had to face in their struggle
to be free and equal. Fulks starts with the blacks in
Africa and traces their struggle through slavery to
the present day. He questions whether the blacks are
free; to him they aren't free yet, and they still have
struggles ahead.

Gerson, Noel B. **Passage to the West: The Great Voyages of Henry Hudson.** Messner 1968.

Hudson's four voyages are interestingly presented,
showing Hudson's personality, his relationships with
men like John Smith and Sir Walter Raleigh, and the
results of his discoveries.

Gilfond, Henry. **Heroines of America.** Fleet 1970.

The lives of thirty-four courageous American women
of the eighteenth, nineteenth, and twentieth centuries
are described briefly. The hardships and contribu-
tions of the following women are highlighted: Eliza-
beth Blackwell, Clara Barton, Jane Addams, Lillian
Wald, Harriet Tubman, Sojourner Truth, Mary Mc-
Leod Bethune, Helen Keller, Margaret Sanger, El-
eanor Roosevelt, Amelia Earhart, Mildred Didrickson
Zaharias, Margaret Chase Smith, Shirley Chisholm,
Phillis Wheatley, Julia Ward Howe, Harriet Beecher
Stowe, Pearl Buck, Rachel Carson, Maude Adams,
Ethel Barrymore, Minnie Fisk, Katherine Cornell,
Marian Anderson, Georgia O'Keefe, Margaret Bourke-
White, Marie Mitchell, and Coretta King.

Goettel, Elinor. **America's Wars—Why?** Messner 1972.

The author traces America's wars from the American
Revolution through Vietnam. She looks into the rea-

sons for America's involvement in each of the wars and also gives her personal comments about the effects of war on our country.

Goldston, Robert. **The Coming of the Civil War.** Macmillan 1972.

This book explains how the Civil War began. It tells about the history of slavery in the United States, about the political issues and discussions concerning slavery and secession, and about the causes of the Civil War.

Goldston, Robert. **The Coming of the Cold War.** Macmillan 1970.

Goldston tells how the cold war between Russia and the United States began and describes the events which led up to it. The foreign policy views of all the countries involved are presented. The roles that Roosevelt, Truman, Churchill, and Stalin played in the development of the cold war are also discussed.

Goldston, Robert. **The Negro Revolution: From Its African Genesis to the Death of Martin Luther King.** Macmillan 1968.

This book about the American Negro begins by destroying the myth that Africa is a savage continent. It then documents the history of the American Negro, through the civil rights campaign of the 1960s and the contributions of Malcolm X and Stokely Carmichael.

Graham, Alberta Powell. **Lafayette: Friend of America.** Abingdon 1952.

This book tells the story of Lafayette's life, first as a wealthy, young Frenchman, trained in the military, who risks his life and gives his own money voluntarily to fight for the colonies' freedom in the American Revolution; later, as a military and political leader in France during its revolution, and finally as a hero returning to a growing America.

Grant, Bruce. **American Forts: Yesterday and Today.** Dutton 1965.

More than 1,200 forts built in America are briefly described—their history and locations as they relate to today's towns and the present condition of the forts. The book is organized by sections of the United States, and forts in each state are listed. More than one hundred drawings and a glossary are included.

Green, Margaret. **Defender of the Constitution: Andrew Johnson.** Messner 1962.

Born into poverty in North Carolina the son of uneducated parents, Johnson learned tailoring at the age of twelve, taught himself to read, and became a student of American history. Moving into Tennessee, he succeeded as a tailor and was elected to state and national political offices. He championed the cause of the poor and the working people and defended the Constitution. Upholding his beliefs, he withstood a trial of impeachment and preserved the Union.

Green, Margaret. **President of the Confederacy: Jefferson Davis.** Messner 1963.

The book gives the life story of Jefferson Davis. A soldier, congressman, Secretary of War, and senator loyal to the South, he showed outstanding courage and ability in establishing a confederate government in perilous times and in raising an army that fought heroically.

Gridley, Marion E. **American Indian Women.** Hawthorn 1974.

This book contains the stories of eighteen prominent Indian women who made significant contributions to their people and their country. Included are such women as Sacajawea, guide for the Lewis and Clark Expedition, and Susan La Flesch Picotte, the first Indian woman physician.

Harris, Janet, and Julius W. Hobson. **Black Pride: A People's Struggle.** Bantam 1970.

This book provides a history of the black man's role in American life, from slavery to the present day.

Haskins, Jim. **Ralph Bunche: A Political Analysis.** Hawthorn 1974.

The life of Ralph Bunche, who rose above poverty and racial discrimination to succeed in school as a scholar and athlete, and as an American leader in the United Nations and winner of the Nobel Peace Prize. This book describes the life of a modest, intelligent, unselfish, kind, and hardworking American statesman.

Hazama, Dorothy. **The Ancient Hawaiians: Who Were They? How Did They Live?** Hogarth 1973.

This booklet tells about the "hale" or ancient Hawaiian home—what people lived in it, how it was built, what tools were used, what ceremonies and chants sanctified it. Drawings and photographs help the young reader see the knots the builders used, the kukui nut candle, the lauhala pillow and other unfamiliar items.

Hiller, Carl E. **From Tepees to Towers: A Photographic History of American Architecture.** Little 1967.

More than one hundred photographs tracing the history of American architecture. Illustrated glossary; index of architects.

Hoag, Edwin. **American Cities: Their Historical and Social Development.** Lippincott 1969.

Tracing the historical and social development of cities in the United States, the author shows the gradual shift from an agricultural to an urban nation.

Hoehling, Mary, and Betty Randall. **For Life and Liberty: The Story of the Declaration of Independence.** Messner 1969.

Beginning in 1761 with the arguments against the Writs of Assistance, this story traces the actions and ideas of leading colonists to the moment in 1776 when the Declaration of Independence was signed.

Hogg, Garry. **Union Pacific: The Building of the First Transcontinental Railroad.** Walker & Co 1969.

The building of the Union Pacific was authorized by President Lincoln. The author tells how the railroad was completed in half the anticipated time despite hostile Indians, weather, mountains, and other hazards.

Hughes, Langston. **Famous Negro Heroes of America.** Dodd 1958.

Defying armed redcoats, operating a wilderness trading post, spiriting slaves to freedom, captaining a ship through submarine-infested waters, and performing other courageous acts, black Americans add their exploits to the American saga.

Ipsen, D. C. **Eye of the Whirlwind: The Story of John Scopes.** A-W 1973.

This book is more than the story of a Kentucky boy, son of a railroad mechanic, who grew up in Illinois, graduated from the University of Kentucky, became a teacher in Dayton, Tennessee, and later an oil geologist. The book tells the dramatic story of the teacher who was the center of the Tennessee Evolution Trial, with William Jennings Bryan and Clarence Darrow battling to determine whether a teacher "could teach any theory that denies the story of the Divine Creation of man as taught in the Bible and teach instead that man had descended from a lower order of animals."

Johnson, Dorothy M. **Warrior for a Lost Nation: A Biography of Sitting Bull.** Westminster 1969.

The Sioux boy called Slow became Sitting Bull, eloquent leader and great warrior of the Plains Indians, in their hopeless struggle against the encroaching white men.

Kane, Joseph Nathan. **Facts about the Presidents.** PB 1968.

Vital statistics, important career dates, election information, and significant national and international events for each president from George Washington to Lyndon Johnson are presented in itemized form.

Keating, Bern. **Famous American Explorers.** Rand 1972.

The excitement of the unknown drew adventurers westward for centuries, until the North American continent held few secrets. Beginning with Leif Ericson and his Vikings nearly a thousand years ago, the author gives brief stories of the voyages and overland treks that opened up America to European settlers. Columbus, the Spanish conquistadores, the French voyageurs, Daniel Boone and other frontiersmen, the seekers for the Northwest Passage to the Pacific, Lewis and Clark, Zebulon Pike, the fur traders of the Northwest, and many others fill these pages. The book is handsomely illustrated with drawings and reproductions of paintings. Western Heritage Juvenile Book Award.

Khan, Lurey. **One Day, Levin . . . He Be Free.** Dutton 1972.

William Still was a fearless fighter for slaves running away from the South. Son of Levin Still, who had bought his freedom, and a mother who had run away, William Still became the executive secretary of Philadelphia's Anti-Slavery Society. He kept accurate and detailed records of runaway slaves and took an active leadership role in the Underground Railroad. From his records he published in 1872 *The Underground*

Railroad. From that book came this biography and history, which includes Levin's work and the letters, newspaper clippings, and records related to the slave problem.

King, Martin Luther, Jr. **Why We Can't Wait.** Har-Row 1964.

In a convincing answer to an old question, King traces the history of the black Americans' fight for equality, explains how it came to a head in Birmingham, and projects his views into the future.

Kohn, Bernice. **The Spirit and the Letter: The Struggle for Rights in America.** Viking Pr 1974.

This book tells how and when civil rights and liberties were acquired. Examples of minority groups such as blacks, women, and homosexuals, who must constantly fight for rights they legally possess, are highlighted in the book.

Kromer, Helen. **The Amistad Revolt, 1839: The Slave Uprising Aboard the Spanish Schooner.** Watts 1973.

This story of a group of Africans, kidnapped on the Gold Coast and sold into slavery, is strewn with quotes from prominent people and observers who actually witnessed some of these historical scenes. The *Amistad* was a schooner used to transport the slaves. After a shipboard revolt, they were imprisoned. Many Americans, led by abolitionists, sympathized and took the case as high as the Supreme Court. Eventually they succeeded in outfitting a ship to return the slaves to Africa. Photographs and drawings illustrate the text.

Lader, Lawrence, and Milton Meltzer. **Margaret Sanger: Pioneer of Birth Control.** Dell 1974.

From her girlhood in the early 1900s, Margaret Sanger was aware of and sensitive to the miseries of people in the slums of New York. This biography tells how, with courage and intelligence, she sought ways to aid these people. For fifty years she crusaded for Planned Parenthood throughout the world.

Lampman, Evelyn Sibley. **Once Upon the Little Big Horn.** T Y Crowell 1971.

This is a narrative about the battle of the Little Big Horn. It is told from the point of view of the military white man as well as from that of the Indian.

Leipold, L. Edmond. **Famous American Teachers.** Denison 1972.

This book tells the stories of ten American men and women teachers who influenced other people's lives through their courage—in overcoming obstacles of racial prejudice, lack of money, and physical handicaps—and introduced new and unpopular ideas: William McGuffey, author of pioneer readers; Booker T. Washington, founder of Tuskegee Institute; Horace Mann, founder of the American Public Education System; Emma Hart Willard, founder of the first women's college; Mary Lyon, founder of Mount Holyoke College for Women; Martha Berry, founder of a school in the Georgia hills; John Dewey, a believer in experiment in the classroom; James Bryant Conant, advocate of individual freedom; Mary McLeod Bethune, founder of the Daytona (Florida) Educational and Industrial Training School for Negro Girls later known as Bethune-Cookman College; and Anne Sullivan Macy, Helen Keller's teacher.

Leipold, L. Edmond. **Famous American Women.** Denison 1967.

The book presents the life stories of ten women who contributed to America's growth and greatness, from the American Revolution to the twentieth century: Willa Cather, writer; Molly Pitcher, heroine of the American Revolution; Susan B. Anthony, suffragette leader; Sacajawea, Indian guide to the Lewis and Clark Expedition; Martha Washington, wife of the General and President of U.S.; Elizabeth Peabody, founder of kindergartens in the U.S.; Emily Dickinson, poet; Clara Barton, founder of the American Red Cross; Emma Lazarus, writer; Amelia Earhart, aviatrix; and Dolly Madison, wife of a U.S. President and heroine of the White House.

Lester, Julius. **To Be a Slave.** Dell 1970.

This book shows the type of life plantation slaves experienced. The reader learns of the poor living conditions, the constant fear, the lack of freedom, and the trauma the blacks faced, from the personal stories of slaves and from the author's short history of slavery.

Levine, Israel E. **Young Man in the White House: John Fitzgerald Kennedy.** Messner 1964.

John F. Kennedy's life story shows a hard-working man, courageous, concerned about others, and determined to help them. The book describes his family and its influence, his schooling, his experiences in World War II, and his political career.

Loh, Jules. **Lords of the Earth: A History of the Navajo Indians.** CCPr Macmillan 1971.

This is the story of the Navajo Indians, the "Dineh" (the people) of Arizona, Utah, and New Mexico. It tells of their persecution by white men such as Kit Carson, of broken treaties and exile, and the "Long Walk" to Fort Sumner near Albuquerque. But it is also the story of how the Navajos have come to be the largest and most prosperous Indian tribe in America today. Western Writers of America Spur Award.

McHugh, Tom. **The Time of the Buffalo.** Knopf 1972.

Everything you ever wanted to know about that exciting animal of the Great Plains, the buffalo, has been gathered into one book by the man who filmed *The Vanishing Prairie*. The author reaches back into prehistory and follows the buffalo through the time when entire Indian cultures of the plains revolved around it. He gives a close-up view of behavior of buffaloes within the herd, from their battles to their playful moments. White settlers reacted to the buffalo first with awe, then with an eye for plunder, almost wiping out the herds and destroying the Indian cultures. The author's photographs and many reproductions of early drawings enrich this book. Western Writers of America Spur Award.

Meltzer, Milton. **Bound for the Rio Grande: The Mexican Struggle, 1845–1850.** Knopf 1974.

This book tells the story of American migration west and how the United States acquired the territories of California, New Mexico, Arizona, Colorado, Nevada, and Utah after the Mexican War. It contains accounts of men who journeyed westward, the intrigue connected with the planning and declaration of war, the dissent among American soldiers, the weak Mexican government, the American war correspondents, and the songs of the period.

Meltzer, Milton, editor. **In Their Own Words: A History of the American Negro 1916-1966.** T Y Crowell 1967.

The third volume in the author's history of black Americans, told through excerpts from present day documents, covers the period of two world wars and today's civil rights movement.

Miller, Douglas T. **Then Was the Future: The North in the Age of Jackson 1815–1850.** Knopf 1973.

This book brings to life the period between 1815 and 1850 in the North, when industrialization was changing America. The problems of slavery, sexism, immigrants, and factory workers, and the work of the reformers are shown vividly through the prints, songs, photographs, letters, diaries, and speeches of well-known leaders of the day, such as William Lloyd Garrison, Charles Dickens, Ralph Waldo Emerson, Martin Delany, Solomon Northup, Davy Crockett, Martin Van Buren, and many others.

Molloy, Anne. **The Years before the Mayflower: The Pilgrims in Holland.** Hastings 1972.

The Separatists or Pilgrims left northern England in 1608 and went to Holland. Remaining there for twelve years, the Pilgrims were influenced in their life-style and thinking by the Dutch. The book describes the Pilgrims' life in Holland, their preparation for the journey to America, and the fate of those left behind in Holland.

Morgan, Edmund A. **So What about History?** Atheneum 1969.

This book tells us why we bother to study history. The author attempts to define history as things or "junk" we have gotten from the past. The author also shows how we have taken ideas from the past and used them to change things in the present.

Myers, Elisabeth P. **Madam Secretary: Frances Perkins.** Messner 1972.

After devoting most of her life to improving conditions for working women, Frances Perkins was appointed Secretary of Labor in President Franklin Roosevelt's administration—the first woman cabinet member in the history of the U.S. This biography tells how her design for labor programs helped to pull the country out of the Depression.

The New York Times, Staff of. **The End of a Presidency.** Bantam 1974.

The resignation of Richard M. Nixon from the presidency of the United States is documented by the staff of *The New York Times.* A pictorial history, a chronological history, and editorials about the event are included. The text of Nixon's letter of resignation and incriminating documents are presented.

Oakley, Mary Ann B. **Elizabeth Cady Stanton.** Feminist Pr 1972.

A biography of Elizabeth Cady Stanton, the first American to suggest in public that women should have the vote. She wrote the "Declaration of Sentiments" for the Seneca Falls convention of 1848; it began, "We hold these truths to be self-evident, that all men and women are created equal."

O'Connor, Richard. **Sitting Bull: War Chief of the Sioux.** McGraw 1968.

Sitting Bull is one of the most famous Indian tribal chiefs and warriors. This story tells of his concerns, his struggles, his strategies for battle, as he tries to keep the Sioux tribes from losing their land and their heritage to the white man.

Orrmont, Arthur. **The Amazing Alexander Hamilton.** Messner 1964.

This book relates the life of Alexander Hamilton from his early years in the Dutch West Indies. It describes his college days in the American colonies, his influence as a brilliant orator and aide to George Washington, his heroic action in the American Revolution, his leadership in ratifying the Constitution, his founding of the fiscal system of our government and finally, his death in a duel by a political opponent, Aaron Burr.

Pearson, Michael. **Those Yankee Rebels.** Putnam 1974.

The fact that they were outnumbered by the British forces was not enough to keep the rebellious American colonists under their mother country's rule. This history shows how both sides in the American Revolution depended on spies and interceptions to outwit the enemy, and how quarrels between King George III and his generals contributed to the failure of the British campaign. It tells how the Americans won their independence and the reputation of fighting rebels in the Revolution.

The People's Bicentennial Commission. **Voices of the American Revolution.** Bantam 1975.

This book traces the American Revolution from its beginning to the final separation of the colonies from

England. Many little-known facts are revealed. The last half of the book contains thoughts and quotations of participants in the Revolution. Included also are biographical sketches.

Phelan, Mary Kay. **The Story of the Boston Tea Party.** T Y Crowell 1973.

The story of the largest "tea party" in history is told in narrative form, bringing clearly to life such historical characters as Sam Adams, John Hancock, and Paul Revere.

Place, Marian T. **Retreat to the Bear Paw: The Story of the Nez Percé.** Four Winds 1969.

This is the story of Chief Joseph and the Nez Percé Indians and their attempt in 1877 to escape being confined on a reservation by fleeing to Canada from their home in eastern Oregon. The Nez Percé traveled 1,700 miles, only to be stopped forty miles from the Canadian border in the Bear Paw Mountains of Montana. Along the way, the Nez Percé managed to outwit and outfight much larger forces of Army troops and volunteer militia. Their tactics are still studied by West Point cadets. In the end, however, the Nez Percé were defeated and sent to a reservation. Chief Joseph, one of the greatest Indian chiefs, seeing his people defeated, made one of the most famous of Indian speeches: "Hear me, my chiefs, I am tired. My heart is sick and sad. From where the sun now stands, I will fight no more forever." Western Writers of America Spur Award.

Raphael, Ralph B. **The Book of American Indians.** Arco 1973.

This book tells the story of the American Indian from prehistory, when the first Indians crossed the land bridge from Siberia at the Bering Strait and settled throughout North and South America, to the present. It tells about the great Indian tribes, chiefs, and battles, and about Indian life—ceremonials, legends, arts, crafts, medicine men, hunting, fishing and agriculture.

Reeder, Colonel Red. **The Story of the Mexican War.** Hawthorn 1967.

The Mexican War and the personalities involved in it such as General Winfield Scott and Lieutenants Lee, Meade, and Grant are presented in a readable and interesting account.

Reimers, Henry L. **Indian Country: Cultural Views of the Spokanes.** Denison 1973.

This is the story of the Spokane Indians, the "Children of the Sun" of eastern Washington. It tells about their culture and their history, about what happened to them when the white man came to their land, about life on the reservation, and about how the Spokanes live today.

Robe, Rosebud Yellow. **An Album of the American Indian.** Watts 1969.

A short history of the American Indian written by an Indian, this book tells in words and pictures about the Indian cultures of long ago, the coming of the white man, and the Indian wars. It also tells about life on an Indian reservation and about Indians today such as Jay Silverheels, better known as Tonto, the Lone Ranger's "faithful Indian friend."

Rosenfelt, Willard E. **The Last Buffalo: Cultural Views of the Plains Indians: The Sioux or Dakota Nation.** Denison 1973.

This is the story of the great plains Indians, the Sioux or Dakota. It tells about how the Sioux lived: about the importance of the horse and the buffalo to their way of life, about tepees, sign language, and the religious beliefs of the Sioux. It is also the story of the persecution of the Sioux by the white man—the broken treaties and battles that forced the Sioux from their lands.

Sanderlin, George. **A Hoop to the Barrel: The Making of the American Constitution.** Coward 1974.

This book clearly outlines the questions and problems that faced the men who met in convention to write the U.S. Constitution. The answers, personalities, confrontations, and compromises that ensued are shown through many first-hand accounts.

Seidman, Laurence Ivan. **Once in the Saddle: The Cowboy's Frontier, 1866–1896.** Knopf 1973.

This history tells in the words of the men and women who lived on the western ranges their experiences on the plains, on the buffalo hunts, in the towns, in the blizzards of 1886 and 1887, and on the Chisholm Trail. Not only autobiographical accounts but also cowboy songs and photographs make this history of cowboys come alive.

Simpson, Colin. **The Lusitania.** Ballantine 1974.

On May 7, 1915, a German submarine torpedoed a British passenger liner, killing 1,198 persons including 124 Americans. This act of war is considered to be a major factor in the United States' entry into World War I. Now Colin Simpson, a *London Sunday Times* correspondent, has gathered evidence supporting the theory that the *Lusitania* was, in fact, armed and carrying munitions, and that it was an explosion of these munitions that caused her to sink in eighteen minutes! He further theorizes that the incident was connived, a plot concocted by the British government to lure the U.S. into the war.

Solomon, Louis. **America Goes to Press: The Story of American Newspapers from Colonial Times to the Present.** CCPr Macmillan 1970.

This book gives a detailed account of the developments that have shaped and changed the American newspaper from colonial times to the present. The public has been the key factor in shaping the newspapers of every age. Newspapers are bought by people, so they must please them. Many other things have influenced newspaper reporting and publishing, such as politics, radio, and television. These influences are discussed in the book.

Steele, William O. **The Old Wilderness Road: An American Journey.** HarBraceJ 1968.

This is the story of the Old Wilderness Road, but especially, the story of the four men who made the road in Virginia: Thomas Walker, Daniel Boone, Elisha Wallen, and John Filson. The author has used journals and other contemporary sources for his book, and supplemented it with maps.

Steiner, Stan. **The Tiguas: The Lost Tribe of City Indians.** CCPr Macmillan 1972.

This is the story of the Tiguas Indians, a tribe of Pueblo Indians which everyone thought was extinct. The Tiguas have lived secretly in El Paso, Texas, since 1682. They fled south to El Paso from the great Revolt of the Pueblo Indians in Arizona and New Mexico against the Spanish conquistadores in the seventeenth century. They have lived secretly in El Paso, preserving their ancient ways by holding religious ceremonies in the streets and hunting on missile ranges. Western Writers of America Spur Award.

Stember, Sol. **Heroes of the American Indian.** Fleet 1971.

This is the story of some of the great American Indian leaders and heroes—men like Sequoya, who created a written alphabet for the Cherokee language; Osceola, Chief of the Seminoles; Chief Joseph of the Nez Percé; Cochise and Geronimo of the Chiricahua Apaches; and Sitting Bull, Chief of the Sioux, who tried to keep the white man from stealing Indian lands and hunting grounds.

Sterling, Dorothy. **Tear Down the Walls: A History of the American Civil Rights Movement.** Doubleday 1968.

Although the book begins with the 1955 bus boycott in Montgomery, Alabama, the author includes much of the history of blacks in America from the coming of the slaves. She enlivens the history through characterization, dialogue, and action. W. E. B. DuBois, Martin Luther King, and several others are vividly portrayed, as are the roles of antagonists like the Ku Klux Klan, the Red Shirts, and the Knights of the White Camelia. Emphasizes the NAACP's activities at the expense of more militant organizations and philosophies.

Taylor, Theodore. **Air Raid Pearl Harbor: The Story of December 7, 1941.** T Y Crowell 1971.

This book tells about the Japanese attack on Pearl Harbor, from both the Japanese and the American viewpoints. It describes Japanese planning for the attack, the attack itself, and the American negligence that made it possible. Heroes of Pearl Harbor are described, and a list of the key figures is included.

Titcomb, Margaret. **The Ancient Hawaiians: How They Clothed Themselves.** Hogarth 1973.

Much Hawaiian ritual and art was once centered on making tapa, the cloth whose patterns and textures today's machines cannot reproduce. As the women pounded the bark of mauke, the cloth-plant, they evolved music and a message system. Photographs show that woodcarvers also developed their art in making fine designs on the tapa boards.

Wade, William W. **From Barter to Banking: The Story of Money.** CCPr Macmillan 1967.

This book traces the history of money through the ages with special concentration on American currency

from the colonial era to the present. The author focuses on the good and bad points of money, the guarding of money, the management of money, the Federal
Reserve, and inflation.

Walton, Richard J. **Canada and the U.S.A.** Parents 1972.

Beginning with a chronological history of conflicts between French and English settlers, this book traces
the course of Canada through the War of 1812 to the
present day. It tells in depth of the assassination of
Deputy Premier Pierre Laporte. The final chapter
discusses American investment in Canada and its
effects.

Williams, Frances Leigh. **Plantation Patriot: A Biography of Eliza Lucas Pinckney.** HarBraceJ 1967.

Largely set in pre-revolutionary America, this authenticated biography of Eliza Lucas Pinckney reveals
much about the uncertainties experienced and courage
required by those living on the colonial plantations of
the South.

Witt, Shirley Hill. **The Tuscaroras.** CCPr Macmillan
1972.

This is the story of the Tuscaroras, the sixth Indian
Nation to join the famous Iroquois Confederacy in the
northeastern United States. It is the story of the Tuscaroras' ancient customs and beliefs and how they are
trying to keep their culture alive in today's modern
world. It also tells about the Iroquois steelworkers,
who have become famous because they are not afraid
to work on the highest bridges and buildings across
America.

Wood, James Playsted. **The Great Glut: Public Communications in the United States.** Nelson 1973.

This book about the media begins with a view of early
American newspapers and goes on to include famous
nineteenth-century journalists, the emergence of radio
and television, press associations, and the prevalence
of advertising. The author suggests ways to cope with
the media.

Wood, James Playsted. **New Hampshire.** Nelson 1973.

One of the Colonial Histories series, this book tells of
the early history of New Hampshire. Many biographical sketches are included, and photographs and drawings are numerous. A guide to historical sites, plus

a listing of important dates in the history of New Hampshire, are at the back of the book. Other books in the series include *Colonial Maryland* by Ann Finlayson, and *Colonial Virginia* by Harold Gill, Jr., and Ann Finlayson.

Yolen, Jane. **Friend: The Story of George Fox and the Quakers.** Seabury 1972.

George Fox was the founder of a religious group called Quakers. This story of his life tells how he was often imprisoned because of his beliefs. His belief in the Inner Light present in everyone led to a Quaker belief in equality of sexes and nationalities. Fox refused to join Cromwell's army, to take oaths, to remove his hat to authority. The book describes his two-year visit to America in 1671.

Young, Bob, and Jan Young. **Fifty Four-Forty or Fight: The Story of the Oregon Territory.** Messner 1967.

In 1843, when settlers in the Northwest organized the first American government on the Pacific Coast, and in 1848 when Oregon became a territory, a long race for possession of this rich area was nearly concluded.

World

Alderman, Clifford Lindsey. **The Wearing of the Green: The Irish Rebellion.** Messner 1972.

An account of twentieth-century Irish struggles for freedom. The Irish Rebellion started with the Easter Week Rising in 1916, and by 1921 there was war with England. Peace negotiations followed, resulting in a peace treaty favorable to England but establishing the Irish Free State. After civil war in the 1920s, the Republic of Ireland was created in 1948.

Carlson, Dale. **Warlord of the Genji.** Atheneum 1970.

The Fujiwaras ruled Japan for two centuries with the loyalty of two warrior clans, the Heike and the Genji, who finally turned against each other. Yoshitsune, a young boy, heir to leadership of the Genji, is imprisoned in a monastery without knowing his real identity. When this story begins, his clansmen are helping Yoshitsune escape to lead the Genji's return to power.

Coolidge, Olivia. **The Golden Days of Greece.** T Y Crowell 1968.

The ancient Greeks' love of freedom and beauty is graphically shown through their everyday life, their wars, their leaders, and their artists.

Drower, Margaret. **Nubia: A Drowning Land.** Atheneum 1970.

This is the story of an ancient Egyptian people, the Nubians, who were forced to leave their homeland along the Nile River because of the building of a new dam. Before the dam was completed, however, scientists from all over the world organized themselves to explore, record for history, and preserve much of what remained of the Nubian civilization. The author describes in detail what these scientists recorded.

Ellis, Harry B. **Israel: One Land, Two Peoples.** T Y Crowell 1972.

This book about Israel tells the story of the Jews and the Promised Land from ancient times to today. The book also discusses Arab claims to the same land and the struggles and wars that have resulted.

Fisher, Tadd. **Our Overcrowded World: A Background Book on the Population Crisis.** Parents 1969.

About the population explosion, this book contains many astonishing facts and many easy-to-understand graphs and charts. The world's population from ancient days to the present is traced, and speculation about future population trends is included.

Grohskopf, Bernice. **From Age to Age.** Atheneum 1968.

This book spans several hundred years of history, life, and literature of Anglo-Saxon England. It discusses the history of the Anglo-Saxons from Roman Britain to Edward the Confessor. Also the book talks about life, society, language, poetry (lyrical, heroic, historical, popular, and religious) and prose. A fine book for anyone interested in history and literature of early England.

Hessel, Milton. **Man's Journey through Time.** S&S 1974.

This history of man begins with the formation of the earth, his home, and ends with a look ahead to his flights to other planets. The nine chapter headings include the periods: five billion years of our earth, two million years of manlike creatures, the ancient civilizations, the classical civilizations, the Dark Ages and the rise of Islam, the crusades and the awakening of Europe, the centuries of European domination, the twentieth century and man's journey through time. Each chapter has a time bar which locates the chapter events in relation to overall historical time, and each chapter's events are divided into five differently colored areas of historical development: the Mediterranean world and Europe, Asia, Oceania, Africa, and the Americas.

Hodges, C. Walter. **The Spanish Armada.** Coward 1968.
Here is a brief, profusely illustrated account of the mighty naval force that threatened England in 1588.

Howard, Cecil, and J. H. Parry. **Pizarro and the Conquest of Peru.** Am Heritage 1969.
Accompanied by excellent illustrations, this volume tells of the Spanish conquest of the Inca Empire, of the conquerors' insatiable desire for gold, and of the violent conflicts among Spanish leaders.

Janssen, Pierre (translator William R. Tyler). **A Moment of Silence.** Atheneum 1970.
Janssen, in *A Moment of Silence,* tells of the Second World War and its effect on the Netherlands. Photographs of sculptures depicting events of the war illustrate the book.

Johnson, Gerald W. **The British Empire: An American View of Its History from 1776 to 1945.** Morrow 1969.
This American author gives his view of the history of the British Empire from the American Revolution to the end of World War II. He evaluates the roles of leading Englishmen during those years.

Lum, Peter. **The Growth of Civilization in East Asia: China, Japan and Korea to the Fourteenth Century.** S G Phillips 1969.
Asian civilization began in China and spread to Japan and Korea. The author traces these civilizations from their mythic beginnings. The emphasis is on the customs, philosophies, art, and inventions, which make the ancient eras come to life for the reader. This book provides a background for its sequel, *Six Centuries in East Asia.*

Lum, Peter. **Six Centuries in East Asia: China, Japan and Korea from the Fourteenth Century to 1912.** S G Phillips 1973.

This book begins with the Mongols in power in East Asia and much of Europe. When they were driven out of China in 1368, the Ming dynasty began an age of brilliance in art, science, and literature. Because the Mongols had instilled a lasting fear of the "barbarian," China, Japan, and Korea have almost always resisted the ever-increasing encroachment of the West.

Paine, Albert Bigelow. **The Girl in White Armor.** Macmillan 1967.

Using authentic records, Albert B. Paine presents the story of the courageous medieval French leader, Joan of Arc, from her early childhood when she heard voices, to her search for a king to lead France against English invaders, her imprisonment, torture, excommunication as a heretic, her trial and execution.

Payne, Blanche. **History of Costume: From the Ancient Egyptians to the 20th Century.** Har-Row 1965.

While investigating costumes, the reader learns about the history, daily lives, and customs of people in other times and places. Besides photographs of paintings and sculptures, the author utilizes re-drawings of museum plates which accurately depict costumes in various stages of physical activities. The fifty pages of patterns will be very useful to the costume-maker.

Rau, Margaret. **The People's Republic of China.** Messner 1974.

Written from a Chinese viewpoint, this up-to-date account of China's people and their ways describes the conditions and circumstances that led to the take-over by the Communists and why Mao Tse-tung was able to make this country a leading world power.

Scharfstein, Ben-Ami. **The Mind of China.** Basic 1974.

Why are some Chinese paintings gray and sad? What is the great message of forests and streams? What is the shape of the universe? The author explores such questions in delightful, well-researched vignettes about the culture, customs, and beliefs of traditional China.

Seeger, Elizabeth. **Eastern Religions.** T Y Crowell 1973.

An introduction to the history, philosophies and rituals of such religions as Hinduism, Buddhism, Taoism, and

Shintoism, this book tells of the teaching of many of the great religious leaders and some legends about them.

Sheldon, Walter J. **Tigers in the Rice: A Short History of Vietnam.** CCPr Macmillan 1969.

Vietnam has a history which dates back to 3000 B.C. This book begins with Vietnam's mythic beginnings and ends with the Paris peace talks. The history of Vietnam is a story of long, courageous struggles against foreign invasions and rulers.

Tamarin, Alfred. **Japan and the United States: The Early Encounters, 1791-1860.** Macmillan 1970.

The first encounters between the Japanese and the Americans were marked with both comic and tragic misunderstandings, as Westerners tried to cajole the Japanese into opening their ports and the Japanese steadfastly tried to isolate themselves. The art work done by Japanese and American eyewitnesses of the period gives especially fascinating views of how two very different cultures saw one another.

Trease, Geoffrey. **This Is Your Century.** HarBraceJ 1966.

With the aid of many excellent maps and photographs, the author graphically presents the twentieth century, highlighting outstanding figures, wars, and the revolutionary social, economic, and political changes. Book World Children's Spring Book Festival Award.

von Däniken, Erich (translator Michael Heron). **The Gold of the Gods.** Bantam 1974.

In this book the author offers more information in support of his belief that there was once a prehistoric earthly "era of the gods." This era, the author says, was one in which beings from outer space landed on earth and were proclaimed gods. Von Däniken offers everything from cave wall drawings of spaceship-like vehicles to Chinese mythology to give more proof to his theory.

Warner, Rex. **Athens at War.** Dutton 1970.

Rex Warner has translated Thucydides' account of the war between Athens and Sparta in 431 B.C. and created an exciting, readable story of the struggle to end Athens' overseas empire and her leadership of the Greek mainland. This history shows not only a war but also its tragic aftermath.

White, Jo Ann. **African Views of the West.** Messner 1972.

Africans tell stories and accounts revealing their pride in what has happened to them in the past, what's happening now, and what they anticipate for the future.

White, Jo Ann. **Impact: Asian Views of the West.** Messner 1971.

This book is a collection of reactions which Asians have had to the impact of the West. The writers include Gandhi on his visit to England, a Chinese commissioner protesting to Queen Victoria about the English opium trade, a Hiroshima kite-maker's impressions of the first atomic bomb. There are also writings from Korea, Java, the Philippines, Thailand, Indonesia, and Vietnam.

Young, Bob, and Jan Young. **The Last Emperor: The Story of Mexico's Fight for Freedom.** Messner 1969.

Although this book opens with the execution of Maximilian in 1867, it briefly details the early history of Mexico under the Spaniards before beginning an account of the struggle for independence.

HOBBIES

Alton, Walter G. **Making Models from Paper and Card.** Taplinger 1974.

This book gives clear instructions for making a variety of designs. Helpful illustrations and detailed diagrams assist the reader and maker of models.

Amster, Shirley. **The Complete Book of Family Boating.** Coward 1967.

A well-written and detailed manual on almost everything a beginner would need to know about boating—what to look for in a boat, what equipment is necessary, rules of the road, winter storage, etc.

Barris, George, and Jack Scagnetti. **Famous Custom and Show Cars.** Dutton 1973.

This book describes in words and photographs more than eighty custom cars by famous designers. Included are show cars, custom Corvettes, sporty customs for the street, and prestige luxury cars.

Brock, Virginia. **Piñatas.** Abingdon 1966.

Piñatas are beautiful objects, usually made of papier mache and clay, filled with treats and made to be broken. This book contains a history and three stories of piñatas. Included are illustrations and step-by-step instructions for making eleven different types of piñatas.

Charlip, Remy, Mary Beth, and George Ancona. **Handtalk: An ABC of Finger Spelling and Sign Language.** Parents 1974.

Colored photographs and black and white inserts show how to form letters and words in sign language.

Coffey, Francine. **Francine Coffey's Celebrity Sewing Bee.** Har-Row 1974.

In her book, Francine Coffey tells with great enthusiasm the origins of her interest in sewing, and how it eventually led her to fascinating careers in Paris and New York. She discusses encounters with many famous people along the way. The author further stimulates one's interest in sewing by describing a hundred unique and versatile items to create yourself, with clear instructions to follow.

Coombs, Charles. **Motorcycling.** Morrow 1968.

This survey of motorcycles begins with a brief history of the motorcycle industry and also describes the most popular models through the 1960s. Operation and safety procedures are explained. Particular attention is given to sports cycles, although road and trail bikes are covered as well.

Cunningham, Chet. **Your Wheels: How To Keep Your Car Running.** Putnam 1973.

This book will help a reader take better care of his "wheels." It shows how to service spark plugs, how to clean the engine, and how to do a tune-up. The author says that knowing a car and how to service it will result in cheaper and safer driving.

D'Amato, Janet, and Alex D'Amato. **American Indian Craft Inspirations.** M Evans 1972.

A book of Indian crafts and how to make them. It tells how to make Indian jewelry out of beads, shells, bone and metal, and how to weave and sew Indian clothing such as moccasins and Hopi dresses. The book has many ideas of things to make, using Indian craft techniques.

DePree, Mildred. **A Child's World of Stamps: Stories, Poems, Fun and Facts from Many Lands.** Parents 1973.

The book contains pictures of over 150 postage stamps, enlarged and in color. Along with the stamps are poems, games, facts and folklore from the more than fifty countries represented.

Durden, Kent. **Gifts of an Eagle.** Bantam 1974.

This is a true story of training a golden eagle. Although eagles are protected by law, the Durden family receives a permit to obtain an eagle for research purposes. The eagle is trained, adopts a gosling as her child, and stars in Disney films and "Lassie" shows. After sixteen years, she flies off with a mate.

Dwiggins, Don. **Riders of the Wind: The Story of Ballooning.** Hawthorn 1973.

A new adventure for man began in Paris, France, in 1783, when the Montgolfiers sent up the first balloon. *Riders of the Wind* presents many first-hand accounts of ballooning from 1783 to 1973. It tells of the successful as well as the unsuccessful flights, including those of the Piccards, Lunard, Pilatre de Rozier, and Madame Thibee.

Engler, Larry, and Carol Fijan. **Making Puppets Come Alive: Method of Learning and Teaching Hand Puppetry.** Taplinger 1973.

This books shows the beginner step-by-step methods leading up to staging a hand-puppet show. Photographs of lively puppets illustrate finger, wrist, and arm exercises, pantomimes, and improvisational skits the authors have chosen for developing skills like speech synchronization.

Fenin, George N., and William K. Everson. **The Western: From Silents to the Seventies.** Grossman 1973.

One hero known worldwide is the cowboy in the tall white hat; one art form that has grown out of the very soul of America, her myths and her history, is the Western. Beginning with "The Great Train Robbery," that famous silent movie of 1903, this book follows the development of the Western. Generously illustrated with movie shots.

Gardner, Martin. **Codes, Ciphers and Secret Writing.** S&S 1972.

In the United States alone, tens of thousands of people

are engaged in, and more than a billion dollars per year is spent on, code-breaking. The author explains systems of making and breaking codes. Included in the book are famous code incidents from history.

Hamilton, Charles (with Diane Hamilton). **Big Name Hunting.** S&S 1973.

This is a guide for the beginning autograph collector. It tells such things as what types of autographs can be collected, how to buy from dealers, how to mount and preserve a collection, how to avoid forgeries and mechanically reproduced signatures, and how to build an historically and financially valuable collection. Appendixes include addresses of autograph dealers, autograph auction houses, autograph periodicals, and the addresses of one hundred notable world figures.

Horvath, Joan. **Filmmaking for Beginners.** Nelson 1974.

The young filmmaker will find this book invaluable for practical, step-by-step instructions. The author gives suggestions on script writing, choosing a camera and film, shooting, editing. Her emphasis is on self-expression and imagination.

Hunt, Douglas, and Kari Hunt. **The Art of Magic.** Atheneum 1967.

This history of magic includes people who believed that they could produce real miracles as well as entertaining "conjurers" like Houdini, Blackstone, and Chung Ling Soo. This book tells about the lives of famous conjurers and the acts they invented. The second part shows the beginning magician many tricks of the trade.

Joseph, Joan. **Folk Toys Around the World and How to Make Them.** Parents 1972.

This is a collection of twenty-three toys from all over the world, with instructions and detailed diagrams on how to make them. Included are a puppet from Indonesia, a Russian bear from the Soviet Union, and a corncob donkey from Venezuela. Histories of the toys and the countries from which they come are also included.

Kuykendall, Karen. **Art and Design in Papier-Mache.** Hearthside 1968.

Basic introduction to the art of papier-mache; easy-to-follow instructions for projects such as jewelry,

Christmas ornaments, puppets, and wall plaques. Many illustrations.

Larson, Rodger (with Ellen Meade). **Young Filmmakers.** Dutton 1969.

A documentary about a grandmother called Bubby. A fantasy about an invisible boy. Animated vegetables. These are some of the movies by young filmmakers that will make you want to try your own hand at the camera. The authors will help you script, shoot, edit, and even distribute your film.

Marks, Mickey Klar. **Collage.** Dial 1968.

Collage is the art of gluing bits of paper and other materials to canvas or cardboard to form a picture. This book includes easy-to-follow instructions and illustrations for making twelve different types of collage.

McFarland, Kenton (with James C. Sparks, Jr.). **Midget Motoring and Karting.** Dutton 1961.

The authors give complete information along with diagrams and photographs on building a midget car, from selecting an engine to building a chassis, constructing wheels, brake systems and engine mountings, and upholstering. In addition, instruction on driving safely, information on buying a kart and forming a club, and lists of manufacturers of midget cars and parts are included in the book.

Meilach, Dona Z. **Creating Art from Anything.** Reilly & Lee 1968.

Meilach shows how to transform familiar materials—including toothpicks, rocks, plastic bottles, and wire—into collages, collographs, and sculptures. Brief instructions and many illustrations are included.

Meyer, Carolyn. **Christmas Crafts.** Har-Row 1974.

This book, with simple instructions and step-by-step illustrations, suggests twenty-four exciting things to make with inexpensive and easy-to-get materials for Christmas. Included also are legends and myths about Christmas celebrations around the world.

Murray, Michael. **The Videotape Book.** Bantam 1974.

A basic guide to portable TV production for everyone, this book includes explanations of a variety of videotaping equipment and shows the advantages of videotaping over filming.

Musciano, Walter A. **Building and Flying Scale Model Aircraft.** Herman Pub 1970.

The author has been building and flying model planes since he was seven years old. He is considered one of the world's top model aircraft authorities. Plans and instructions are given for building and flying fifteen carefully selected models. Included are simple beginner's models and complex, radio-controlled craft. Photos and captions show and describe many models.

Paul, Aileen. **Kids Camping.** Doubleday 1973.

A complete guide for beginning campers. It has sections on how to buy camping equipment, good places to camp in North America, preparation and suggested supplies, basics like pitching a tent, tips on backpacking, and safety measures. There's plenty of common sense advice to help you get the most out of your camping trip.

Peltier, Leslie C. **Guideposts to the Stars: Exploring the Skies through the Years.** Macmillan 1972.

This book is helpful for locating stars, constellations, and planets without the aid of a telescope. Everything is clearly illustrated with charts giving times and locations of planets, constellations, stars, and even meteorite showers. Individual explanation is given to each constellation in the middle northern latitudes.

Pountney, Kate. **Make a Mobile.** S G Phillips 1974.

This book with colorful illustrations and diagrams describes the different kinds of mobiles—twisting, flying, twirling, and humming. The author explains step-by-step how to make various mobiles and gives ways for designing original mobiles.

Reid, Peter C., and Don Lehrbaum. **The Motorcycle Book.** Doubleday 1967.

This informative book covers all aspects of motorcycles—varieties, choosing a bike, safety techniques, what to wear, and taking care of your cycle.

Waters, Barbara, and John Waters. **Salt Water Aquariums.** Holiday 1967.

A how-to-do-it book on setting up an aquarium, what fish to buy, problems a beginner may face, and some extremely practical advice for anyone interested in marine life.

Zaidenberg, Arthur. **How To Draw Flowers, Fruit, and Vegetables.** Abelard 1964.

While flowers, fruit, and vegetables can "hold a pose," they have a vitality and freshness that the artist must capture. This book gives basic shapes but urges the young artist to see for himself and not just make copies.

OCCUPATIONS

Clark, Dorothy, Jane Dahl, and Louis Gonzenbach. **Look at Me, Please Look at Me.** D C Cook 1973.

This is the story of two women who dedicate themselves to helping the mentally handicapped. At first they are shocked and repulsed by the sight of the children. Through many of their stories and experiences, the reader sees these women learning to accept the children and discovers what hidden beautiful qualities the handicapped can have.

Cole, Doris. **From Tipi to Skyscraper: A History of Women in Architecture.** Braziller 1973.

Women were the first architects. In many North American tribes, Indian women designed, fabricated, and constructed the dwellings. From its beginnings, the author shows the many contributions women have made to American architecture. Photos include the Shaker village at Canterbury, New Hampshire; San Simeon, the Hearst castle; and a house in Massachusetts heated with solar energy.

Deschin, Jacob. **Photography in Your Future.** Macmillan 1965.

Readers interested in a career in photography will find here the steps which can be followed in preparing for photography-related jobs. Thirty-four areas of specialization are described in detail.

Gardner, Martin. **Codes, Ciphers and Secret Writing.** S&S 1972.

In the United States alone, tens of thousands of people are engaged in, and more than a billion dollars per year is spent on, code-breaking. The author explains systems of making and breaking codes. Included in the book are famous code incidents from history.

Gerrold, David. **The Trouble with Tribbles.** Ballantine 1973.

This is the story of one television segment of the show "Star Trek." It covers all aspects of that one show, from script-writing through the final production as it was seen on television. Much information about the behind-the-scenes work that goes into a TV show is included.

Gerrold, David. **The World of Star Trek.** Ballantine 1973.

This book covers the television series "Star Trek" from its inception as an idea through its production to the aftermath of its being dropped as a series. The author recreates all facets of the process with interesting narrative about each.

Griese, Bob, and Gayle Sayers. **Offensive Football.** Atheneum 1974.

Two topnotch pros discuss the topics they each know best. The techniques for passing, running, and team execution are tied into the strategy of game situations. Both photographs and diagrams illustrate appropriate moves and procedures.

Grumich, Charles A., editor. **Reporting/Writing from Front Row Seats.** S&S 1971.

Twenty-five staffers of the Associated Press discuss journalism, offering advice about gathering news, putting a story together, and developing writing techniques. Photographs of the newsmen in action are included.

Heaps, Willard A. **Wandering Workers: The Story of American Migrant Farm Workers and Their Problems.** Crown 1968.

This is compelling study of the American migrant farm workers—who they are, what they do, where they work, why they do what they do.

Hopke, William E., editor. **Encyclopedia of Careers and Vocational Guidance.** Doubleday 1972.

Two volumes—*Planning Your Career* and *Careers and Occupations*—include vital information about many careers: definition, history, and nature of the work; requirements; opportunities for experience; methods of entering and advancing; employment outlook; earnings; working conditions; and social and psychological factors.

Kane, Betty. **Looking Forward to a Career: Dentistry.**
Dillon 1972.

What do dentists do? What kind of education do you
need? What alternatives are there in the field of
dentistry? These and dozens of other questions are
answered and illustrated by photographs showing
equipment, dental students, and dentists in action.

Krueger, Starry. **The Whole Works: Autobiography of a
Young American Couple.** Random 1973.

Tape-recorded interviews tell the story of Bruce and
Gail Erickson, twenty-one and nineteen, who grow up
in Michigan, marry, and move to California, where
they live in a migrant labor camp. The book is a
picture of two people who do temporary farm work.

Lee, Essie E. **Careers in the Health Field.** Messner 1974.

This book contains 144 articles and photographs on
careers in the health field, with discussions on opportunities, requirements, duties, salaries, and advance-
ment possibilities. A list of sources of additional information is included.

Liston, Robert A. **On the Job Training and Where to
Get It.** Messner 1973.

Descriptions of training opportunities for high school
graduates in major occupational fields such as industrial production, building trades, retail sales, and
service, with special emphasis on technical fields. Examples from companies are given.

Liston, Robert A. **Your Career in Civil Service.** Messner
1966.

This book contains general information about civil
service careers, including how to get jobs, descriptions
of specific jobs with the government, and the advantages, and disadvantages of civil service work.
There are over 150 types of jobs, employing over
ninety per cent of the people in government.

Liston, Robert A. **Your Career in Law Enforcement.**
Messner 1973.

This career book gives details about the qualifications,
opportunities, duties, salary, and methods of law
officers in various jobs at every level—city, state, and
national. Case histories are included to give examples
of the kind of personality and training needed, and
risks taken by the officers.

McCall, Virginia, and Joseph R. McCall. **Your Career in Parks and Recreation.** Messner 1974.

Beginning with a brief history of the national park system and the establishment of state parks, the authors proceed to discuss outdoor recreation in the cities, counties, states, and in the national parks and forests. Four states were selected to represent each of the four regions: New York—East; Florida—South; Michigan—mid-North; California—West. Park systems in each of the states are discussed in detail.

McKown, Robin. **Heroic Nurses.** Putnam 1966.

Here are twelve biographical sketches of famous nurses including Jeanne Mance, Florence Nightingale, Clara Barton, Elizabeth Kenny, and Mary Breckinridge, as well as some less famous ones. This book is good background reading on the nursing profession and gives the reader insight into the lives and times of these women.

McLeod, Sterling, and editors of Science Book Associates. **Careers in Consumer Protection.** Messner 1974.

This book includes background in the field of consumer protection, the challenges of protecting the consumer's safety, food, drugs, and money, and a discussion of the following careers requiring college training: home economists; dieticians and nutritionists, food inspectors; investigators and consumer counselors; life scientists (biochemists, embryologists, geneticists, marine biologists, pathologists, pharmacologists, physiologists); food scientists; chemists; physicists; engineers—agricultural, chemical, civil, electrical and mechanical. In addition to careers requiring college, the book contains information about noncollege jobs for technicians in medical and chemical laboratories and in consumer protection in food processing.

Melendez, Carmelo. **A Long Time Growing.** Childrens 1970.

Even after leaving Puerto Rico with his mother to find his father in East Chicago, Carmelo's life did not improve: he still had to live with his father's drinking and his parents' fights, and had to suffer doing poorly in school, having few friends, and being called a momma's boy. In a simple, straightforward style, Carmelo Melendez describes how he broke away from home, decided to become an X-ray technician, and, with the help of his young wife, found the determination to work and go to school full time to achieve success in his new career. Supplemented with information about careers in X-ray technology.

Meredith, Scott, **Writing to Sell.** Har-Row 1974.

This well-written book will be useful to students who hope to write novels. It gives the sort of information needed by creative writers who want to get their work published, and discusses the writer's market.

Millard, Reed, and editors of Science Book Associates. **Careers in Environmental Protection.** Messner 1974.

This book on careers in ecology has two parts: the first describes the challenges to society in protecting the air, water resources, forests, land, fish, and wildlife, and in fighting noise. The second part describes careers in various professions in ecology and life sciences and in environmental protection that do not require college training. At the end of the book are lists of sources for further information and of the U.S. agencies concerned with environmental protection.

Neal, Harry Edward. **Your Career in Electronics.** Cornerstone 1968.

Here are facts about career opportunities in the field of electronics. This detailed handbook discusses qualifications, educational requirements, salaries, and growing demands in the world of electronics.

Olney, Ross R. **Air Traffic Control.** Nelson 1972.

This book gives information about air traffic control—radio and radar, methods of navigation, duties of control-tower operators, training of operators, and the Federal Government departments involved. A glossary of terms is included.

Seide, Diane. **Careers in Medical Science.** Nelson 1973.

A guide for those choosing a career in the health sciences. Careers in the field of medicine, such as nurse, inhalation therapist, mental health technician, optometrists, psychiatric social worker, physician's assistant, doctor, dentist, hospital administrator, podiatrist, and speech therapist, are analyzed. There is also a list of names and addresses of organizations, hospitals, and associations that will give more information on careers.

Sine, Jerry (with Gene Klinger). **Son of This Land.**
Childrens 1970.

White Beaver, a small Indian boy, helped his parents
earn a living by demonstrating Indian dances. He
worked hard at getting an education, but was pulled
into World War II. When he returned, he found jobs
hard to get. He began by doing paste-up work for a
large firm, but soon became a commercial artist and
improved so much that a prestigious advertising agency
hired him. When he married and started a family, he
knew his hard work had been rewarded. Information
about work as a commercial artist is given.

Solomon, Louis. **America Goes to Press: The Story of
American Newspapers from Colonial Times to the
Present.** CCPr Macmillan 1970.

This book gives a detailed account of the developments
that have shaped and changed the American newspaper from colonial times to the present. The public
has been the key factor in shaping the newspapers of
every age. Newspapers are bought by people, so they
must please them. Many other things have influenced
newspaper reporting and publishing, such as politics,
radio, and television. These influences are discussed
in the book.

Splaver, Sarah. **Nontraditional Careers for Women.**
Messner 1973.

This book gives guidance to the young liberated
women, who has more career choices than ever before.
The author has researched over five hundred occupations and gives not only encouragement but much
practical information, such as qualifications and training, future outlooks for jobs, and addresses of professional organizations.

Splaver, Sarah. **Paraprofessions: Careers of the Future
and the Present.** Messner 1972.

This book first defines paraprofessions, then, in categories, discusses the kinds of opportunities in the paraprofessions. The author also lists schools offering programs in the various paraprofessions and sources of
further information.

Splaver, Sarah. **Your Career If You're Not Going to
College.** Messner 1971.

In the first four chapters of this book the student is
helped to evaluate his/her interests and abilities and

to choose a job matching personal qualifications. Requirements to hold the job and make progress in it are given. Separate chapters describe jobs requiring little or no training and those requiring apprenticeship and/or study. Lists of regional offices, the U.S. Bureau of Apprenticeship and Training, State Apprenticeship Councils, and sources of additional information also are included.

Squire, Elizabeth D. **Heroes of Journalism.** Fleet 1973.

Heroes of Journalism is the story of men and women who have defended freedom of the press in America. Journalists such as Benjamin Franklin, Daniel Craig, Joseph Pulitzer, Margaret Bourke-White, and Edward R. Murrow struggled to bring the news speedily and truthfully to the people. The book also tells why the journalist's job is exciting and important.

Standerford, Betsy (with R. Conrad Stein). **No Hablo Inglés.** Childrens 1970.

Vincente (Betsy) Standerford grew up in New Mexico in a primitive village, speaking only Spanish, full of superstition, and yet curious about the world. When her family moved to Colorado, she was frightened by the city and teased by her classmates. When her father tried to marry her off to a stranger, she left home and eventually found an employer who understood her fright and self-consciousness. She married and moved to Chicago, where she became a personnel manager, helping others like herself find themselves and their places in life. Information on work as a personnel manager is provided.

Viscott, David S. **The Making of a Psychiatrist.** Fawcett World 1974.

What does it really take to become a psychiatrist? The author describes his experiences, from student to practicing psychiatrist. He relates his fears, frustrations, the long hours on the job, and the uncertainties on and off the job. This is a good insight, especially for anyone interested in psychiatry as a profession.

Whitfield, Stephen E., and Gene Roddenberry. **The Making of Star Trek.** Ballantine 1973.

This is a complete description (including pictures, authors, and sketches) of the conception and production of the television series "Star Trek." The author, an outside observer, discusses all the technical and practical aspects of writing, planning, financing, and filming *Star Trek*.

Wilkinson, Burke, editor. **Cry Sabotage!** Bradbury Pr 1972.

Here are twenty-seven true stories about acts of sabotage. Most of them take place in the twentieth century; they range from the sinking of the *U.S.S. Maine* (which led to United States' declaration of war on Spain in 1898) to more recent acts of sabotage, such as those in the Vietnam War.

Williams, Billy (with Rick Simon). **Iron Man.** Childrens 1970.

Billy Williams Day was one of the biggest thrills of Billy Williams' life. It made him think back on how he became what he was, a major league baseball star. He reflects on the racial prejudice he met in his baseball career, the excitement of getting into the minor leagues, and the thrill of knowing he had made it in the majors. Information on the life of a professional athlete is provided.

Wood, James Playsted. **This Little Pig: The Story of Marketing.** Nelson 1971.

This book explores the past history and present methods of selling products and the creation of chain stores, famous department stores, and discount houses. It also shows the rise of such companies as Coca Cola and their place in the modern world.

Yates, Elizabeth. **Someday You'll Write.** Dutton 1969.

Elizabeth Yates gives practical suggestions on writing— how to select a subject, to keep the reader interested, to develop plot and characterization, and to use conversation and description.

PERSONAL GROWTH AND DEVELOPMENT

Bayly, Joseph. **The View from a Hearse.** D C Cook 1973.

Many views of death are discussed as well as death-related subjects such as terminal illnesses, funeral parlors, and grief. The viewpoint presented is religious.

Berry, James. **Heroin Was My Best Friend.** CCPr Macmillan 1971.

This book reveals actual conversations the author had with seven young ex-addicts who began using drugs

in their teens, and with an addict's mother. Each ex-
addict explains why he took drugs as well as the
reasons for quitting. Some smoked pot. Others popped
pills. But Donny took heroin—up to twenty bags a
day.

Breisky, William. **I Think I Can.** Doubleday 1974.

At the age of two, Karen suffered massive brain injury when the oxygen supply to her brain was cut off.
Suddenly she could no longer talk or see. She could
scarcely move. This is her father's remarkable journal
of her courageous struggle to get well, covering five
years of vigorous daily training with special slides and
ladders, masks, lights, and special diets. A testament
to the power of faith against all odds.

Chase, Stuart. **Danger—Men Talking: A Background
Book on Semantics and Communication.** Parents 1969.

This book tells how people can improve their communication channels by using semantics. It points out
the benefits and disadvantages of language. It also
shows ways advertisers and politicians get people to
agree with them and tells how to be on the lookout
for their tactics.

Chinnock, Frank W. **Kim—A Gift from Vietnam.** Paperback Lib 1971.

The true story of a young father's dedicated struggle
to adopt a homeless Vietnamese orphan. The author
describes the almost insurmountable barriers of red
tape encountered in Vietnam before being allowed to
bring Kim to America, her special needs, the difficulties
the family faced in instilling love and trust in this
frightened child, and their final struggle to obtain legal
adoption.

Colton, Helen. **Our Sexual Evolution.** Watts 1971.

This book helps the young understand how their upbringing influences their sexual attitudes. The author
discusses masturbation, venereal disease, homosexuality, pregnancy, and many other aspects of sexuality.

Gibran, Kahlil (translator Anthony Ferris). **Spiritual
Sayings of Kahlil Gibran.** Bantam 1970.

Kahlil Gibran, author of *The Prophet,* probes life,
death, and our innermost thoughts and feelings in a
collection of spiritual sayings that each individual must
read and interpret in relation to his or her own life.

Griffin, John Howard. **Black Like Me.** HM 1961.

In a racial attempt to find out what it is like to be a black man in the American South, John Griffin decides that the only way to learn the truth is to experience it himself—as a black man. Risking the disapproval of his friends and the security of his family, Griffin has his skin temporarily darkened by medical treatments, shaves his hair, and moves to New Orleans, where he spends several months living as a black.

Hook, Diana ffarington. **The I Ching and You.** Dutton 1973.

Traditionally no one under fifty can knowledgeably consult the *I Ching*, the 5000-year-old *Chinese Book of Changes*, the world's oldest book. Diana ffarington Hook guides the youthful seeker step by step in approaching the *I Ching* as if it were a human being and using it as spiritual teacher. Beautifully printed diagrams include a transparent overlay and fold-out chart.

Hua, Ellen Kei. **Kung Fu Meditations and Chinese Proverbial Wisdom.** Bantam 1974.

Chinese teachings are presented in the form of seventy-five meditations or thoughts and twenty-four proverbs. A short introduction explains the purpose and method of meditation. Meditations range from one line to one page in length. One meditation reads, "He who knows that enough is enough will always have enough." "Mischief results from too much opening of the mouth" is an example of a proverb.

Johnson, Eric W. **Love and Sex in Plain Language.** Bantam 1974.

A candid and straightforward discussion of the physical, emotional, and moral aspects of love and sex. Written with reserve, objectivity, and good taste.

Landau, Elaine. **Woman, Woman! Feminism in America.** Messner 1974.

This book is the "herstory" of women's roles and how many organizations such as the National Organization for Women have brought women together to improve those roles. The author gives much practical information on women's rights—and the lack of them—in various jobs and life-styles.

Melendez, Carmelo. **A Long Time Growing.** Childrens 1970.

Even after leaving Puerto Rico with his mother to find his father in East Chicago, Carmelo's life did not improve: he still had to live with his father's drinking and his parents' fights, and had to suffer doing poorly in school, having few friends, and being called a momma's boy. In a simple, straightforward style, Carmelo Melendez describes how he broke away from home, decided to become an X-ray technician, and, with the help of his young wife, found the determination to work and go to school full time to achieve success in his new career. Supplemented with information about careers in X-ray technology.

Plowman, Edward. **The Jesus Movement in America.** D C Cook 1971.

This book presents the facts about the "Jesus Movement"—the pros and cons, and what young people today think about the church. Much religious terminology is used.

Powell, John. **Why Am I Afraid to Tell You Who I Am?** Argus Comm 1969.

This book deals primarily with communication, awareness, and understanding between people. A catalogue of games and roles people play is included.

Reingold, Carmel B. **How to Cope: A Guide to the Teen-Age Years.** Watts 1974.

This book deals with the many facets of being a teenager. It discusses parent-teen relationships, peer relationships, and boy-girl interaction. It also deals with drugs, school involvement, and community awareness.

Robertson, Dougal. **Survive the Savage Sea.** Bantam 1974.

When the Robertson family decides to take a pleasure cruise on the schooner "Lucette," they have no idea what is going to happen before they complete that trip. The "Lucette" is attacked by killer whales, and all six of the family have to survive on a small raft and lifeboat. With a lot of determination, very little fresh water, and ten days' supply of food, they try to find land. They learn many techniques of survival.

Ross, Pat, editor. **Young and Female: Turning Points in the Lives of Eight American Women.** Random 1972.

Women have had to fight courageously to fulfill their

talents and ambitions. In this book Shirley Chisholm says that her femaleness has been more of a handicap than her blackness. Eight women tell how their childhoods prepared them to become pioneers.

PLACES AND PEOPLE OF THE WORLD

Alden, Carella. **Sunrise Island: A Story of Japan and Its Arts.** Parents 1971.

Myths and legends exploring the birth and history of Japan begin this trip into a culture completely different from our own. There are dozens of pictures showing the art of Japan, as well as some photographs of old and modern Japanese buildings. Old Japanese customs and traditions, some of which are still observed today, are explained.

Alderman, Clifford Lindsey. **The Wearing of the Green: The Irish Rebellion.** Messner 1972.

An account of twentieth-century Irish struggles for freedom. The Irish Rebellion started with the Easter Week Rising in 1916, and by 1921 there was war with England. Peace negotiations followed, resulting in a peace treaty favorable to England but establishing the Irish Free State. After civil war in the 1920s, the Republic of Ireland was created in 1948.

Baldwin, Gordon C. **How the Indians Really Lived.** Putnam 1967.

This comprehensive but very readable description of the nine areas of Indian culture north of Mexico includes information about food, homes, clothing, hair styles, social units, recreation, warfare, religion, and many other aspects of Indian life.

Bourdeaux, Michael. **The Evidence That Convicted Aida Skripnikova.** D C Cook 1973.

Aida Skripnikova, a Russian Christian, stood up for her religion in spite of persecution. Some Christians in Russia were jailed for their religious convictions.

Carr, Albert B., and Robert S. Hopkins. **Islands of the Deep Sea.** John Day 1967.

The origin of oceanic islands in the Pacific, from undersea volcanoes and coral polyps, is clearly presented along with information on weather, plant and animal life on the islands, and early islanders.

Chapin, Henry. **The Search for Atlantis.** CCPr Macmillan 1968.

Atlantis, as legend says, was a vast continent and kingdom that sank beneath the sea before history. Did it really exist? All clues are considered: the legend itself, related history, and the latest research techniques. Reasons for its existence are fully covered and explained in detail with accompanying pictures and maps.

Christie, Trevor L. **Antiquities in Peril.** Lippincott 1967.

Fourteen monuments of the past threatened with destruction—including Westminister Abbey, the Leaning Tower of Pisa, the Parthenon, Angkor, and the U.S. Capitol—are described with information about efforts being made by modern scientists to rescue them. Excellent photographs.

Coolidge, Olivia. **The Golden Days of Greece.** T Y Crowell 1968.

The ancient Greeks' love of freedom and beauty is graphically shown through their everyday life, their wars, their leaders, and their artists.

Crane, Louise. **Ms. Africa: Profiles of Modern African Women.** Lippincott 1973.

Louise Crane, born in the Belgian Congo of missionary parents, writes profiles of successful African women of today. Whether a judge, singer, or physician, each woman has struggled to overcome difficulties and achieve equality and recognition.

DePree, Mildred. **A Child's World of Stamps: Stories, Poems, Fun and Facts from Many Lands.** Parents 1973.

The book contains pictures of over 150 postage stamps, enlarged and in color. Along with the stamps are poems, games, facts and folklore from the more than fifty countries represented.

Drower, Margaret. **Nubia: A Drowning Land.** Atheneum 1970.

This is the story of an ancient Egyptian people, the Nubians, who were forced to leave their homeland along the Nile River because of the building of a new dam. Before the dam was completed, however, scientists from all over the world organized themselves to explore, record for history, and preserve much of what remained of the Nubian civilization. The author describes in detail what these scientists recorded.

Dunlop, Richard. **Great Trails of the West.** Abingdon 1971.

A modern-day narrator invites the reader to travel the historic trails of the Old West, camping outdoors at night. He visits gold mines, and sometimes travels by covered wagon or stagecoach.

Edwards, Harvey. **Scandinavia: The Challenge of Welfare.** Nelson 1968.

The differences and similarities among modern Denmark, Norway, Sweden, Finland, Iceland, and Greenland, with a special chapter on Lapland, are presented in this attractive volume.

Ellis, Harry B. **Israel: One Land, Two Peoples.** T Y Crowell 1972.

This book about Israel tells the story of the Jews and the Promised Land from ancient times to today. The book also discusses Arab claims to the same land and the struggles and wars that have resulted.

Fraser, Amy Stewart. **The Hills of Home.** Routledge & Kegan 1973.

A true account of life in a small glen in Scotland during the late 1800s and early 1900s, this book includes comments on the laws, religious beliefs, and morals of Amy Stewart Fraser's community.

Heilman, Grant, and J. W. McManigal. **Farm Town: A Memoir of the 1930's.** Greene 1974.

A beautiful pictorial record of rural life in the United States between 1935 and 1940. The photographs were taken by J. W. McManigal and purchased by the author. The barnyard flock of hens, the family's cows, the hand-turned separator, and the pigs butchered in the back yard—they're all in this book.

Henderson, Larry. **Vietnam and the Countries of the Mekong.** Nelson 1972.

Through a brief examination of the past of those Southeast Asian nations—Vietnam, Laos, Cambodia, Thailand, and Burma—touched by the Mekong River, Henderson views the present and appraises the viewpoints of the Vietnamese, and the Western nations, principally the United States. Written during the Vietnam War.

Jenness, Aylette. **Along the Niger River: An African Way of Life.** T Y Crowell 1974.

This photo documentary reveals the differing life styles of nearly a dozen African tribes which come together peacefully at the marketplaces. The tribes, of necessity, rely on each other for goods not produced within their own societies.

Kaula, Edna Mason. **The Land and People of Rhodesia.** Lippincott 1967.

This nation in southeast Africa, once a sort of crossroads for warring tribes, is seen primarily through its cultural heritage. The development of modern Rhodesia is also traced.

Keating, Bern. **Chaka, King of the Zulus.** Putnam 1968.

Chaka was born a nobody in southern Africa in 1787 and as a boy, wandered with his disgraced mother from village to village. He grew up to be a military genius who became a mighty king and made the Zulus great and powerful.

Lifton, Betty Jean, and Thomas C. Fox. **Children of Vietnam.** Atheneum 1972.

This book presents the effect war has on children, from the rich to the poor—on those with parents, on orphans, on runaways. The authors give this description a personal touch by writing about children they knew. National Book Award.

Mead, Margaret. **People and Places.** Collins-World 1972.

In a book written especially for young people, Margaret Mead discusses five cultural groups—the Eskimo, Indians of the Plains, the Balinese, the Minoans of Crete, and the Ashanti of West Africa. Her emphasis in each case is on how the group developed in relationship to its environment and its contact with other people. Especially concerned with how the young learn their culture and its values. The chapter on the Plains Indians discusses the Blackfoot and Cheyenne Indians in depth. This book has been called a "young people's encyclopedia of man."

Nazaroff, Alexander. **The Land and People of Russia.** Lippincott 1972.

This informative and readable account describes Russia's geography and history and in a final section discusses recent economic, political, scientific, and technological developments.

Nickel, Helmut. **Arms and Armor in Africa.** Atheneum 1971.

In pictures and words, Nickel describes the ancient weapons of African tribes and the weapons used today by groups of people in different parts of Africa: in the Sudan, in the Congo, in South Africa, and in North Africa. Pictures and drawings show both the weapons and people.

Pratson, Frederick J. **New Hampshire.** Greene 1974.

Take a pictorial trip through New Hampshire, a state rich in culture. The charm and character of New Hampshire's small towns are enhanced by the diversity of its rich landscape. This is a place that reminds one of home, whether real or imagined.

Raiff, Stan. **Get Ready, Get Set, Go: A Young Travellers Guide to Europe.** Doubleday 1970.

This European travel guide for young people describes the histories of each of eleven European cities, their museums, shops, restaurants, and places to visit.

Rau, Margaret. **The People's Republic of China.** Messner 1973.

Written from a Chinese viewpoint, this up-to-date account of China's people and their ways describes the conditions and circumstances that led to the takeover by the Communists and why Mao Tse-tung was able to make this country a leading world power.

Reynolds, Charles R., Jr. **American Indian Portraits from the Wanamaker Expedition of 1913.** Greene 1971.

This group of 120 photographic portraits of American Indians lay in neglected files for more than fifty years—a byproduct of the third Rodman Wanamaker expedition. The photographs, printed in their original size, are representative of Indian men, women, and children from tribes across the country in 1913. The introduction describes the rediscovery of this picture gallery.

Roland, Albert. **Profiles from the New Asia.** Macmillan 1970.

Through the life stories of Asian leaders the author, Albert Roland, has shown the problems of the new Asia and the progress being made toward solving the problems. Mochtar Lubis, an Indonesian journalist, is working for freedom from oppression from without and repression within; in Singapore Lim Kim San is working for better housing for the increasing urban population; Nilawan Pintong, a Thai magazine editor, is informing the public and encouraging women to participate in youth, education, and professional associations; Elvino and Rosario Encarnacin of the Philippines have established and are managing a credit union; and Akira Kurosawa of Japan, a film director, is emphasizing the humanity of man.

Spring, Norma. **Alaska: Pioneer State.** Nelson 1967.

The author glowingly describes the forty-ninth state in terms of people at work and play, and their relation to the geographic and economic situation.

Sutton, Felix. **West Virginia.** Coward 1968.

Beginning with the making of this mountain state, this profile describes West Virginia's forests and farms, its laboratories, mines, and mills, as well as its people and some of the tales told about them.

Tamarin, Alfred. **Japan and the United States: The Early Encounters, 1791–1860.** Macmillan 1970.

The first encounters between the Japanese and the Americans were marked with both comic and tragic misunderstandings, as Westerners tried to cajole the Japanese into opening their ports and the Japanese steadfastly tried to isolate themselves. The art work done by Japanese and American eyewitnesses of the period gives especially fascinating views of how two very different cultures saw one another.

Tuck, Jay Nelson, and Norma Coolen Vergara (translator Elsie E. González-Paz). **Heroes de Puerto Rico.** Fleet 1971.

This moving history of the people of Puerto Rico describes their achievements, their devotion to the cause of liberty, and their contributions to the culture of their island country. It captures the distinctiveness of each hero's personality and the flavor and excitement of his own time.

von Däniken, Erich (translator Michael Heron). **The Gold of the Gods.** Bantam 1974.

In this book the author offers more information in support of his belief that there was once a prehistoric earthly "era of the gods." This era, the author says, was one in which beings from outer space landed on earth and were proclaimed gods. Von Däniken offers everything from cave wall drawings of spaceship-like vehicles to Chinese mythology to give more proof to his theory.

Voss, Carl Hermann. **In Search of Meaning: Living Religions of the World.** Collins-World 1968.

The major religions are extensively described in this discussion of the origins of religion, the evolution of world faiths, and the role of religions in contemporary society.

White, Jo Ann. **African Views of the West.** Messner 1972.

Africans tell stories and accounts revealing their pride in what has happened to them in the past, what's happening now, and what they anticipate for the future.

White, Jo Ann, editor. **Impact: Asian Views of the West.** Messner 1971.

This book is a collection of reactions which Asians have had to the impact of the West. The writers include Gandhi on his visit to England, a Chinese commissioner protesting to Queen Victoria about the English opium trade, a Hiroshima kite-maker's impressions of the first atomic bomb. There are also writings from Korea, Java, the Philippines, Thailand, Indonesia, and Vietnam.

Yolen, Jane. **The Wizard Islands.** T Y Crowell 1973.

Islands have always been intriguing and mysterious. Most real islands have tales about them. Certain islands, called ghost islands, have tales of pirates, a lady in black, a dreaded black dog, and multiple ghosts. Island mysteries involve strange stones and creatures that time seemed to forget. The disappearing islands include volcanic ones, and those that completely vanish and then return.

Young, Margaret. **Hawaii's People from China.** Hogarth 1973.

To make Hawaii their home, the Chinese had to overcome tremendous hardships. Some were chained on ships, others whipped for talking in the cane fields. The Hawaiians enforced a Chinese exclusion law between 1892 and 1942. Yet half of those who did manage to come to the islands chose to remain, and they added to the cultural richness of Hawaii.

SCIENCES

Ancona, George. **Monsters on Wheels.** Dutton 1974.

This book describes the machines on wheels that man
has made and harnessed to do many jobs. The book
illustrates in sequence the kinds and functions of the
machines in different industries: land machines for
earth moving and road building; machines for shipping
and cargo transfer; agricultural machines; construction
machines; and machines used in exploration of space.

Angrist, Stanley W. **Other Worlds, Other Beings.** T Y
Crowell 1973.

The author begins by describing the probability the-
orem and then goes on to explain what life is and
what conditions are needed to host life as we know it.
The author also explores the possibility of life that
isn't like ours and suggests ways we could communicate with the other beings of our universe.

Aylesworth, Thomas G. **The Alchemists: Magic into
Science.** A-W 1973.

Alchemy was the chemical science of the Middle Ages,
with added touches of superstition, sorcery, religion,
and experimentation. Those who practiced alchemy
were called alchemists—scientists who were dreamers,
honest men and frauds. Some famous alchemists are
described: Merlin of King Arthur's court, Paracelsus
of Switzerland, Cagliostro of Sicily who was a fraud,
Democritus of Egypt, and many others.

Babun, Edward. **The Varieties of Man.** Macmillan 1969.

The author describes the thirty-six races of mankind
and tells how these many races have been formed over
the centuries. He explains how the old categories of
race (Negroid, Caucasoid, and Mongoloid) are inadequate to describe the many "varieties of man." He
also discusses how men's and women's bodies have
adapted to the earth's different climates in order to
survive, how races change over time. Illustrated with
photographs of men and women who represent races
around the world.

Barbour, John A. **In the Wake of the Whale.** Macmillan
1969.

The author tells how man's greediness for wealth has
resulted in the near-extinction of earth's largest creatures, the whales. Man's advance from the small row-

boat and spear to the motorized boat and harpoon has resulted in mass killing. The whale is now considered an endangered species.

Barnett, Lincoln. **The Universe and Dr. Einstein.** Bantam 1974.

The foreword by Albert Einstein states: "The main ideas of the theory of relativity are extremely well presented. Moreover, the present state of our knowledge in physics is aptly characterized." It is exciting to be able to read this clear account of Einstein's thinking about our universe.

Batten, Mary. **Discovery by Chance.** Funk & W 1969.

The book discusses the qualities of mind involved in scientific inquiry. The discoveries of ten scientists are discussed, among them Fleming, Pasteur, and Daguerre.

Berry, Graham. **Life on Mars? The Incredible Photographic Mission of Mariner Nine.** Ritchie 1973.

This is a pictorial essay on Mars, containing pictures brought back to earth by Mariner 9. Berry gives a brief history of man's interest in the possibility of life on Mars. Astronomy buffs in particular will like this book.

Berry, James. **Exploring Crystals.** CCPr Macmillan 1969.

This history of man's knowledge of crystals traces the discovery of such scientists as Huay, Thompson, Dalton, Frank, and Boyle. It also shows crystals at work and suggests experiments for the reader to try.

Bova, Ben. **In Quest of Quasars: An Introduction to Stars and Starlike Objects.** CCPr Macmillan 1970.

One of the newest discoveries in astronomy is the discovery of quasars. These new star-like objects have astronomers puzzled. They may be the answers to the origin of the universe. This book explains why these star-like objects are so unusual and exciting.

Bova, Ben. **Workshops in Space.** Dutton 1974.

This book describes the sky lab space program from its beginning. The author discusses the future of the program and stresses the benefits of nations working together to help mankind. There are many diagrams, photographs, and drawings in the book to help the reader.

Branley, Franklyn M. **Comets, Meteoroids, and Asteroids: Mavericks of the Solar System.** T Y Crowell 1974.

Comets, meteoroids, and asteroids are the mavericks of the solar system. The author includes lists and accounts of meteorites that have hit earth, describes asteroids, tektites, and other little-known features of the solar system.

Briggs, Peter. **Men in the Sea.** S&S 1968.

This book gives short biographies of nine men who made important contributions to the scientific study of the seas. It describes many of the now-famous experiments which first allowed man to live for days at hundreds of feet below the ocean's surface. The importance of the oceans is clearly shown, as well as their potential for future exploration and development.

Brindze, Ruth. **Charting the Oceans.** Vanguard 1972.

This book is about the world's biggest mapping job: charting the oceans. The author gives the history of sea charts and tells about work done in that area of oceanography today. Pictures, maps, and diagrams make the story of charting the oceans exciting and more understandable.

Brindze, Ruth. **Hurricanes: Monster Storms from the Sea.** Atheneum 1973.

This book identifies the sizes, shapes, and causes of hurricanes, one of the most destructive kinds of storms. It describes the terrifying Great Hurricane Camille (1969) and tells how other hurricanes played a large part in the discovery and development of America. Ruth Brindze also explains how radar, satellite pictures, hurricane-hunting airplanes, and special communication systems track the paths of hurricanes and warn people when danger is coming.

Calder, Nigel. **Violent Universe: An Eyewitness Account of the New Astronomy.** Viking Pr 1970.

Radio astronomy and the discovery of quasars and pulsars are developments of the late 1960s, and this book presents up-to-date information through words, photographs, and charts.

Caras, Roger. **The Roger Caras Nature Quiz Book #2.** Bantam 1974.

One hundred and one short quizzes about the natural

world are included in this book. Fish, birds, animals, trees, and naturalists are some of the quiz subjects. The quizzes may be used to test your knowledge, or as a learning tool.

Carr, Albert B., and Robert S. Hopkins. **Islands of the Deep Sea.** John Day 1967.

The origin of oceanic islands in the Pacific, from undersea volcanoes and coral polyps, is clearly presented along with information on weather, plant and animal life on the islands, and early islanders.

Chapin, Henry. **The Search for Atlantis.** CCPr Macmillan 1968.

Atlantis, as legend says, was a vast continent and kingdom that sank beneath the sea before history. Did it really exist? All clues are considered: the legend itself, related history, and the latest research techniques. Reasons for its existence are fully covered and explained in detail with accompanying pictures and maps.

Cohen, Daniel. **ESP: The Search beyond the Senses.** HarBraceJ 1973.

The author examines parapsychological investigation and brings in the work of the Society for Physical Research. The book discusses telepathy, clairvoyance, and precognition with cases from history and modern times as evidence.

Cottrell, Leonard. **Reading the Past: The Story of Deciphering Ancient Language.** CCPr Macmillan 1971.

This book reveals how the writings called Egyptian hieroglyphics, Babylonian cuneiform, and Cretan Linear B came to be understood. The author provides a great deal of information about the linguists whose work led to major breakthroughs in the decipherment and the processes they employed. There are brief synopses of the lives of these men plus discussions of the cultures which each of these three languages represented. New York Academy of Sciences Children's Science Book Award.

Davis, Phillip, and William G. Chinn. **3.1416 and All That.** S&S 1969.

A collection of entertaining essays in the field of mathematics. Topics covered include prime numbers, postulates, geodesics, and number theory.

De Bell, Garrett, editor. **Environmental Handbook.** Ballantine 1970.

Prepared for the first nationwide environmental "teach-in" in 1970, this book contains extensive background information and a thorough examination of the problems facing man in saving the earth.

Dowden, Anne Ophelia. **Wild Green Things in the City: A Book of Weeds.** T Y Crowell 1972.

This book is about the interesting and beautiful weeds of New York City. The author follows them through the year, telling also of their survival and their relationships to people. The author's illustrations show the beauty of these stubborn inner-city representatives of nature.

Ebon, Martin. **Test Your ESP.** NAL 1971.

Can you read the thoughts of others? Forecast events? Influence matter with your mind? This book contains an array of experiments designed to analyze the four major areas of ESP experience. Each experiment is simple enough to perform in your own living room. Correctly performed and evaluated, the exercises will give an indication of the psychic power you may very well possess.

Farmer, Gene, and Rosa J. Hamblin. **First on the Moon, A Voyage with Neil Armstrong, Michael Collins, Edwin E. Aldrin, Jr.** Little 1970.

The actual voyage to the moon is presented through transcripts from the crew's communication with earth. An epilogue by Arthur C. Clarke helps evaluate the importance of this voyage.

Gannon, Robert. **What's Under a Rock?** Dutton 1971.

Springtails, mites, pseudoscorpions, nematodes, slime molds, slugs, snails, earthworms, centipedes, crickets and spiders, termites, and ants come alive when the author explores the world under a rock. The life of the rock also is described. The appendix contains information on how to stalk insects.

Hellman, Hal. **Transportation in the World of the Future.** M Evans 1974.

This book describes transportation as it may be in the future on land, in the air, and on the sea. Reasons for the inefficiency and failure of our present means of transportation are given as well as possible alternatives for both the near and distant future. Imagined for the future are jet propulsion in tunnels and tubes, electric cars, and planes reaching speeds of 5,000 m.p.h.

Hey, Nigel, and the editors of Science Book Associates. **How Will We Feed the Hungry Billions? Food for Tomorrow's World.** Messner 1971.

This book discusses the food crisis—what is being done by scientists all over the world and what still must be done to solve the problem. Among discoveries already made, the book discusses the new wonder wheat, the improved rice, and the high-protein corn. Problems that remain unsolved include finding enough water, getting the most from the soil, producing crops without chemicals, discovering food savers, using food from the sea, and inventing ways to preserve the protein in food. The text is accompanied by many photographs.

Hilton, Suzanne. **How Do They Get Rid of It?** Westminster 1970.

Old cars, planes, trains, refuse, radioactive materials— these leftovers from modern society continue to plague us. The author discusses methods of disposal, both old and new, and also many problems still to be solved.

Hirsch, S. Carl. **Meter Means Measure: The Story of The Metric System.** Viking Pr 1973.

This book describes the scientific creation of the metric system during the French Revolution. Nation after nation has adopted the metric system, because it is logical and precise. The author explains why he feels America will have to accept the metric system.

Holmes, Sandra. **Flowers of the World.** Bantam 1974.

Descriptions of flowers from around the world, including size of the plant, best growing conditions, and botanical classification. Illustrated with color photographs.

Holmes, Sandra. **Trees of the World.** Bantam 1974.

Descriptions of trees from around the world, including size, best growing conditions, and botanical classification. Illustrated with color photographs.

Hutchins, Ross E. **Scaly Wings: A Book About Moths and Their Caterpillars.** Parents 1971.

All types of moths are discussed in this well-illustrated

book. The author warns us about dangerous or poisonous moths, as well as those which are beneficial to nature. Technical terms are clearly defined, and stages of growth and development are detailed. Pictured are different types of moths at various stages and their "homes."

Kay, Helen. **Apes.** Macmillan 1970.

Citing actual experiments and field research involving young apes and children, the author supports the theory that man evolved from apes.

Leek, Sybil, and Stephen Leek. **The Bicycle: That Curious Invention.** Nelson 1974.

The authors, Sybil and Stephen Leek, give a detailed account of the bicycle: its history, its uses in peace and war times; freaks of the cycling world, and "sky-cycling." Line drawings and photographs add interest and information.

Limburg, Peter R., and James B. Sweeney. **Vessels for Underwater Exploration: A Pictorial History.** Crown 1973.

In this pictorial history of underwater exploration vessels, the authors trace development from the crudely built diving bells and diving suits of old to the complex submersibles of today. The book shows the importance of these vehicles in many types of scientific study, salvage work, and peaceful underwater tasks. The book tells about the process of inventing some of these vehicles and explains why they are accepted or rejected by the military.

Lukashok, Alvin. **Communications Satellites: How They Work.** Putnam 1967.

The story of the development of early communications satellites, with explanations in simple language of how they work and some excellent illustrations.

Mackenzie, Katherine. **Wild Flowers of the North Country: Northern New York, Vermont, New Hampshire, Maine.** Tundra Bks 1973.

Katherine Mackenzie's watercolors of wild flowers make this an unusual field guide. Her comments about each flower are for the novice and filled with her personal reactions as well as useful information.

McKown, Robin. **Giant of the Atom: Ernest Rutherford.**
Messner 1962.

Ernest Rutherford has led the world in major discoveries about the atom and radioactivity. This book
tells about his early life in a large New Zealand
family, his education in England, his experiments, discoveries, and honors, and his work with other eminent
scientists.

McLeod, Sterling. **How Will We Move All the People?
Transportation for Tomorrow's World.** Messner 1971.

What kind of car will you be driving twenty years
from now? Can you picture yourself riding in a rapid-
transit train or careening above ground at 300 miles
per hour in a wheelless vehicle? These are the types
of questions this book tries to answer.

Michelsohn, David R. **Atomic Energy for Human Needs.**
Messner 1973.

The peaceful use of atomic energy in anthrophology,
medicine, and agriculture is the major subject of
Michelsohn's book. It also contains information about
the way atomic energy performs "detective work" in
industry and criminology.

Michelsohn, David R. **Housing in Tomorrow's World.**
Messner 1973.

What can be done to develop natural resources and
find new sites for housing developments? Michelsohn
has found some answers to housing demands by using
more plentiful materials such as plastic, concrete, and
recycled wood to achieve a new type of complex suit-
able for the family of tomorrow.

Michelsohn, David R. **The Oceans in Tomorrow's
World: How Can We Use and Protect Them?** Messner
1972.

One of the ways man can use the ocean in the future
is by "fish-farming." Mining minerals and drilling for
oil are additional uses. Among the most important
uses of the sea is as a source for fresh water. The
author also explains the fundamentals of ocean ecology.

Millard, Reed, and editors of Science Book Associates.
**How Will We Meet the Energy Crisis? Power for
Tomorrow's World.** Messner 1971.

We will solve the energy crisis by developing new

sources of energy from the earth, the sun, and the oceans, writes Millard. But these new sources will require additional technological advances which may prove hazardous to the environment.

Millard, Reed, and editors of Science Book Associates. **Natural Resources: Will We Have Enough for Tomorrow's World?** Messner 1972.

This book is about conserving America's natural resources. The author writes about the ways people consume them. The book shows how people are wasting these resources and making beautiful places ugly.

Neal, Harry Edward. **From Spinning Wheel to Spacecraft: The Story of the Industrial Revolution.** Messner 1964.

Moving swiftly from its beginning in the United States to the present age of automation, this story of the Industrial Revolution tells of inventions, relates human-interest incidents concerning inventors, explains terms, and treats problems created by the revolution.

Peltier, Leslie C. **Guideposts to the Stars: Exploring the Skies through the Years.** Macmillan 1972.

This book is helpful for locating stars, constellations, and planets without the aid of a telescope. Everything is clearly illustrated with charts giving times and locations of planets, constellations, stars, and even metorite showers. Individual explanation is given to each constellation in the middle northern latitudes.

Pringle, Laurence. **Ecology: Science of Survival.** Macmillan 1971.

This book gives the reader an idea of man's effects on the different eco-systems of our earth. It describes how food chains and other biological cycles work. It also gives the reader an understanding of what ecologists do and the changes that they want to make in the way we use our natural resources.

Pringle, Laurence. **One Earth, Many People: The Challenge of Human Population Growth.** Macmillan 1971.

Laurence Pringle discusses problems of underdeveloped countries, where shortages of food, water, energy, resources, and living space are resulting from population growth of as many as 40,000 people a day. People need to become better educated about this problem before the population problem can be solved.

Pringle, Laurence. **Pests and People: The Search for Sensible Pest Control.** Macmillan 1972.

Laurence Pringle examines the problems involved in the challenge of pest control. He tells how pests destroy our food, water, and land, and how, by carrying diseases, they kill humans and animals. He talks about the widespread use of chemical poisons, which causes destruction to our environment and endangers our lives. He also points out that biological alternatives—such as radiation, natural enemies, and changing natural growth—would not only control pests but would also help us remain healthy and save our environment.

Richey, B. J. **Apollo Astronauts: First Men to the Moon.** Strode 1970.

This book is a biographical retelling of the exciting events which have occurred in recent United States space exploration. Much of the material has come from newspaper reports by the author.

Ross, Frank, Jr. **The Metric System: Measures for All Mankind.** S G Phillips 1974.

Frank Ross, Jr. gives the early history of weights and measures, information about British weights and measures, an account of the birth of the metric system, a description of measurement in the U.S., and the pros and cons of the U.S. going metric. In simple terms he explains the metric system.

Sagan, Carl, and Jerome Agel. **Other Worlds.** Bantam 1975.

Our first halting steps into space have shown us other worlds far stranger and more interesting than imagined by the authors of the most exotic fiction. Is there life out there? It is possible. This light and airy ramble through a gallery of the moon, sun, planets, and comets contains many black and white photographs.

Sanderson, Ivan T. **More "Things."** Pyramid Pubns 1969.

Are there really dinosaurs still roaming unexplored territory in Africa? Are the Moas, a tribe of primitive

people believed extinct, still living in the vast New
Zealand wilderness? What is the Bermuda Triangle?
These and other fascinating stories of unexplained
phenomena will intrigue any reader who enjoys
delving into the natural mysteries of earth.

Schuman, Benjamin N. **The Human Skeleton.** Atheneum
1965.

Utilizing illustrations and simple language, Dr. Schuman details the functions of the individual parts of the
human skeletal frame.

Silverberg, Robert. **Clocks for the Ages: How Scientists
Date the Past.** Macmillan 1971.

Roving the vast earth, scientists past and present seek
the history of our planet and of man. Using the
evidence of seemingly fragmentary clues gathered by
geologists, archeologists, and chemists, scientists date
the earth's age, climate changes, and relics and skulls
of early man.

Silverstein, Alvin, and Virginia B. Silverstein. **Bionics:
Man Copies Nature's Machines.** Dutton 1970.

The book deals with the new science, bionics—the
study of systems in living creatures and their applications for the improvement of man-made systems. The
author clearly describes machines that see and hear;
animals that have keen senses of smell and use odors
to help find and win mates; nature's clocks and com-
passes; nature's mechanics, bioluminescence—living
lights; bioelectricity—living generators.

Silverstein, Alvin, and Virginia B. Silverstein. **Sleep and
Dreams.** Lippincott 1974.

The authors explain what research has been done on
sleep and dreams. The sleep patterns of humans and
animals are described. Although one-third of our life
is spent asleep, we actually know very little about sleep
and dreams. The Silversteins mention ancient myths
and make some predictions concerning future research
about sleep and dreams.

Sterling, Philip. **Sea and Earth: The Life of Rachel
Carson.** Dell 1974.

The life of a famous twentieth-century biologist and
writer. Rachel Carson was determined to succeed in
college although she had little money for an education.
She was recognized early for her writing ability, her

sensitivity to nature, and concern for ecology. Pursuing science as a career, she combined her literary talent with her scientific findings to awaken the world to the widespread destruction of the natural environment. Christopher Award Children's Book Category.

Stoiko, Michael. **Pioneers of Rocketry.** Hawthorn 1974.

Five men who pioneered in rocketry are described— William Congreve of England, who developed in the early nineteenth century the first barrage rockets; Konstantin Tsiolkovsky of Russia, who furthered the principle of jet propulsion; Robert Esnault-Pelterie of France, who designed a liquid-propellant rocket engine; Robert Goddard of the United States, who was the first to prove a rocket would work in a vacuum; Hermann Oberth of Germany, who designed a rocket combustion chamber and cone nozzle. Included are a history of rockets and ideas about the future of rocketry.

Sullivan, Navin. **Pioneer Astronomers.** Atheneum 1964.

This book tells the progress man has made through the years in exploring the universe. The contributions of pioneer astronomers show how each man helped the others after him make new discoveries. The work of these astronomers is described: Copernicus, Kepler, Galileo, Newton, Herschel, Bessel, Adams, Leverrier, Frainhofer and Kirchoff, Huggins, Shapley and Hertzsprung, Hubble, Jansky and Reber, and Smith and Baade.

Teale, Edwin Way. **The Junior Book of Insects.** Dutton 1972.

This book provides information about the habits of beetles, butterflies, moths, ants, and wasps. Photographs and a chapter on insect warfare are included.

Valens, Evans G. **The Number of Things: Phythagoras, Geometry and Humming Strings.** Dutton 1964.

This book shows how the ideas of Pythagoras and his followers grew and spread. The book is concerned with those things that can be described with numbers. Chapter titles include "Three Four Five," "Filling Space," "A Sine of the Time," "From Square to Crescents," "Cut-Up," "Stars and Double Cubes," "Geometry for Listening," "Means and Ends," "Harmony and Harmonics," and "Music of the Spheres."

SOCIAL ISSUES

Adoff, Arnold. **Black on Black.** Macmillan 1968.

Blacks speak out on blacks through a series of speeches, letters, excerpts from books, personal interviews, and exhortations. Authors such as Dick Gregory, Malcolm X, Langston Hughes, and Martin Luther King are represented.

Aymar, Brandt, and Edward Sagarin. **Laws and Trials That Created History: A Pictorial History.** Crown 1974.

Beginning with the trial of Socrates in 399 B.C., the authors discuss twenty-four trials that have important places in history. Included are, for example, the trials of Joan of Arc, John Thomas Scopes, Angela Davis, the Salem Witchcraft Trials, and the Nuremberg Trials.

Bayly, Joseph. **The View from a Hearse.** D C Cook 1973.

Many views of death are discussed as well as death-related subjects such as terminal illnesses, funeral parlors, and grief. The viewpoint presented is religious.

Cavanah, Frances. **Freedom Encyclopedia: American Liberties in the Making.** Rand 1968.

Brief articles arranged alphabetically give accurate information on events, ideas, documents, organizations, landmarks, and men, contemporary as well as historical, who have contributed to American freedom.

Chase, Stuart. **Danger—Men Talking: A Background Book on Semantics and Communication.** Parents 1969.

This book tells how people can improve their communication channels by using semantics. It points out the benefits and disadvantages of language. It also shows ways advertisers and politicians get people to agree with them and tells how to be on the lookout for their tactics.

Collier, Peter, **When Shall They Rest? The Cherokee's Long Struggle with America.** HR&W 1973.

This book traces the struggle of the Cherokee Indians, from colonial times to today. Mainly about the fight of the Cherokees for land, the book contains descriptions of such events as "The Trail of Tears," the forced march of the Cherokees from their eastern homeland to the Oklahoma Territory.

Conn, Frances G. **Ida Tarbell, Muckraker.** Nelson 1972.

The life of a crusading journalist. Born in her grand-father's log cabin in the oil-producing area of Pennsylvania, Ida Tarbell early saw the miseries of economic depression, the effects of a standard oil monopoly on independent oil men such as her father, and the discrimination against women after the passage of the Fourteenth Amendment to the Constitution. After graduation from college, she became a head mistress at Poland College in Ohio, a member of the staff of the magazine *Chautauquan,* a biographer and historian of Lincoln's life and period, and a journalist with *Mc-Clure's* magazine, exposing corruption.

Coolidge, Olivia. **Women's Rights: The Suffrage Movement in America, 1848-1920.** Dutton 1973.

The fight for the ratification of the Nineteenth Amendment granting American women the right to vote began in 1848 with the Women's Rights Convention in Seneca Falls, New York, and continued until 1920. This book tells about the courageous leadership of such women as Susan B. Anthony, Alice Paul, and Carrie Catt. To win the vote, women picketed, lobbied, paraded, and went to jail.

Crary, Margaret. **Susette La Flesche: Voice of the Omaha Indians.** Hawthorn 1973.

A biography of Susette La Flesche, who traveled to meetings all over the United States telling people about the Omaha and Ponca tribes, their hardships, and their plans for the future.

Davis, Daniel S. **Mr. Black Labor: The Story of A. Philip Randolph, Father of the Civil Rights Movement.** Dutton 1972.

Asa Philip Randolph, son of a southern minister, learned early of the injustices the blacks suffered and the courage needed to bring them racial freedom, social justice, and economic equality. This biography tells how, as a young man, Randolph went to New York for an education, accepted socialism as a way to help the blacks, started a newspaper, *The Messenger,* and worked at many jobs. He brought blacks into the labor movement in the twenties and thirties and organized the civil rights movement in spite of powerful opposition.

Edwards, Harvey. **Scandinavia: The Challenge of Welfare.** Nelson 1968.

The differences and similarities among modern Denmark, Norway, Sweden, Finland, Iceland, and Greenland, with a special chapter on Lapland, are presented in this attractive volume.

Fisher, Tadd. **Our Overcrowded World: A Background Book on the Population Crisis.** Parents 1969.

About the population explosion, this book contains many astonishing facts and many easy-to-understand graphs and charts. The world's population from ancient days to the present is traced, and speculation about future population trends is included.

Fulks, Bryan. **Black Struggle: A History of the Negro in America.** Dell 1969.

Fulks writes of the conflicts, burdens, and problems blacks in America have had to face in their struggle to be free and equal. Fulks starts with the blacks in Africa and traces their struggle through slavery to the present day. He questions whether the blacks are free; to him they aren't free yet, and they still have struggles ahead.

Gutman, Judith Mara. **Is America Used Up?** Grossman 1973.

Judith Gutman takes a critical look at America, from the early 1900s to the present. She uses photographs to portray people's lack of interest in our society.

Harris, Janet, and Julius W. Hobson. **Black Pride: A People's Struggle.** Bantam 1970.

This book provides a history of the black man's role in American life, from slavery to the present day.

Haskins, James. **Street Gangs Yesterday and Today.** Hastings 1974.

Street gangs date back as far as the early 1800s. This book traces the historical development of street gangs with special emphasis on New York City gangs. Vivid black and white pictures illustrate why people join street gangs and what happens to them once they are members.

Heaps, Willard A. **Wandering Workers: The Story of American Migrant Farm Workers and Their Problems.** Crown 1968.

This is a compelling study of the American migrant

farm workers—who they are, what they do, where they work, why they do what they do.

Hilton, Suzanne. **How Do They Get Rid of It?** Westminster 1970.

Old cars, planes, trains, refuse, radioactive materials—these leftovers from modern society continue to plague us. The author discusses methods of disposal, both old and new, also many problems still to be solved.

Hirsch, S. Carl. **Cities Are People.** Viking Pr 1968.

This book traces the development of cities, from Babylon to the modern megalopolis. America's largest cities and their problems are given particular attention.

Hirsch, S. Carl. **The Riddle of Racism.** Viking Pr 1972.

In America, three great racial groups—the Indians, white colonizers, and blacks of Africa—met in large numbers. From the 1850s to the present, the search for scientific knowledge of race as a biological phenomenon is traced against the political background that reveals the sociological aspects. The personal stories of many individuals are included. Jane Addams Book Award.

King, Martin Luther, Jr. **Why We Can't Wait.** Har-Row 1964.

In a convincing answer to an old question, King traces the history of the black Americans' fight for equality, explains how it came to a head in Birmingham, and projects his views into the future.

Kohn, Bernice. **The Spirit and the Letter: The Struggle for Rights in America**. Viking Pr 1974.

This book tells how and when civil rights and liberties were acquired. Examples of minority groups such as blacks, women, and homosexuals, who must constantly fight for rights they legally possess, are highlighted in the book.

Landau, Elaine. **Woman, Woman! Feminism in America.** Messner 1974.

This book is the "herstory" of women's roles and how many organizations such as the National Organization for Women have brought women together to improve those roles. The author gives much practical information on women's rights—and the lack of them—in various jobs and life-styles.

Lester, Julius. **To Be a Slave.** Dell 1970,

This book shows the type of life plantation slaves experienced. The reader learns of the poor living conditions, the constant fear, the lack of freedom, and the trauma the blacks faced, from the personal stories of slaves and from the author's short history of slavery.

Liston, Robert A. **The Right To Know: Censorship in America.** Watts 1973.

Americans tend to fear both too much censorship and complete absence of control over what is shown, written, said, or broadcast to the public. This absorbing book looks into the reasons some of us favor various degrees of restriction—upon TV and radio, movies and book sales, and information about "classified" government activities—as well as the reasons other people oppose some or all restraints. The author doesn't take sides. He sets forth plenty of information about both poles of opinion and leaves it to the reader to decide how he or she feels. Christopher Award Children's Book Category.

Liston, Robert A. **Violence in America: A Search for Perspective.** Messner 1974.

By comparing acts of violence in the past with acts of violence today, the author shows that violence is not as prevalent as the mass media would have citizens believe. Many types of disturbances have virtually disappeared today.

Matturri, Joanna, and Hy Dales. **Inner City Reflections in Black and White: A Collection of Visuals by Young Photographers.** WSP 1973.

Starting with the minimum essentials—a couple of cameras, several rolls of film, the encouragement of two adults—ten inner-city teenagers learned to express their feelings about the city through photography. As diverse as the city itself, their visions are by turn hopeful, poignant, desolate: children playing, children alone, houses deserted, old men musing on sidewalk stoops. The photographs are accompanied by commentary from the young photographers; many of the pictures were exhibited at museums in New Jersey and New York.

May, Charles Paul. **Probation.** Hawthorn 1974.

This book traces the history of probation from its origin in 1841 to the present. The author notes the changes in juvenile rights and laws as well as changes in the probation programs. Actual case histories are given. Since there is a great need for more probation officers, he discusses qualities of a probation officer and careers in the area of probation.

Medea, Andra, and Kathleen Thompson. **Against Rape.** FS&G 1974.

This well-written book for mature readers gives straightforward, realistic advice on how to prevent rape and what to do in case of rape. The authors are a self-defense teacher and a member of Chicago Women Against Rape. The suggest self-defense techniques for women and analyze the causes and effects of assault. Included is a list of existing rape crisis centers.

Meltzer, Milton, editor. **In Their Own Words: A History of the American Negro 1916-1966.** T Y Crowell 1967.

The third volume in the author's history of black Americans, told through excerpts from present day documents, covers the period of two world wars and today's civil rights movement.

Paradis, Adrian A. **Economics in Action Today.** Messner 1967.

This book deals primarily with economic systems around the world. It tells how money is circulated through society, why we pay taxes, and how the American economy has developed during the past two centuries.

Paradis, Adrian A. **Inflation in Action.** Messner 1974.

The author defines inflation, gives some historical background, tells whom inflation hits, and suggests ways inflation can be controlled.

Plowman, Edward. **The Jesus Movement in America.** D C Cook 1971.

This book presents the facts about the "Jesus Movement"—the pros and cons, and what young people today think about the church. Much religious terminology is used.

Roebling, Karl. **Is There Healing Power?** D C Cook 1971.

Karl Roebling describes his personal experiences while visiting with faith healers and attending healing services. The author gives accounts of apparent healings.

Ross, Pat, editor. **Young and Female: Turning Points in the Lives of Eight American Women.** Random 1972.

Women have had to fight courageously to fulfill their talents and ambitions. In this book Shirley Chisholm says that her femaleness has been more of a handicap than her blackness. Eight women tell how their childhoods prepared them to become pioneers.

Rover, Constance. **Love, Morals and the Feminists.** Routledge & Kegan 1970.

This book for mature readers explores the impact of feminism on sexual morality. From the French Revolution to today, women have fought to enlighten social attitudes about marriage, divorce, free love, prostitution, birth control, the "double standard," etc. Particularly interesting are the personal life-styles feminists such as Mary Wollstonecraft and Margaret Sanger chose while working for liberation in the face of moral pressures.

Stein, M. L. **Blacks in Communications: Journalism, Public Relations and Advertising.** Messner 1972.

In the past, blacks have been excluded from responsible positions in the media, but now they are being accepted. In this book, blacks tell of the difficulties they have had to overcome in making careers for themselves in the media. Biographical sketches are included.

Sterling, Dorothy. **Tear Down the Walls: A History of the American Civil Rights Movement.** Doubleday 1968.

Although the book begins with the 1955 bus boycott in Montgomery, Alabama, the author includes much of the history of blacks in America from the coming of the slaves. She enlivens the history through characterization, dialogue, and action. W. E. B. DuBois, Martin Luther King, and several others are vividly portrayed, as are the roles of antagonists like the Ku Klux Klan, the Red Shirts, and the Knights of the White Camelia. Emphasizes the NAACP's activities at the expense of more militant organizations and philosophies.

Stricker, George, and Fred Weiss. **Kicking It.** Pyramid Pubns 1971.

Through words and pictures this book conveys the setbacks, struggles, and victories of the young people who find hope and help in Topic House. It is a story of drug abusers and drug addicts in distress and contains interviews with nine of the residents, who reveal how they kicked the habit and found new hope.

Strouse, Jean. **Up Against the Law: The Legal Rights of People Under 21.** NAL 1970.

A clearly written explanation of the legal rights of young adults. Recent court decisions are reviewed and historical perspective is presented in a lively fashion.

Thum, Gladys, and Marcella Thum. **The Persuaders: Propaganda in War and Peace.** Atheneum 1972.

This book explains how propaganda is and has been used to control people. Propaganda is used in wartime, but is also used in advertising, politics, and many other aspects of American life.

Tobin, Richard L., editor. **The Golden Age: The Saturday Review 50th Anniversary Reader.** Bantam 1974.

Celebrating its first half century, *The Saturday Review of Literature* presents this fabulous collection of articles which have appeared in the magazine. Early reviews of some great novels, biographical sketches of famous writers, articles by Eleanor Roosevelt, Norman Cousins, Albert Schweitzer, and Robert F. Kennedy, and, finally, a short humor section are included.

Uden, Grant. **A Dictionary of Chivalry.** T Y Crowell 1969.

Many illustrations and cross-references add to the excellence of this volume, which gives information about people, events, places, terms, and almost anything concerned with feudalism.

Van Voris, Jacqueline. **Constance de Markievicz: In the Cause of Ireland.** Feminist Pr 1972.

This is the story of Constance de Markievicz, who lost her wealth and beauty fighting for the liberation of Ireland and of women. In 1922 she wrote, "The question of votes for women, with the bigger thing, freedom for women and opening of the professions to women, has been one of the things that I have worked for and given my influence to procuring all my life. . . ."

Werstein, Irving. **Strangled Voices: The Story of the Haymarket Affair.** Macmillan 1970.

On May 1, 1886, a nationwide strike of American workers took place. On the fourth day of that strike (May 4, 1886) a bomb exploded at a workers' rally in

Chicago's Haymarket Square. This is the story of that bloody affair which came to be known as the Haymarket Affair.

Wood, James Playsted. **The Great Glut: Public Communications in the United States.** Nelson 1973.

This book about the media begins with a view of early American newspapers and goes on to include famous nineteenth-century journalists, the emergence of radio and television, press associations, and the prevalence of advertising. The author suggests ways to cope with the media.

Yates, Elizabeth. **Amos Fortune: Free Man.** Dell 1971.

This is the true story of an African slave, Amos Fortune, who in 1725 at the age of fifteen was captured and brought to Massachusetts. Sold at auction, he lived as a slave until sixty years of age, when he purchased his freedom. He saved his money to purchase the freedom of other slaves. As a tanner, Christian, and citizen of Jeffrey, Massachusetts, he was a respected member of the community. Book World Children's Spring Book Festival Award. John Newbery Medal.

Yates, Elizabeth. **Prudence Crandall: Woman of Courage.** Dutton 1955.

Running a boarding school for girls in the 1800s wasn't easy, but Prudence Crandall found it was even harder when the school was for black girls. Nothing stopped her, however, not even broken windows and being thrown in jail.

SPORTS

Abodaher, David J. **Mag Wheels and Racing Stripes.** Messner 1973.

This book shows the development of the high performance cars of the sixties. It gives inside information on how the automobile companies decide on a car design, how "muscle" cars are rebuilt for drag racing, and what to expect at a sportcar "rallye." More than 60 photographs are included.

Axthelm, Pete. **The City Game.** PB 1971.

This is the New York Knicks' story, personifying basketball at its best. New York loves the game, from the

young children in the streets to the national championship team. Big stars like Willis Reed, Walt Frazier,
Dave DeBusschere, and others take part in some
exciting and important games. We begin to understand
the mystique of "the city game."

Berger, Phil. **Great Moments in Pro Football.** Messner
1969.

Twelve of the most exciting and sometimes unexpected
moments in the crucial games of the history of football, from Ernie Nevers' singlehanded slaughter of the
Chicago Bears, to Joe Namath and the underdog Jets
springing the biggest upset in pro football's championship series. These are accounts of men who refused
to give up, even at the last minute, when everyone else
said they couldn't make it.

Butler, Hal. **Roar of the Road: The Story of Auto Racing.** Messner 1972.

This book tells of auto racing's development from its
beginning in 1894 to the present. All types of races
are described, including the Grand Prix Circuit, the
sports car circuit, oval track racing, stock car racing,
drag racing, and midget car racing. Short biographies
of the most famous Grand Prix and oval track racers
are given, as well as detailed descriptions of some of
the actual races in which they drove.

Butler, Hal. **Sports Heroes Who Wouldn't Quit.** Messner 1973.

A collection of short biographical sketches about sports
heroes who had handicaps of different kinds or were
members of minority groups. They include Jackie
Robinson, Johnny Unitas, Gertrude Ederle, and Pete
Gray, a one-armed outfielder. These are stories of
people who succeeded against great odds.

Caldwell, John. **The New Cross-Country Ski Book.**
Greene 1973.

The range of possibilities for the enjoyment of cross-
country skiing is unlimited. The fourth edition of this
guide tells the what/how/where of basic equipment,
efficient method, clothing, waxing, and family fun.
Illustrated with black and white photographs.

Carmichael, John P. **My Greatest Day in Baseball.**
G&D 1968.

The greatest stars in baseball tell about their most

outstanding achievements, as well as some personal insights into baseball itself. You'll read about Sandy Koufax pitching his fourth no-hitter, Babe Ruth's historic home run in the 1932 World Series, Dizzy Dean pitching the last game of the 1934 World Series, and many others. Stars include Mickey Mantle, Willie Mays, Carl Yastrzemski, Joe DiMaggio, and many others.

Casewit, Curtis. **The Hiking-Climbing Handbook.** Hawthorn 1969.

The book will provide the enthusiast with information on equipment, techniques, trails, rescues, first aid, clubs, and schools.

Coombs, Charles. **Motorcycling.** Morrow 1968.

This survey of motorcycles begins with a brief history of the motorcycle industry and also describes the most popular models through the 1960s. Operation and safety procedures are explained. Particular attention is given to sports cycles, although road and trail bikes are covered as well.

Csonka, Larry, and Jim Kiick (with Dave Anderson). **Always on the Run.** Bantam 1973.

Running backs for the Miami Dolphins, Larry Csonka and Jim Kiick, tell their life stories in rough, realistic language. They tell about professional football and many individual players. In an up-to-date final chapter, they negotiate contracts with the WFL for the 1975 season involving over one million dollars each.

Darby, Ray. **The Space Age Sport: Skydiving.** Messner 1964.

The author traces the history of skydiving, flying, and parachuting and describes the thrills men and women get from trying to conquer the unknown. The equipment needed and what the sport costs is also discussed, with many good photographs included throughout the book.

Dixon, Peter L. **Where the Surfers Are: A Guide to the World's Great Surfing Spots.** Coward 1968.

All the vital information is given on surfing in the U.S., Mexico, Hawaii, Australia, Africa, Europe, South America.

Dunaway, James O. **Sports Illustrated Book of Track and Field: Running Events.** Lippincott 1972.

A how-to-do-it manual on running events—sprinting, hurdling, and long distance running, with specific directions on warming up and gaining endurance. Well illustrated and very helpful to anyone interested in the running events in track.

Durant, John. **The Story of Baseball.** Hastings 1973.

Who invented baseball? How is it related to the English game "rounders"? How many different versions of baseball existed in America before 1900? These and other questions are answered in Durant's book. *The Story of Baseball* in words and pictures lets a reader be present at some of the most exciting moments in baseball history, such as the day Babe Ruth hit his sixtieth homer.

Dwiggins, Don. **Riders of the Wind: The Story of Ballooning.** Hawthorn 1973.

A new adventure for man began in Paris, France, in 1783, when the Montgolfiers sent up the first balloon. *Riders of the Wind* presents many first-hand accounts of ballooning from 1783 to 1973. It tells of the successful as well as the unsuccessful flights, including those of the Piccards, Lunard, Pilatre de Rozier, and Madame Thibee.

Edmonds, I. G. **Minibikes and Minicycles for Beginners.** Macrae 1973.

How to choose the right bike for you, how to ride, how to make repairs, safety measures, the mechanics of the engine, and places to ride are some of the things covered in this manual. There are lots of photographs to help illustrate and explain the text.

Edwards, Harvey. **Skiing to Win.** HarBraceJ 1973.

This informative book focuses on major international ski races, especially the Alpine Ski Cup, with interviews of key members of U.S. ski teams.

Gogolak, Pete. **Kicking the Football Soccer Style.** Atheneum 1972.

Pete Gogolak of the New York Giants was the first player to kick the football soccer style. His book describes and illustrates the stance, approach, contact, and follow through in this style. Gogolak explains the conventional place kick as well. Pete also recalls some unusual moments in his kicking career.

Griese, Bob, and Gayle Sayers. **Offensive Football.** Atheneum 1974.

Two topnotch pros discuss the topics they each know best. The techniques for passing, running, and team execution are tied into the strategy of game situations. Both photographs and diagrams illustrate appropriate moves and procedures.

Gutman, Bill. **New Breed Heroes in Pro Baseball.** Messner 1974.

All twelve of these superstars are highly individualistic. Yet the author shows us what players like Nolan Ryan, Johnny Bench, and Vida Blue have in common. They are men who worked hard to overcome hardships and personal tragedy to become stars.

Gutman, Bill. **New Breed Heroes of Pro Football.** Messner 1973.

Here are brief sketches of the lives of twelve pro football superheroes. Included in the sketches are descriptions of the players' most outstanding football games. The author tries to show how each player has added new excitement to the game of football.

Hall, Moss. **Go, Indians: Stories of the Great Indian Athletes of the Carlisle School.** Ritchie 1971.

This is the story of the Carlisle School for Indians and the famous Indian athletes who went there. It tells how the Carlisle Indians became one of the best football teams in América in the early years of the twentieth century, and how they went on to beat even mighty Harvard. It also tells the stories of such famous Indian athletes as Jim Thorpe, who not only was a great football player but also won both the Pentathlon and the Decathlon in the 1912 Olympics; and Louis Tewanima, the Little Hopi, one of the greatest long-distance runners of all time.

Hano, Arnold. **Roberto Clemente: Batting King.** Dell 1973.

Roberto Clemente overcame racial prejudice to become a great baseball player. His talent and hard work helped him to make three thousand hits. The book describes his career and his projects to help other people have happier and more successful lives.

Harrelson, Bud. **How to Play Better Baseball.** Atheneum 1973.

Ability counts in baseball, not size. This is how Bud Harrelson became a major leaguer. In pictures and words, Bud shows how to play the position of shortstop successfully, as well as how to field, catch, throw, hit, and run the bases.

Hirshberg, Al. **Henry Aaron: Quiet Superstar.** Putnam 1969.

This book details the life of Hank Aaron, who was born in a ghetto in Mobile, Alabama, and who pursued a career in baseball.

Libby, Bill. **Heroes of the Heisman Trophy.** Hawthorn 1973.

This book gives the history of the Heisman Trophy, a brief account of many of the thirty-eight winners and runners-up, with high points in their football careers, and comments of sports writers and broadcasters. Heisman Trophy voting results from 1935 through 1972 are listed.

Liss, Howard. **Bowling Talk.** Archway 1974.

This bowling dictionary defines terms and explains many techniques from A.B.C. (American Bowling Congress) to Y.B.A. (Youth Bowling Association). How to score a bowling game is explained and illustrated in detail. Different approaches and the best way to knock down a split are also explained. There are many diagrams and sketches to illustrate the text.

Liss, Howard. **Hockey's Greatest All-Stars.** Hawthorn 1972.

Howard Liss selects twelve hockey stars and places them on two teams. He describes these players from their beginnings in hockey through their professional careers and their most exciting experiences in hockey. On the first team are Gordie Howe, Bobby Hull, Jean Beliveau, Eddie Shore, Doug Harvey, and Terry Sawchuk. For the second team the author picks Maurice "Rocket" Richard, Ted Lindsay, Stan Mikita, Bobby Orr, Leonard Patrick, "Red" Kelly, and Jacques Plante.

McWhirter, Norris, and Ross McWhirter. **Guiness Sports Record Book.** Bantam 1974.

The most interesting, up-to-date facts about the major

sports have been collected from the sports section of the Guiness Book of World Records. For example, the section on football includes how it started, all-American selections, college records, longest winning streaks, all-star games, and both college and professional individual records for rushing, passing, gaining, etc. Do you know the distance of the longest punt in football history? Who kicked it? Other sports included in this book range from auto racing to sailing, from bullfighting to chess and pigeon racing.

Morris, Jeannie. **Brian Piccolo: A Short Season.** Dell 1972.

This book is written in part by Brian Piccolo, the football star, and was finished after his death by Jeannie Morris, the wife of Brian Piccolo's friend, Johnnie Morris. The career and character of the football player who died at twenty-six from cancer are described. His fighting spirit on the football field and in the hospital and his genuine concern for others are shown in this biography.

Osgood, William E., and Leslie J. Hurley. **The Snowshoe Book: A Complete Guide to How, Why, When, and Where.** Greene 1974.

A factual book which provides prime reading in the field of snowshoeing. What will it cost? Which snowshoes to buy? Where do you go? How about emergencies? These are only a few of the questions answered in this comprehensive book.

Palmer, Arnold (with William Barry Furlong). **Go for Broke! S&S 1973.**

Arnold Palmer tells about his whole life in golf: hardships, fame, personal traits, great tournaments, and hints about the game. His philosophy in golf is to win by thinking boldly and taking chances. He gives the thoughts and ideas that come to him while actually playing golf, and how he overcame his problems and difficulties.

Radlauer, Edward. **Drag Racing: Quarter Mile Thunder.** Abelard 1966.

This book describes the fundamentals of drag racing, its history, types of cars entered, and the qualifications and rules that must be observed to enter a race. Includes over eighty photographs.

Shapiro, Milton J. **A Treasury of Sports Humor.** Messner 1972.

Told here are humorous and embarrassing moments of sports heroes. Well-known athletes such as Dizzy Dean, Leo Durocher, and Lou Gehrig, tell of hilarious situations they have encountered on the field or in the locker room.

Smith, Robert W. **Chinese Boxing: Masters and Methods.** Kodansha 1974.

The author lived on Taiwan for three years and was determined to learn all he could about Chinese boxing. He met many wonderful masters who taught him their secrets and told him stories. His book is packed with information about kung fu, tai chi, and other forms of martial arts.

Sullivan, George. **The Complete Book of Family Bowling.** Coward 1968.

A good beginner's manual on bowling—equipment, scoring, tips for the beginner and the advanced bowler, tournament rules—with excellent illustrations.

WITCHCRAFT, MAGIC, AND THE OCCULT

Alderman, Clifford Lindsey. **A Cauldron of Witches: The Story of Witchcraft.** Messner 1971.

This book contains a history of witchcraft. The author defines the subject, gives examples of witchcraft from the ancient world, and shares information about King James and Scotland, English witches, Johann Schüler in Germany, Joan of Arc in France, and witches in Africa, the West Indies, and Salem, Massachusetts. Modern witches—Sybil Leek and Aleister Crowley—and their influence are discussed.

Alderman, Clifford Lindsey. **The Devil's Shadow: The Story of Witchcraft in Massachusetts.** Messner 1973.

In this dramatic account of Salem, Massachusetts, in 1692, the reader sees the madness of a mob, a community of suspicious people, and the unjust trials of five women.

Appel, Benjamin. **Man and Magic.** Pantheon 1966.

Magic is a universal language which has been found in all ages throughout the world. What magic is and the relationships between people and magic are discussed.

Bayly, Joseph. **What about Horoscopes?** D C Cook 1970.

Written from a skeptical viewpoint, this book discusses witches, gypsies, seers, psychics, palmistry, communication with the dead, spiritism, ESP, voodooism, and astrology.

Cohen, Daniel. **ESP: The Search beyond the Senses.** HarBraceJ 1973.

The author examines parapsychological investigation and brings in the work of the Society for Psychical Research. The book discusses telepathy, clairvoyance, and precognition with cases from history and modern times as evidence.

Cohen, Daniel. **A Natural History of Unnatural Things.** Dutton 1971.

Witchcraft, the werewolf, the vampire, demons and the devil, giants, fairies and other little people, the mummy, the zombie, and man-made monsters are introduced with accounts of their history and importance today.

Cowan, Lore. **Are You Superstitious?** Auerbach Pubs 1969.

Even if you deny you are superstitious, as many do today, you could probably start with black cats and quote popular superstitions by the yard. The author has collected interesting superstitions from all over the world, relating to home, days and seasons, love and marriage, omens and signs, the evil eye, charms and talismans, colors, numbers, cards, wishes, dreams, and you-name-it. There are special sections on superstitions of the theatre and of sailors and the sea.

Greenhouse, Herbert B. **In Defense of Ghosts.** Essandess 1970.

Herbert Greenhouse has researched and documented these sixty accounts about friendly ghosts. Some return to help their living spouses, others protect and advise. One ghost even got lost trying to visit her daughter! The author offers tips on how best to communicate if a ghost should visit you, and some do's and don'ts for making them feel at home.

Heaps, Willard A. **Superstition.** Nelson 1972.

The author has made a study of superstition. He explores what superstition is, how we become superstitious, and who in history was superstitious. He discusses unfounded beliefs, superstitions about good luck, and others related to music, theater, sports, folk medicine, predicting weather, love, marriage, and death.

Hook, Diana ffarington. **The I Ching and You.** Dutton 1973.

Traditionally no one under fifty can knowledgeably consult the *I Ching,* the 5000-year-old *Chinese Book of Changes,* the world's oldest book. Diana ffarington Hook guides the youthful seeker step by step in approaching the *I Ching* as if it were a human being and using it as spiritual teacher. Beautifully printed diagrams include a transparent overlay and fold-out chart.

Hunt, Douglas, and Kari Hunt. **The Art of Magic.** Atheneum 1967.

The history of magic includes people who believed that they could produce real miracles as well as entertaining "conjurers" like Houdini, Blackstone, and Chung Ling Soo. This book tells about the lives of famous conjurers and the acts they invented. The second part shows the beginning magician many tricks of the trade.

McHargue, Georgess. **The Impossible People.** Dell 1974.

"A history natural and unnatural of beings terrible and wonderful" describes this collection of mythological beings. Giants, trolls, fairies, witches, pixies, demons, mermaids, sphinxes, and swanmaidens are only a few in the book. These "people" are gathered from all over the world. The tales are told, and sometimes the origins of the beings are traced. National Book Award.

POETRY

The people who say they don't like poetry have probably never looked through the collections of poetry annotated here! There are poems for all occasions written by both professional and amateur poets. There are poems by children as well as adults. There are poems about living in the city, poems about exploring nature, and poems about discovering yourself. There are short poems, long poems, medium-length poems, and concrete poems that come in many sizes and shapes. There are poems that will make you laugh, some that will make you smile, and some that will turn up the corners of your mouth just a bit.

You may not like all of the poems included in these books, but if you give them a chance to work their magic on you, you will certainly like a lot of them.

Adoff, Arnold, editor. **City in All Directions.** Macmillan 1969.

This collection of poems about the city covers all aspects of its life—morning and evening, rich neighborhoods and poor. All the poets have lived in the city and talk about things that concern them most directly. These poets have a way of examining ordinary things in unusual ways that may surprise readers who expect poetry to be dull.

Adoff, Arnold, editor. **I Am the Darker Brother: An Anthology of Modern Poems by Negro Americans.** Macmillan 1968.

"I, too, sing America. I am the darker brother." These lines from a poem by Langston Hughes are the source of the title and a theme of this anthology of modern poems by black Americans. Twenty-nine poets, including Gwendolyn Brooks, Robert Hayden, Margaret Walker, and Hughes, write on how it feels to be black, to be poor, to live in a city ghetto or in the South.

Adoff, Arnold, editor. **It Is the Poem Singing into Your Eyes: Anthology of New Young Poets.** Har-Row 1971.

An anthology of poetry selected by the editor from more than six thousand manuscripts by young people, many of them in their teens. The poems, in free verse, are based on contemporary life.

Allen, Samuel, editor. **Poems from Africa.** T Y Crowell 1973.

Poems in this book introduce other culltures in ways that a history or social studies book cannot. They give a sense of how other people feel, what they worry about, what they wish for, what they worship. Some of the poems contain wisdom and sadness that have been handed down for generations. Other poems deal with modern themes such as the problems that arise when two cultures meet and clash.

Arnold, Edwin. **The Light of Asia, or, The Great Renunciation.** Routledge & Kegan 1971.

Written in blank verse, this present-day epic poem celebrates the life of Gautama Buddha, who wins freedom from money, family, ego, hate, sorrow, and other traps to teach human beings the way to spiritual enlightenment.

Arnold, Edwin. **The Song Celestial, or Bhagavad-Gita.** Routledge & Kegan 1967.

Sir Edwin Arnold has given us another translation of the Bhagavad-Gita, this time in English blank verse which in some places sounds like Milton. During a crucial battle, the god Krishna appears to Prince Arjuna in the form of his charioteer; they discuss how a human being can free himself. Krishna gives instructions on yoga and meditation.

Baron, Virginia Olsen, editor. **Here I Am: An Anthology of Poems Written by Young People in some of America's Minority Groups.** Dutton 1969.

A collection of poems by young people from some of America's minority groups. These young poets talk about things that matter most—being lonely, being loved, being happy, being scared—in ways that make readers feel as well as understand what they're talking about.

Baron, Virginia Olsen. **Sunset in a Spider Web.** HR&W 1974.

A collection of sensitive Korean poetry. These sijo

poems present both new and familiar points of view.
Since most students write haiku and tanka, this book
will introduce the reader to a new form to try.

Belting, Natalia. **Our Fathers Had Powerful Songs.** Dutton 1974.

American Indians had no written alphabet. They remembered their traditions and beliefs using songs
which they passed down from generation to generation.
This book explains that the Indians' songs were more
than just ways to remember important things: they
were powerful magic.

Belting, Natalia. **Whirlwind Is a Ghost Dancing.** Dutton 1974.

These poems show how important nature was to the
American Indian, and how the American Indian used
beautiful images like these, drawn from nature, to
explain the world: "Whirlwind is a ghost dancing."
"Icicles are the walking sticks of winter winds." "The
stars are night birds with bright breasts/Like hummingbirds." "Twinkling stars are birds flying slowly/
Shooting stars are birds darting swiftly."

Bettenbender, John, editor. **Poetry Festival.** Dell 1972.

Poems in this anthology cover a wide variety of subjects, although more than half of them are ballads
or folk songs. Authors range from William Shakespeare to Langston Hughes. Introductions to each section provide a good idea of the theme of each section.
The book includes some good, brief biographies of
authors.

Brewton, Sara, and John E. Brewton, editors. **Shrieks
at Midnight: Macabre Poems, Eerie and Humorous.**
T Y Crowell 1969.

The subject matter of these poems seems grim—death,
ghosts, doom. But most of these poems manage to be
humorous, with just a slightly frightening twist. Illustrations are excellent. With both the poems and the
illustrations, readers can feel the chill and mystery
and yet can know "it will never happen to me." Readers can share frightening experiences safely.

Brewton, Sara, John E. Brewton, and G. Meredith
Blackburn, III, editors. **My Tang's Tungled and Other
Ridiculous Situations.** T Y Crowell 1973.

Poems in this volume range from the humorous to the

absurd, showing both fanciful and everyday situations. There are many plays on words and a lot of the poems show the funny side of embarrassing situations.

Brooks, Gwendolyn, editor. **A Broadside Treasury.** Broadside 1971.

This is a collection of poems by the black poets of today, poets who are trying to come to grips with the black experience, to define their "blackness." There are poems that express black people's growing pride in their culture and heritage and poems of protest against "whitey."

Clare, John. **The Wood Is Sweet: Poems for Young Readers.** Watts 1968.

Anyone who enjoys the outdoors should enjoy these poems. The beauty of nature and wonder at what it includes are the subjects of these sixty-one poems.

Cole, William, editor. **A Book of Animal Poems.** Viking Pr 1973.

This volume contains a huge variety of poems about all sorts of animals. Some are witty; some are sad; most will provoke a really strong reaction of some sort. There are enough different poems in this volume to appeal to readers of almost any level. An introductory note warns that "This isn't a book to gulp down at one sitting." It's not, but taken in small bites it's delicious.

Cole, William, compiler. **A Book of Nature Poems.** Viking Pr 1969.

A splendid collection of nature poems from varied sources and centuries (many are modern) arranged by theme. Delightful illustrations.

Cole, William, editor. **Pick Me Up: A Book of Short, Short Poems.** Macmillan 1972.

Poems in this volume are short and can be, as the title suggests, picked up and read for pleasure. This might be a good book for someone who has not read much poetry; rhythm and rhyme patterns are familiar, and the poems are easy to understand. A lot of the poems are fun. And funny.

Cole, William, editor. **Rough Men, Tough Men.** Viking Pr 1969.

A collection of vigorous ballads about adventurous

men, both heroes and villains, which ranges from
Alaska to Australia.

Cole, William, editor. **The Sea, Ships and Sailors.** Viking Pr 1967.

A collection of eighty-five poems, songs, and shanties
representing the moods of the sea.

Doob, Leonard W. **A Crocodile Has Me by the Leg:
African Poems.** Walker & Co 1967.

Africans have verse for almost every occasion, and this
collection of simple, direct African poems provides an
interesting glimpse into the everyday life of African
people. Illustrated with woodcuts by a Nigerian artist.

Dunning, Stephen, Edward Lueders, and Hugh Smith,
compilers. **Reflections on a Gift of Watermelon Pickle
. . . and Other Modern Verse.** Scott F 1966.

Dozens of modern poets, such as Langston Hughes,
May Swenson, Theodore Roethke, and John Updike,
express feelings and experiences that we have each
felt in our own lives—humor, sorrow, love, loneliness.
Beautiful and thought-provoking photographs are scat-
tered throughout the book. Each poem is rich and
full of meaning because of what we put into it when
we read, so take Eve Merriam's advice in the first
poem: "Don't be polite. Bite in."

Dunning, Stephen, Edward Lueders, and Hugh Smith,
compilers. **Some Haystacks Don't Even Have Any
Needle: And Other Complete Modern Poems.** Lothrop
1969.

The poetry in this book was selected especially for
teenagers. The poems deal with a wide range of subjects including sports, cars, romance, war, and pets.
Even though the book was published in 1969, it continues to be one of the most popular collections of
poetry for young people. Take a look at it, and you'll
understand why.

Gibran, Kahlil. **Tears and Laughter.** Bantam 1974.

This is a collection of some of the Lebanese writer
Gibran's works, both poetry and prose, including his
short story, "The Bride's Bed."

Gonzales, Rodolfo. **I Am Joaquin.** Bantam 1972.

This is the first work of poetry to be published by

Chicanos for Chicanos. The "I" in the poem could be almost any Chicano who has felt the indignities and frustrations of trying to make it in an Anglo-Saxon society. The complete text is given in both English and Spanish. Almost every page has a photograph of Chicanos in various settings, or an art reproduction illustrating the text.

Grigson, Geoffrey, editor. **The Cherry Tree.** Vanguard 1962.

A collection of all sorts of poems that appeal to all ages. The poems are grouped according to topic; chapter headings include "Never Stew Your Sister," "The Grief of Love," "Life and Death," and "I Think You Stink." There is much in this book that will appeal to people who think they don't like poetry.

Grohskopf, Bernice, editor. **Seeds of Time: Selections from Shakespeare.** Atheneum 1966.

These brief excerpts from Shakespeare, written in poetic form, help one to understand Shakespeare the poet rather than the playwright. This book is enjoyable for skimming or reading through carefully. For sophisticated readers.

Hannum, Sara, and John Terry Chase, editors. **To Play Man Number One.** Atheneum 1969.

This is a collection of contemporary poems, poems that "play man number one." The poets dare to tell the truth about modern society and to explore the effects of today's social crisis and change. There are poems about love, about the tragedy of war, about doubting and questioning, and about death.

Hannum, Sara, and John Terry Chase, editors. **The Wind Is Round.** Atheneum 1970.

A collection of nature poems by modern poets who love nature and are concerned about what humans are doing to their environment. Perhaps these poets' visions of nature, its beauty and wonder, will make us all concerned about what we are doing to it, before it is gone forever.

Hesse, Hermann (translator James Wright). **Poems by Hermann Hesse.** Bantam 1974.

Thirty-one poems by the German poet, dealing with the theme of homesickness, appear in this translation by the 1972 Pulitzer Prize-winning poet James Wright.

The poem by Hermann Hesse in German appears opposite the English translation.

Houston, James D., editor. **Songs of the Dream People: Chants and Images from the Indians and Eskimos of North America.** Atheneum 1972.

American Indians and Eskimos expressed their sense of the magic of life in songs and chants. These songs and chants, about the world of spirits, about dreams and the hunt, were usually quite short, but they might be repeated over and over again for a whole night. Here is a collection of these songs and chants from the tribes of the eastern woodlands, the central plains, the northwest coast, and the far North.

Howard, Vanessa. **A Screaming Whisper.** HR&W 1972.

Vanessa Howard is a young black poet. She writes about what it is like to be a black living in America today, about what it is like to live in a ghetto, about wanting to be really free.

Hsu, Kai-Yu, translator and editor. **Twentieth Century Chinese Poetry: An Anthology.** Cornell U Pr 1970.

Twentieth century China has undergone at least three political revolutions as well as major literary revolutions. The poets included in this anthology range from traditional classicists (like Mao Tse-tung) to experimentalists influenced by their travels in the West and by communism. The many concentrated changes make this modern period one of the most lively and important literary eras of Chinese poetry.

Jablow, Alta, translator. **Gassire's Lute.** Dutton 1971.

This story from West Africa has been handed down for generations as part of the long poem about the Soninke tribe. *Gassire's Lute* explains how a great warrior became his people's first poet and began a tradition of singing and storytelling that has lasted for hundreds of years. Some unfamiliar words and the story's poetic form may seem confusing at first, but readers—especially those who can imagine how the poem would sound when read aloud—should be able to enjoy it as an adventure story and as an introduction to a culture they know little about.

Jordan, June. **Who Look at Me.** T Y Crowell 1969.

A montage of poems created by Ms. Jordan hauntingly probes the black person's question of "Who me?"

The book will appeal to both teenaged and adult readers. The poems examine ways blacks look at others, and how blacks are looked at. They show the varying aspects of blacks' feeling of invisibility, and ponder the question, "Why you can't see us?" James Baldwin, a black writer, says America can never be white again. June Jordan's poems capture that sentiment.

Jordan, June, and Terri Bush, editors. **The Voice of the Children.** HR&W 1970.

This is a collection of poems by young blacks and Puerto Ricans—poems that express how they feel about being black or Spanish, about America, politics, war, and riots; poems that tell about their hopes and fears, about what they would do if they were the President.

Keats, Ezra Jack, editor. **Night.** Atheneum 1969.

A collection of photographs and brief quotations from poetry and prose. The photography is beautiful, and the excerpts are thought-provoking.

Keys, James. **Only Two Can Play This Game.** Bantam 1974.

James Keys finds paradise and happiness when he falls in love and lives with a girl. He also experiences pain and heartbreak when his girl decides not to marry him. The broken love affair triggered this book. It is an expression of his insights and feelings about love and life.

Kherdian, David, editor. **Visions of America: By the Poets of Our Time.** Macmillan 1973.

This is a collection of modern poems about America, about growing up and living in America, and about America's cities. There are poems about everything from "Puerto Ricans in New York" to "A Supermarket in California."

Kramer, Aaron, editor. **On Freedom's Side: An Anthology of American Poems of Protest.** Macmillan 1972.

In this anthology of American poems of protest, over 160 poems and prose selections are arranged chronologically under the following subjects: the red man, the black man, war, justice, the mob, and the poor. Historical notes explain some of the poems. A poem by Roger Williams protesting Englishmen's treatment of the Indian in 1643 is the earliest.

Larrick, Nancy. **On City Streets: An Anthology of Poetry.** M Evans 1968.

This collection of poems—all of which were selected by young people—gives a good picture of the sights, sounds and problems one encounters in cities. Readers who live in the city—especially the inner city—will find familiar things seen in a new light. Readers who don't live in a large city will begin to get a feeling of what life is like.

Lewis, Richard. **I Breathe a New Song: Poems of the Eskimo.** S&S 1971.

Poetry is as important to the Eskimo as eating and breathing. In this collection of Eskimo poems there are magical chants, lullabies, stories and myths, and dream songs. There are also examples of the song duels of the Greenland Eskimos, who use poetry to resolve disputes and arguments.

Lewis, Richard. **Miracles: Poems by Children of the English Speaking World.** S&S 1966.

Poetry is like television. It lets us see how other people think and feel, how they see their world. This is a collection of poems written by children from the English speaking countries of the world—the United States, New Zealand, Ireland, Kenya, Uganda, Canada, England, Australia, India, and the Philippines. These poems are windows through which we can see their worlds.

Lewis, Richard. **The Park.** S&S 1968.

With words and photographs, this book explores the world of a city park through the four seasons of the year.

Lewis, Richard, editor. **There Are Two Lives: Poems by Children of Japan.** S&S 1970.

The young Japanese poets in this book view the world with such freshness that no two poems are alike. A seven year old writes about wetting his bed, a ten year old, about being a grape completely eaten by a hen. Each poet gives a sharp, new insight into familiar themes like mother, school, animals. The illustrations are also done by talented children.

Lewis, Richard, editor. **The Wind and the Rain.** S&S 1968.

This is a book of poems about wind and rain. The poems are written by young people, and express the many different ways people perceive and feel about wind and rain. Each poem is complemented by a black and white photograph which tries to capture the mood of the poem.

Livingston, Myra Cohn. **Listen, Children, Listen: An Anthology of Poems for the Very Young.** HarBraceJ 1972.

A lively collection of simple poems by well-known poets for the young or young-at-heart.

Livingston, Myra Cohn. **The Malibu and Other Poems.** Atheneum 1972.

These are contemporary poems for young people about nature, ecology, and living in our modern world.

Livingston, Myra Cohn, editor. **Poems of Lewis Carroll.** T Y Crowell Co., 1973.

The book contains whimsical verse from *Alice in Wonderland* and other Lewis Carroll books, a parody of "Hiawatha," and a lot of riddles. The fantasy and playfulness of most of these poems would seem to make them (especially when read aloud) attractive to young children or to mature readers, but perhaps not so appealing to some adolescents.

Livingston, Myra Cohn. **Speak Roughly to Your Little Boy: A Collection of Parodies and Burlesques.** HarBraceJ 1971.

Here is a fine collection of original poems, classic poems, and more modern parodies written about them. The tone is generally humorous.

Mackay, David, compiler and annotator. **A Flock of Words: An Anthology of Poetry for Children and Others.** HarBraceJ 1970.

The poems in this book offer something for everyone. Poetry from Biblical days to today is represented by poets from the entire world—Japan, Switzerland, Nigeria, Spain, Australia, America, etc. It's a personal scrapbook in which the author's favorite poems are collected. This sensitive book will encourage readers to start their own collection.

Madgett, Naomi Long. **Pink Ladies in the Afternoon: New Poems 1965-1971.** Lotus 1972.

These clear, straightforward poems gain their appeal from their use of the common, everyday details of life. To such themes as childhood, searching for one's identity, and lost love, the author brings her personal perspective as a woman and a black.

Marshall, Shirley E., editor. **A Young American's Treasury of English Poetry: From the Early Middle Ages to the Twentieth Century.** WSP 1968.

Intended for the teenager who is interested in the serious study of poetry, this anthology chronologically presents poems of the major English poets from the early Middle Ages to the twentieth century.

McCullough, Frances Monson. **Earth, Air, Fire and Water.** Coward 1971.

This is a collection of modern poems: poems of protest against war and racial prejudice, poems that look at America past and present with a critical eye, poems about love and death, friends and parents. Some of the poets are well known, like LeRoi Jones and Yevgeny Yevtushenko; others are having their poems published for the first time in this book.

McKuen, Rod. **Lonesome Cities.** Random 1968.

Rod McKuen, America's best-selling poet, presents thirteen of his songs and several love poems. Other poems record his impressions of several cities, including Paris, Venice, London, Cheyenne, Los Angeles, Tokyo, and Gstaad.

Merriam, Eve. **Finding a Poem.** Atheneum 1970.

Eve Merriam writes poems about today, about alarm clocks, transistor radios, television commercials, subways, and auto junkyards. Her poems protest what our modern way of life does to people. She looks at the way language is used today, and, at the end of the book, shows the reader how she writes a poem.

Merriam, Eve. **It Doesn't Always Have to Rhyme.** Atheneum 1972.

Poems don't always have to rhyme . . .
    " . . . but there's the repeat of a beat somewhere
    an inner chime that makes you want to
    tap your feet or swerve in a curve;
    a lilt, a leap, a lightening-split:—

> thunderstruck the consonants jut,
> while the vowels open wide as waves in the noon-
>   blue sea."

Molloy, Paul, editor. **Beach Glass and Other Poems.**
Four Winds 1970.

Poetry doesn't always have to be hard to understand.
This collection of American poems proves it. Here are
poems about everyday life in everyday language, poems
about people, nature, love, and even supermarkets.

Moore, Lilian, and Judith Thurman, editors. **To See the
World Afresh.** Atheneum 1974.

This is a collection of poems by poets who "see the
world afresh." There are poems about nature, about
the earth, about people and places—poems for the
seventies like "Kent State" by Paul Goodman, and
"A Bummer," a poem about Vietnam by Michael
Casey.

Morse, David, editor. **Grandfather Rock: New Poetry
and Old.** Delacorte 1972.

A fascinating juxtaposition of traditional and modern
poems dealing with similar themes. The implications of
these pairings and the editor's excellent discussions
make this book absorbing for older adolescents but
difficult for some younger readers.

Morton, Miriam, editor. **The Moon Is Like a Silver
Sickle.** S&S 1972.

This is a collection of poems written by Russian children, poems that reflect a way of life, ideas, and
beliefs that are very different from our own. But
these poems also reveal the similarities that unite
people worldwide regardless of different national
ideals. These young Russian poets write about themselves, about family and friends, about loving, about
war and peace, and about their thoughts and hopes.

Peck, Richard, editor. **Mindscapes: Poems for the Real
World.** Dell 1972.

In this collection of poems, serious themes—love, death,
identity—are dealt with honestly. The poets are good
storytellers and choose vivid details that create strong
feelings. Poems are likely to produce varied but intense reactions, especially for more mature readers.

Peck, Richard, editor. **Sounds and Silences.** Dell 1970.

Called by the editor "poetry for now," the poems in

this book are arranged under such topics as the family, childhood, identity, love, and war. The poetry is by contemporary writers.

Randall, Dudley. **After the Killing.** Broadside 1973.
Dudley Randall is a black poet. He writes about the black experience, about a visit to Ghana, about famous blacks like Frederick Douglass and Gwendolyn Brooks, and about man the killer.

Randall, Dudley. **Black Poetry: A Supplement to Anthologies Which Exclude Black Poets.** Broadside 1969.
This is a sampling of poems by black American poets from the beginning of the twentieth century to the young poets of today, including poems by Langston Hughes, Gwendolyn Brooks, and LeRoi Jones.

Townsend, John Rowe, editor. **Modern Poetry.** Lippincott 1974.
This is a collection of poems by modern English and American poets, poems about war, supermarkets, space travel, and even about a computer trying to compose its first Christmas card.

Wilbur, Richard. **Opposites.** HarBraceJ 1973.
These are funny poems about "opposites" like these, for instance:
"What is the opposite of string?
It's gnirts, which doesn't mean a thing."
and,
"What is the opposite of riot?
It's lots of people keeping quiet."

Wood, Nancy. **Hollering Sun.** S&S 1972.
This is the story of the Taos Indians of New Mexico, their customs, their beliefs, and some of their history, retold in poems and photographs. The poems tell of how the Coyote brought the buffalo to Taos from the faraway plains of the rising run, of why it's bad luck to whistle in the night like a bear or an elk or an owl, and of the meaning of a Taos Indian's blanket.

REFERENCE TOOLS

Do you want to find a Christmas play? Do you want to find out who holds the world's record for running the 50-yard dash? Do you want to find out who the world's most famous women are? Do you want to find out how people dress in other parts of the world? The books annotated in this section will answer these questions as well as many more.

Aymar, Brandt, and Edward Sagarin. **Laws and Trials that Created History: A Pictorial History.** Crown 1974.

Beginning with the trial of Socrates in 399 B.C., the authors discuss twenty-four trials that have important places in history. Included are, for example, the trials of Joan of Arc, John Thomas Scopes, Angela Davis, the Salem Witchcraft Trials, and the Nuremberg Trials.

Berndt, Fredrick. **The Domino Book.** Nelson 1974.

This is a book of games to play with dominoes, including solitaire and games for two or more.

Burack, A. S. **A Treasury of Holiday Plays for Teen-Agers.** Plays 1963.

These twenty-five royalty-free one-act plays commemorate fifteen special days or weeks. Included are historical plays, comedies, and dramas of family life and of problems of young people. Most of the plays require fewer than ten characters, but two could be presented by an entire class.

Burack, A. S., and B. Alice Crossley. **Popular Plays for Classroom Reading.** Plays 1974.

A collection of many different kinds of plays—adventures, mysteries, comedies. Most have a lot of action that takes place within a very short time. Realers who like to feel that characters in plays are real, believable people and readers who like plays that deal with difficult subjects may not be attracted to these plays. But readers who enjoy reading aloud—

even hamming it up—should enjoy the plays in this collection.

Caras, Roger. **The Roger Caras Nature Quiz Book #2.** Bantam 1974.

One hundred and one short quizzes about the natural world are included in this book. Fish, birds, animals, trees, and naturalists are some of the quiz subjects. The quizzes may be used to test your knowledge, or as a learning tool.

Charlip, Remy, Mary Beth, and George Ancona. **Handtalk: An ABC of Finger Spelling and Sign Language.** Parents 1974.

Colored photographs and black and white inserts show how to form letters and words in sign language.

Dickson, Roy Ward. **The Greatest Quiz Book Ever.** Har-Row 1974.

A very interesting and challenging quiz book. Among the many kinds of puzzles are ones that will intrigue people of all ages.

Fontaine, Robert. **Humorous Monologues for Teen-Agers.** Plays 1971.

The twenty-five humorous monologues in this book are based on modern problems such as a "normal fellow's" experiences with fathers of girls, a young girl's thoughts and actions before her first dance, a boy's thoughts before taking "Miss Snowflake" to the prom, and a husband's attempt to do the housework while his wife is sick.

Garrison, Webb. **How It Started.** Abingdon 1972.

The wonder of discovering "how things started" is satisfied with over three hundred brief descriptions listed under fifteen headings as diverse as festivals, games, sports, music, medicine, customs, business, and law. Halloween, checkers, superstitions, football, the ferris wheel, drive-ins, and calendars are traced back to their beginnings.

Gassner, John, and Edward Quinn, editors. **The Reader's Encyclopedia of World Drama.** T Y Crowell 1969.

Dealing with drama as literature, this generously illustrated volume offers the story of drama from all continents, concentrating on aspects of each country's dramatic history, its playwrights and significant plays.

Grant, Bruce. **American Indians: Yesterday and Today.** Dutton 1960.

Everything you always wanted to know about the American Indian from "Abnaki," a tribe of Northeastern Indians, to "Zuni," a tribe of Southwestern Pueblo Indians, including famous chiefs, battles, arts and crafts, all alphabetically listed.

Grohskoph, Bernice. **From Age to Age.** Atheneum 1968.

This book spans several hundred years of history, life, and literature of Anglo-Saxon England. It discusses the history of the Anglo-Saxons from Roman Britain to Edward the Confessor. Also the book talks about life, society, language, poetry (lyrical, heroic, historical, popular, and religious) and prose. A fine book for anyone interested in history and literature of early England.

Hiller, Carl E. **From Tepees to Towers: A Photographic History of American Architecture.** Little 1967.

More than one hundred photographs tracing the history of American architecture. Illustrated glossary; index of architects.

Holmes, Sandra. **Flowers of the World.** Bantam 1974.

Descriptions of flowers from around the world, including size of the plant, best growing conditions, and botanical classification. Illustrated with color photographs.

Holmes, Sandra. **Trees of the World.** Bantam 1974.

Descriptions of trees from around the world, including size, best growing conditions, and botanical classification. Illustrated with color photographs.

Hopke, William E., editor. **Encyclopedia of Careers and Vocational Guidance.** Doubleday 1972.

Two volumes—*Planning Your Career* and *Careers and Occupations*—include vital information about many careers: definition, history, and nature of the work; requirements; opportunities for experience; methods of entering and advancing; employment outlook; earnings; working conditions; and social and psychological factors.

Horvath, Joan. **Filmmaking for Beginners.** Nelson 1974.

The young filmmaker will find this book invaluable for practical, step-by-step instructions. The author gives suggestions on script writing, choosing a camera and film, shooting, editing. Her emphasis is on self-expression and imagination.

Kauffmann, Stanley. **Figures of Light: Film Criticism and Comment.** Har-Row 1971.

Stanley Kauffman's book is a valuable document in two senses. First, it gives detailed analyses of many important films, both American and foreign, of the late sixties. Second, in discussing the themes and values, implicit and explicit, which pervade these films, the author pictures a time in the recent past that future histories of American culture will undoubtedly see as a watershed.

Laurie, Rona, editor. **One Hundred Speeches from the Theater.** CCPr Macmillan 1973.

Students of drama and competitive speaking can use this book as a tool in selecting plays and finding practice, audition, and contest material. A hundred speeches from plays spanning five hundred years are introduced with summaries of the plays from which they are taken. Parts for men's voices and women's voices are divided into the following categories: dramatic speeches, character and dialect, comedy, verse plays.

Levy, Elizabeth. **Lawyers for the People: A New Breed of Defenders and Their Work.** Knopf 1974.

This book contains the stories of nine lawyers who are working to wipe out injustices in American society. Linda Huber works to help juveniles; Bernie Clyne works for and with the poor; Charlie Halpern promotes the Public Interest Law; Tom Kline is trying to make the Public Interest Law self-supporting; Fay Stender concentrates on prison reform; Carol Broege defends radicals; Carol Libow helps women attain their rights; Eleanor Holmes Norton works for equal rights; and Beverly Moore labors for the consumers' best interests.

Loeper, John L. **Men of Ideas.** Atheneum 1970.

This book tells briefly the ideas of world-famous philosophers—Socrates, Plato, Aristotle, Lucretius, Lao-Tzu, Confucius, Augustine, Thomas Aquinas, Francis Bacon, Descartes, Spinoza, and Voltaire. A discussion of philosophy is included.

Lum, Peter. **The Growth of Civilization in East Asia: China, Japan and Korea to the Fourteenth Century.** S G Phillips 1973.

Asian civilization began in China and spread to Japan and Korea. The author traces these civilizations from their mythic beginnings. The emphasis is on the customs, philosophies, art, and inventions, which make the ancient eras come to life for the reader. This book provides a background for its sequel, *Six Centuries in East Asia*.

Lum, Peter. **Six Centuries in East Asia: China, Japan and Korea from the Fourteenth Century to 1912.** S G Phillips 1973.

This book begins with the Mongols in power in East Asia and much of Europe. When they were driven out of China in 1368, the Ming dynasty began an age of brilliance in art, science, and literature. Because the Mongols had instilled a lasting fear of the "barbarian," China, Japan, and Korea have almost always resisted the ever-increasing encroachment of the West.

Magary, Allan, and Kerstin Fraser Magary. **East Africa: A Travel Guide.** Har-Row 1975.

East Africa holds a strong fascination for many people. For anyone who hopes to see it for himself, this book is a complete and invaluable guide, with information about the most economical and efficient ways to travel in Kenya, Tanzania, and Uganda. Also included are facts about the cultures of East Africa, maps, drawings, and photographs.

Martens, Anne Coulter. **Popular Plays for Teen-Agers.** Plays 1968.

Eighteen one-act plays chosen to reflect the moods and interests of young people.

McWhirter, Norris, and Ross McWhirter. **Guinness Book of World Records.** Sterling 1975.

The oldest horse, the most expensive dog, the smallest handwriting, and the fattest man—these are just a drop in the bucket of the largest collection of records ever collected for one book. The oldest, tallest, smallest, longest, and shortest of everything imaginable are here. (Did you know a woman once sneezed continuously for 155 consecutive days?)

McWhirter, Norris, and Ross McWhirter. **Guinness Sports Record Book.** Bantam 1974.

The most interesting, up-to-date facts about the major sports have been collected from the sports section of the Guinness Book of World Records. For example, the section on football includes how it started, all-American selections, college records, longest winning streaks, all-star games, and both college and professional individual records for rushing, passing, gaining, etc. Do you know the distance of the longest punt in football history? Who kicked it? Other sports included in this book range from auto racing to sailing, from bullfighting to chess and pigeon racing.

Ortego, Philip D., compiler. **We Are Chicanos: An Anthology of Chicano Literature.** WSP 1973.

A variety of Mexican-American writers, young and old, men and women, have contributed to this anthology. Each thematic section is preceded by an introduction to provide a background for better understanding. The themes cover a broad spectrum including: Backgrounds, Folklore, Days in the Lives, Voices and the Movement, Poetry, Drama, and Fiction. There is also a list for suggested further reading.

Osmond, Edward. **Animals of Central Asia.** Abelard 1968.

Strange and interesting animals inhabit this remote and forbidding area. The author, who is an art historian and illustrator, provides much information, not only on the animals, but also on the people of Central Asia who are dependent on them for their needs. Superb illustrations.

Osteen, Phyllis. **Bears around the World.** Coward 1966.

This comprehensive book describes bears by size, includes some information about the history of bears and bears in folklore, and gives information about their lives and behavior.

Payne, Blanche. **History of Costume: From the Ancient Egyptians to the 20th Century.** Har-Row 1965.

While investigating costumes, the reader learns about the history, daily lives and customs of people in other times and places. Besides photographs of paintings and sculptures, the author utilizes re-drawings of museum plates which accurately depict costumes in various stages of physical activities. The fifty pages of patterns will be very useful to the costume-maker.

Ruskin, Ariane (editor Howard Smith). **Nineteenth Century Art.** McGraw 1973.

A well-organized survey of nineteenth century European and American art and artists. Descriptions of the lives, personalities, and influence of the major artists. Many illustrations in full color.

Scheuer, Steven H., editor. **Movies on TV.** Bantam 1974.

This is a listing of the movies shown on TV, including brief plot descriptions, names of stars, and ratings.

Smith, Eleanor G. **Horses, History, and Havoc: Through the Ages with Hoof in Mouth.** Collins-World 1969.

Horse lovers will enjoy this wealth of fact and fancy about the horse through the ages in art, history, and legend.

Splaver, Sarah. **Nontraditional Careers for Women.** Messner 1973.

This book gives guidance to the young liberated woman, who has more career choices than every before. The author has researched over five hundred occupations and gives not only encouragement but much practical information, such as qualifications and training, future outlooks for jobs, and addresses of professional organizations.

Streatfeild, Noel. **The First Book of the Opera.** Watts 1967.

A useful introduction to opera—its history, production, performers. Numerous illustrations.

Turner, Frederick W., III. **The Portable North American Indian Reader.** Viking Pr 1974.

A collection of literature of and about the American Indian: myths, tales, poetry, oratory and autobiography from the Iroquois, Cherokee, Sioux, Navaho and many other tribes.

Uden, Grant. **A Dictionary of Chivalry.** T Y Crowell 1969.

Many illustrations and cross-references add to the excellence of this volume, which gives information about people, events, places, terms, and almost anything concerned with feudalism.

Witt, Shirley Hill, and Stan Steiner, editors. **The Way: An Anthology of American Indian Literature.** Knopf 1974.

This is a collection of speeches, prophesies, poems, songs, prayers, legends, essays, proclamations and underground parodies and satires written by American Indians. The selections reflect the Indians' pride in their heritage and their anger at what the white man has done to them from the time of Tecumseh to the Red Power movement of today.

SHORT STORY COLLECTIONS

Good short stories are always fun to read, and there are some really good collections of short stories included in this section. Some are by a single author; others include the work of many writers. Because all these collections center on one theme or another—science fiction, folk tales, mysteries, stories of minority groups, for example— the complete descriptions of these books are found in the appropriate places, throughout the fiction section of this booklist. The short story collections listed here are arranged by the last name of the author or editor. But if you skim quickly through the titles, you'll find that they, along with the descriptive phrases, tell you a lot about the kinds of stories to be found in each book. You shouldn't have any problems finding some good reading here.

Adoff, Arnold, editor. **Brothers and Sisters.** Macmillan 1970. Stories of black youth, by black writers.

Aiken, Joan, et al. **Authors' Choice 2.** T Y Crowell 1974. Favorite stories of seventeen well-known authors.

Aiken, Joan. **The Green Flash.** Dell 1973. Tales of horror, suspense, fantasy.

Allen, Elizabeth. **You Can't Say What You Think and Other Stories.** Dutton 1974. Stories about high school students struggling with familiar problems.

Allison, Leonard, Leonard Jenkin, and Robert Perrault, editors. **Survival Printout: Science Fact, Science Fiction.** Random 1973. Science fiction tales by famous writers.

Asimov, Isaac. **Asimov's Mysteries.** Dell 1968. Fourteen science fiction mysteries.

Baumann, Hans. **The Stolen Fire: Legends of Heroes and Rebels from Around the World.** Pantheon 1974. Twenty-seven legends of heroes and rebels from around the world.

Benedict, Stewart H., editor. **The Crime Solvers: 13 Classic Detective Stories.** Dell 1966. Anthology of famous writers.

Blish, James. **Star Trek 11.** Bantam 1975. Adventures of the crew of starship *Enterprise* in space.

Brackett, Leigh. **The Halfling and Other Stories.** Ace Bks 1973. Seven science fiction stories.

Bradbury, Ray. **The October Country.** Ballantine 1972. Nineteen science fiction tales by a master.

Brooks, Charlotte, editor. **The Outnumbered.** Dell 1967. Stories, poems, and essays about minority groups.

Burland, C. A. **Gods and Heroes of War.** Putnam 1974. Stories from around the world and throughout history.

Carr, Terry, editor. **Into the Unknown: Eleven Tales of Imagination.** Nelson 1973. Fantasy-reality stories to make you laugh, then think.

Carr, Terry, editor. **Worlds Near and Far: Nine Stories of Science Fiction and Fantasy.** Nelson 1974. Stories of science fiction, ghosts, and fantasy.

Clarke, Arthur C. **Expedition to Earth.** Ballantine 1953. Eleven science fiction stories.

Creel, J. Luke. **Folk Tales of Liberia.** Denison 1969. Tales from West Africa.

Dickinson, Susan, compiler. **The Drugged Cornet and Other Mystery Stories.** Dutton 1973. Fifteen classic and contemporary mysteries.

Dickinson, Susan, compiler. **The Usurping Ghost and Other Encounters and Experiences.** Dutton 1971. Nineteen stories of "ghostly pleasure."

Elwood, Roger, editor. **And Now Walk Gently through the Fire and Other Science Fiction Stories.** Chilton 1972. Ten stories that mix biochemistry and religion.

Elwood, Roger, editor. **Children of Infinity: Original Science Fiction Stories for Young Readers.** Watts 1973. Ten stories about young people in the future.

Elwood, Roger, editor. **Continuum 1.** Putnam 1974. Science fiction by four authors.

Elwood, Roger, editor. **Continuum 2.** Putnam 1974. Sequels to the four stories begun in *Continuum 1*.

Elwood, Roger, editor. **Crisis: Ten Original Stories of Science Fiction.** Nelson 1974. Ten science fiction characters face varied crises.

Elwood, Roger, editor. **The Learning Maze and Other Science Fiction.** Messner 1974. Stories of life in the future and fantastic happenings in the present.

Elwood, Roger, editor. **The Many Worlds of Poul Anderson.** Chilton 1974. Science fiction ranging from the humorous to the heartbreaking.

Elwood, Roger, editor. **The Other Side of Tomorrow: Original Science Fiction Stories about Young People of the Future.** Random 1973. Young people look at the future in stories by nine science fiction writers.

Elwood, Roger, editor. **Survival from Infinity: Original Science Fiction Stories for Young Readers.** Watts 1974. Eight science fiction tales about young people.

Feldmann, Susan, editor. **The Storytelling Stone: Myths and Tales of the American Indians.** Dell 1965. Stories to explain creation, the acquisition of fire, and the development of Indian culture.

Furman, A. L. **Haunted Stories.** S&S 1965. Young people unravel a series of eerie mysteries.

Gates, Doris. **Two Queens of Heaven: Aphrodite & Demeter.** Viking Pr 1974. Eight stories of the Greek goddess of love, Aphrodite.

Ghidalia, Vic, and Roger Elwood. **Beware the Beasts.** Macfadden 1971. Ten stories about legends.

Graves, Robert. **Greek Gods and Heroes.** Dell 1973. Twenty-seven short tales of the adventures of Greek mythological characters.

Haining, Peter, editor. **The Monster Makers: Creators and Creations of Fantasy and Horror.** Taplinger 1974. Eighteen tales of monster-makers and their creations.

Haldeman, Joe, compiler. **Cosmic Laughter: An Anthology of Humorous Science Fiction.** HR&W 1974. Humor is the unifying thread in this science fiction collection.

Harrison, Harry, and Brian W. Aldiss, editors. **Best SF 73.** Putnam 1974. Nineteen science fiction stories.

Heinlein, Robert A. **The Worlds of Robert A. Heinlein.** Ace Bks 1972. Five stories, with an introduction on science fiction.

Herbert, Frank. **The Worlds of Frank Herbert.** Ace Bks 1971. Nine stories in which science fiction dominates.

Hesse, Hermann (translator Ralph Manheim). **Stories of Five Decades.** FS&G 1973. Twenty-five stories by the German master.

Hodges, Margaret. **The Other World: Myths of the Celts.** FS&G 1973. Ten tales from ancient Britain and Ireland.

Hunter, Kristin. **Guests in the Promised Land.** Scribner 1973. On being young and black, in the ghetto.

Johnson, Dorothy M. **A Man Called Horse and Other Stories.** Ballantine 1970. Indians and white on the frontier, from Minnesota to Montana.

Kissin, Eva H., editor. **Stories in Black and White.** Lippincott 1970. Fourteen stories about race relations.

Knight, Damon, editor. **Orbit 12.** Putnam 1973. Fourteen science fiction stories.

Knowles, John. **Phineas.** Bantam 1969. Stories of young boys facing personal problems.

Leiber, Fritz. **Swords against Death.** Ace Bks 1970. Stories of science fiction, featuring Fafhrd and the Gray Mouser.

Leiber, Fritz. **Swords against Wizardry.** Ace Bks 1968. Four science fiction stories.

Leiber, Fritz. **Swords and Deviltry.** Ace Bks 1974. Four hero tales.

Leiber, Fritz. **You're All Alone.** Ace Bks 1972. Three science fiction stories.

Leodhas, Sorche Nic. **XII Great Black Cats: And Other Eerie Scottish Tales.** Dutton 1971. Tales of the supernatural, ghosts, and hauntings in Scotland.

Lessing, Doris. **The Temptation of Jack Orkney and Other Stories.** Bantam 1974. Stories for mature readers, on love themes.

Lester, Julius. **Long Journey Home.** Dial 1972. Stories of slave life in the south in the 1880s.

Levoy, Myron. **The Witch of Fourth Street and Other Stories.** Har-Row 1972. Stories of ethnic groups in New York City.

Luckhardt, Mildred Corell, editor. **Spooky Tales about Witches, Ghosts, Goblins, Demons and Such.** Abingdon 1972. Stories from around the world.

Manley, Seon, and Gogo Lewis, editors. **Shapes of the Supernatural.** Doubleday 1969. Tales of banshees, werewolves, and other weird creatures.

McKay, Don. **On Two Wheels: An Anthology about Men and Motorcycles.** Dell 1971. The drama of cycling, and its mystique.

Momaday, Natachee Scott, editor. **American Indian Authors.** HM 1971. Stories about what it means to be an Indian.

Norton, Andre. **High Sorcery.** Ace Bks 1971. Five stories about survival in the future.

Norton, Andre, compiler. **Small Shadows Creep.** Dutton 1974. An anthology of young ghosts.

Norton, Andre, and Ernestine Donaldly, editors. **Gates to Tomorrow: An Introduction to Science Fiction.** Atheneum 1973. Twelve science fiction stories tenth-graders have enjoyed.

Nourse, Alan E. **PSI High and Others.** McKay 1967. Three science fiction tales.

Pohl, Carol, and Frederik Pohl, editors. **Science Fiction: The Great Years.** Ace Bks 1973. Stories by seven authors.

Pohl, Frederik, editor. **Nightmare Age.** Ballantine 1970. Thirteen stories of the strange tomorrows that today's technology could bring.

Reed, A. W. **Myths and Legends of Australia.** Taplinger 1973. Creation stories, hero tales, and animal legends.

Schulman, L. M., editor. **A Woman's Place.** Macmillan 1974. Famous women writers examine the lives of women.

Silverberg, Robert. **Beyond Control.** Dell 1972. The excitements and dangers of scientific experiments.

Silverberg, Robert. **Mind to Mind: Nine Stories of Science Fiction.** Dell 1971. Stories about unusual mental powers.

Silverberg, Robert, editor. **Infinite Jests: The Lighter Side of Science Fiction.** Chilton 1974. Eleven science fiction tales with humorous twists.

Silverberg, Robert, editor. **The Science Fiction Bestiary.** Dell 1971. An anthology of stories about fantastic beasts.

Singer, Jane, and Kurt Singer. **Folk Tales of Mexico.** Denison 1969. Ten stories from south of the border.

Smith, Cordelia Titcomb. **Great Science Fiction Stories.** Dell 1964. Eleven tales, from Jules Verne to those of present-day writers.

Spinner, Stephanie, editor. **Feminine Plural: Stories by Women about Growing Up.** Macmillan 1972. Modern writers explore the theme of women as victim.

Sutcliff, Rosemary. **Heather, Oak and Olive.** Dutton 1972. A story each, from ancient Wales, Greece, and Rome.

Turner, Mary, editor. **We, Too, Belong: An Anthology About Minorities in America.** Dell 1973. Minority groups in America, seen through short stories, poetry, and prose.

Weiss, M. Jerry, editor. **Tales Out of School.** Dell 1973. Fourteen yarns by American humorists.

Whedbee, Charles Harry. **Legends of the Outer Banks and Tar Heel Tidewater.** Blair 1971. Legends of the North Carolina coast.

Whitney, Alex. **Stiff Ears: Animal Folktales of the North American Indian.** Walck 1974. Stories to entertain and teach, from many tribes.

Whitney, Thomas P., editor. **The Young Russians: A Collection of Stories about Them.** Macmillan 1972. Ten stories from Russian literary journals.

Wilhelm, Kate, editor. **Nebula Award Stories, No. 9.** Har-Row 1974. Science fiction stories with a psychological twist.

Windham, Kathryn Tucker. **Jeffrey Introduces 13 More Southern Ghosts.** Strode 1971. Ghost lore from the south.

Yolen, Jane, editor. **Zoo 2000: Twelve Stories of Science Fiction and Fantasy Beasts.** Seabury 1973. Twelve science fiction stories about animals.

Zolotow, Charlotte. **An Overpraised Season: Ten Stories of Youth.** Har-Row 1973. Joys and trials of teenage life.

LIST OF STANDARD BOOKS

Alcott, Louisa May. *Little Women.*
Aldrich, Bess. *A Lantern in Her Hand.*
Annixter, Paul. *Swiftwater.*
Austen, Jane. *Pride and Prejudice.*

Bagnold, Enid. *National Velvet.*
Benary-Isbert, Margot. *The Ark.*
Brink, Carol. *Caddie Woodlawn.*
Brontë, Charlotte. *Jane Eyre.*
Brontë, Emily. *Wuthering Heights.*
Burnford, Sheila. *The Incredible Journey.*

Cather, Willa. *My Antonia.*
Conrad, Joseph. *The Secret Sharer.*
Cooper, James Fennimore. *The Last of the Mohicans.*
Crane, Stephen. *The Red Badge of Courage.*

Daly, Maureen. *Seventeenth Summer.*
Defoe, Daniel. *Robinson Crusoe.*
Dickens, Charles. *David Copperfield; Great
    Expectations; Oliver Twist.*
DuMaurier, Daphne. *Rebecca.*

Edmonds, Walter. *Drums along the Mohawk.*

Farley, Walter. *Black Stallion.*
Fast, Howard. *April Morning.*
Forbes, Esther. *Johnny Tremain.*
Frank, Anne. *The Diary of a Young Girl.*

Gallico, Paul. *The Snow Goose.*
Gipson, Fred. *Old Yeller.*

Hemingway, Ernest. *The Old Man and the Sea.*
Heyerdahl, Thor. *Kon Tiki.*
Hilton, James. *Goodbye, Mr. Chips.*

Kipling, Rudyard. *Captains Courageous; Kim.*
Kjelgaard, James. *Big Red.*
Knight, Eric. *Lassie Come Home.*

Knowles, John. *A Separate Peace.*
Krumgold, Joseph. *. . . And Now Miguel.*

Lawson, Robert. *Ben and Me.*
L'Engle, Madeleine. *A Wrinkle in Time.*
London, Jack. *Call of the Wild; The Sea Wolf.*

McCloskey, Robert. *Homer Price.*

O'Hara, Mary. *Green Grass of Wyoming; My Friend Flicka.*
Orwell, George. *Animal Farm; 1984.*

Pease, Howard. *The Tattooed Man.*

Rawlings, Marjorie K. *The Yearling.*
Richter, Conrad. *The Light in the Forest.*

Schaefer, Jack. *Shane.*
Sewell, Anna. *Black Beauty.*
Speare, Elizabeth. *The Witch of Blackbird Pond.*
Sperry, Armstrong. *Call It Courage.*
Steinbeck, John. *The Pearl.*
Stevenson, Robert Louis. *Kidnapped; The Black Arrow; Treasure Island.*
Street, James. *Goodbye, My Lady.*
Swift, Jonathan. *Gulliver's Travels.*

Twain, Mark. *A Connecticut Yankee in King Arthur's Court; The Prince and the Pauper; The Adventures of Huckleberry Finn; The Adventures of Tom Sawyer.*

Ullman, James. *Banner in the Sky.*

Verne, Jules. *Around the World in Eighty Days; Journey to the Center of the Earth; Mysterious Island; 20,000 Leagues under the Sea.*

Wells, H. G. *The Time Machine.*
West, Jessamyn. *Cress Delahanty.*
Wilder, Laura Ingalls. *The Little House on the Prairie.*
Wolfe, Thomas. *Look Homeward, Angel.*
Wyss, Johann. *Swiss Family Robinson.*

DIRECTORY OF PUBLISHERS

A-W Addison-Wesley Publishing Co., Inc., Jacob Way, Reading, Ma 01867

Abelard Abelard-Schuman Ltd., 257 Park Avenue, South, New York, NY 10010

Abingdon Abingdon Press, 201 Eighth Avenue, South, Nashville, TN 37202

Ace Bks Ace Books, 1120 Avenue of the Americas, New York, NY 10036

Airmont Airmont Publishing Co., Inc. Orders to: Associated Booksellers, 147 McKinley Avenue, Bridgeport, CT 06606

Alaska Northwest Alaska Northwest Publishing Co., P.O. Box 4EEE, Anchorage, AK 99509

Am Heritage American Heritage Publishing Co., 1221 Avenue of the Americas, New York, NY 10036

Apollo Eds Apollo Editions, 201 Park Avenue, South, New York, NY 10003

Arc Bks Arc Books. Orders to: Arco Publishing Co., Inc., 219 Park Avenue, South, New York, NY 10003

Archway Archway Paperbacks. Orders to: Simon & Schuster, Inc., 1 W. 39th Street, New York, NY 10018

Arco Arco Publishing Co., Inc., 219 Park Avenue, South, New York, NY 10003

Argus Comm Argus Communications, 3505 N. Ashland Avenue, Chicago, IL 60657

Arno Arno Press, 330 Madison Avenue, New York, NY 10017

Assoc Bk Associated Booksellers, 147 McKinley Avenue, Bridgeport, CT 06606

Atheneum Atheneum Publishers. Orders to: Book Warehouse, Inc., Vreeland Avenue, Boro of Totowa, Paterson, NJ 07512

Auerbach Pubs   Auerbach Publishers. Orders to: Mason & Lipscomb Publishers, 384 Fifth Avenue, New York, NY 10018

Avon   Avon Books, 959 Eighth Avenue, New York, NY 10019

Ballantine   Ballantine Books, Inc. Orders to: Random House Inc., Order Department, 457 Hahn Road, Westminster, MD 21157

Bantam   Bantam Books, Inc., 666 Fifth Avenue, New York, NY 10019

Basic   Basic Books, Inc., 10 E. 53rd Street, New York, NY 10022

Berkley Pub   Berkley Publishing Corp. Orders to: G. P. Putnam's Sons, 200 Madison Avenue, New York, NY 10016

Blair   John F. Blair, Publisher, 1406 Plaza Drive, S.W., Winston-Salem, NC 27103

Bradbury Pr   Bradbury Press, 2 Overhill Road, Scarsdale, NY 10583

Braziller   George Braziller, Inc., 1 Park Avenue, New York, NY 10016

Brigham   Brigham Young University Press, 205 University Press Building, Provo, UT 84601

Broadside   Broadside Press Publications, 12651 Old Mill Place, Detroit, MI 48238

CCPr Macmillan   Crowell-Collier Press. Orders to: Macmillan Publishing Co., Inc., Front & Brown Street, Delran Township, Riverside, NJ 08075

Childrens   Childrens Press, Inc., 1224 W. Van Buren Street, Chicago, IL 60607

Chilton   Chilton Book Co. Orders to: Sales Service Department, Chilton Way, Radnor, PA 19089

Chris Mass   Christopher Publishing House (Mass), 53 Billings Road, North Quincy, MA 02171

Collins-World   William Collins, & World Publishing Co., Inc., 2080 W. 117th Street, Cleveland, OH 44111

Cornell U Pr   Cornell University Press, 124 Roberts Place, Ithaca, NY 14850

Cornerstone   Cornerstone Library, Inc. Orders to: Simon & Schuster, Inc., 1 W. 39th Street, New York, NY 10018

Coward   Coward, McCann & Geoghegan, Inc., 200 Madison Avenue, New York, NY 10016

Criterion Bks Criterion Books, Inc. Orders to: Intext Educational Publications, 257 Park Avenue, New York, NY 10010

Crown Crown Publishers, Inc., 419 Park Avenue, South, New York, NY 10016

D C Cook David C. Cook Publishing Co., 850 N. Grove Avenue, Elgin, IL 60120

D White Davide White Co., 60 E. 55th Street, New York, NY 10021

Delacorte Delacorte Press. Orders to: Dial Press, 750 Third Avenue, New York, NY 10017

Dell Dell Publishing Co., Inc., 1 Dag Hammarskjold Plaza, 245 E. 47th Street, New York, NY 10017

Denison T. S. Denison & Co., Inc., 5100 W. 82nd Street, Minneapolis, MN 55437

Dial Dial Press, 1 Dag Hammarskjold Plaza, 245 E. 47th Street, New York, NY 10017

Dillon Dillon Press, Inc., 500 S. Third Street, Minneapolis, MN 55415

Dodd Dodd, Mead & Co., 79 Madison Avenue, New York, NY 10016

Doubleday Doubleday & Co., Inc., 501 Franklin Avenue, Garden City, NY 11530

Dutton E. P. Dutton & Co., Inc., 201 Park Avenue, South, New York, NY 10003

Essandess Essandess Specials. Orders to: Simon & Schuster, Inc., 1 W. 39th Street, New York, NY 10018

Exposition Exposition Press, Inc., 50 Jericho Turnpike, Jericho, NY 11753

Fawcett World Fawcett World Library, 1515 Broadway, New York, NY 10036

Feminist Pr Feminist Press, SUNY/College at Old Westbury, Box 334, Old Westbury, NY 11568

Fleet Fleet Press Corp., 160 Fifth Avenue, New York, NY 10010

Follett Follett Publishing Co., 1010 W. Washington Blvd., Chicago, IL 60607

Four Winds Four Winds Press. Orders to: Scholastic Book Services, 50 W. 44th Street, New York, NY 10036

FS&G Farrar, Straus & Giroux, Inc., 19 Union Square, West, New York, NY 10003

Funk & W Funk & Wagnalls Co. Orders to: Thomas Y. Crowell Co., 666 Fifth Avenue, New York, NY 10019

G K Hall G. K. Hall & Co., 70 Lincoln Street, Boston, MA 02111

G&D Grosset & Dunlap, Inc., 51 Madison Avenue, New York, NY 10010

Greene Stephen Greene Press, P.O. Box 1000, Battleboro, VT 05301

Grossman Grossman Publications, Inc. Orders to: Viking Press, 625 Madison Avenue, New York, NY 10022

Hale E. M. Hale & Company, Eau Claire, WI 54701

Har-Row Harper & Row, Publishers. Orders to: Keystone Industrial Park, Scranton, PA 18512

HarBraceJ Harcourt Brace Jovanovich, Inc., 757 Third Avenue, New York, NY 10017

Hastings Hastings House, Publishers, Inc., 10 E. 40th Street, New York, NY 10016

Hawthorn Hawthorn Books, Inc., 260 Madison Avenue, New York, NY 10016

Hearthside Hearthside Press, Inc., 445 Northern Blvd., Great Neck, NY 11021

Herald Pr Herald Press, 616 Walnut Avenue, Scottdale, PA 15683

Herman Pub Herman Publishing, 45 Newbury Street, Boston, MA 02116

HM Houghton Mifflin Co., 2 Park Street, Boston, MA 02107

Hogarth Hogarth Press, P.O. Box 6012, Honolulu, HI 96818

Holiday Holiday House, Inc., 18 E. 56th Street, New York, NY 10022

HR&W Holt, Rinehart & Winston, Inc., 383 Madison Avenue, New York, NY 10017

Independence Pr Independence Press. Orders to: Herald House, 3225 S. Nolan Road, Box 1019, Independence, MO 64051

John Day John Day Co., Inc. Orders to: Intext Educational Publications, 257 Park Avenue, South, New York, NY 10010

Knopf Alfred A. Knopf, Inc. Orders to: Random House, Inc., 400 Hahn Road, Westminster, MD 21157

Kodansha Kodansha International, Ltd. Orders to: Harper & Row Publications, Inc., Keystone Industrial Park, Scranton, PA 18512

Lancer Lancer Books, 1560 Broadway, New York, NY 10036

Lanewood Lanewood Press, Inc., 89 Franklin Street, Boston, MA 02110

Lippincott J. B. Lippincott Co., E. Washington Square, Philadelphia, PA 19105

Little Little, Brown & Co. Orders to: 200 West Street, Waltham, MA 02154

Lothrop Lothrop, Lee & Shepard Co. Orders to: William Morrow & Co., Inc., 6 Henderson Drive, West Caldwell, NJ 07006

Lotus Lotus Press, P.O. Box 601, College Park Station, Detroit, MI 48221

M Evans M. Evans & Co., Inc. Orders to: J. B. Lippincott Co., E. Washington Square, Philadelphia, PA 19105

McGraw McGraw-Hill Book Co., 1221 Avenue of the Americas, New York, NY 10036

McKay David McKay Co., Inc., 750 Third Avenue, New York, NY 10017

Macmillan Macmillan Publishing Co., Inc. Orders to: Riverside, NJ 08075

Macfadden Macfadden-Bartell Corp., 205 E. 42 Street, New York, NY 10017

Macrae Macrae Smith Co., 225 S. 15th Street, Philadelphia, PA 19102

Meredith Corp Meredith Corp. Orders to: Consumer Book Division, 1716 Locust, Des Moines, IA 50336

Messner Julian Messner, Inc. Orders to: Simon & Schuster, Inc., 1 W. 39th Street, New York, NY 10018

Morrow William Morrow & Co., Inc. Orders to: 6 Henderson Drive, West Caldwell, NJ 07006

NAL New American Library, 1301 Avenue of the Americas, New York, NY 10019

Nash Pub Nash Publishing Corp., Order Service Center, 50 Liberty Avenue, Freeport, NY 11520

Nelson Thomas Nelson, Inc. Orders to: 407 Seventh Avenue, South, Nashville, TN 37203

Norton W. W. Norton & Co., Inc., 500 Fifth Avenue, New York, NY 10036

P-H Prentice-Hall, Inc., Englewood Cliffs, NJ 07632

Pantheon Pantheon Books. Orders to: Random House, Inc., 457 Hahn Road, Westminster, MD 21157

Paperback Lib Warner Paperback Library, 75 Rockefeller Plaza, New York, NY 10019

Parents Parents Magazine Press, 52 Vanderbilt Avenue, New York, NY 10017

PB Pocket Books, Inc. Orders to: Simon & Schuster, Inc., 1 W. 39th Street, New York, NY 10018

Pendulum Pr Pendulum Press, Inc., Academic Building, Saw Mill Road, West Haven, CT 06516

Plays Plays, Inc., 8 Arlington Street, Boston, MA 02116

Popular Lib Popular Library, Inc., Unit of CBS Publications, 600 Third Avenue, New York, NY 10011

Putnam G. P. Putnam's Sons, 200 Madison Avenue, New York, NY 10016

Pyramid Pubns Pyramid Publications, 919 Madison Avenue, New York, NY 10022

Rand Rand McNally & Co., P.O. Box 7600, Chicago, IL 60680

Random Random House, Inc. Orders to: Order Department, 457 Hahn Road, Westminster, MD 21157

Reilly & Lee Reilly & Lee Co. Orders to: Henry Regnery Co., 114 W. Illinois Street, Chicago, IL 60610

Ritchie Ward Ritchie Press, 474 S. Arroyo Parkway, Pasadena, CA 91105

Routledge & Kegan Routledge & Kegan Paul, Ltd., 9 Park Street, Boston, MA 02108

S G Phillips S. G. Phillips, Inc., 305 W. 86th Street, New York, NY 10024

S&S Simon & Schuster, Inc., 630 Fifth Avenue, New York, NY 10020

Schol Bk Serv Scholastic Book Services, 50 W. 44th Street, New York, NY 10036

Scott F Scott, Foresman & Co., 1900 E. Lake Avenue, Glenview, IL 60025

Scribner Charles Scribner's Sons. Orders to: Shipping & Service Center, Vreeland Avenue, Totowa, NJ 07512

Seabury Seabury Press, Inc., 815 Second Avenue, New York, NY 10017

Signet Signet Books. Orders to: New American Library, 1301 Avenue of the Americas, New York, NY 10019

St Martin St. Martin's Press, Inc., 175 Fifth Avenue, New York, NY 10010

Sterling Sterling Publishing Co., Inc., 419 Park Avenue, South, New York, NY 10016

Strode Strode Publishers, 6802 Jones Valley Drive, S.E., Huntsville, AL 35802

T Y Crowell Thomas Y. Crowell Co., 666 Fifth Avenue, New York, NY 10003

Taplinger Taplinger Publishing Co., Inc., 200 Park Avenue, South, New York, NY 10003

Time-Life Time-Life Books. Orders to: Little, Brown & Co., 34 Beacon Street, Boston, MA 02106

Tundra Bks Tundra Books of Northern New York, 18 Cornelia Street, Box 1030, Plattsburgh, NY 12901

U of Okla Pr University of Oklahoma Press, 1005 Asp Avenue, Norman, OK 73069

Vanguard Vanguard Press, Inc., 424 Madison Avenue, New York, NY 10017

Viking Pr Viking Press, Inc., 625 Madison Avenue, New York, NY 10022

Vin Random Vintage Trade Books. Orders to: Random House, Inc., Order Department, 457 Hahn Road, Westminster, MD 21157

Walck Henry Z. Walck, Inc., 19 Union Square, West, New York, NY 10003

Walker & Co Walker & Co., 720 Fifth Avenue, New York, NY 10019

Washburn Ives Washburn, Inc. Orders to: David McKay Co., Inc., 750 Third Avenue, New York, NY 10017

Watts Franklin Watts, Inc. Orders to: Grolier, Inc., 845 Third Avenue, New York, NY 10022

Western Pub Western Publishing Co., Inc. Orders to: 1220 Mound Avenue, Racine, WI 53404

Westminster Westminster Press, Witherspoon Building, Philadelphia, PA 19107

World Pub World Publishing Company. Orders to: 2080 W. 117th St., Cleveland, OH 44111

WSP Washington Square Press, Inc. Orders to: Simon & Schuster, Inc., 701 Seneca Street, Buffalo, NY 14210

AUTHOR INDEX

419

TITLE INDEX